BESA

A True Story

Pertef Bylykbashi

NEWMAN SPRINGS PUBLISHING
320 Broad Street
Red Bank, NJ 07701

First originally published by Newman Springs Publishing 2019

ISBN 978-1-64531-096-9 (Paperback)
ISBN 978-1-64531-098-3 (Hardcover)
ISBN 978-1-64531-097-6 (Digital)

Printed in the United States of America

BESA is a story of unrelenting courage and perseverance in the face of adversity. This true account of Pertef Bylykbashi's life stirs a deep range of emotions including laughter, anger and sorrow. Pertef's dedication to family and country is a shining example for our younger generations. BESA is a must-read book that is hard to put down.

Catherine Beasley, Captain, Retired, USAF, NC

BESA – An excellent read! This should be required reading for every high school student in America!

Mary Ellen Epps, State Senator, Colorado (1999-2003)

In his memoir, Bylykbashi narrates his story of survival while living under the dictatorship of Enver Hoxha and recounts the events leading to his escape to America and freedom. The stories told in BESA memorialize thousands of other victims and their unheard voices.

It is an excellent book that will help our younger generations in America see the pitfalls of communism through the eyes of a survivor.

Mithat Gashi (escaped Albania in 1986) - Board Member of the Holocaust, Genocide, Interfaith Education Center, Manhattan College; teaches at Lehman College, City University of New York

I humbly dedicate this book to my family. Without their love and support, I would not have been able to finish this manuscript. It is from family that I have learned the true meaning of love and honor. For this, I am eternally grateful.

Acknowledgments

I owe a special debt of gratitude to Carrie Cook who has spent hundreds of hours in typing my manuscript, helping me review and incorporate my research notes, and getting my book to a stage where it could be published.

A special thank you to Mr. and Mrs. Gurali Skoti, who generously donated the land in Bilisht where the monument was erected.

And thank you to those special people who helped to weave the fabric of my life. I am proud to call you my friends.

Foreword

For nearly half a century, my family lived through torture, degradation, humiliation, and suffering when the communists took over our beloved Albania.

This is the story of our struggle for freedom. It is a story that was forever etched in my memory as I made my own escape into Greece; a story that found its form in the suffering and courage of my loved ones—many of whom died in communist labor camps. Most of all, it's the story of how our commitment to family and to honor, our BESA, endured to find its expression in the undying spirit of liberty.

Journey with me as I relive some of the horrific (and sometimes hilarious) events that shaped my own life. Join with me as I claim the joy that only free people can know. Rejoice with me as I share my eternal gratitude and deep love for my adopted homeland—America!

Pertef Bylykbashi
July 2017

Introduction

A few days before my birthday, I was helping my brother Gezim groom a calf when the little devil turned his head to scratch himself and accidentally gashed my forehead with his horn. For the first hour or so, I didn't realize how badly I was hurt, but then the wound became infected and my temperature began to rise. It was 1951, and by now, the Communist had their thumb over my beloved Albania, which left my choices for medical care few at best.

My sister Lumturje (we called her Lumka for short) was just a teenager at the time but very mature for her age. She was the one caring for me when it became clear that there was nothing she could do to break my fever. Only after my illness seemed too dire to ignore did Lumka seek help from our grandmother. She was the only elder for the job, as the men in the family had already made their escape to Greece, my mother had been taken to a labor camp by the Communists, and the regime had confiscated our land.

Grandmother Aishe was a shade over eighty at the time, and waking her from her afternoon nap was often a frightening proposition. I was later told that Grandmother woke the moment Lumka stepped through the door as if she'd had a premonition that something was terribly wrong. Grandmother had not been able to see for over five years, but her mind and memory remained excellent, and she always did seem to have a sixth sense about her.

"There is something wrong, Lumka," she said and it was not a question.

"It's Pertef," Lumka said. She was so frantic that I could hear her from the next room, even over my feverish breathing. "He has a very high fever, and it is getting worse. His head is badly swollen around the wound. It looks infected."

"Take him outside to the balcony, girl," Grandmother said. I'm sure she would have followed my sister into the room I was occupying, were she able to walk. She had limited ability to stand by this time in her life. Whenever she needed to be somewhere else, a few of the children would have to carry her on her cot. She was frail but certainly strong of mind, will, and spirit. "Make a pallet for him to lie on so he can get some fresh air," she called after my sister. "Then come back with the others and fetch me. I'll stay with him and watch his fever."

Despite the fever, I was able to find humor in the situation. "How can she watch my fever?" I bleated at my sister. "She can't see a thing!"

Lumka and Gezim moved me onto a cot and carried me to the balcony then went back to retrieve Grandmother. Outside, the autumn air was mild, but to my warm flesh, it felt at once like the dead of winter and then again like roaring August heat. As I curled myself into a shivering ball, Grandmother was telling Lumka how to mix some raw onion, roux, and a few other ingredients into a poultice for my wound. She prepared the poultice as Grandmother instructed then put it on the wound and covered it with a thin cloth to keep the flies and gnats at bay.

My head throbbed, and my body shook. Someone laid a blanket over me then another. In this way, I spent the afternoon on the balcony with Grandmother. I could sense that my face had swollen like a balloon. Not only was it difficult to see, but my forehead felt as if someone had dumped a pot of stew on it. When the poultice began to take hold, I finally found sleep. It couldn't have been more than twenty minutes later when I felt a sharp pain that jolted me from my fever dream. But reality felt more like a dream than the dream. It was all wings and screeching and fluttering agony. Through my confusion, there emerged the sense that I was battling with a bird that had perched just beside my head and was feeding off the poultice.

Frantically, I swung my arms in defense. The bird flew away, but the damage was already done. In the excitement, its beak had punctured my wound. The pus was like a fountain flowing over my head and dripping down to my chest.

Grandmother, blind as she was, didn't realize what was happening until I started screaming. "What happened?" she bellowed. "What happened?"

When all I could do was wail in reply, she went to the edge of the balcony and started calling out to the other children present. "Please help! Somebody *help*!"

My cousin Myrset was the first to answer the call. When she saw the mess I had become, she asked me what had happened then explained the situation to my panicking grandmother.

"Pertef is okay," Myrset said. "Everything is under control." And she was right. In a matter of minutes, the pus had drained from my face, my temperature began to drop, and the swelling subsided.

I've often wondered what would have become of me had I not been on the balcony with Grandmother that afternoon. Truly, it seems possible that the bird's appetite for that poultice saved my life.

As it turned out, birds were more likely saviors than the doctors were for me and my family back then. Even if there had been a doctor in our small village of Pilur, we wouldn't have been allowed to see him. For many generations before the Communists began their brutal takeover, the Bylykbashi family had been landowners and shop owners. This meant that the elders of our family were highly respected by the villagers, something for which the Communists never much cared. They would focus considerable effort on the task of discrediting my family and turning the villagers against us. This, they believed, was the only way to gain full control of Pilur and the surrounding region. Owed to the carefully orchestrated stigmatization, the villagers couldn't risk helping anyone in the Bylykbashi family. If they were caught helping us, no matter how minor the help might be, their punishment would be severe.

One might think that a state-sponsored effort to break us would have led us to toe the party line, but the truth was that it had the opposite effect. From the outset, my family took a public stand for democracy, openly refusing to bend to the rules and laws of communism. The regime cared little about the women and children in my family—they did all they could to make us suffer. To them, we were believers in what they called "American imperialism." We were branded *Kulaks* (a Marxist derogatory term for "rich farmers"), which lined us up for destruction by the party.

After the bird incident, I kept up with a more manageable fever, which left me weak and in constant need of rest. They moved me back to the bed I shared with one of my siblings, and there I stayed, day and night. My only entertainment was Grandmother's stories, which was fine by me because she always had a storyteller's flare.

*****

"Can you tell me about Grandfather?" I asked her one day as I was on the mend. I knew so little about him, so I wanted to hear any story she could tell about when he was a young man.

Grandmother's eyes widened in surprise. The long, hard years of her life showed on her frail but delicate face. Her eyes were cloudy from the blindness, but when she heard that I wanted to know about Grandfather, a hint of their old twinkle returned. She lifted her head, straightened her slouching body, and beat back a soft smile.

"I remember like it was yesterday," she said with a proud, commanding voice. She paused for a moment before continuing. "Oh, your Grandfather Ramo was so handsome. Tall and strong too! He was good-hearted and courageous. He spent most of his life fighting the invaders. Ramo, God rest his soul, suffered through the most unfortunate situation." She seemed to trail off into distant memory.

"What was that, Grandmother?" I asked, trying to snap her back to the moment.

Grandmother pursed her lips as if struggling to find her next words. "Your poor grandfather killed a man when he was only twelve years old."

I sat up straighter in bed, bunching my blanket in my hands and fidgeting with the fabric that the women in my family had sewn.

"To save his young life," Grandmother continued, "he had to leave his village. You may know him as a Dervish (holy man), but for a time, he dedicated himself to fighting for the cause of Albania's independence." Grandmother's blank gaze grew even more distant as if she was traveling backward through time.

My heart leapt when I pondered whether to ask the question on my mind. "Why would Grandfather kill this poor man?" I asked nervously.

"Show patience, my grandson, and I will tell you the story of Ramo Bylykbashi." Grandmother let her head roll back as she reclined and began rocking in her creaky wooden chair. "One morning, the family shepherd took ill, so Ramo was asked to take the herd of sheep to the riverbank for the day. When he arrived at the river, he saw someone fishing.

"Ramo approached the man and very politely said, 'Good morning, sir! Would you like to exchange some fish for some fresh milk?'

"The man turned around, took a good look at your grandfather, and replied, 'The only fish you are going to get are the ones that I'll shove in your mouth after I have my way with you!'"

I had to work hard to stifle a laugh.

Grandmother didn't seem to share my delight at the strange reply. "At the same time," she said gravely, "the man was touching himself and making obscene gestures.

"'Now go away, you little bastard!' the man said.

"Ramo could not believe his ears. An Albanian in the right frame of mind would never insult anyone with words such as these, unless he was trying to be killed. Wanting to be certain of what he had heard, Ramo said, 'Did I hear you correctly, sir?'

"The man abruptly answered, 'Yes, and I meant what I said!'

"Ramo was too young and too small in stature to face this giant of a man, and he was unarmed and alone besides. But as he turned to leave, he told the man that he would be back tomorrow. Then he headed home with his sheep. Your grandfather was very upset. He could not eat supper that night, and when he finally went to bed, he lay awake all night, tossing and turning. His honor, as well as his family's honor, was at stake and had to be defended."

"What do you mean, it had to be defended?" I asked of my grandmother. I was still feverish enough that even furrowing my brow caused me to ache, but I was so deep into the story that I hardly noticed.

"You are too impatient, child," Grandmother said with a playful frown. "I am getting to that." Then she rocked back as if she needed to consult with God about where she had left off in the story. "Ah yes," she added with a nod. "Your Grandfather Ramo knew what had to be done. He carefully mulled it in his head, running through the plan time and time again.

"Morning came, and he quickly gathered the sheep and headed toward the river. This time, he had a gun with him. When he reached the riverbank, he began searching for the man that had insulted him the day before and, within a few minutes, spotted someone standing on the edge of the river. Ramo felt as if an electric charge was running through his body as he slowly approached the fisherman. When he was within sixty feet of his target, he stopped, took a deep breath, and put his plan into action.

"'Good morning, sir,' he said. 'Would you consider exchanging some of your fresh fish for some fresh milk?'

"The man lifted his head and very politely answered, 'Good morning to you, young fellow. Certainly! The first catch will be yours, and it won't be necessary for you to give me anything.'

"Ramo was not thinking logically. His heart was pounding so loudly that he could barely hear the man speak. The only thought running through his mind was that he must follow his plan no matter what. *I must kill the man that humiliated me*, he thought. *It's not just my honor at stake; it is the honor of the Bylykbashi name!*"

My intrigue soaring, I pulled my aching knees to my chest and made myself into an excited little ball.

"Ramo could not see the man's face clearly," Grandmother said, "but he felt as if this had to be the man he was after. Then his mind began to race. *But why is he being so nice today? He must have seen my gun and thought I would change my mind about shooting him, so long as he was polite.* Ramo gave a profound nod. *That's it! He was speaking kindly to me simply out of fear.*" Grandmother raised a finger to the air. "*Or maybe he* did *insult me again and I just didn't hear him correctly.* What do you think about that, child?"

So enrapt was I by the story that it took me a moment to realize that Grandmother had asked me a question. "What? Oh yes," I said.

"You were not paying attention," Grandmother said defensively. "No, I was, I—"

"You children these days have no respect for your history."

"No, Grandmother, I promise. I was listening." My fever pains meshed with the anxiety of upsetting my grandmother, which only heightened the sense that I wanted desperately to hear the end of the story. "Grandfather was just deciding whether he should shoot the kind fisherman."

Grandmother raised her pencil-thin eyebrows and gave a faint smile. "Good. Then I will continue."

She leaned back again, returning to her storytelling posture. "Ramo could not wait a second longer. He had to shoot while he still had the nerve. So as he was advancing toward his target, he quickly lifted the gun and pulled the trigger. His aim was exact. The poor man's body collapsed face down in the river. Ramo's excitement rose, his heart pounding as he tasted his first victory."

"Wait," I said, regretting the interruption immediately. "To shoot someone is a victory?"

For a moment, Grandmother made a face as if she meant to scold me again, but then she shrugged. "This is a good question, child. Whether it is victory or not, I cannot say. I can only say that this was what it felt like to Ramo at the time."

"But why?"

"Ramo thought that everyone would praise him for his bravery and his willingness to defend his honor. He thought his family would be proud."

"And were they?" I asked sheepishly.

Now Grandmother seemed to be losing patience, if only slightly. "Were they what?"

"Proud?"

"Of course!" she bellowed. "Your grandfather did what had to be done."

I nodded. I wasn't sure yet whether I understood the lesson in the story, but I was sure there was one to be found. Grandmother's stories always had lessons.

"As proof that he had restored his family's honor, Ramo decided to take the man's ear back to his family. He jumped into the water, took the knife from his pocket, and—without hesitation—flipped his victim over to take one last look." Grandmother suddenly rocked forward, her dull gray eyes going wide. "But then a sudden devastation consumed his body. *What's this?* he thought. *What have I done? I have killed the wrong man.*"

Grandmother fixed her sightless gaze on me for a long, silent moment. "You see the dilemma here."

I nodded. "Grandfather killed the wrong man?"

"Yes. To kill the man that insulted him was honor. But to kill an innocent man? That was a shameful action."

I tensed at the thought. "What did he do?"

"Ramo had only one alternative. He would have to leave his home and family. So he told his father what happened then went into hiding. His father worried about him day and night, knowing the danger he faced. But his father also knew that he had to act quickly and properly to resolve the situation between the two families, or it would prove catastrophic for everyone, possibly creating a vendetta that could last for many generations and cost the lives of innocent men in both families.

"Ramo's father went immediately to the dead fisherman's family to explain how the killing had happened and that it was accidental. As was customary in that time, he offered an apology, along with large sums of money as his expression of regret. Both families gave their BESA that this incident would not bring more bloodshed between the two families."

"What does this mean, Grandmother?" I asked.

This time, she didn't look annoyed to be interrupted. Rather, it was as if she had anticipated it. "What does what mean?"

"BESA."

"BESA is to give your word. It is a code of honor, loyalty, and nobility. In this case, the BESA between these two families was that they would not seek retribution for the accidental killing. In the spirit of true BESA, I am happy to say that the families have kept their promise all these years."

We sat in silence for a time as a mild breeze drifted through the lacy curtains my mother had made. The reminder that she had made these put me in a sour mood, for my mother was now toiling away in a labor camp run by the Communists.

I became suddenly aware that it was nearing dusk. The room had grown dark enough to light the lamps, but Grandmother, blind as she was, hadn't noticed. So here we sat in the darkening room, Grandmother pondering the depth of her story and I pondering the meaning.

"What happened to Grandfather after that?" I asked.

"Ramo never returned home after the incident. He fled to the mountains and made his life there. As the years passed and times began to change, so did Ramo. He turned his devotion to his homeland and fought to defend his country. When the Turkish Empire withdrew from Albania, Ramo joined the fight against the Greeks. Your grandfather made such a name for himself that the Greek government placed a large bounty on him, but Albanians in the southern region were supportive of Ramo and his cause and kept him hidden from his enemies."

I watched Grandmother Aishe as she ruminated. Somehow, I knew she could see every detail in her mind as if it had happened yesterday.

"There were many troubles for your grandfather after that," Grandmother continued. "One day, he and eleven of his men were fighting their way through a terrible snowstorm and came upon a Teqe (small mosque), where a priest and his wife lived. They were invited in and, once inside, saw a table with plates set for twelve. As they took their meal at the table, the priest began telling them of a dream he had earlier that night of twelve men travelling his way. In his dream, it was revealed that he should light torches in the night so the men could find their way to the Teqe in the storm. Ramo listened in amazement as the Dervish (holy man) told him the story of his dream.

"'I have always known that God was close to me, and this is yet another proof.'

"After that day, Ramo separated from his followers, put his rifle away, and became a clergyman. He died when he was seventy-five years old. His last wish for his sons and his daughter was that they should always stay together and help each other through difficult situations. He was buried as a common man in the cemetery. But a few months after his death, the people of the village helped his sons build a mausoleum for Ramo's body. Your Grandfather Ramo was known to the people in the region as a Dervish." Grandmother Aishe seemed to swell with pride. "So you see, child, there are lessons to be learned from your grandfather."

"Yes, Grandmother."

"You must always defend your family," she urged. "You also have a duty to defend your beloved Albania." She clenched her teeth as if in frustration about the current condition of Albania. Indeed, there were many people who believed our country needed defending from the Communists but far too few who acted. "You must honor God," she said then brightening up. "And through it all, you must keep to your BESA."

"I understand, Grandmother," I said.

"When you are a grown man, you will do these things, yes?"

"I will." There are moments in any boy's life where it feels like he grows up all at once. This was one of those moments for me.

Grandmother fell silent after that—so silent that for a time, I thought maybe she was sleeping. But then she began to grumble and then chuckle intermittently as if reliving an old conversation with Grandfather Ramo in her mind.

I will never forget that day, for even though I was sick, I scarcely noticed the pain. By the time the sun had set, we were both so content with the story that we dozed into a peaceful sleep, dreaming our own dreams of my future and of a shared history so fresh in our memories.

Chapter 1

The last time our family was together was a happy occasion for most of the people present but not at all happy for me. I have good reason. This was the day that I, along with my brother Medi and my cousins Agron and Fevri, was ritualistically circumcised.

It was midmorning when Mother asked the four of us to assemble in the loft we used as a bedroom. We milled around there for a time, not knowing what was happening. Then she brought four long shirts and told us to put them on. "Nothing else," she explained. "Just the shirts."

My mother, petite and fiery in her humor, was a beautiful woman inside and out. She loved everyone, and everyone loved her. She was the kind of woman who could blend into any conversation and make anyone feel comfortable and at ease in her presence. This was partly why it was so odd to see the unsettled expression that crossed her face as she urged us not to delay.

When she left us, we threw our shirts over our heads and made our way down from the loft, the summer air from the open windows breezy against my bare thighs. My family was considered reasonably wealthy by the standards of rural Albania. Together, we owned two orchards, stores, and a great deal of farmland. On that land rested a compound consisting of two houses separated by a picturesque courtyard. The houses, one to the north and the other to the south, were nearly identical in layout. Both featured a pair of bedrooms, a loft, and an attached bathroom (but without running water). As I reached the bottom of the stairs on the balcony outside, I could see that all the family members had gathered in the courtyard, along with many other members of our extended family and dozens of family friends.

"What's going on?" I asked of Medi.

"Quiet, Pertef," Agron answered for him. "Can't you see it's a party?"

"Then why are we wearing these shirts?" I asked.

"Isn't it obvious?" Agron said, tossing his hands in exasperation. "We're the guests of honor!"

Indeed, as we stepped into the sunny courtyard, all eyes fell on us, and I thought for a moment that maybe my cousin was right. My heart swelled. I had never been the guest of honor before! I had always loved family gatherings, for they meant plenty of food and a host of children my age with whom I could play. But my momentary pride melted away when I noticed that the laughter and revelry seemed to die down as more and more of the people realized that the four of us had joined them. Slowly, the smiles faded from every face, and a strange sort of solemnity washed over the crowd. I became keenly aware of how drafty my shirt felt.

Suddenly, Father was there, wearing that same contemplative expression he always wore. He wasn't a tall man, but he was stocky and well-built. He kept a thick, well-groomed mustache that blunted at the edges, and he wore a fine suit complete with tie. At the time, seeing him in a suit was strange to me, for he nearly always wore work clothes so he could tend to the farm. Later in life, when he no longer had to do manual farm labor, he would wear a suit like this one every day, no matter the occasion. He would wear them even at leisure. He was always a handsome man, with his high, sharp cheekbones and strong jaw. That jaw seemed to tense as he reached out with his hand to lead us.

"This way, boys," he said. "Don't keep him waiting."

When the main entrance to the courtyard was opened, in strode a man whose face I didn't recognize. The attention was on us now—every member of my family and more friends than I could ever remember visiting our house at one time. I still had no idea the meaning of this occasion, but the ample turnout was unmistakable. The collective gaze of the guests seemed to combine with the heat of the sun, making me break out in a sudden, beading sweat.

"Medi, what is this?" I asked. "What is that man doing?"

"I don't know," my brother said. "But I think we should keep quiet."

Medi seemed to have a point. Apart from the fact that everyone had their eyes trained on us, the other striking feature of the party was that everyone, even the children, had fallen silent. It was so quiet that I could hear the breeze carrying through the orchard that bordered the courtyard at a distance.

There was nothing but the four of us, the quiet crowd watching, and the man entering through the gate. My mouth felt dry. My palms were sweaty. My heart was pounding.

Then just when I thought I could take no more of the waiting, the man began striding toward us. The closer he came, the more of him I could make out. I didn't know him, but he was a large man—broad of shoulder and with a thick neck supporting a big, sober head. From the way he was looking at us, I could sense that we weren't going to be fast friends.

In one hand, he held a long, sharp razorblade, and in the other hand, he carried a black leather bag. I recognized the razor as the kind I had seen the town barber use to shave his customers. As the man drew within a few strides of us, my legs began to shake in fear, for it was then that I understood what this celebration meant. From the way my cousins began sniveling and my brother grew straight and stony as a statue, I could sense that they were coming around to understanding as well.

So now I faced my coming of age. This was my Sunnet (circumcision). I knew very little of what was about to happen or of just how much of my penis would be cut away, I just knew I wasn't going to like it. I was terrified. The man holding the razor looked like a butcher at the meat market, and my childish imagination began to soar. I pictured our local butcher hacking at sausage and reflexively covered my penis with my hands.

Since I was the youngest, I would be the first one circumcised. I quivered in fear as the butcher knelt before me and slowly opened his leather bag. He produced a little hook-like tool and a tube of cream. I turned my face away as he lifted my shirt and applied the cream to my penis. Everything went numb. I had heard about people going into shock—the body defending itself from pain by becoming completely detached from reality—but this was my first brush with the phenomenon.

By the time I clenched my teeth and tightly closed my eyes, it was done. I could feel the warm blood on my thighs, but there was almost no pain. I found my father's face in the crowd. He was nodding with pride. I had faced my fear and my suffering like a man, and here I was the youngest of the four.

Being that I was a man now and much wiser in the ways of the world, I took an odd sort of delight in the notion that now I would get to watch my brother and cousins suffer as I had suffered. I was no longer a member of the spectacle; I had become one of the crowd. I might have still been standing on the edge of the courtyard as part of the attraction, but I felt separated somehow like I was privy to information that the other boys could not yet possibly understand. I slowly turned my head and looked down the row with a faint smile on my face.

When it was over, Uncle Nevrus presented me with a majestic white filly in honor of my Sunnet. To receive a horse when you are such a young boy is every bit the dream come true that it might seem. I named her Flutur (Butterfly), and even though I was still too small to ride, everyone knew that Butterfly belonged to me. In the years that followed, Butterfly and I would form the kind of bond that can only exist between a rider and his beloved horse. On the day of my Sunnet, I couldn't imagine loving anything more dearly than Butterfly or anyone more admiringly than Uncle Nevrus. Even as I write this, it is difficult to explain the depths of terror that came from losing them both to the Communists.

*****

The story of Uncle Nevrus began, as these stories often do, with our ancestors. After Albania became independent, it took another thirteen years of turmoil before the country was able to form its first government. That landmark achievement came to pass thanks to a man called Ahmet Zogu, who was anointed king of Albania in 1928. By then, my late grandfather Ramo had a daughter and three sons. They had prospered, and life was good.

Uncle Arif was the oldest, and as Albanian tradition goes, the unquestioned head of the household. He was naturally smart and a hard worker with a wonderful personality that could win your heart instantly. In all these ways, Uncle Arif's sister Vajbe was identical to him. My father Zenel was the middle child. He was a calm, quiet, and simple man, honest and dedicated to his beliefs—both in terms of his family and his faith. Uncle Nevrus, the youngest, was more like Grandfather Ramo than the other children. He was steadfast in his beliefs and so dedicated to the honor of his family and his country that it would one day cost him his life.

All of grandfather's children married. Uncle Arif and Aunt Sibe had two sons and four daughters. My father and mother (Zenel and Resmije) had four sons and two daughters. Aunt Vajbe married into a very nice family and lived in the village of Vishotice. She and her husband Pasho had six sons and a daughter. Uncle Nevrus married my mother's sister Idajet. Unfortunately, they did not have children.

Albanian culture was quite different when I was a child. Families remained close even when they reached their adult years. It was not uncommon to have siblings live together with their wives and children in the same house, like my father and his brothers did. There was never a question of children taking care of their mothers and fathers when they grew older. Including Grandmother Aishe, we were nineteen people living together. Grandmother took charge of the women and made a schedule of household chores for her daughters-in-law to follow on a rotating weekly basis. She was tough as nails and gave the orders like a general, but she was fair and honest. She reserved a specific set of chores for her granddaughters as well. Grandmother was stricter with her granddaughters because she wanted them to learn and be prepared for the future.

That same year of my Sunnet, I turned six years old. The early years of my childhood were wonderful. Every day, aunts, uncles, cousins, or good family friends would visit, and often the guests would stay for days or even a week at a time. I loved the company because everyone always seemed so festive. The adults would stay up until the wee hours of the morning, telling stories and laughing. Of course, it helped that their constant need to cater to our guests prevented them from watching me as closely as they might have otherwise, which in turn freed me up to do the things little boys normally get scolded for doing.

In hindsight, it's hard to believe we all lived together under one roof. Even with all those differing personalities running around, I can't remember a single time that we argued. The elder male in the family always had the final say on any issue, and we all respected his decision. Our home was one of kindness, respect, structure, and discipline, but what I remember most is the warmth and love that permeated the house. The memories of my childhood will remain in my heart forever. It was a perfect life and too good to be true, as we would soon discover.

The atmosphere in Albania was changing. You could feel the uncertainty in the air just as surely as a winter chill. It was like this for a long while, that sense that our lives as we knew them would never be the same again. Then it began. A violent civil war broke out between the Nationalists and the Communists. I was just a child and did not understand the nature of war, but I could tell that all the adults carried the heavy burden of something terrible that was happening outside the walls of our house.

Eventually, though, not even a six-year-old's blissful naiveté could maintain its immunity to the harsh realities of a country at war. The happy afternoons in the courtyard grew less frequent then ceased altogether. Friends and family stopped coming over for celebrations. The smiles and laughter of the people I had grown up around had turned to worry and even fear. Those joyful gatherings were replaced by somber discussions around the dinner table, the elders of the family speaking in hushed, histrionic tones.

Grandmother Aishe wore her anxiety more clearly than did anyone else in the family. She looked utterly drained, physically as well as emotionally. Grandmother had faced hard times in her life, but now it looked like her last years would be fuller with turmoil and heartbreak than any that came before them.

It all started with the loss of her grandson. Iqmet had just returned home after fighting the Communists. The next day, he called on the village barber to get a haircut and a shave. When the barber arrived that afternoon, Iqmet's sister Refijan brought a chair outside to the courtyard to accommodate the process. Iqmet knew the possibility of the enemy advancing on him was ever present, so he brought his rifle with him and propped it up against the chair to keep it close in case any Communists came calling.

Iqmet's decision to have his haircut under the warm sunshine attracted a few other members of the family. Soon, there was something of a lighthearted gathering around Iqmet and the barber.

Setali was Iqmet's adopted brother. He was not wise in the ways of warfare which leant him the unfortunate combination of fascination with Iqmet's rifle and ignorance in how to use it. While Iqmet was having a shave, Setali picked up the rifle.

"If you're going to play with that," Iqmet said, "you'd better remove all the bullets. I don't want you accidentally shooting yourself or anyone else!"

With an eager smile, Setali quickly agreed to the condition and started removing all the bullets, or so he thought. Setali's first and last act with the rifle was to playfully point it at its owner and pull the trigger. The bullet he had failed to clear from the chamber struck Iqmet in the temple, killing him instantly. I can only imagine the pain and horror Setali must have felt at accidentally taking the life of a brother he so dearly loved.

Over the weeks that followed, the only thing that managed to break through the pall hanging over our house was news that Uncle Nevrus would once again be returning home from the war front to spend some time with his wife and family. Everyone was thrilled to hear this, especially Grandmother Aishe, who had been living in crippling fear that her sons would meet a dark fate at war. She had always loved Uncle Nevrus best among her children because he reminded her most of Grandfather Ramo. The excitement was contagious as Grandmother ordered the women around with their planning and cooking for the huge feast that would accompany Uncle Nevrus's return and last for at least a week following.

I was still young enough then that I wasn't entirely aware of the reasons for the change in mood in our house. I just knew that I was glad to see my grandmother smile, glad to smell all that food cooking in the kitchen and the bread oven once more, and glad to have the adults at least pretending that we had finally moved beyond the scarcities leveled by war. Mostly, I was just excited, like everyone else, to see Uncle Nevrus after many months apart.

When Uncle Nevrus arrived, the courtyard was packed with people waiting to welcome him home. He made his way joyfully through the crowd, and when he reached Grandmother Aishe, he lifted her completely off the ground and hugged and kissed her. Then he went to his wife and greeted her with a warm, long, passionate kiss. I blushed at the sight, but I couldn't turn away. Tradition had it that public shows of affection were strictly forbidden, so the kiss didn't set well with some of the older women, but I and everyone else loved and respected Uncle Nevrus enough to allow him the moment with the elders just pretending as if nothing out of the ordinary had happened.

Uncle Nevrus was an attractive man at thirty-five, tall and slim and arrestingly handsome. He was dressed in an officer's uniform, as was one of the two friends he had brought along with him to the party. The other man in uniform, Fuhat Ecmeniku, was short and stocky with dark, curly hair and a pair of binoculars dangling around his neck. Demirsha Qose was a few years older than the other officers and was dressed in a dark brown shepherd's poncho made of heavy wool and a round, white, woolen cap adorned with a gold Albanian double eagle pin. He was an attractive man and his garb quite sharp. He and Fuhat enjoyed plenty of admiring gazes from the women in the family.

This day was not like any other I had ever experienced, but when I think back on it now, I can only describe it as bittersweet. That day, I laughed and played with cousins and siblings as any child would, but the elders still seemed to carry a sense that the political unrest would soon bring an end to everything we knew and loved.

They were right, of course. That would be the last week our family would ever be together.

The night before Uncle Nevrus and his friends were to leave, the men sat down with cocktails and appetizers. They talked jovially and would occasionally break into song. Some of the songs I knew, but others were bawdy and told of war. After a couple hours of this, the women brought the main course, and everyone praised Mother Resmije and Aunt Sibe for their delicious meal. I ate ravenously as I watched the men and listened to their songs.

After dinner, the men continued drinking while the rest of us retired to other rooms to tend to the cleanup or play our childish games. I was just thinking about gathering the other children for a game of hide-and-seek when it happened. I am still humbled by the notion that everything a family can build over the course of generations can be lost in a single instant. For my family, that instant came when that first bullet shattered the glass of the dining room window.

Everyone froze and looked in the direction of the broken window. The men freshest from war were the first to react.

"Gather the children," Uncle Nevrus called out to the women. "Everyone get in the basement."

As everyone started scrambling to take cover, more shots rang out. Uncle Nevrus hustled the women and children toward the basement door while his fellow freedom fighters overturned the dining table to make cover. Our idyllic evening had become a war zone. Every non-fighting member of the family was in the basement now—everyone except me. In the confusion, the women had not been able to take a head count, so I was left behind.

I still remember snippets of hollering from my uncle and the other men. I remember more glass shattering and the walls behind exploding from the force of the bullets. But the thing I remember most is the sound. There is no way to do justice to the harrowing loudness of a gunfight. You can't appreciate the sheer cacophony of it all until you're right there in it. As a young boy, it was the most terrifying thing I had ever experienced. I didn't know what to do or where to go. Everyone had left, save for the men with guns, and I didn't have anyone to turn to.

So I did what I guess comes naturally to a child in those situations: I backed myself into a corner of the room just beside the kitchen. I curled up and put my head between my knees. I tried plugging my ears to drown out the sound, but it seemed to have no effect. The fear gripped me so coldly that I couldn't move. All I could do was keep my eyes shut tight and wait. I was too afraid even to pray.

In my terror, I barely noticed when the fighting moved from out of the house and onto the property. Later, I was told that the men had taken the Communists by surprise and beaten them back. Then they patrolled the outer wall of the compound and searched through the garden and orchards to make sure there were no snipers left behind.

When it was over, Uncle Nevrus called down to the women that it was safe for everyone to come upstairs. Grandmother Aishe was frantic, as I guess at some point during the raid, she had noticed that I was missing. Uncle Nevrus was the one who found me in the corner. I was so afraid that I had gone numb. To the observer, I must have looked docile—*calm*, even—and at first, I probably was. But then when Uncle Nevrus picked me up and started looking me over for bullet wounds, my mind returned to me, and I began to sob. The women were shaken as well, and the men stood in reverent awe.

Uncle Nevrus embraced me gently, my head resting on his shoulder. When he turned around with me in his arms, I saw the wall where I had been sitting. Everywhere—to the left, to the right, and above—my position, in an almost perfect outline of my tiny body, there were bullet holes. It was a matter of inches that had spared my life.

Uncle Nevrus looked serious as he paced about the room. "All right, boys," he said to the others, "it looks like there are only two kinds of Albanians these days: Nationalists and Communists. We know what category we're in, and we have just seen what the others think of us."

The other men nodded gravely.

"I was hoping we could stay out of trouble here at home," Uncle Nevrus continued, "but it seems the Communists have decided otherwise."

A strangely tense sort of silence hung in the air. I curled up with my mother, not wanting to even look at the corner where I had nearly lost my life.

It was Grandmother Aishe who first spoke. "What will you do now?" she asked, and from the way she spoke, I could sense that she was haunted by the similarities she was seeing between her son and her departed husband.

"Well, we've beaten them back for now," Uncle Nevrus said. "We've shown them that we'll be ready if they come calling again." He steeled up, standing tall and clenching his fists. "But we still have some unfinished business. I think the first step is to try to recruit people from the villages to help combat the Communist propaganda." Fuhat gave a grim look. "They're telling our people they can have the moon! They're being promised that, thanks to Russian technology, soon, they'll be able to turn on their taps and get milk instead of water."

"The trouble is some of our people believe this nonsense," Uncle Nevrus agreed.

"Worse than that," Demirsha said as he looked gravely at me, "the children are told to disregard what their parents say and join the Communist ranks, as Father Stalin wants them to do. The young people are being brainwashed. The villagers are being offered bouquets of sweet-smelling roses, but when they get them in their hands, they'll find only a handful of thorns."

Uncle Nevrus was pensive for a time. "The Communists have gained a lot of ground," he said finally. "We have to admit it and go on from here. We fought against the Italians and Germans, and now we must fight our own people. I personally don't like the idea at all, but it has to be this way."

Despite the protests from the women, Uncle Nevrus and his friends left that night, as did the rest of the houseguests. It was the end of a day in hell and the beginning of a nightmare that would last for many years to come. No one could predict the outcome of this dreadful war, but we could only pray that freedom and democracy would prevail.

For months after, my uncle and his friends fought the Communists night and day but always found themselves pushed back by the enemy's superior numbers. It wasn't long before Uncle Nevrus and his men started falling short on ammunition and supplies. The wounded, dead, and deserters began to outnumber those still fighting. After weighing the odds, the survivors decided to attempt escape across the Adriatic Sea into Italy, the hope being that they could reassemble there and return to fight for their freedom at another time.

It wasn't until later that I would learn the details of the plan, but I can still picture it as if I had been there. They gathered near the town of Shkoder. The moonlight faded and came on again as the clouds moved across the sky on the back of a gentle evening breeze. As they came closer to the shoreline, they could hear the combined sounds of the waves breaking on the rocks blending with the pounding of their own hearts. The boat they would use for their journey was carefully concealed under an outcropping of rock just along the shoreline.

I would later learn that my Uncle Nevrus took pause right as the group was on the cusp of fleeing.

"I feel like a deserter, leaving Albania," Uncle Nevrus said. He explained that despite the odds, he was compelled to remain, to fight to the death for freedom.

Some of the men objected.

"So what happens if we do escape?" Uncle Nevrus replied. "There will be those who will call us traitors."

A growl went up from the men. Traitor was a word that no true Albanian would tolerate.

It was Demirsha who served the opposing viewpoint. "If we stay, then eventually we must surrender. And if we surrender, the Communists will make examples out of us. They'll use us as proof to the villagers that our fight is hopeless and that they have no choice but to fear and succumb to the regime."

"The Communists are nothing but liars," someone said. "We've given them enough examples for one lifetime."

Demirsha paused for a moment, nodding in thought. "But if you decide to stay and fight now," he said to Uncle Nevrus, "then I will stay too. I don't want to be called the only traitor among you."

So rather than escape to freedom, Uncle Nevrus and his following fought for a time before ultimately giving themselves up. When they surrendered to the authorities, they were promptly arrested and put in prison. A few short days passed before they were tried in military court.

I was too young to attend the proceedings, but I would later learn from Asan Talo who witnessed the trial in person that Uncle Nevrus, along with the rest of his freedom fighters, stood in handcuffs before a panel of military judges and a large crowd of people from the town of Bilisht. Armed soldiers of the People's Socialist Republic of Albania stood guard behind them. Not one of the condemned men could speak in his defense. For four days, they were shuffled back and forth to court, where they were forced to stand and listen to the fabricated charges shouted against them. They were accused of every major crime, from murder to rape to theft on a grand scale.

At one point, Uncle Nevrus was so overcome by all the lies and fabrications that he interrupted the prosecutor. "These charges are not true," he said. "We want nothing more than to have a free Albania—to free it from you Communist thugs! Your beliefs are destructive to the Albanian people and our country. You have no principles or morals."

One of the judges pounded his gavel, trying to silence my uncle, but he kept on.

"I know the day will come that you will pay for your crimes," Uncle Nevrus said. "We stand here before you today as Albanians. You may have been born Albanian, but as you sit here today in judgment of us, it cannot be determined what you have become!" More chaotic objections erupted.

Uncle Nevrus kept on. "You are called the Butchers of Russia, and your father is called Father Stalin, among other things. We did not know that Stalin came away from Moscow and had his way with your mothers."

By now, the judge was choking in his anger. His face turned pale and spittle flew from his mouth as he shouted, "Guilty as charged, you filthy pigs! The sentence is death. You will all be shot." Then he turned to the guards and said, "Get them out of here. Lock them up."

Uncle Nevrus and the others were taken to the prison to await their execution. By that time, Father and Uncle Arif had also been arrested as political objectors. With all the adult men in prison, only the women and children were left in the Bylykbashi household. But Grandmother Aishe stood firm and brave, not letting anything bend her courage or her spirit. She was like an old oak tree—as she grew older, she also grew stronger. As each new dire situation arose, she calmly and collectively planned her retaliation strategy. She would plot and organize every maneuver as if she were an officer in the military.

When Grandmother received word that family members would be allowed to see the prisoners, she sent Mother to visit my father. The following week, Aunt Sibe went to visit Uncle Arif in a different prison. Uncle Nevrus's wife had to wait over a month before permission was granted for a visit with her husband. Finally, the opportunity came, and Aunt Idajet asked Mother to go with her. They prepared some of my uncle's favorite food and packed some clean clothing for him. The next morning, Mother, Aunt Idajet, and I arrived in the town of Bilisht, where we were directed to the prison holding Uncle Nevrus.

After being ushered through the guard detail, we entered a small room manned by a single bureaucrat at a desk. Mother handed over the documentation allowing for the visit. The bureaucrat checked it over, his bald spot gleaming under the single overhead light bulb, and then stamped the papers in red ink.

The heavy door behind him was unlocked, and we were escorted to another room. This room was divided by a wall interrupted only by a small window covered in thick iron bars. There was one stool on our side of the wall, and through the bars, I could see that there was a similar stool set up on the other side. Aunt Idajet took a seat on the stool, and the three of us waited nervously for Uncle Nevrus's arrival. I held my mother's hand as we waited, my palms sweaty and my knees weak.

A few minutes later, Uncle Nevrus was brought in and seated on the other side of the wall. The armed guards that had served as his escort remained behind him throughout our allotted time.

Being a young boy, I naively asked, "When are you coming home, Uncle Nevrus? It's been a long time, and we miss you."

He smiled sadly but did not reply. He just continued to smoke a cigarette and look us over as if he knew it would be the last time.

All through the time we had waited for him, Aunt Idajet behaved as if nervous and upset, but now that he was here before her, she began talking about trivial matters—talking just for talking's sake as if she were talking against time they no longer had.

Suddenly, Uncle Nevrus interrupted her, "Idajet, you know we don't have much time left. The guards will take me away in a few minutes, and this is the only time we have to say what we need to say to each other."

Aunt Idajet lowered her head, but she couldn't hide her tears. I could see her lips quivering and see her chest seize through her silent sobs.

"This is difficult for me," Uncle Nevrus said, "but it will be even more difficult for you." He reached through the bars to touch his wife's fingers, but one of the guards stepped forward and intervened.

"Idajet, you are a young woman, and you must go on with your life," Uncle Nevrus said softly. "You must find happiness again. I want you to promise me you will remarry once I'm gone."

My aunt could no longer hold her silence as she pressed a hand-kerchief to her face and moaned in sorrow.

"We never had children," Uncle Nevrus was saying, "and you should be a mother. Please marry again and do this in my memory."

It was then that I began to cry as well, not because I understood what was going on but because my aunt's sorrow upset me. By the end of our time there, Aunt Idajet was in a state of near collapse, and Mother quickly moved to her side to support her from falling. Uncle Nevrus looked on but was unable to help.

A guard motioned that it was time to go, and my aunt raised her hands as if in prayer. "Goodbye," she whispered through her tears.

Mother waved to her brother-in-law and spoke loudly, "Nevrus, we will never forget you!"

At the sound of my mother crying out, two guards appeared on our side of the wall. One of them shoved Mother to the floor with such violence I feared she might never rise. In defiance, she climbed shakily to her feet and screamed, "You are murderers! Someday, you will pay for your vicious acts!"

They started dragging Mother through the door where we had entered and took Uncle Nevrus back to his cell. As I followed Mother, I could hear Uncle Nevrus's cell door slam shut. The guards marched away through an empty corridor as we were escorted in the opposite direction. Then suddenly, we were outside the prison walls. I would never see my uncle again. He was left inside that cell, all alone, with only his memories of better times and the uncertainty of when would be the last day of his life. Never again would he get to enjoy his birthright: the streams, the mountains, his country, his family, his life. I know he must have felt helpless and, even worse, that there was no use for harboring hope.

One thing was certain: in the eyes of those who knew him and for those that would hear his story told years after he was gone, he would die bravely. Even as thousands of his countrymen turned their backs on him and his cause, he had defended the country he so loved.

All the way home from the prison, Aunt Idajet's mind seemed to be elsewhere.

Mother had to lead her sister along by the arm, or she would wander off aimlessly as if she had forgotten where she lived or even what her purpose was in this world. As we traveled past the places we had favored in happier times—the meadows and the streams that our family had enjoyed together—nothing seemed to register in Aunt Idajet's mind.

That was when I first came to realize what we had just done, how we had just said goodbye for the very last time to a man we loved dearly. My heart filled with such sorrow that even I lost the sense of where we were or what we were doing. I'm not sure how we got home, but I am certain we would not have made it without my mother's strength.

A few months later, I would learn the details of my uncle's execution.

Uncle Nevrus and the rest of the prisoners were transferred to a prison in Korce, where they remained until they officially received their death sentence. With hands and feet chained, they were ushered into a truck under heavy guard. As an extra precaution, a truck of armed guards preceded the prisoner escort, and another similar truck followed them. I guess the Communists feared an ambush along the route to Bilisht.

Included with the prisoners in the truck were a Muslim Imam named Qerim Shehu and his son Sali, condemned to death for their beliefs. I have heard that the Imam was so concerned for his son that he spent most of the journey fervently praying that God would give Sali the courage he needed to face what awaited them. He also prayed for the rest of the prisoners, asking that they be granted strength.

"These men are innocent," he prayed, "and their convictions were as unjust as mine and my son's."

Fuhat was observing the Imam as he prayed and, in a low voice, said, "He has never committed any crimes. Why would they want to execute him and his son? It doesn't make any sense to me."

"Don't try to make sense out of this, Fuhat," Nevrus replied. "Logic in the mind of a Communist does not exist. They can only gain control through torture and terror. It's all they know. My dear friend, this regime wants to play God. These pigs will do anything Moscow tells them."

"But the merciful thing—"

"Mercy?" Uncle Nevrus interrupted his friend. "Stalin executed millions of his own people, so why would you think he is capable of mercy? When we had the power and captured these monsters, what did we do? We let them go so they could fight us again. We should have known that the old rules no longer apply."

The long silence that followed was abruptly punctuated when the Communist soldiers riding in the lead truck began shouting at the passersby in the villages.

"You!" they would shout. "Come along with us and see what happens to traitors and anyone else who opposes the blessings of communism."

"Death to counterrevolutionaries!" they would call. "Death to Kulaks!"

As they continued through the villages, the soldiers chanted and recited the magnificent things that would result from their Russian friends under the leadership of Father Stalin's dictatorship, all the while encouraging the villagers to follow them and see what happened to those who refused to succumb to communism.

The trucks arrived at a clearing along the edge of Bilisht, where the soldiers quickly jumped out to surround the prisoner transport vehicle. The stage was set. All the machine guns were in place. A sizeable crowd had gathered, some of the people forced by the Communists to attend and others drawn to the place purely out of curiosity. All that was left was to perpetrate the bloody massacre of innocent men.

The officer in charge ordered the tailgate of the prisoners' truck to be opened.

From the gossip of the villagers and the tales of my family, I later learned that Uncle Nevrus was the first to jump down from the truck. He quickly turned to give encouragement to his comrades. "Come on, you freedom fighters! We have lived like lions, and now we will die like lions! We will have pride in ourselves until our last breath, and then because of what we stood for, our families will have pride when they speak of us long after we are gone."

The guards tried to silence Uncle Nevrus with the butts of their rifles, but he kept on.

"The only contempt we will carry to our grave is for these traitors, whose only strength is in numbers and treachery. Long live Albania and its people! Know in your hearts that the day is coming when our blood will be avenged!"

As the guards converged on Uncle Nevrus once more, his companions jumped down from the truck and joined him. They held their heads up high with their shoulders proudly back, forming a straight line with my uncle as they bravely awaited their final stand.

An army judge appeared and, in a pompous voice, announced, "If anyone has anything to say, this is your last chance."

"I have a last request," the Imam said. "I wish to be the first to die."

"No, you religious old fool," the judge replied. "You will not be the first to die." With a snort of contempt, he added, "In fact, I am going to be sure that you are the *last* to die. Maybe you can use your time to pray to your God. Ask him to save you from the firing squad if he is so powerful!"

The Imam bowed his head and prayed, "May God the merciful forgive you for what you are saying and for what you are about to do."

"Oh yes!" Demirsha screamed. "These pigs know what they are saying and doing, all right. If I had my hands loose, I would tear them apart!"

The judge fumed. "Take these traitors away from the rest of the group," he barked at the guards. "Give them a lesson they will not forget. Maybe then when they stand in front of our firing squad again, they'll give us the respect we deserve."

Only seconds after the Imam, his son, and Demirsha were dragged away, the judge gave the order to fire on Uncle Nevrus, Fuhat, and the rest of the prisoners. The machine guns blazed away, and the prisoners fell backward into pools of their own blood. I am told that my Uncle Nevrus died with his head held high and that as he fell, no one spoke, not from among the crowd and not from among the Communists.

Our enemy left my uncle and his comrades to lie in the sun until nightfall—a grim reminder of what happened to those they called "traitors." Then under cover of darkness, they disposed of their bodies in an undisclosed location. To this day, we have never learned where my brave uncle Nevrus's body was taken.

A few weeks passed before there was another execution. This time, Gani Kulla, the leader of the Devolli Region, and his nephew Ajdin Kulla were sentenced to die by firing squad. It wasn't until this day that Demirsha, along with the Imam and his son, were finally released from their torture and executed.

War makes monsters of men, but I still can't justify how something like this happens in the real world. I have to believe that most of the people who witnessed the slaughter of my uncle and those that followed him—and even some of those who had taken part in the killings—could not fully grasp the reality of what was happening. How could this be possible, Albanians operating under the banner of communism, killing fellow Albanians while other Albanians stood by and watched? With the massacre of these innocent men, it was clear to everyone, even the six-year-old me, that the future of our country was grim. More brave men were gunned down for defending their country. More bodies were collected and moved to unmarked graves throughout Albania. Week after week, it was the same thing.

For many Albanians, including myself, I think it was easier to stand by and watch what the Communists were doing to us simply because it is not possible to comprehend such brutality when it is happening in the moment. It wasn't so much war that we were witnessing as it was cold-blooded murder committed in full view of the public.

The grief was unbearable, but somehow in the face of it all, the Bylykbashi family was learning to endure the nightmares we had faced and the hell yet to come. Our lives were all about survival now.

Chapter 2

A few months after the executions, a Communist delegation invaded our house, and "for the good of the State," one third of our property, including our livestock, was confiscated. Some of the people with the group had been our former neighbors. Now they wore the brown uniforms with the thick, woolen overcoats and called themselves Communists. They were led by a high-ranking officer who ordered what remained of my family to be rounded up and herded into the courtyard. The patches on his uniform were different. He had more of them than the other soldiers I had seen which made me suspect that he was of high rank—a suspicion confirmed when I heard one of the others address him as colonel.

There, the officer opened a briefcase and removed a crisp, official-looking letter. From the steeliness of his jaw to the way he carried his head thrown back like a rooster, it was clear to all that this was a man of exceptional arrogance who took great pleasure in stealing our land and livestock as he cleared his throat and began to read: "Direct from the national capital at Tirana, the property of Nevrus Bylykbashi now belongs to the national government."

From my position just behind the officer, I could see that another Communist official had duly and officially stamped the letter. After he finished reading, he told his men to keep my family at gunpoint while he inspected our horses and other livestock.

A cold numbness gripped me when he reached the stall where I kept Butterfly. I loved that horse for who she was but also because she was a gift from my beloved Uncle Nevrus, the only reminder of him I had left in the world. I felt a knot form in my stomach as the colonel made an abrupt halt and stood sizing up my horse.

Butterfly was four years old by then and at the peak of her unrivaled beauty. My throat went dry, and my eyes began to water as I watched this wretched stranger put a saddle and bridle on my horse. When he was finished, he turned and, with a hungry grin, told one of his soldiers to write something down.

Even at gunpoint, I couldn't help but step forward to get a better listen.

"You heard me," he told the soldier. "Mark this horse on the list as my own personal property."

A white-hot rage surged within me. I swatted the rifle out of my face and charged toward the colonel. "Get your filthy hands off my horse, you dog!" I heard myself screaming. "This is my horse, given to me by my uncle as a present, and you're not stealing him, you thief!" When I reached him, the colonel casually pushed me to the ground. I tried to rise, but he kicked me swiftly in the ribs, sending me toppling back into the dirt.

"If you want him alive," he hissed at Mother, "then keep him away from me. If he lays another finger on me, I'm going to put a bullet in his head."

Mother went rigid, but Grandmother Aishe refused to cow to this man. She was old, but she still had plenty of life left in her. "How dare you say that you will kill my grandson," she said, her voice stronger and more authoritative than I could ever remember hearing. "You've already murdered my younger son, along with his friends. And now today, your thugs are robbing our house. You viciously threaten to kill women and children. What kind of monsters are you?"

The colonel chuckled derisively. He said something to the soldier nearest him, but I couldn't make out the words.

"Go ahead and kill us all," Grandmother was saying. "We'd rather die than live under your rules."

Now the colonel had lost his sense of humor. His expression hardened, and his proud jaw tensed. "Shut up or I'll cut out your tongue!"

With that, he threw his boot into the stirrup and tried to mount my horse. Butterfly must have sensed danger, for she resisted the mount, and the colonel stumbled back to his feet. When he tried again, Butterfly shied away wildly, her eyes rolling in fear.

The tears streamed down my face as I rose to my knees and reached out. I felt like a newborn reaching blindly and helplessly at the sky. There was nothing in the world I wanted more than to save my horse, but there was nothing I could do.

On the colonel's third attempt to mount, Butterfly had calmed enough to allow the rider to take the saddle. I'll never forget the look of complete satisfaction etched on that man's face when he found his mount. But then in his pride and revelry, he made a mistake. He turned Butterfly toward the gate then whipped her harshly. Startled and in pain, Butterfly reared back and whickered in a piercing cry. When she found her feet again, she turned and bucked violently before bolting through the gate at top speed, the colonel holding onto the saddle for dear life.

I rushed to the main entrance to watch. Just at the end of the road, the colonel lost his grip, and Butterfly tossed him into the dirt. There the pompous officer lay, stunned and clearly hurt.

My tears turned to hysterical laughter at the sight of the colonel lying in the middle of the street. For a moment, as I watched Butterfly trot and shake her head magnificently, I hoped that maybe the colonel had learned a lesson here—that maybe he would choose another horse, one that he could handle. But the colonel clearly knew a good horse when he saw one. He was not going to let my Butterfly go.

Young as I was, even I could see what was happening here. Because my family was somewhat wealthy, the invading party clearly saw that wealth as a threat. In response, they had launched a campaign to systematically eliminate the men in the Bylykbashi clan one by one. Uncle Nevrus was executed. Nuri and Asan were in prison on trumped-up charges. Father and Uncle Arif had been locked away as well. Uncle Emin, as well as Aunt Vajbe, were sent to Tepelena, a labor camp with the reputation as the most brutal such camp in Albania. They wound up in Tepelena specifically because they both had sons that had escaped Albania to join the freedom fighters in Greece.

One of those sons, my cousin Seit, escaped Albania and joined the resistance in Greece that was led by the British Intelligence

Service. They formed a group of freedom fighters to infiltrate and work within Albania, the goal being to stir the people into an uprising that could topple the Communist regime. In charge of the operation was a British officer named Colonel Kim Filby. The men trained in Malta then returned to Albania, but the mission was doomed from the start.

They barely had time to organize before the entire group was captured. Soon after, they would learn that the leak had come from the top. Colonel Kim Filby was working with the Russians and had notified the Albanian secret police (the Sigurim) of the mission.

Months passed before they were dragged before the military court. Seit had been trained as a short-wave radio operator, and the chief judge asked him how he had learned to operate the radio so well since he had no formal schooling. Seit was only twenty-five years old and knew there was no hope for a future, so he gave an honest answer.

"The flame of hatred I feel for you and your criminal regime compelled me to learn it well," he said. "You are traitors to our country and to the Albanian people. You're nothing more than butchers, and you will all pay with your lives someday!"

Seit and the others were executed. After that, it seemed like the Communist Party thought they had finally brought the Bylykbashi family under control. For a while, it was true. We were a family very much in mourning over all the losses we had suffered.

*****

By now, I had many reasons to hate communism. It had murdered my Uncle Nevrus and my cousin Seit. It had stolen my horse. It had imprisoned my father and Uncle Arif. My family and many of our friends suffered daily under its thumb. The Communists treated my family as if we were criminals, but we had done nothing more than kept our minds free from their tyranny. For a long while after Butterfly was taken from me, uniformed Communists would enter our home, any time day or night, and remove family treasures and heirlooms. They would take food, livestock, clothes—whatever their hearts desired. It hurt us to have people we used to live alongside in our village taking our belongings without cause or concern, but we never gave them the satisfaction of knowing just how much it hurt.

Mostly, we were bewildered by the intrusions on our daily life. We had no one to turn to for sympathy either. The Communists had made the other people in our village too afraid to offer us help of any kind. We stood alone now. In many ways, everyone stood alone. Paranoia ran rampant in the villages. There was no longer any trust between Albanians. Even those who had once called themselves friends were turning on each other. We had to be careful what we discussed because spies and informants were everywhere. The most casual and innocent of remarks could invoke a death sentence at worst and a life sentence in either prison or a labor camp at best.

We discovered this the hard way when my cousin Agim arrived at the house to tell my mother that both her brothers had been arrested.

"Where are they being held?" Mother asked urgently. Young Agim lowered his head. "I don't know," he said. "I've tried tracking them for the past two days, but no one knows where they were taken."

With so many of the Bylykbashi family now in prison, the oldest free males in the family were my brother Fejzi and my first cousin Sybi, both only fifteen years old. Despite their youth, Mother had no choice but to tell them to go with Agim and try to get information.

"Find out what you can about where they took my brothers," she told them. "And see if you can learn how they are doing physically."

I stepped forward as if she might ask me to help as well, but her eyes never left my brother.

"Go right away," she said as she placed her quivering hands on his shoulders. "I'm worried sick."

Two long, anxious days passed. Then finally, Fejzi and Sybi returned.

Mother greeted them warmly and hugged them close to her. "I thank God with all my being that you have come back to us safely."

"Mother," Fejzi said, "we have found where they are holding our uncles. No one would tell us the charges, but they have been brutally tortured and beaten."

My mother gasped, "When will they be sentenced?"

My heart sank as Fejzi and Sybi traded forlorn glances.

"They have already been sentenced," Sybi said sadly.

With wide eyes, my mother went to her nephew and held his face in her hands. "Please tell me, child."

Sybi seemed to shrink in that moment, and words failed him. It was my brother who answered.

"Uncle Seit will only have five years in prison," he said. "But Uncle Hysen received a death sentence."

I had seen my mother upset many times before. The Communists had seen to that. But that was the first time I ever saw her crumble. She went to the floor, where she began crying hysterically. I wanted to comfort her, but there was no controlling my own tears. The four of us sobbed for a time until Mother pulled herself together and stood once more.

"Why, Mother?" I asked. "Why would they do this? My uncles are good men."

She shook her head. "The choices we make in our youth often come back to haunt us," she said cryptically. With a handkerchief she had made with her own hands, Mother wiped away the last of her tears and shuddered through a sigh. "Your Uncle Hysen went to the United States several years ago and lived in New York City for a while. Your uncle was tall, slim, charming, and very handsome. There he met a very beautiful woman who was recently divorced. They fell in love and wanted to spend the rest of their lives together." Mother was sitting in the rocking chair, and now for the first time in my life, I noticed her age. She reminded me a little of Grandmother Aishe in that moment—proud and resolute but old and tired. Mother appeared to have aged many years in several minutes. She looked hollowed out and weak.

"What does this have to do with the Communists?" I asked Mother.

"I'm getting to that," she said. "Just be patient." And again, she reminded me of my grandmother. "Your uncle and his new bride named Reshide returned to Albania and made their home here. And from that day forward, everyone knew your uncle as the man who had lived in America." She took on a distant, resigned expression. "So you see, Pertef, that was his dreadful mistake. The Communists fear him because he has known real freedom in the United States. They fear he will expose them for what they are and spread the word of freedom to the people. And now they've condemned my brother to death."

Mother had to act without delay to see if she could save her brother's life. That same day, I went with her to her old village of Cangonj to see her father. She informed him of his son's sentence, and together, they made plans to free Uncle Hysen. They decided to gather up all the family gold in the hopes that it would be enough to bribe some high official to remove Uncle Hysen's death sentence.

To our great surprise, the plan worked. Through a friend of a friend, we learned that somehow the orders were changed and my uncle's death sentence was reduced to life in prison. Grandfather had spent his entire fortune, but he would later tell me that it was a small price to pay in exchange for his son's life.

For the next couple of years, we lived in this nightmarish place where everyone distrusted everyone else and the Communists took from us whatever and whoever they wanted. Then much to our surprise, Father was released from prison. The day after his return home, the head of the local Communist tax department marched into our house unannounced and told Father in the most insulting tone that he had not paid his taxes for the time he had been away in prison.

"I'm sorry," Father said. "But I did pay those taxes."

The notion that a man should be expected to pay taxes on earnings he didn't make while locked up should have angered us, but we had gotten used to the Communists writing their own rules. What frustrated Father was that he had indeed paid the taxes to the legitimate tax office. When he tried to explain that to the official, his explanation fell on deaf ears.

"If you don't pay the taxes by tomorrow," the official said, his eyes growing dark, "you will be sent back to prison. This time, you will be shown no mercy."

My father replied without any sense of fear. "You are dead wrong," he said and the way he said it caused me to swell with pride for him. "My wife paid these taxes when you had me in prison. Here are my tax receipts. See for yourself."

The official sneered as he looked over the documents my father handed him. Then he waved his hands in dismissal. "These taxes don't apply to people like you because you're rich and have to pay double taxes." He glared at each of us in turn. "We know you have piles of money hidden away. That's not how we do things in this country anymore. Now we share the wealth and make everyone equal. That's what Father Stalin teaches us." He clicked his heels together. "So pay up or I'll handcuff you and send you back to the same prison cell you had before."

The truth of the matter was that there was no money left. The Communists had already wiped us out with illegal taxes and confiscations. But my family was desperate.

Father had no choice but to borrow the money and pay the taxes for the second time.

I would like to write that this was the end of the matter, but of course, the fact that he was able to pay only confirmed the party's distorted notion of my family's wealth. We were only made to suffer more in the future.

*****

The school I attended was about a twenty-minute walk from our house. It was in a lovely spot, located at the base of the forest-covered hills that led up to the high mountains, and overlooking a river that roared from the snowmelt. The building itself was constructed of stone and covered with a tile roof. It housed four classrooms with an additional room for the teachers' office. Each of the classrooms had a wood-burning stove with enough wood stacked inside to last three or four days. For the coldest of days, there was extra wood stored under the building. To the side of the building was a dirt playground reserved for soccer and gymnastics. At the far end were separate outhouses, one for boys and one for girls.

The school served the villages of Pilur, Vranisht, and Bicke. After the Communist takeover, a man named Fhari Spaho acted as school principle. He had only five years of formal schooling, but because he was a party member, the authorities placed him in charge. Including Fhari, there were four teachers. The other three actually had teaching credentials, so it was always better to learn from them.

One such credentialed teacher was Olga, the only woman in the group. Remzi, Mero, and Mustafa Xama were the others. Teacher Remzi was highly intelligent and could easily have been a college professor, but the Communists did not trust him. In fact, the only reason he was even allowed to remain at the school instead of being carted off to prison was because he was needed to keep the school open.

The so-called "Comrade Fhari" knew absolutely nothing about teaching or running a school, but any time there were accolades to be passed down, they would all go to him, the loyal member of the party. He regularly called school assemblies for the purpose of brain-washing the children.

One day, all the students were called together to discuss religion.

"Do any of you believe there is a God?" Fhari asked of us.

We were young and naïve. All of us raised our hands.

Fhari sneered in that way only the Communists seemed capable. "Well, since you believe there is a God, then call upon him and see if he will bring you some candies."

Anxious to try this experiment, the pupils in the first through fourth grades called out, "God the merciful, please send us some candy!"

The principal made his students repeat their prayer for candy four or five times. I shook my head, knowing that this was a fool's errand and that Fhari would never give in. No candies would be forthcoming, and with every passing prayer from the decreasingly hopeful children, the ignorant principal's smile would widen.

I looked to the corner of the room, where teacher Remzi was standing. I kept hoping that he would speak out against this absurd propaganda, but he would only look at me and gently shake his head in disapproval as if telling me not to believe what was being said.

"All right," Fhari was saying. "Now I want all of you to say, 'Father Stalin, we want you to bring us some candies.'"

The children did as they were ordered. "Father Stalin, please bring us some candy!" came the cry.

Immediately, the door to the classroom opened. Several adult men entered the room with baskets full of candies and began throwing them around on the floor. Naturally, the children were excited enough to jump from their seats and frantically collect the candy. My cousin Bedri and I never moved from our chairs to take part in this charade. Our parents had warned us of the tactics used by the Communist government. In fact, just the mention of Stalin's name would make any member of our family sick to their stomach.

We were in the minority. With sessions such as these and through lectures in the school, the Communists gradually brought doubts and ridicule to bear on established religious faiths. The brainwashing was particularly effective on the children. It worked so well, in fact, that eventually my classmates would not speak to me or my cousin Bedri. Some of them even went so far as to betray their own families by turning them in to the authorities for perceived crimes against the party.

The great irony in it all is that many of the people who welcomed the regime so willingly and eagerly were ultimately made to suffer from its machinations. Even with all their power well established, the secret police (Sigurim) began recruiting informers to spy on Albanian families, the very families that had already shown them loyalty. In many instances, when they couldn't find anyone to prosecute, they would fabricate charges that guaranteed a prison sentence or internment in a labor camp.

There seemed no way to fight back against the tide, at least not en masse. The propaganda and paranoia were too strong for that. The Communists ensured their tight grip on the national consciousness by clamping down on foreign influences as well. Albania was now completely isolated from the outside world, with no counteracting influences like foreign news media, and no conversation with foreign travelers.

Sometime after my father's release from prison, Uncle Arif was finally released from prison as well and placed under house arrest. Even though his arrival was a joyous occasion for the family, we were saddened to share the news with Uncle Arif that Mentka, his daughter who was ten years old, had died from a childhood illness while he was imprisoned. That night, the adults talked warmly, but I couldn't help noticing how they didn't speak as freely as before. Now there was a heightened awareness among us regarding spies and informants. I remember feeling angry about this. To learn that there were informants embedded in other families was one thing, but to think that my family believed it possible within the walls of the Bylykbashi household? It didn't make sense to me. But then the Communists had ensured that no one was beyond suspicion, not even the children.

Whenever the conversation started to get interesting, someone would say, "We must be very careful now because even the walls have ears." Then the conversation would change to a lighter subject.

The situation in the country was getting worse by the day, and as each new day passed, new rules and regulations would come. Those rules would often get changed again the next day. When the Albanian people weren't so busy focusing on how disappointed, overworked, and starving they were, they had nothing but confusion to carry them through.

By this time, the government had done almost every landowner in the country the same way they had done my family. They took their land and formed cooperatives. Now the land and the people belonged to the state, and all were at the mercy of one evil man, Enver Hoxha, and his followers. The Stalinist puppet in charge of the Communist takeover of Albania was one of the most vicious criminals the world has ever known. The only property that thief hadn't stolen from us yet was our house and two apple orchards.

Since my family had been marked as enemies of the state, we were not allowed to participate as members of any of the local cooperatives. Since these were the only jobs available, it effectively meant that we weren't allowed to work.

*****

"What are we supposed to do?" Uncle Arif asked of my father one morning.

They sat in the dining room around the same table Uncle Nevrus had used as a barricade that first night the Communists started firing into our house. They thought they were alone, but the walls did indeed have ears. Fortunately for them, I was the only one eavesdropping, and my loyalties remained with my family as ever.

"There is nothing we can do," Father replied.

"But how do they expect us to feed our families?" Uncle Arif said.

My father sighed. "Arif, you know exactly what they're planning for us. They're trying to humiliate and degrade us."

Uncle Arif gave a cheerless chuckle. "They're trying to starve us out, is what they're doing."

The men were right, of course. With no food, no work, and no one to help us, we would eventually die of starvation. The party had aligned its problem in such a way that it would eliminate itself.

The truth is that there is only so much pushing a man can take before he starts to either fight or flee. As the oldest remaining male in the family, Uncle Arif was in charge of all the family matters in those days. He often spoke of our circumstances as if he could feel the weight of our fate in his hands. It was in 1950 that he made his decision, one that would change my family forever.

He gathered us all in the living room, where we sat shoulder to shoulder and watched him pace back and forth as he carefully planned in his head exactly what he wanted to say to us. He was always a slender man, but by now, the Communists had rendered him thin as a rail.

"As things stand right now," Uncle Arif said, and I remember being stunned by how loudly he was speaking, "there is simply no future for us in Albania. Even if it means crossing over into Greece temporarily, our only alternative is for the men to organize a resistance movement and arm themselves. Then hopefully, we will have a better chance of defeating the enemy." A few of the women gasped.

But Father was nodding his agreement. "The longer we wait, the more chance we have of being caught by their trumped-up charges and traps."

"Let's be men again," Uncle Arif said. "Men with rifles in our hands and Communist in our sights!"

Now even I began to tense up at how freely my uncle was speaking of treason.

"Start spreading the word among our relatives and trusted friends," he told Father.

"But do it quietly. Be cautious. It's our necks if this gets to the wrong people."

My mother began to object. "But what if—"

"I don't intend to be stopped," Uncle Arif interrupted. "We've waited long enough. It's now or never."

The next morning, Uncle Arif and his son Sybi went to the orchard. My brother Fejzi had planned to meet them there later in the day. That afternoon, Mother made lunch and asked me to take it to them. I was very happy to oblige since I knew Fejzi would be there and I was quite fond of him.

I had walked about a kilometer when I saw a man coming toward me. "Hold on there!" he shouted.

I stopped. "What can I do for you, sir?"

"What's your name, boy?"

With a furrowed brow, I looked up at him. "Who wants to know?"

"I want to know," the man said, pointing at his chest. "I'm the taxman. My name is Ymer Mulla." He was quite a handsome man with hollow eyes and a tattered suit. With the way he was sizing me up, I could sense that he was trying to scare me.

For as long as I have lived, I have never frightened easily. "My name is Pertef Bylykbashi," I said, giving him my full name just so he knew I wasn't afraid.

The taxman raised a bushy eyebrow. "Are you related to Arif?"

"Yes. I am the son of Zenel. Arif is my uncle."

"Do you know where your uncle is?"

At first, I hesitated. I wanted to make sure I knew what effect my answer would have and whether it would implicate anyone in our circle of family and friends. A thought flashed into my mind: *Why did he ask me about Uncle Arif and not my father?* I tried to smile agreeably. "My uncle is in the orchard. I'm on my way there now. Perhaps, sir, you would care to come along with me?"

The taxman made a face like he hadn't expected such compliance. "Thank you. I would like that."

Together, we trudged through fields that used to be lush with crops but had become little more than rows of dirt. We passed Grandfather Ramo's mausoleum, and the sight of it gave me strength.

"Do you go to school?" the taxman asked.

"Yes, sir."

Since I wasn't sure of the man's motives, I was wary about accidentally giving him too much information. He seemed to sense this. So as we walked along, we talked casually about unimportant things, and I was always careful to keep my answers brief.

As we neared the orchard, our old dog Kuqo (Red) began to bark violently. Once we had kept four or five dogs to help with working the livestock, but as the times became more difficult, we couldn't afford to keep them. We couldn't really afford Kuqo either, but he was such a good watchdog that we couldn't bear to part with him.

"Kuqo," I shouted at the snarling dog, "stop that immediately!"

Uncle Arif must have heard me hollering because he called out, "Is that you, Pertef?"

"Yes, it's me," I replied. I gave my companion a sidelong glance before adding, "Comrade Ymer from the tax department is with me. He wishes to talk with you."

My uncle emerged from among the young fruit trees and greeted the taxman.

"I'm glad to find you well," the tax man replied.

Uncle Arif turned to me, smiling. "Why don't you go to the edge of the orchard and wait for your brother to join us."

I immediately recognized this as an effort to get rid of me while the men talked, but what I didn't know was that Ymer was part of the plan for an escape into Greece. A few minutes later, Fejzi arrived. He was the oldest son, and so we all depended on him. He was tall and strong, had blue eyes like our mother's, and was gifted with an excellent physique. Moreover, he was well disciplined, courteous, and pleasant—qualities that made him instantly accepted and liked by anyone he met. My other siblings and I knew that he was our parents' favorite, but we loved him so much that we were not jealous of him. He was very special to all of us. Fejzi had good words for everyone—everyone except the Communist regime. For them, intense hatred ran through his veins, and he always stood ready to fight.

When I ran up to greet him, he put his hand on my head and playfully mussed my hair. In his other hand, he held a watermelon carved halfway open. Suddenly, he became very serious. "You have to be a good boy, Pertef," he said gravely. "The next time we meet, little brother, you'll probably be all grown up!"

I was bewildered. "I don't know what you're talking about, Fejzi. Are you going away somewhere? Can't I come too?"

He smiled. "Forget it. I'm just fooling around." He pulled a red, ripe chunk out of the watermelon he was enjoying. "Here. Have a piece. It's good."

Later, I would come to understand that Fejzi and Sybi had already learned of the escape plans from Father, and both had been warned not to share details of the escape to anyone—not even their mothers.

It began to rain hard, but I was chilled by something other than the storm. A vague premonition of something disastrous enveloped me but soon passed as Fejzi began playfully teasing with me again.

That evening, there was an uneasy feeling at home. Uncle Arif looked troubled as he kindly ordered all the women and children to leave the dining room.

"We men have some private affairs to discuss," he explained. "And only Zenel, Fejzi, and Sybi and my nephews Nazmi and Ilmi are to remain."

No one noticed when I also stayed behind to watch and listen.

When the room was clear, an excited Uncle Arif, puffing heavily on his pipe, remarked in agitation, "I've called you together to let you know that I received word from a reliable source that a meeting was held today in the town of Korca. It seems we have been singled out to be executed this very week. If we do not escape Albania right now, the next time we are together will be in front of a firing squad."

The men uttered curses. Everyone was upset because the time-table must now be changed quickly and having to rush could lead to careless mistakes.

"Let's not all go to pieces," Uncle Arif commanded. "Here is what we must do. Nazmi, this evening, you must say goodbye to your wife and your daughter, and the rest of you boys should say your farewells to your mothers. We're leaving Albania for the time being, but once we have organized with other supporters, we'll come back to overthrow these ignorant Communist *so-called* Albanians and free our families!"

The meeting broke up, and the men dispersed. Father and Uncle Arif slipped unseen from the house and, a long while later, returned with some wrapped packages containing weapons hidden since the old days. They spent a good part of the night cleaning, oiling, assembling, and loading regular and automatic rifles in preparation for the next day. When they had finished, we all went to bed, but none of us could sleep.

The next morning, a family friend named Idaet Bushka paid us a visit. He bore a piece of paper listing the names of individuals marked for execution within a few days. Among the names were my father, Uncle Arif, and Alil Bushka, Idaet's father. Uncle Arif sent word to the village of Cangonj to alert Ymer the taxman and his brothers to the existence of the list. They were advised to ready themselves, as their escape was now planned for that same evening. The letter contained information on where they would all meet and the exact time to be there.

Uncle Arif also sent a message to our good friend Refik Talo and his brother Asan, advising them of the change in plans for the escape. Refik and Asan lived close to the border, so their knowledge of those lands put them in charge of leading the group through the wooded mountains to Greece.

That night, Father and Uncle Arif said goodbye to their wives, their mother, and to all the children. The women and children were fighting back tears, but there were no tears from the men. Grandmother Aishe did not appear upset when she was told that her sons were fleeing the country—or at least, if she was, she didn't show it. Either way, it shouldn't have surprised anyone, given that her husband Ramo had spent most of his life fighting and hiding in the mountains.

"May God the merciful and compassionate watch over and guide you, my sons," she said solemnly. "Avenge the death of my son Nevrus and my nephew Seit. Give your BESA that you will preserve the family name and honor."

Those were to be the last words Grandmother would ever speak to her sons.

"Don't worry, Grandmother," Fejzi said. "When we get over the Greek border, we'll fire off a volley from our rifles. You'll be able to hear the echo from here, and that will tell you that we have made it safely." He looked to the window as if checking the position of the setting sun for the time. "But don't fret if it takes a long time. Under the best of conditions, it's about four hours of hard mountain walking. So don't be alarmed if it takes us a while."

Fejzi kissed all of us younger children then said goodbye to Mother, who pulled him into her arms and held him.

"Don't you dare forget me," she said to Fejzi. "But most of all, my son, be careful. You are very precious to all of us." Then Mother turned to my father and regarded him with a loving gaze. "Dear husband, please be careful with our son and return him safely to me. May God bless you and protect you."

In the midst of tears, hugs, and prayers, everyone exchanged BESA that we would never forget each other and would not forget that we were united in our cause, no matter what might come to pass. As a child at the time, I had no idea what lay ahead for us. I never could have guessed that our future would change with every choice we would make from that day forward.

With darkness setting in, those of us that were to remain behind held each other and fought back tears as we sadly but proudly watched the men leave for Greece and freedom.

It would be many years before I would learn the details of their escape from the iron grip of communism, but when the story was told to me, it was told with the kind of detail reserved only for fresh or indelible memories.

The night was hampered by cold, unceasing rain and high winds that blew viciously down from the higher peaks. The men climbed over the rocks and rough places, straining up the sharp cliffs, panting in the thin mountain air, slipping, sliding, falling, skinning hands and knees, and bruising their bodies as they struggled and sweated upward toward freedom. Several times, they had to stop and rest. The weather was not kind to them, and the mountain terrain was brutal.

Uncle Arif, his clothes filthy from mud and rain dripping in channels down his face, would occasionally burst into laughter, in an effort to keep the momentum high. "Come on, boys," he would say. "It's only a bit further to sunny Greece, the land of enchantment—our vacation spot!"

His mood proved infectious. All the men began to laugh from their perches on the tree roots and jagged pieces of stone that would serve as their footholds on the ascent.

"Let's have a swallow of raki (whiskey) to warm us," Uncle Arif suggested.

"Mind you, not too much. We wouldn't want to lose our heads or our bodies." The closer they came to the summit, the higher their spirits soared. They knew it wasn't much farther to the top, and yet their hardships were not at an end. Even if they managed to reach the peak, their next and last obstacle to tackle would be the border guards.

With aching arms and tired bodies, they moved like shadows through the pass. It was with great surprise that they slipped past the guards without incident. They had come prepared for a firefight, but none would greet them. There were rumors that many Albanian guards had deserted their units and escaped to Greece. The men in my family found evidence of that rumor's truth in every abandoned post they passed.

"Maybe the Communists don't have the borders secured as well as they thought," Father said with a chuckle.

In this way, my heavily armed family and friends made it into Greece without firing a shot. I have been told that it was a seminal moment for all them. In a single night, they had come from a place heavily oppressed by a party that had taken everything from them, including their hope of winning a fight from their own soil. Now they stood in a country that promised great hope for Albania. They all paused, smiling at the possibilities that now lay before them.

Then for my father at least, stark reality took hold. They were fugitives from their homeland.

It was Fejzi who broke the somber moment. "Uncle, I think it's time for the message to our families."

"Yes, of course, my boy!" Uncle Arif said.

With wild whoops and shouts, the men pointed their firearms into the Grecian sky and fired volley after volley, the sound of which echoed from mountain range to mountain range. Delirious with joy, they hugged each other and started to sing as they made their way into Greece.

Chapter 3

Hours had passed since the men said their goodbyes, but to us, it felt like weeks. Between us, not a word was spoken as we waited and listened for the volley of gunfire we were promised.

Finally, the echoes of the gunshots broke through the intense silence. I leapt at the sound. They had made it! They had made it, and my heart could not have been filled with more pride. With every passing volley, our happiness redoubled until laughter rang through the house. It had been a long time since I had heard genuinely joyful laughter—so long that I had almost forgotten what it sounded like.

They were alive, and they were free. For this, we were grateful, but for this, we were also concerned. Now that the men had made it, the focus could return to the home front. How would the Communists react when they learned of the escape? Would we be made to pay for their actions? We knew that there would be retribution of some kind, but it was the unknown that kept us up at night.

The next day, we stayed close to home in fear of being questioned by the authorities. The excitement and tension we had endured over the previous few days left me and my family physically and mentally drained, so we decided to go to bed early and try for a decent night's sleep. Before we went off to our bedrooms, we huddled together and bowed for our nightly prayers.

"God," my mother prayed, "we ask that you keep us safe and together, and if that is not possible, then please give us the wisdom and strength we need to face the future and what may come with it. We ask that you also give us the courage needed to honor the BESA we have given to our family, to hold steadfast and protect the values that have been instilled in us, and to bring honor to our name and to you."

I slept in the southern part of the house with Gezim, Medi, Lumka, Yllke, and Mother. Grandmother Aishe and Aunt Sibe slept in the northern quarters with Aunt Sibe's two daughters.

We had been asleep for only four or five hours when we received a stark wake-up call. A dozen or more soldiers crashed through all three entrances of our courtyard. They quickly posted guards at each entrance before entering our quarters, breaking every door in the house along the way.

"You're all under arrest!" the officer in charge screamed.

Mother jumped from the bed and frantically yelled for us to get up quickly. Medi and Gezim were not completely awake and could not seem to grasp exactly what was going on. Lumka ran toward Mother and then turned to pick up Yllke, who was crying hysterically.

My mother was a blur of movement as the soldiers began pouring in. She would later tell me that she had no doubt that we were going to prison—or worse—so she felt she had to gather everything we might need to survive the troubled days ahead. My mother was a beautiful woman, or else I'm not sure the guards would have let her pack anything. But she was slender and petite and had twinkling blue eyes and soft brown hair, so they allowed her to gather clothing and blankets. She formed them into bundles that we could carry over our shoulders.

After a time, the officer had seen enough. "You there!" he barked. "Don't take so many things. You will have to walk for many days, and you'll never make it with those loads."

I don't know what compelled me to say it, but I told Mother not to believe him. "There are trucks near Grandfather's tomb," I whispered. "And besides, they won't let us walk too far because they'll be afraid it would give us a better chance to escape."

The officer overheard me and assumed a stunned expression. "How did you know that, boy? I have been with you from the moment we arrived, and no one has spoken to you. It is impossible for you to know that information, but you have named the exact location of our trucks."

For the first time, the officer didn't look like a monster. His expression softened, and there was the human in him again. I wondered if he felt any remorse about all he was doing to his countrymen.

He looked around to see if anyone was near before he stepped to Mother and whispered just loudly enough for me to hear, "Listen to what your son is saying. Gather up every last thing that you can possibly carry for a distance of about one kilometer. After that, you'll be put into trucks and driven the rest of the way."

Minutes later, the secret police ordered us to join Grandmother and Aunt Sibe in the northern half of the compound. As we shuffled by with our heavy sacks, the soldiers pushed and kicked us, calling us every name imaginable. It was a humbling and frightening experience, but my concern lay not with myself but with my grandmother.

By the time we reached her, I could see that she was plenty capable of holding her own. Despite her age, she showed more fighting courage than all the rest of us combined. "Leave us alone, you monsters!" she was hollering. "And get out of our house! How dare you come here? Such brave men you think you are, picking on women and children! Such heroes! And you call that courage?"

Being defied by a weathered old woman appeared to anger the officer in charge. He took the pistol out of his holster and pointed it at her. We all froze in fear, thinking he was going to kill Grandmother Aishe right then.

"Shut up, you old hag," he said, all the evil returning to his face, "or I'll use this on you. The only thing that stops me is knowing the bullets are worth more than your life."

Blind as she was, I knew that Grandmother couldn't see the pistol pointed at her head and didn't know she was only a split second away from death. Silently, I prayed that she wouldn't speak another word, but I knew my grandmother better than that.

"Go ahead, you great brave man," she hissed. "I assume you're pointing a gun at me. Well, shoot and get it over with. What are you afraid of? Do you think I'll be able to hurt you, sonny?"

Her courage should not have surprised any of us. She had always been strong in the face of danger, particularly where her family was involved. To Grandmother, no one crossed the line and threatened her family, not without consequences.

We were all ordered outside to the courtyard, where the officer in charge started shaking his head and fuming. "The old hag will have to stay behind," he announced in disgust.

We were speechless. For as long as I can remember, I had thought that Grandmother would always be with us. I never could have imagined that we wouldn't be the ones to care for her in the end.

"But she is a blind old woman," Mother pleaded with the soldier who had shown her some compassion earlier. "Who will take care of her?"

And for the second time, I saw something of the man within the monstrous shell appear on the officer's face. "Do you have any family nearby?"

Mother nodded. "My husband's first cousin. Please let me send one of my children to ask them to take her."

An image of Uncle Maliq flashed in my mind just then. He too had a son in prison. He too had the Communist boot crashing down on him. I knew that Grandmother would be well cared for at Uncle Maliq's home. We had no alternative, so when the officer nodded, Mother quickly summoned for Medi to bring his cousins to our house. Then mother raced to Grandmother's side and started giving her instructions. I am sure that one of the instructions was to avoid provoking the soldiers further, but Grandmother roundly ignored it.

The secret police refused to let us hug her or even say goodbye. Medi returned in just a few minutes with Uncle Maliq's sons, Teki and Minir, who arrived with a stretcher to carry Grandmother Aishe to her new home. As they shuffled her off through the main gate, with Grandmother spouting invectives at every armed man she was carried passed, I wondered if I would ever see her again. I knew she would be in good hands but also knew I would miss her so. She was the strongest woman I had ever known. She had always given the family courage and always made me feel safe despite the turmoil raging all around us.

The secret police made us form a single column. Two officers led us, two more brought up the rear, and the rest of the soldiers guarded our flanks. Bent beneath the heavy loads we carried, we were herded along the slippery, muddy road through the fields we once called our own. Whenever we slipped or fell, we were prodded to our feet by rifle butts. Drops of rainwater tumbled from the old, proud trees that lined both sides of the road. The trees cast ominous shadows. We staggered past the houses of our neighbors, all them huddling in the dark and watching. Surely, they knew that we faced prison or death, so their fear prevented them from doing anything more.

I had known for quite some time that this day would come, but even now as it was happening, it all felt so surreal. The guns propelling us forward were real enough, and so was my fear, yet my mind was clear and my body strong. I just kept putting one foot in front of the other, determined to do everything I was told so I could avoid provoking further ire.

By the time we reached the cemetery, I was panting from exhaustion, my every muscle aching from the weight I carried. We drew closer to Grandfather Ramo's tomb, where, strangely enough, the trucks awaited us exactly as I had predicted. I am still not sure how I had known. I simply *knew*.

The guards didn't even give us a chance to catch our breath.

"All right, you imperialist traitors!" one of them shouted. "Get into the truck and keep quiet, or you'll get a bullet in your head!"

With rifles and machine guns all around us, we didn't argue. My hands and knees were shaking from fatigue as we wearily clambered aboard the vehicle. I found my place on a cold metal seat near the far end.

A few minutes later, under heavy guard, Alil Bushka's family appeared, and then my Uncle Qani and his family.

Uncle Qani was an old man worn down by long years, but he was still nearly as tough and free-spirited as Grandmother. When the guards forced him into the truck, he didn't hold back. "You rotten pieces of shit!" he shouted. "You sons of bitches! Why don't you leave us alone? We haven't done a damned thing to you. I hate everything about you and your lousy communist/socialist regime, and I only wish I was young again just long enough to show you what a real Albanian is all about."

He was so completely riled, so warlike and wild—like a fiery little gamecock with his gnarled old fists striking the air, his thin hair flying about, and his words challenging the night. He made such a scene that we all started to laugh. Even through my pain and fear, I laughed heartily. His defiance was good for my soul—for *all* of our souls.

When things quieted down a bit, the adults started talking in hushed tones.

"What's going to happen now?"

"Are they going to take all of us to prison, or will they dream up some reason to kill us out here on the road somewhere?"

"If they wanted to execute us, all they would have to do is claim we tried to escape."

"They would have no trouble scaring up witnesses on their behalf." After much talking in circles, a consensus was never reached.

We spent the night traveling through the countryside over rutted, potholed roads. The truck bounced and jostled constantly. Every time it came to a rollicking stop, we would wait for the better part of an hour for the soldiers to break into another home and arrest the women and children of men who had escaped with my father. I looked at the people in the truck, all wearied from being rooted out of their beds and homes in the dark. Some of them were defiant, some frightened, and some angry, but all were looking scruffy and often only partly dressed. One thing was certain to me: they didn't look like desperate enemies of the people, as the Communists called them. After all, we *were* the people, weren't we?

For the invaders of our land, it was never a matter of what was right and what was wrong. The Communists knew that any resistance to their overthrow would come mainly from upper class families. If they could destroy the spirit of these people, they would control all Albania. So little by little, one family at a time, they carried out their plan to break us.

On that night, several of my village's upper- and middle-class families—exhausted, cold, wet, tired—were packed like sardines in the back of an uncovered truck. After a while, no one talked. We rode for what seemed an eternity over rough roads, each of us silently fighting our own fears. No one slept that night.

Around five o'clock the next morning, we arrived in the town of Korca. With a population of thirty-five thousand, Korca was considered to be a large town in Southern Albania. By then, there were around ten families in our little procession of trucks.

When the secret police threw open the tailgate and woke me, I was groggy and confused by the dawn's light. They snapped at us to get out and form a line. After looking us over once more, they escorted us toward a prison crowned by a wooden sign bearing a quaint name: Hani me dy Porta. I thought the name proper, given that the place had high, forbidding walls interrupted by two heavy steel doors.

Moments after we entered the guardhouse just inside the gates, Uncle Qani was dragged away and put in a cell in the basement of the building. He cursed the authorities all the while as they separated him from the rest of us. I, along with the women and children, was forced into a small cell on the first floor. There were about thirty of us that they jammed into a cell of maybe four hundred square feet. It was all we could do to fit, but the guards kept pushing us in like animals shoved into a pen. We were so unnerved and exhausted by our ordeal that we eventually collapsed on top of each other, and some of us actually slept.

The claustrophobia would come over us in waves. There is nothing quite like the feeling that you are being suffocated. Even when I wasn't panicking, breathing was difficult. It felt like I was being slowly asphyxiated. I kept my consciousness throughout the ordeal, but many of the other children would faint from time to time. Even for the adults, their physical conditions were worsening.

The air became so stagnant that I could hardly see. There was only one small, steel-barred window, and it didn't even open to the outside. Rather, it looked into the neighboring cell, which was unoccupied. There was a woman standing near that window—far enough away that I never got a look at her—who suggested that we wave our blankets over our heads to circulate the air in the room. There was so little space that following her suggestion proved difficult, but it did help a little and probably saved a few lives in the process.

After a few more hours, some of the women began pounding on the doors and bars, screaming for help. The guards never so much as came to the door to listen to us.

Hour after hour drifted past like the weeks in a long winter. None of us had any idea what our captors had planned for us, which made our situation even more terrifying. To be packed in like that as you awaited transport to a permanent prison is one thing, but to think that you might have to live out the rest of your days in this way is entirely another. Add to that not knowing how many more days you had to live. Execution could come at any time.

Of course, a person's natural bodily functions don't cease in situations like this. Those closest to the door began to plead for a chance to go to the toilet, but the cries went unheeded.

"What's the matter with you animals?" one woman yelled. "Can't you see what's happening to us?"

Another woman in the cell across the hall also pleaded for help. "For the love of God," she begged, sounding hysterical. "Open the door! My baby is dead!" She pounded on the door, but I never heard the sound of it opening.

I don't know how long it had been before our cell door finally opened. At gunpoint, guards directed us to file out, and so we staggered into the corridor. I was among the lucky few allowed to use the toilets. After thirty minutes or so, the guards pushed us back into the cell. The short time did not allow everyone a chance to use the toilet, despite desperate need. In response, we decided to make two holes in the floor by breaking some floorboards. These would serve as our makeshift toilets. Some of the women even suggested that we could provide privacy by forming a human partition or by holding up some of the blankets we had with us in the cell. Some objected to using a hole in the floor, but others pointed out that it would at least keep the waste from sloshing around at our feet.

Only seconds after the makeshift toilet was used for the first time, we heard loud screams from below. We had no idea there were people locked in a cell directly beneath us.

"What the hell are you doing?" someone bellowed. "There are people down here!"

The practice stopped immediately, replaced by a plan to designate a small corner of the cell for our toilet needs.

This was just one of the many tactics designed and executed by the Communists to embarrass, shame, and destroy the morale of our people. On top of this shame, we had been caged for two days, and still we hadn't learned what was in store for us.

On the third day, the tiny barred window opened, and someone handed in a few loaves of bread. This was the first food we had received since our arrest, so we all scrambled to get a piece. The same lady that had suggested we wave the blankets for air was the first to pipe up about the danger the bread posed.

"Hold on!" she commanded. "Let's size up the situation. If you don't think this through, we won't have to wait for the firing squad because we'll be killing each other." My fellow prisoners quit scuffling long enough to hear her out.

"Don't you people understand this is exactly what they want?" she said. "They're trying to create distrust and hate among us so we'll begin fighting each other." The woman paused for just a moment as she looked around the cell. "We have a couple of young men here." She pointed to my brother Medi and Myfit Bushka. They were both fifteen years old, and I could see that even in these conditions, their chests swelled with pride to hear the lady refer to them as men. "Let them distribute the bread evenly."

Empowered by their newly dubbed manhood, Medi and Myfit shoved into the center of the crowd and took charge. They gathered up the four loaves and began handing out chunks evenly and fairly, ensuring that everyone got their proper share. The bread was old and stale, and my portion was as small as everyone else's, but I ate it ravenously and was grateful.

The incident changed the collective mindset of our group. It became clear that if we were going to survive this ordeal, we would have to remain unified and supportive of each other. It was one of the most valuable lessons I have ever learned, and I learned it in the unlikeliest of places.

For days, we remained in the same small holding cell with no opportunity to bathe or even splash water on our faces. Between the body odor, the smell of excrement from the corner, and the lack of airflow, the stench had become difficult to bear. But no matter how the communist tried to break us, to make us weak, it wasn't working. Even after two weeks in the cell, which felt like a lifetime, most of us remained unbroken. The conditions became so deplorable that I couldn't imagine even a caged animal surviving this long, and yet there we all stood, in unity, waiting for something. We weren't sure what we were waiting for, but we waited all the same.

Some of the adults would pass the time by talking and telling stories, but I spent most of my time in my own head. Slowly, I came to the realization that this war was different, more terrible than any other that I had heard about coming to Albania before. I had grown up hearing stories about invaders to our country that arrived to massacre and maltreat the people. But they were invaders. This was what made this war so different: those who oppressed us were by and large Albanians themselves. At least with an invader, one can find the proper place to pin his scorn, but these were traitors torturing their own countrymen. My focus became to determine who our true enemy was. Was it Stalin, who was killing and torturing innocent men, women, and children in the name of communism? Or was the enemy our own people, our fellow Albanians? After all, it was Enver Hoxha in Albania who was behind the regime and giving the orders to commit these war crimes, but the Albanians standing outside my cell were the ones committing the unspeakable crimes.

I lost track of the days after that.

Sometime later, the door opened again and in stepped an authoritative little man in an officer's uniform. "There are some among you who have been scheduled for a hearing and sentencing in the people's court," he said. Then he listed off a series of names. My family's names were among them.

"For what?" someone asked. "What crimes have we supposedly committed?"

By then, the officer had already let the door shut behind him. The question went unanswered.

"Our only crime is being the sons, daughters, wives, and family of men who were brave enough to fight back," someone said.

"We're here because our men left us behind," said another.

I had been pressed close to Mother for weeks, so by then, I could anticipate her thoughts before she spoke them. I reached up as if to quiet her, but she pulled her face away from my hand and spoke. "If they hadn't fled, they would've been tortured and killed for crimes they never committed," she insisted.

That seemed to quiet the dissenters.

Given the official nature of the officer's pronouncement, I had thought that we would be taken to court immediately, but the door didn't open again for a long while. Of course, they knew being forced to wait indefinitely can be hazardous to the mind. And not knowing exactly what it is that you're waiting for only adds to the danger. There were those among us that seemed alarmingly close to coming unhinged.

When the time finally came, we weren't taken to any people's court. Instead, the Communists led us into the prison's chilly, gray courtyard. There, the officers began to divide us into separate groups. They ushered the adults to one corner of the yard and the children to another.

The adults included my mother, Aunt Sibe, and her daughter Feruze. My cousin Myrset was shoved off into the children's corner along with Lumka, Medi, Gezim, Yllke, and myself.

It was a tall, angular man dressed in the drab garb of the secret police who finally informed us of our fate. He faced the children first. "Young children and infants are of no use to us," he said in a high, quavering voice. "You are free to go."

The same quiver of relief I felt echoed in the sighs and bellows of the other children. But then just like the others, I tensed up when I realized the man was only speaking to us and not to our parents.

"However," he continued, as he turned toward the adults looking as if he were taking a healthy sense of joy from the news he was about to deliver, "the rest of the prisoners have been marked as enemies of the state and deserve to be punished as such."

We all began to cry. Just like my siblings, I wanted to go with Mother, whether that meant having to join her in a labor camp or otherwise. It wasn't until later that I understood what was happening. The Communists intended to use the adults as slave laborers but had little use for the children, who were too small and weak to use as workers. Instead, they planned to use us as bait, hoping that once our father got word we were alone, he would return to save us and would be captured and executed.

We were all concerned about what would happen to us, of course, but our first thoughts were for our baby sister Yllke. She was still young enough to desperately need Mother's care. Even if the rest of us had to be sent away, we knew that something had to be done to try and keep her with Mother. So when the guards returned to us a suitcase full of many of the possessions we had brought along, we dragged it into the corner of the courtyard and started emptying it. My siblings and I frantically stashed our belongings into our tattered clothing, leaving only a few items behind to pad the bottom of the suitcase. Using sharp sticks, we poked holes in the suitcase to allow for air. Then we coaxed our sister inside, closed the lid, and gently handed it to Mother.

Her eyes filled with tears, Mother kissed each of us in turn and begged us to be careful. "I'll pray for each of you every day. I'll ask God to protect you from all harm until we're together again."

I could see that mother's concern for her children far outweighed any she might have held for herself and her uncertain future. She hugged and kissed us again and again right up until the guards grabbed her by the shoulders and started dragging her toward the truck idling near the prison's entrance.

Mother was trying to be gentle with her suitcase, even as the guards jerked her violently to the back of the truck. She had difficulty climbing into the truck while caring for her suitcase, which caused one of the guards to lose his patience. Without warning, he snatched the suitcase from Mother's hand and slung it into the back of the truck. Even from the other side of the prison yard, I could hear the loud clunk as my baby sister smacked against the far wall of the truck.

There was a long, tense moment of silence as I prayed that Yllke would remain quiet. Then the cry came, long and loud.

When the guards heard the baby crying, they pointed a rifle at Mother's head and demanded that she open the suitcase.

"What the hell is this?" one of them snarled. "What are you trying to pull over on us? Get that suitcase off this truck before I fill it full of bullet holes!"

They all looked to the nearest officer who sneered. "You'll be dealt with when we arrive at the camp," he said. "This will go hard for you, bitch."

By the time Mother got my baby sister out of the suitcase and had her standing on the ground, little Yllke was crying uncontrollably. I could see that she was in pain from the collision with the wall, but mostly, she was crying for her mother. We all were. Yet the heartless Communists remained untouched by the sad scene.

I stood in disbelief as they hauled Mother into the truck and slammed the tailgate shut. I wanted to hope that this wouldn't be the last time I would ever see her, but then quickly, the bleakest thought of my young life came to me. *Soon, it won't make a difference*, I told myself. *We'll all be dead at the hands of these thugs anyway.*

For a long while, I stared at the truck that bore my mother. I kept expecting them to leave, but then I saw that the proceedings hadn't yet come to an end. Next into the courtyard was my Uncle Qani and his family, along with Axhire, the wife of Alil Bushka. She had her two daughters and five sons with her, their ages falling with the range of me and my siblings. The authorities sent her children to wait with us as the secret police dragged Axhire toward Mother's truck.

Uncle Qani never lost his courage as the guards beat and kicked him toward another truck bearing the men. After they had him inside, the trucks finally began to roll slowly away. I watched for as far as I could see them, straining my eyes until they were not even a speck on the horizon.

There is no way to describe the emptiness that comes from realizing that you and your brothers and sisters have become orphans. We had no direction and no understanding of how to make it in any world, not to mention a world led by fellow countrymen who would rather have seen us dead. We were utterly alone.

It was at this point that the magnitude of our loss set in. We were a group of children with no guiding hands—no adults to guide us, feed us, or keep us going. I wasn't too young at the time to see that this was exactly what the Communists wanted. Their plan was that if we wanted to stay alive, we would have no choice but to succumb to their government, no choice but to live under their dictatorship.

What the Communists did not count on was our BESA, the strong fiber that ran through my family's blood. Our name was Bylykbashi, and even though we were just children, we *would not* surrender to the regime nor would we ever stop fighting them.

My oldest sister, Lumka (not to mention one of the toughest of the Bylykbashi children), had to take over the role of a mother, as well as head of the household. "Stop that crying," she told Yllke, who was the youngest among us. "We have to look after ourselves for Mother's sake. And we *will* do anything necessary to survive as a family until she comes home." She looked to the west, where it looked to me like an inky darkness had settled. "Speaking of home, that's where we must go, beginning right now."

"How far do you guess it is?" Myrset asked.

Medi shrugged. "Based on our time in the truck, I'd say it's at least four or five hours on foot."

"You mean they won't drive us?" Myrset asked naively.

Lumka strode forward, scooped Yllke out of Myrset's hands, and started walking.

"These pigs won't be giving us any help, Myrset," she said. "I can promise you that." Hungry, tired, and dismayed, we gathered up what we could and followed Lumka and Myrset. Even as we walked, I was struck with the notion that the girls had become women in an instant.

There was only one road that would take us to our village in Pilur. It was paved years earlier by the Italians, but by now, it was potholed and uneven. We walked that road for three hours or more before we had to leave it behind in favor of another direction with a dirt road. We encountered rough ground for the rest of the journey home. As we trudged through the mud and underbrush, cold rain dripped down from the tree branches overhead.

When we finally arrived home, we found the house locked and the windows boarded up. We checked with the authorities in the village and were told we would not be allowed into the house until we received approval from the government officials of Tirana, which would take some time. The only place left for us to find shelter was outside our old grocery store. The Nazis had bombed the store in the early forties, so all that remained were four walls and a partial roof. This was enough, at least, to provide shelter and a place to try for sleep.

Of our ordeal, word spread quickly through the village. Some of the villagers were sympathetic, but most were afraid to help for fear of punishment at the hands of the Communists. As a result, we could find very little to eat.

A month or so passed before we finally received permission to return home. The first thing we did was pay a visit to Uncle Maliq so we could pick up Grandmother Aishe. She was overjoyed when we came for her. We told her about how the Communists had taken Mother, Aunt Sibe, and Feruze to a labor camp. Grandmother was heartbroken.

"But at least we have you home now," she said with a shuddering sigh. "That will be our starting point."

From afar, the place looked like a warzone. It was dark and haphazardly fortified with shoddy wood. Where before, there had been an orchard, a farm, and stables full of life, now there were empty fields and not a single sound. Then out of the silence came a great, joyful baying. My heart leapt when I heard it, for I knew exactly who it belonged to. The government had confiscated our herds and livestock, but somehow, they had missed our dog Kuqo.

He appeared from behind the stables, his hair matted, his face muddy, and his skin stretched taut over his ribcage, but his was the happiest face I had seen in months. I couldn't help but laugh as he sprinted toward us. When Kuqo reached us, he jumped with joy, licking us all over, one by one. I could hardly believe he had made it.

"You're a survivor, Kuqo," I said.

"Like us," Lumka said somberly.

I knew a hollow sort of relief at finally being able to return home. It would never be the same without Mother and Father here, to say nothing of all the others we had lost to war, prison, or the labor camps. It felt like the life had been sucked out of the house.

On top of that, the place was a mess.

"God only knows what those dogs were doing in here before they boarded it up," Grandmother said.

From the sights and smells, there was no question that whatever they had been doing, it wasn't savory. If this hadn't been my lifelong home, I might have preferred the half shelter of that old grocery store, but we were determined to make this place feel like our home again.

For more than a month, Lumka and Myrset worked to bring the house back as close as they could to the shape it was in before we were arrested. Our plight could have been worse if not for the keen insights of Grandmother Aishe. We had no jobs or income, so food would have been extremely difficult to come by, but Grandmother Aishe recalled how our parents had hidden food in and around the house whenever the Communists would order raids on our property. As children, we had not paid attention to the places where our parents had hidden the food, but our blind Grandmother Aishe had listened as the hiding places were carefully chosen, so she knew exactly where to look.

She shared this information with only Lumka and Myrset and warned them not to tell any of the other children or anyone outside the family.

"The fewer people that know where the food is stored," she told them, "the better our chances of keeping it from the authorities."

So while I tried to keep our spirits up with games in the yard, Lumka and Myrset took inventory. Later, I would learn that they believed we had enough food to last for at least six or seven months.

"If we eat one small meal a day," Myrset said, "we might just survive through the winter."

In any normal scenario, a child who learns he can only expect one small meal a day would be likely to complain and complain loudly. But being crammed in that cell in the prison had taught us a good lesson: a person must have faith, hope, and determination. If you do the best you can throughout your life and trust that God will guide you through the difficult times, there is no power on this earth that can overturn your destiny. Before the Communists started leveling my family with tragedy, I was much like any other young child with occasionally selfish thoughts. I knew how to pity myself and how to pout if I didn't get what I wanted. But the Communist take-over taught me what true pain and suffering were like. The pain of hunger is different—and much deeper—if you don't know when and from where your next meal will come. The pain of cold is more har-rowing when you've walked through freezing rain and ice for miles, only to sleep in a place with no true shelter over your head. The pain of humiliation is more encompassing when modesty becomes a for-eign concept. The pain of loss is greatest when you know it has struck and can strike any member of your family at any time.

Even though the Bylykbashis's were decreasing in number, we were stronger than we had ever been. With God's help, we would not lose our esteem or our will to survive.

By then, I was old enough to harbor an intense hate for the Communists. With each abuse on my family, that hatred burned hotter. Every night, I would fuel the fire with thoughts of my mother toiling in the labor camp. I had heard the stories of what they did to true Albanians there. Every night after I said my prayers, I swore quietly to Mother that I would survive this nightmare, free her from her prison, and avenge her pain and suffering by killing as many Communists as I could.

Chapter 4

The winter of 1950 was brutal, but it taught us a valuable lesson that would carry us through the more difficult times ahead. We learned that from then on, if we wanted to survive, we had to think and work as a team. In this way, we managed to pull the boards down from all the unbroken windows, clean the house as best we could, and settle all our needs for the long winter. We were fortunate to have enough wood left at the house, or we might have frozen to death. We kept the wood-burning stove running constantly that winter.

Grandmother delegated to the older girls in tones that to an outsider might have seemed harsh, but it was necessary, and besides, she had always been just strict enough to prepare us for times like these. We loved her very much and never stopped showing her just how much she meant to all of us. Even during the most difficult times, she would often lead us in stories, and we would all break into laughter. We always made time to hug and kiss each other. We freely said, "I love you," especially to Grandmother Aishe. In her long life, she had been through hell and back, but she never hesitated to show us that beautiful smile framed with those rosy cheeks of hers.

The tragedies we had endured had been extremely hard on Medi. His daily routines had become daily struggles. Having our parents taken away was devastating. We each had to find our own way to deal with the pain. Gezim was going to school, so he would spend his afternoons after school at home, helping with the household chores.

One day, I was wandering in the fields when I came upon a stray donkey that I decided to keep for my own. Every morning, I would take the animal to the fields with me. Every sunset, I would load him with a few bales of hay to secure his food for the coming winter. Since he was our only work animal, I took special care of that donkey. I fed and groomed him every day. I had plans for this beautiful creature, so I wanted him to be strong and ready when the time came to put my plan into action. The previous winter, I had seen just how valuable firewood can be. So in time for this coming winter, I was going to use him to bring enough firewood home for us to stay warm with some extra wood to sell in the nearby town of Bilisht. The money would help buy the necessities required to get us through the hard times ahead.

When winter came, I was disheartened to see that my plan was not working as I had expected. I knew there were people in the town that needed firewood, but I realized that many of them feared the government and the consequences they would suffer if they helped my family in any way. So I began making my visits to deliver firewood in the late evenings, carefully rotating my delivery times to avoid being detected by the authorities. It didn't take long for me to build a steady stream of customers willing to buy wood from me under cover of night. Business was going well, and I was making a little money for my family, but eventually, the loads I had to carry into town were too heavy for me. On top of that, between my chores during the day and my sales during the wee hours of the morning, there was very little time left for sleep. But somehow, I managed, as we all did. Scarcity had become a way of life for all of us. It seemed as if all of Albania lived in chaos and fear, hunger, and despair.

One evening, as I was delivering firewood, the inclement weather slowed me down a bit. I finished my deliveries later than usual. Most of the night, it had been snowing lightly, but as I began my walk home, the weather took a turn for the worse, and the snow soon turned into a hard, freezing sleet. It was bitterly cold, and the wind was blowing so hard that the sleet felt like nails hammering into my body. My poor donkey tried with all his might to keep pace, but the slippery road caused him to lose footing and his legs would buckle. It would take all the determination he could muster to climb to his hooves again and try to push his way through. Eventually, it got to where I couldn't even see where we were going. If not for the donkey, we wouldn't have made it home. He took the lead as I held on to his tail and staggered blindly through the dark and cold.

It took almost six hours to reach Grandfather Ramo's mausoleum, a distance that would normally take almost two hours in good weather. Just when I thought I could take no more of the cold, the temperature dropped, and the winds picked up, and in that torrent of ice, I lost all hope that we would be able to make it home. Icicles clung to my eyelashes, threatening to freeze them shut. My donkey's ears were frozen. Neither of us could walk a straight line any longer.

There was only one thing to do. Fighting against the wind and rain, I opened the door to the mausoleum and led my trusty friend inside. I removed his saddle then covered his back with a few of the larger sheepskins kept in the mausoleum to serve as prayer mats. This had once been recognized by the people in the surrounding villages as a sacred place for prayer, but that was before the regime took over and declared we were all atheists now. On that day, I felt thankful that they hadn't thought to destroy this monument or even remove the prayer mats.

I covered myself with a few of the remaining sheepskins, and we passed the rest of the night in that place of the dead. I slept fitfully.

By eight o'clock the next morning, the storm had subsided enough for us to finish the journey home. I could see immediately that Lumka and Myrset had been awake all night worrying, for as soon as I entered the house, my sister began yelling and screaming at me.

"How could you be so irresponsible?" she barked. "You have no idea how much we depend on you, and you're out in this blizzard, risking your life?"

She went on and on about how we were a team and how everyone served a role in the family. I let her rant because I knew it came from a place of love, and really, I would have reacted the same way if our positions had been reversed. When she finally paused for a moment, I explained to her what had happened.

"It was a miracle we came to that tomb when we did," I pointed out. "Or we both would have frozen to death."

I guess she must have seen something of ingenuity in my point because she calmed down after that. Sleeping in the mausoleum was in fact the only choice I had at the time, so we were both glad it had been the right one. Of course, it helped that I had made more money that blustery night than any night that had come before.

Even though our situation continued to worsen, we were doing whatever was necessary to survive, and it seemed to be working. We always managed to get by and always had a sense that it was because we were not fighting this battle alone. There was, after all, a supreme power on our side, seeing us through each day. Every time we had to face a situation that seemed too desperate to overcome, somehow a miracle would occur, and we would find a way to make it through. Yes, we had God on our side.

More than a year had passed since our father and his group escaped, but we had not received any news either from or about them since that last volley of gunfire when they crossed the border. We didn't even know for sure if they were dead or alive. That all changed late one night when Grandmother heard a knock on the front window of the house.

"There's someone at the window," she said just after waking me. "Can you go see who it is?"

As I fought off the remaining tendrils of sleep, my heart raced. Anyone who called on us in the middle of the night tended to be from the secret police. I feared that some new hell had come calling. I had been hearing stories lately about party members terrorizing, torturing, and arresting young men and women.

Grandmother seemed to sense something entirely different. "There is no reason to worry, child," she said softly. "They are not police. They are our friends."

Myrset had just entered as Grandmother was saying this. "Don't tell us not to be afraid, Grandmother," she snapped. "How could you know who it is? You're blind. I just looked downstairs, and I could see those pigs through the window. They are armed with rifles; I could spot those ugly uniforms from miles away!"

But Grandmother was undeterred. "These are friendly people. Go and open the door immediately, young lady."

My cousin had no choice but to obey. I went with her as she cautiously made her way toward the door. I held my breath as she reached for the handle and swung it open. I expected guns and loud shouting, but instead, right there, standing in the doorway in front of us, was my brother Fejzi. My first thought was that he looked so courageous with his guns strapped and hanging from his neck. My second thought was that I had missed him so much that he seemed like the most beautiful person I had ever seen!

"Fejzi!" I said breathlessly.

We all toppled together, hugging and laughing and pulling Fejzi into the house.

He had two friends with him, also well-armed, young, fearless, and eager. They looked ready to free Albania singlehandedly. All three were dressed in Albanian Sigurim uniforms so they could not be differentiated from the Albanian secret police.

"That was a perfect idea," I said. "Dressing in the pigs' uniforms is brilliant. But where did you get them?"

Fejzi explained that he and his friends were working with the American CIA in Greece, as well as the Greek government, to overthrow the Communist regime in Albania.

When we led Fejzi up to Grandmother, she pulled him into her arms and kissed him on the cheek again and again. My tears reflected the happiness I felt in that moment, but even the joyful mood in the room couldn't take away the fear of the unknown future.

After Fejzi let Grandmother go, he introduced his friends. We greeted them warmly and with much respect, for their willingness to fight made them our brothers. Lumka filled the pockets of their jackets with apples as a show of hospitality and gesture of kindness.

We asked Fejzi and his friends many questions, and the answers were exactly what we wanted to hear. They told us not to worry because the plan was to free Albania within a year.

"You just have to be patient," Fejzi said. "The United States of America and England are the two most powerful countries in the world, and they are supporting us." We were thrilled to hear such good news.

"I heard about Mother," he said, his mood darkening.

Lumka was inviting the other men to take seats around the dining room table while Myrset prepared some tea. Both girls looked up sadly when they heard Fejzi's words.

"Do you know anything about where she is?" he asked.

No one seemed to want to answer, so the burden fell to me. "We don't know which camp they're holding her in. We've been trying to find out as much as we can, but there is never anything."

"How is her health?"

"We don't even know that," I said sadly. "We've had no word about her at all."

Fejzi shook his head in disgust. "Well, we all know she is tough enough to make it in one of those hellholes."

We all murmured our agreement.

"And anyway," he continued, his proud, fearless expression returning, "Albania will soon be free, and our family reunited."

"Speaking of reunions," Lumka said, "where are Father and Uncle Arif?"

"They are still in Greece," Fejzi said. "They're in good health and anxious to return home, but they were deemed more useful to the cause if they remained behind."

I don't know why but hearing this made me angry. I suppose it was having to listen to Fejzi about how it would take at least another year to free us from tyranny.

"You say we need to be patient," I said bitterly. "But how can we survive one more year under this oppressive regime? Do you have any idea what's going on in this bloody country of ours? If we stay here and be patient, we'll starve to death before the year is out!"

"Pertef, please—" Lumka tried to say, but Grandmother cut her off with a wave of her hand.

"What good will freedom do us then?" I asked of Fejzi.

"Freedom takes time," Fejzi said. "We can't just—"

"For the past four days," I interrupted, "the only thing any of us have had to eat is a single apple a day. The apples will run out soon. We have no money to buy food. We might not survive another winter, let alone another year."

"So what do you suggest?" Fejzi said.

I steeled up my jaw and looked around at my family. "We're coming with you, brother."

When his friends tried to protest, Fejzi held up his hands for silence.

"This isn't the time to take you out of here," he said. "We're on a mission—an assignment that's vital to the ultimate goal of freedom. If we are successful on this mission, hopefully, we will begin to see changes for the better of Albania within the next few months."

"And when this assignment is over? If things are not better, what then?" I asked.

"We have hard work ahead of us, little brother."

"So do we all."

With a sigh, Fejzi rose from the table. I regretted the tension between us as he sized each of us up in turn. In a moment, he started digging in the pockets of that awful uniform he wore. He produced some money and placed it on the table.

"If the situation for Albania hasn't improved by the time we return for our next mission," he said, "then I'll take you out of here and get you to Greece."

From outside, the sound of our dog kicked up. When his bark turned ferocious, I feared that Fejzi had lingered too long. Kuqo was the best guard dog I had ever seen.

Surely, this bark meant the secret police had come.

"You must go at once," Grandmother said quickly.

The alarm turned out to be false—perhaps Kuqo had spotted an animal in the orchard—but Fejzi and his companions hurried off all the same. That left the rest of us alone with thoughts of solitude and another yearlong sentence in the prison our own home had become.

It was difficult for me to find sleep that night. Grandmother and my siblings seemed to be having the same trouble, so eventually, we gathered in one of the bedrooms and started talking about Fejzi.

"One thing that's been bothering me, Grandmother," Medi said. "How did you know the knock on the window wasn't the Sigurim?"

Grandmother Aishe chuffed. "My dear child, if that had been the secret police, they wouldn't have knocked softly on the window. They'd have broken the door down." We all nodded.

"I heard that knock all my life from your Grandfather Ramo," she said, sounding suddenly wistful. "He would use it whenever he would come down from the mountain to see me and the children in the middle of the night."

Although it was difficult for me to imagine surviving for another year in those conditions, the unexpected visit from Fejzi and his friends was a spirit boost for all of us. And a year might have seemed like an eternity, but at least we now had a timetable to imagine as we pondered our futures.

The money Fejzi had given us was considerable as well. After Lumka finished counting it, she informed us that it would be enough to get us through the next couple of months.

*****

The Communists were gaining more control every day. Most of the party members were now carrying concealed weapons and keeping the people under constant surveillance. The Sigurim were using children my age to act as informants. One day, while a friend and I played together, he began to taunt at me, trying his best to provoke me. I noticed him closely watching my facial expressions as if studying my reactions. Then suddenly, he blurted out, "Pertef, a couple of days ago, the Sigurim captured your father and brother."

I knew immediately that he was trying to get information from me. I tried to remain expressionless, but my insides were aflame with fury. It was the first time in my life when I genuinely wanted to kill someone. This boy called himself my friend, but here he was using my father and brother as leverage to try to get information from me.

With a straight face, I casually replied, "Is that so?"

"Yes," he said. "I heard it from my own brother with my own ears. My brother is a party member, and he always tells the truth."

I almost laughed when I heard the words "party member" and "truth" in the same sentence. Instead, I managed to say dispassionately, "Well, don't believe that story, whoever told it."

"How can you be so sure?" he said, as he looked me up and down contemptuously.

"Simple, you dummy. My father and uncle are somewhere in Greece, and I'm certain they won't come back here for a long time. And if they did come back to Albania, the first thing they would do is visit us, so I would know if they were here, and they're not."

Now he looked away as if pretending at disinterest. "You mean they have never come to see you?"

I shook my head. "No."

He thought for a minute before answering. "Well, this time, they did come back all right, but they didn't come to see you because they were captured by the People's Army."

"Like hell they were captured!" I scoffed. "They're too smart to get caught."

I thought that would be the end of it, but he wouldn't let it go, and we began to argue violently. He had revealed himself for what he was: not a friend but an informer for the regime trying to get information about my family. So I decided to leave, knowing that it would be most prudent to avoid saying something that could be used against us. I started for home, but he had planted a seed, and deep down inside me, that seed was sprouting into a tree of doubt that would consume me more and more with every passing minute. As much as I tried to dismiss the thought from my mind, I was worried that there might possibly be some truth to what he had said. Was it possible that Father and Uncle Arif had come back into Albania, only to be captured before they could reach us?

A sense of urgency made me pick up my pace. When I arrived at the house, Lumka and Myrset were in the living room, knitting and talking. They looked puzzled by the ruckus I had created as I rushed into the house. The run home left me short of breath, but I was finally able to tell them what had happened.

"So," I said when I had finished explaining, "do you think it's possible he's telling the truth?"

Myrset rolled her eyes. "Of course not, Pertef."

"The party members will say anything to get information," Lumka agreed, but from her expression, I could see that she had her doubts as well.

We kept talking about it, and the more we talked, the more it seemed like the girls were on my side in believing it was possible.

"I think you should go over and see Aunt Vajbe (father's sister)," Lumka suggested. "Ask her if she's heard anything about all this. Or ask her if she even thinks there might be some truth in it."

I knew my sister was right. Aunt Vajbe was very smart. If anyone knew anything, she would know it too.

The next day, I awoke earlier than usual and got on my way to my aunt's house. I kept to the narrow trails through the fields so it would be easier to detect if anyone was following or watching me. Three hours later, I reached Aunt Vajbe's house.

"Why, what a pleasant surprise, Pertef," she said when the door swung open. "It's been too long since I've seen you."

"I bring you greetings from Grandmother," I said as I stepped inside. "She is well and hopes that you are too."

She put her arm around my shoulder and led me into the kitchen. "My boy, come along and have something to eat. You've walked a long way, and boys your age are always hungry."

I didn't say a word, but she was correct. I was starving.

Almost as soon as she finished the sentence, her daughter and four sons entered the house through the back door. It had been quite a long while since I had seen my cousins, so we spent the time talking and laughing as Aunt Vajbe prepared our food. Then we all sat down to a hot meal. Up to that point, I had kept the reason for my visit quiet. It was evening before I was finally able to talk to Aunt Vajbe.

"Allo (Auntie)," I said, "we have heard that Father and Uncle Arif came back to Albania and were captured. Have you heard anything like this? Could this possibly be true?"

Aunt Vajbe could see the great concern on my face. "No, my son. I think it's all a pack of lies, intended to make us even more unhappy and distrustful of one another." I gave a great sigh of relief.

"Have no fear and put those thoughts out of your mind," she said, running her fingers through my hair. "Arif and Zenel are fine and are now working for our freedom. I know my brothers, and if something had gone wrong, they would get word to us."

"You're right, Auntie," I said.

Aunt Vajbe looked to the window, where we could see that the sun had set. "You had better stay the night and leave early tomorrow morning. When you get home, relieve your siblings' minds also. Tell them that they have nothing to worry about when it comes to their father and uncle."

Now that I could rid myself of images of my father tortured at the hands of the Communists, I felt like a stone had been lifted from my back. I enjoyed the rest of the evening visiting with my aunt and wrestling with my cousins. As the evening grew late, we stopped our fooling and went to bed. That night, I slept peacefully.

My peace shattered quickly. At about six o'clock the next morning, my cousin Refijan burst in and woke me. "The village is full of Sigurim," she cried. "They're tearing around like thugs on horses and motorcycles."

When we had gathered in the living room, Aunt Vajbe was shaking her head in alarm. "Pertef, my son, there is no way of telling what's going to happen around here, so please get dressed and go right away."

"But, Auntie—"

"No," she cut in. "I'm sorry, but you shouldn't be here. You need to get home as quickly and as quietly as you can. It seems like something big must have happened in the village. I'm sure everyone is under suspicion. Go before the hornets reach us."

I did as she requested, pulling on my clothes as quickly as I could. She wrapped my face with a scarf, so no one would be able to recognize me, and soon, I was on my way home.

It was not until later that afternoon that I heard what had caused all the fuss in the village. The night before, some Albanian freedom fighters had slipped unseen into the village of Vishotice to try and disrupt the meeting held by the party. They hurled hand grenades into the meeting place, scaring the hell out of the party faithfuls. We never learned whether any Communists were killed because the party kept that information secret, but we did hear that many of them had been injured.

Unfortunately, acts of revolution never went unpunished. Even when there was no proof about who was responsible, the

Communists would always make an example of someone. Because of the attack on the meeting in Vishotice, a young village boy named Mendu Voci was hanged without trial. There was ample evidence that he had nothing to do with the grenade attack, but the Communists were always quick to save face. They left his small body swinging in the morning breeze, an abject lesson to all perceived enemies of the state.

When I returned home from the visit at Aunt Vajbe's, I gave them the news about Father and Uncle Arif. Somehow, it made us feel better.

The boost in morale wouldn't last, however, as with every passing day, the authorities would put more and more pressure on us. One day, they barged into the house and told us that they were commandeering every room in our house except for the living room. So they had taken our livestock, our fields, our food, our money, and now ninety-five percent of our house. It was apparent to us now that they were still trying to set a trap for my father Zenel hoping he would return and try to take us across the border.

"You should be thankful to our Supreme Leader Enver Hoxha for being kind enough to let you stay here at all," one of the invading party members said. "After all, you have done nothing to deserve such a nice place to live."

None of us spoke in reply as we ushered what few belongings we had remaining from our bedrooms into the living room.

That appeared not to satisfy him, for he sneered. "And don't get too comfortable here either because very soon we have other surprises for you." He looked back over his shoulder as if seeking approval from his fellow invaders. "You are the children of traitors and the puppets of American imperialism, and you will be treated accordingly."

I looked to my siblings, who shook their heads in wonder. It seemed to me that this crook wanted us to thank him in the literal sense. This criminal psychopath named Enver Hoxha wanted thanks for allowing us to stay in the house our parents had built with their own hands, their own sweat, and their own blood.

"We don't deserve this house?" I wanted to scream. "This is our parents' house. Who deserves to live here more than we do?"

Fortunately, I kept my silence, or I'd have found myself in a prison cell again and probably my siblings and grandmother as well.

It took a day or two for the anger about the takeover to subside enough before we began to realize how completely this decision was going to work out in our favor. What should have been a disastrous situation turned out to be a true godsend. For once, the Communists hadn't seized something for no reason other than to prove they could. Rather, this time, they apparently needed the space. They used the entire north end of our house as a storeroom for apples from the orchards that used to belong to our family. In the south end, they stored potatoes from our former fields. The plan was for them to stockpile as many apples and potatoes as possible in these rooms and then schedule them to be shipped out to other Communist countries, including Russia.

This was our salvation. The food meant for our Communist overlords was right there at our fingertips. Now even if we had to huddle together in one room, at least we knew we wouldn't starve to death. All we needed was a plan to pilfer the stores without getting caught.

To that end, Myrset and I found two strong sticks and drove a nail into the end of each one. Then we picked a pair of reasonably well-hidden locations at each end of the barricade separating our living room from the newly converted storerooms. With our makeshift pickaxes, we got to work removing a few bricks from each end of the barricade. It was a slow, painstaking process that wound up taking several days, but when we finally broke through, we saw piles of apples and potatoes so large that we knew we could take enough to stay alive without any of it being missed.

Each night, when we felt it was safe, we used our former pickaxes as spears to poke at apples and potatoes through the holes. We would snake out the produce in this way until we had enough food to last us through the next few days. All winter, the only thing we had to eat were potatoes and apples, but it was enough to keep us alive.

In the spring, I was resting against the barricade when I overheard some of the men speaking on the other side. When I pressed my ear to the wall, I could just make out the conversation. They were discussing the date the remaining apples and potatoes were going to be shipped away.

I hissed to get Myrset's attention. She was sleeping, but when she heard me, she stirred.

"What is it, Pertef?" she said, sounding annoyed at having been woken.

"From this moment on," I said, "we're going to step up our program of securing the food. Until now, we've been getting just enough to feed us for a few days at a time, but soon, they'll be shipping the last of the potatoes and apples, and without this supply to draw from, we'll go hungry."

"I agree with you," she said. "But how do we do it?"

"We'll find a way." I shook my head. "Cousin, if we get caught, they'll probably hang us. But if we don't have food for the weeks and months ahead, we'll die of starvation. So what do we have to lose?"

With the way she furrowed her brow, I could see that she knew I was right. She looked at my siblings, who were sleeping on the other side of the living room, along with Grandmother.

"You want to wake them and tell them too?" Myrset asked.

"Grandmother always said that the fewer who know about a plan, the safer you are."

Myrset nodded.

"If the rest of the family doesn't know about this," I continued, "the authorities may leave them alone if we get caught. So let's keep this between us."

Even though Myrset agreed with me, I could tell by her expression that it bothered her. We were taught all our lives to be honest, and even though we were now facing a matter of survival, I could tell she felt like we were doing something wrong. "So you just want us to steal everything we can get our hands on, is that it, Pertef?" she asked finally.

The question angered me. It was as if Myrset had blocked out what was going on all around her almost as if she had succumbed to the Communist propaganda and lies.

"Don't talk to me about stealing," I whispered loudly. "I want you to put that out of your head. We are *not* stealing. We're taking back what's ours and has always *been* ours."

She blanched, looking away.

"I shouldn't have to remind you that the apples we're *stealing* came from our orchards," I continued. I slid closer to her, so I didn't have to strain so hard to whisper. "The fruit and potatoes stored here aren't even an eighth of what our orchard and fields once produced— not to mention the grain farm that was taken from us, and not to mention what we had in our stores at the time they stole our land."

Even in the lowlight, I could see the tears coming to her eyes. She agreed with me, I knew, but there was still something of defiance in her.

"All the wealth our family has worked for and accumulated through the generations now belongs to the state," I spat. "We've had family members murdered, arrested, and disappeared to places we don't even know. And now they have the seven of us living here together like cattle in one room."

At that, Myrset's expression finally softened. She nodded demurely and told me I was right. "So when do we start?" she asked.

"Tomorrow night."

At around three o'clock the next morning, we took our boldest action yet. Rather than removing our bricks, Myrset and I sneaked outside under cover of night and went to the entrance of the store-rooms. I picked the lock on one of the doors, then quietly, I pulled back the big wooden door and stepped inside. Myrset kept a look-out while I began filling several large burlap bags with potatoes. We would hide these bags in a hole we had dug in the courtyard just outside the living room.

For three consecutive nights, we performed this same routine successfully. But on the fourth night, my blood turned to ice when I heard the voice.

"Just what do you think you're doing?"

Myrset's voice seemed to catch in her throat, and all that came out was a whisper.

"Pertef," she said.

Then on flicked the beam of a flashlight. When it turned on us, I began to shake. It advanced slowly as visions of my terrible future swirled in my head. I knew the penalty for betraying the government. I had seen it too many times. Myrset and I would be beaten and turned over to the authorities. I was certain they would hang us. After all, they had hung Fuat Kulla and Avdyl Kalaja, two young men from the neighboring village of Zemblak just for accidentally burning a few bales of straw that belonged to the cooperative. Burning food meant for the horses was one thing, but stealing food meant for the Communists—it would be a death sentence for sure!

When the owner of the flashlight finally pulled the beam away, I saw that it was Shefqet Xama, the man in charge of the storerooms. He had long suspected us of stealing, so I could see from the glint in his eyes and the way he licked his lips that he felt quite gratified in this moment.

With a snarl, he lashed out and grabbed me by both wrists, shaking me fiercely.

"What are you doing here, you foolish boy?" he barked. He shook me for a while longer before finally letting me go.

I was so scared that it took me a moment to realize what was happening. Gone was the hungry sneer and the gritting teeth. Behind that mask there emerged a softer expression that looked almost sympathetic. I couldn't remember ever seeing such a look on his face, so at first, it was foreign—something I had no way to interpret.

"Don't you understand, boy?" he said. "Don't you get it? If someone else was with me now, I would have no choice but to turn you in. Don't you realize this could mean the rope for both of you?"

I nodded, my whole body numb.

He looked back over his shoulder as if making sure no one else was around. "Now get the hell out of here as fast as you can before someone sees us together, or we'll all be hanged!"

I was dumbfounded. "You mean you're really not going to turn us in?" I asked.

"Look, boy, I'm sorry for what's happened to you up to now, but you have to know that it's never been my plan. I'm just following orders. If I disobey, it'll cost me my life and my family's lives. You of all people should understand how that works."

Myrset and I were frozen in place from fear and disbelief. A part of me still suspected that this was some kind of plot—a test to see what we would do. Shefqet Xama, a man I had believed a monster, was standing here, talking about how he wanted to spare our lives.

"Thank you," I said finally. Then I grabbed Myrset, and together, we bolted back toward the house.

But then I remembered the potatoes. We had spent so much time and energy filling those bags that there was *no way* I was going to leave them! *I may be hanged by these pigs*, I thought, *but I won't let them make me die an agonizing death from starvation.*

"We have to get the bags!" I called out to Myrset.

"Pertef, are you crazy?" she shouted back, but it was too late. I was already heading back to the storeroom.

Shefqet's eyes went wide with disbelief when I turned and came back for the potatoes. Then I could see that his disbelief had become fear that he would be caught helping us.

"Just take them and get the hell out of here," he said, throwing his hands in the air.

"Quickly!"

A few months later, we received another unscheduled visit from the authorities.

This time, they ordered us to evacuate the house.

"Why are you doing this?" Myrset asked.

"Why are we being thrown out of our house?" I echoed. "You've taken everything from us, and now you're stealing our last room!"

The leader of this group had a long, pointed nose, and he held that nose high as he read from an official looking sheet of paper. "This residence has been sold to a party member, and the Bylykbashi family is hereby ordered to vacate at once." There was more party-line babble, but by then, it had started to sound like a broken record, so we left without putting up a fight.

We returned to our rundown old store with its half-roof and broken windows. Upon seeing it again after so many months of having a proper roof over my head, I remember thinking that it almost would have been better to sleep outside. The place was an absolute rat hole. The walls were rotting. There was no real respite from the winds. Standing puddles remained from the last rain. It didn't make much difference to me where the Communists shoved us, but I felt sad for Grandmother. Before, we at least had a roof over our heads and a stall for our animals, but now we all had to bundle together with our donkey and two goats, shoving into the corner of that lean-to just so we could keep the rain off our heads.

We were fortunate that the situation didn't last long. Indeed, the very man who had elbowed us out of our ancestral home would soon learn that retribution comes to all who take what isn't theirs.

Chapter 5

A month later, through word of mouth from the other villagers, I heard the story of a group of freedom fighters who infiltrated a nearby village called Ocisht. Their mission was simple: to eliminate the Communist-appointed mayor of the village. They posed as Sigurim, and when he answered the knock, they told him that they were investigating a tip that Albanian infiltrators had been sent from Greece to overthrow the regime.

"We need your help to draw up a plan to capture these traitors," they told him.

I was told that the mayor swelled with pride at the thought that his military insight would be useful. In this way, the infiltrators were able to lure him out of Ocisht. When they had him in a place where they felt safe, they dropped the neighborly act.

"We are the true Albanians," they told him. "We are the freedom fighters for our country. We have interrogated you, tried, and sentenced you, and now you are going to pay with your life for all the crimes that you and the others have been committing against our people."

I heard that the cowardly mayor begged for his life.

"Have you spared the lives of any of the thousands of innocent men, women, and children your regime has killed?" the leader of the freedom fighters asked. The emotion behind the question must have set off one of the other freedom fighters, for the story is that he stepped in, and before anyone realized what was happening, he gruesomely and brutally took the mayor's life.

The freedom fighters hoped this would be a warning to the other party members to let them know they would be coming for them.

War is a terrible thing. It makes some men act in ways that would normally be unthinkable. Somehow, even though we had faced inhumane treatment at the hands of the Communists for years, the news of this latest atrocity saddened me and my family. We had not become so hardened that news like this didn't turn our stomachs.

Even so, as harrowing as I found the story, I couldn't help but hope that it would give the Communist leaders something to think about—that it would make them recognize that Albanians wouldn't stand by forever while their neighbors were tortured and murdered.

The incident did in fact curtail some of the harsher behaviors from the party. It even seemed to put the fear into some of them. There was such a sea change in their arrogance that our friend's son, Idajet Bushka, managed to enter into Albania from Greece with a group of freedom fighters, and right under the noses of the Communist guards, he took his four younger brothers and two sisters and crossed them into Greece.

Meanwhile, many of the higher-level party members were running like scared rabbits. One of them was the man who had moved into our house. He was so overcome with the fear of meeting the same fate as the mayor from the neighboring town that he immediately moved out.

We were thrilled to move back into our own house. It was wonderful to sleep on a bed again, and Grandmother gave thanks to God for such a wonderful blessing and for making it possible for us to return home.

*****

In May 1952, my brother Medi left the village in search of work and was lucky enough to find a job. It paid very little, but the main perk was that they fed him while he was on the job. That gave us one less mouth to feed at home, but it also took our brother away from us since the job was too far away for him to commute. Now we were only six in number.

Grandmother was concerned for the safety and welfare of Lumka and Myrset, who were maturing into beautiful women sure to catch the often-animalistic eyes of certain party members and the Sigurim. We had heard accounts of how some of the harder-line members among them had been violating women just for the pleasure of it. For instance, a party member named Servet Avdo and some of his comrades had raped a woman in her own house.

"We should have them shave their heads," she told me.

"Why would we want to do that?" I asked, confused.

"To make them as unattractive as possible."

That seemed reasonable to me, so Lumka and Myrset were informed that they would be lopping off their locks.

"I want you to look as much like a man as you can, so you will be less appealing to those unscrupulous animals," Grandmother said as the girls cried but did as they were told.

When they were finished, I had to admit that it was amazing how masculine they looked. Even though we were all saddened by the realities we faced, I never missed an opportunity to tease the girls about their heads. They took the teasing in good spirits, for they knew it was just a product of our wise old grandmother trying to keep them safe.

In July that same year, Fejzi returned to Albania with his friends Demir Agolli and Enver Danglliu on what was to be another secret reconnaissance mission and an effort to extract us from Albania. Unfortunately, there had been a leak about their return, and over the course of that week, everywhere they went, they found themselves under attack. Overcome with hunger and exhaustion, they were living from moment to moment, expecting at any time to give their lives in an unfair fight.

On the first Wednesday morning in July 1952, Fejzi and his friends faced heavy opposition. During a fierce volley of gunfire, in an effort to save their lives, they decided to split up, hoping to divide the attention of the Sigurim. This would prove to be Demir and Enver's last mission. They were killed as they heroically fought for their right to live as free men.

Meanwhile, Fejzi moved from place to place, searching for safe cover. He fled as far as the Greek border but saw that the border guards had doubled. Rather than try to break through enemy lines and return to Greece, he decided it would be better to remain in Albania a while longer. He had no more ammunition for his rifle, so he discarded it, keeping only his handgun, which he concealed under his shirt.

Fejzi made his way through the forest to the home of an Albanian family he met while going back and forth between Albania and Greece. The home belonged to a trusted friend who was also an informer for the freedom fighters. This friend provided Fejzi with civilian clothes to replace his uniform and offered him a bed for a few hours of much-needed rest.

When dawn broke, Fejzi was on his way, dressed like any other civilian. He was confident that he could walk safely about during the daylight hours. As he passed through a valley not far from our house, he noticed several cooperative farmers tending the fields ahead. Fejzi knew that he had already been seen, so turning back would look too suspicious. He had learned through the reconnaissance missions that the communists had expropriated all the land and had placed government agents on the farms to prevent the workers from organizing against the regime, so he continued toward the farmers, hoping all the while they were Albanian civilians.

As it happened, members of the party were present as Fejzi strolled up. They too were dressed as civilians, so he didn't recognize them as the enemy.

After they exchanged greetings, Fejzi sarcastically said, "Comrade Farmers, this will be a most productive year for us, thanks to the good leadership of our government. We will produce more grain than we ourselves need."

A party member named Eshref Mancka eyed him distrustfully. "Who are you, Comrade?"

Fejzi, still unaware of who he was talking to, responded in a mocking tone, "I'm a government technician." He bent down and scooped up some wheat grains, rolling them in his palm as if he was inspecting the quality. "It's through the knowledge, experience, and cooperation of our Russian allies that we have such marvelous crops." He bent down once again, but this time, his shirt hiked up, revealing his pistol.

Eshref straightened up. "Comrade show me your identification!"

"Yes, Comrade," Fejzi said, the stark realization striking him all at once. "Of course." Quickly, he drew his pistol, aimed, and pulled the trigger. His pistol misfired.

Another of the party members fired at Fejzi, who by now was looking for cover.

By one of those unexplainable acts of fate, the man missed his target.

Fejzi did not wait for second shots. He ran as fast as he could, zigzagging through the wheat field, crouched over to present as small a target as possible to the Communist agents behind him as he headed for the forest and the mountains beyond.

Many times throughout the years, I've pondered the events of that Thursday morning and the coincidences that added to that tragic day. I was merely a sad spectator to what happened, although initially, when the calamity began, I was quite far away from the action. I have asked myself time and time again, why did my cousin Nijazi have to appear on the scene of that particular place at that very moment?

But as fate would warrant, Nijazi, on route to Bilisht to buy some food for his family, decided to take a shortcut across the very same wheat fields from which Fejzi was trying to escape. Suddenly, they met face-to-face.

"Fejzi!" Nijazi said. "My God, what are you doing here?"

Fejzi stopped but only long enough to alert his cousin to the situation. "I'm being chased by Communist pigs. They're after my life. Please go immediately, cousin, because if you are seen with me, you'll surely suffer for it. Take care!"

As he dashed away, he left a bewildered Nijazi behind him, standing in the wheat field.

By then, the Sigurim had already notified the regular army units in the area, so a massive manhunt was sweeping through the valley. To Nijazi's grave misfortune, a party member spotted the meeting with Fejzi. Before Nijazi reached Bilisht, the secret police surrounded him and held him at gunpoint.

"We saw you stop and talk to that man running in the field," one of them said as the horde advanced on him. "Who is he?"

"Confess immediately or you'll get a bullet in your head," snarled another.

Nijazi shrugged. "I really don't know. I was headed for town when I literally bumped into him. I said something about it being a good morning, and he ran away. I am just going to town to buy some food for my family. Is there any harm in that?"

"You expect us to believe you didn't have the meeting prearranged, you traitor?"

One of them stepped forward and grabbed Nijazi by the hair. "You're coming with us. We'll take you to a place where they'll teach you not to lie!"

"The two of you can die together," said another with a laugh.

Meanwhile, it took nearly an hour of hard running before Fejzi crossed the valley and reached the cover of the forest. As he paused to get his breath, he thought about what to do to elude his pursuers. When an idea came in his mind, he smiled to himself in approval. As part of his strategy, he climbed into full view atop a commanding hill and stood there for a few minutes, just to make sure he was seen by the oncoming soldiers. Then he climbed down the hill, taking precautions not to be seen, dodging from tree to tree and rock to rock, drifting like a shadow toward the soldiers, who were now advancing into the forest. His intention was to infiltrate their lines as they went past since they were expecting him to continue to flee away rather than toward them. Fejzi hid himself deep in a clump of thick brush as the soldiers hurried by, looking ahead, intent on catching their victim.

Bedri and I were in the hills that day gathering firewood. It was a gorgeous day, and we were enjoying the nature around us. I looked off across the valley at the wide and wild river called Lumi I Devollit, which passed down the valley. The surrounding mountains were covered with a green mantle of hardwood trees, the green a nice complement to the gold of the wheat field in the lowland. Shepherds moved their flocks along the hills, the bells tied on the sheep sounding faint and peaceful. The few clouds were high, and there was no threat of rain.

Since I was very close to the action at this time, I could see a man running in the distance, although initially, I didn't recognize

him as my brother. I watched as the man flitted among the trees, trying to find a hiding place. Then suddenly, my heart began to pound
until I could hardly breathe. Something about the way he moved or
his slender figure told me that this must be my brother Fejzi darting
in and out of the trees.

"God, please let me be mistaken," I prayed. "Please, God, I ask
that it is not my brother that I see being chased to the ground by the
Communist pigs."

But as I strained my eyes, I saw the familiar features and knew
it was Fejzi. I was so consumed by what I was witnessing that I didn't
hear the Sigurim that stepped up behind me.

I was startled by him when he hissed, "Have you seen anyone running around through the forest? We are chasing an Anglo-
American spy."

With my hands going numb from the nerves, I turned slowly
to look back at him.

"We've lost him for the moment," he said. "But not for long.
Have you seen him?"

The huge lump in my throat made it difficult to talk. "No,
I've seen no one other than you. I have just come here to cut some
firewood."

Apparently satisfied by my reply, the officer disappeared into
the trees.

When I was sure I was alone, I returned desperately to my
prayer. "Please save my brother. He is so young and innocent and
deserves to live." I prayed a long while. There was nothing else I
could do.

Meanwhile, the soldiers penetrated farther and farther into the
forest, moving away from my brother. A couple of them remained
behind, and it was those soldiers that spotted a shepherd boy tending his sheep on a nearby hill. From where I stood, I could see the
soldiers questioning him, and I could see that he refused to answer.
I gasped when they lashed out and slapped him several times. Then
my blood ran cold when I saw him speaking and pointing in the
direction where he had last seen Fejzi, for I knew he had just condemned my brother to his death.

One of the officers blew his whistle loudly and repeatedly, the sound echoing among the hills. Before long, the soldiers started to work their way back through the forest, and within fifteen minutes or so, the place was crawling with troops. They concentrated on the general area where Fejzi was hiding, surrounding it quickly.

My brother had chosen his sanctuary well, as it allowed him to move about and change his position readily. A strange silence fell over the forest. I know that I stopped breathing for a moment. Then the soldiers opened fire with rifles, pistols, and automatic weapons. The noise was unbelievable, and its volume increased as the reverberations rang through the hills and mountains. It sounded as if a full-scale war had broken out.

Bullets whined around, ricocheting off trees and rocks in all directions—a storm of hot metal tearing up the forest.

Fejzi didn't return fire since he had only the pistol and a very limited supply of ammunition. Because they were not certain of his exact location, a couple of the Sigurim decided to pin him down. They brought their patrol dog to track my brother's scent. In this way, they crept carefully toward Fejzi, who let them come closer. When they were close enough, he rested his pistol barrel on the branch of a tree to steady it, aimed carefully, shot, and wounded Servet Avdo, one of the party members involved in the rape of a woman in Cangonj. The soldiers returned with a cacophony of gunfire. As I looked on, it seemed to me that nothing could possibly live in the midst of all that shooting. Hundreds of rounds were sprayed around my brother's hiding place, smashing into the trees, throwing chips of rocks into the air, plowing through the brush and the ground like a deadly whirlwind. Tree splinters hit Fejzi in the face and rock fragments cut his hand. Bullets passed through his clothing but did not hit him. It seemed impossible that my beloved brother could still be alive. The shooting continued for quite some time, and still they were unable to capture or injure my brother.

At this point, as I would later learn, Fejzi realized that he was out of ammunition and turned his thoughts to the one cartridge he had tucked away. He reached deep into his pocket and pulled out his last bullet—the one on which he had scratched the word BESA into the casing. His eyes locked into a dead stare, and I can only imagine that his mind wandered back to the day in September 1950, when the entire family gave their BESA to never forget each other or what they were fighting for: freedom for themselves and for the generations of our family to come. And suddenly, realizing that BESA was the highest principle he had ever known, even higher than life itself, he felt compelled to honor it. He carefully loaded the cartridge into the chamber and set it in firing position.

When the officer in charge called for a cease fire, I could see that he was filled with frustration and anger that his men, with all their firepower, had not been able to put an end to a single man. "Cease fire!" he commanded in a loud yell. "Cease fire!" The noise of the battle stopped, but the ringing in my ears continued.

"I call on you to surrender, in the name of the party," the same officer said. "Give yourself up, and I'll see that you're treated fairly. You have my word on it."

My brother's laughter drifted through the trees. "And just what is your lousy Communist idea of 'fairly?' Is it the 'fairly' of the Communist mock trials 'fairly?' Is it the 'fairly' of your 'fair' imprisonment? The 'fairly' of your 'fair' executions? The 'fairly' of your 'fair' torture? The 'fairly' of your 'fair' repression of all kinds, from starvation to degradation of the spirit? Don't talk to me of fair, you rotten pig! The Bylykbashi's have had a gut full of your 'fair' propaganda."

"I may be just one lone Albanian here today," he continued, "but you and your cutthroat gang will never have the satisfaction of taking me alive of torturing and murdering me. Death is far sweeter than living under your stinking regime. I have enough friends. There are enough Albanian nationalists to avenge me. So you better fear us, you bastards! Fear us in the day and fear us in the night because we are coming to get you!"

I saw him stand up tall and proud among the trees, in full view of the Communist soldiers, dignity and honor his only shield. Even though he was surrounded and nearly out of ammunition, he stood undefeated. His courage was indomitable, and the soldiers looked at him in awe. No one shot at him—a sign of acknowledgement of his bravery. A strange silence fell over the forest, and then in noble tones and with a strong, clear voice, my brother Fejzi declared, "The only way I'll surrender is this way, my own way! Rrofte Shqiperia! Rrofte Populli Shqipetar! (Long Live, Albania! Long Live the Albanian People! Death to communism! Death to Albanian Traitors!)"

Then as I looked on in a dazed, unbelieving stare—as if I were watching phantom shapes through a mist—I saw my brother, my beloved Fejzi, put his pistol under his chin and, without hesitation, pull the trigger. His body leaped into the air with the impact of the cruel bullet, and he fell to the ground, rolling down, down the hill.

My cousin Nijazi, who was being held at bay by the Sigurim, struggled fiercely and managed to get free. He ran to Fejzi, dropped to his knees, and took him into his arms. He kissed my brother as tears dropped onto Fejzi's face.

Nijazi moaned his sorrow and hissed through his teeth. "Don't worry, Fejzi, they will pay! Because of your courageous stand here today, we shall never forget you—never, even in our darkest night! The Albanian people will quickly learn of your magnificent fight, and they too will never forget you. Your courageous story will be told and remembered for generations to come! Now, my dear cousin, go to sleep knowing that the fight for freedom rages on."

The officer in charge of the operation was a man named Gjergos, a man as widely known for his brutality as he was for his complete devotion to communism. I later learned that after examining Fejzi's pistol, Gjergos looked as if he had tasted something sour. "He killed himself with his last cartridge," he said begrudgingly. "If I had ten men like him under my command, I could catch every last one of these Anglo-American imperialist spies."

It was a fitting epitaph for my brother: words of praise from the very man who had led him to death.

Then as if to give vent to his disappointment, Gjergos began kicking and beating Nijazi with the butt of his rifle. After my cousin collapsed unconscious, Gjergos ordered his men to haul him away to prison, where he would spend the next twenty-five years. Gjergos finished his day by arranging for Fejzi's body to be desecrated. He had his men tie a rope around Fejzi's ankles and attach the rope to a horse's saddle. In this way, they dragged my brother's body through the trees, across the fields, and over rough and uneven ground into the town of Bilisht. There, they laid Fejzi's body on the roadside so everyone could watch as high-ranking party members did anything they could to defile and shame the body of a man who had openly defied the regime.

At the end of that dreadful day, with night hanging like a cloak, they took my brother's body to a secret spot and threw it into an unmarked grave. We have never learned where Fejzi lies after all this time.

As for me, I wandered down from the mountain where I had just witnessed the ultimate show of courage, followed by the dreadful death of my beloved brother. Shock numbed me to the point that I didn't know where I was or what I was doing. Fejzi had been destroyed and desecrated before my eyes. I was completely shattered. I felt as if I no longer had a reason for living.

I don't recall how I got back to the village, what route I took, or how long I was in getting there. My clothes were torn and dirty, my hands and face scratched. I was sweating, and the dust made it more difficult for me to see where I was going. Word had spread like lightning about the day's events. In town, the village counselors laughed and derided me, belittling Fejzi and the family. It was too much for a young boy to endure. The rest of my family had heard of Fejzi's death by now, and they were all as devastated as I was, but I couldn't feel anyone's hurt because it was all so overshadowed by my own. I had lost my dear brother, and with it went my hope for the future of my family.

Death, I decided, would be better than life.

In our courtyard, we kept a deep well for our water. I went there with the intention of drowning myself. If Lumka had not been outside at the time, I might have succeeded. As it was, she ran swiftly through the courtyard, grabbed me just as my weight shifted over the lip of the well, and—with all her strength—pulled me back to where my feet were touching the ground.

"Pertef," she said, panting, "you have no right to do this thing. You have no right to increase the sorrow of this family. We've had enough sadness already to last us a lifetime."

Then using both of her hands, she grabbed me by the hair and the back of my shirt and dragged me into the house, putting me to bed. I lay there unmoving for days, too shaken to do anything else.

*****

A few months after Fejzi's death, we received a letter from my mother. It seemed that the government had joyfully informed her of the death of her "traitorous" son. She wrote:

> Dearest beloved children,
>
> This morning during roll call, the authorities told me about my son Fejzi and of his death. I want all of you to keep your heads high and your courage up. I want you to be very proud of Fejzi, as I am, and as thousands of dear brothers and sisters are at the camp of Kamze! I love you all!
>
> May God the Merciful and Compassionate be with you always.
>
> Your loving mother

This was the first evidence we had received that Mother was still alive. Her message was clever in that it informed us of the exact location of her labor camp as well. How the authorities managed to let this letter escape the camp, I am not certain, but I do know that it was the one thing that restored my faith that there was something left in life worth saving.

My brother's death left a scar on my heart, but more than that, it deepened my hatred for our oppressors. If hatred could kill, there wouldn't have been a Communist left alive in the world for all my vengeful daydreams.

Chapter 6

The year 1953 brought continued harassment and humiliation for my family, as the village authorities grew more obnoxious and arrogant by the day. A rumor had spread that we planned to escape into Greece, as our father had done before us, so that led to round-the-clock surveillance from the Sigurim. We often talked about how important it was to keep our spirits high, so we took every opportunity to tell jokes about the enemy's ignorance and stupidity.

The Communists weren't our only enemy in those days, however. We were also at war with time. Our food supply was almost exhausted, and the longer we went without finding another source, the closer we came to losing the battle. As it was, we were only able to find a small meal about every third day—just enough to stay alive, but not nearly enough to sate our hunger. The Bylykbashi pride prevented us from asking anyone for food. We would have rather died from starvation before we turned to begging. We had no interest in caving in to the regime in any sense of the word. Strangely, it was that same pride that gave us such an uncommon will to live.

Our safe harbor was ever at Grandmother's side. Often, whenever we were hungry and full of despair, we would go to Grandmother's bed, cuddle close with her, and ask her to tell us stories of better times. Those stories always made me feel safer somehow.

At some point, there was talk of the government giving corn rations to citizens who supported their cause. By then, I was fed up with being excluded from the ration. We were starving, and I was determined to find food. So one day, I pulled Lumka aside and told her about my plan to end the madness.

"I'm going to get some of that corn from the government," I whispered.

"But, Pertef, they only give that to the people that support their political party."

I scoffed. "I can't think of anyone who deserves it more than we do. It was probably taken from one of our fields to begin with."

She clenched her jaw tight in that look of defiance she often wore. "Don't do it. Don't even try. If they find out, they'll surely beat you to death! We'd rather starve than have you suffer at their hands."

I smiled and held up my hand. "Don't worry, Lumka. I won't be found out. But please don't try to stop me. I'm going to Progri. I *must*. I'll give you my best guarantee that I'll come back and with something to eat."

"If you must, you must," she said, shaking her head doubtfully. "And I know I can't stop you since you're so completely stubborn. But you're asking for trouble. If they catch and kill you, don't come telling me your problems."

We both realized the silliness of her remark at the same time and had a good laugh.

Progri was about five kilometers from our village, so I put a packsaddle on my donkey's back. The saddle was meant to carry me there and carry back the food I planned to take from the government storehouse. I must confess that at this point, I was pondering whether there was truly any wisdom in making the trip. Ultimately, it was my pride that won out, and I made the trip into Progri. I had told Lumka that I would bring food, and going back with an empty packsaddle would make me look foolish.

I was frightened to the core by the time I arrived at the government building where the corn was stored and saw the long line stretching down the road. I decided to wait awhile to take my place in line because I didn't want anyone to recognize me or my plan would surely fail. So my donkey and I sauntered around for a while, killing time and waiting.

At around four o'clock, I wandered back and saw only a couple of people standing in line. Fearing it was time for them to close, I said a small prayer, plucked up my courage, and briskly walked into the warehouse office as if I had the right to be there.

The official looked up from some papers he was checking. He was an ugly man with a hooked nose. "Yes, boy? And what is your family name?"

"Kadri Tale, Comrade," I lied. I used the name of a man whose brother was one of the most vicious party members in Pilur.

He checked a list on his desk and nodded in satisfaction. "Correct! You may have fifteen kilos of corn."

"Thank you, Comrade."

As I went down the stairs, I felt a mixture of happiness and fear. I couldn't believe I had pulled it off. It was so *easy. This must be a trap*, I thought. *As soon as I pick up the corn, they'll arrest me.* I felt my heartbeat in my throat as I headed toward the storeroom. But God was surely with me, as I was given the fifteen kilos of corn. When my donkey was loaded, the two of us hurried away from Progri and toward home as quickly as we could go, never looking back.

At home, I proudly carried the corn into the house and put it on the floor, not saying a word. Lumka and Myrset stared at me in disbelief.

Lumka nodded. "Brother, you were right. You said you would bring food, and you did it. You truly did it!"

It had been a while since we had eaten bread, but now that we had the corn, we could end our drought. Once the corn had been ground into meal, the women quickly baked us some cornbread, and we ate it right from the oven, so hot that it burned our mouths. As hungry as we were, this felt like a veritable feast. All this time, we had survived on apples and potatoes, which of course we were glad to have, but the change in menu was most welcome.

Not long after, Grandmother's health began to falter noticeably. One day, she called us to her bedside. "You children should go and get my daughter," she said.

"Because I'm going to die."

We were shocked. It was true that she was very old and couldn't last forever, but Grandmother had always been and was a part of everything we loved. We sent Gezim to Aunt Vajbe's, and they returned the same day, their eyes filled with concern.

Two days later, Grandmother died peacefully, but before she left us, she whispered, "Please bury me in a casket. I want my sons to see me one last time, and my body will hold up better if you do as I ask."

The Muslim custom is to bury our dead by sunset of the same day of their death. The body washer in our village was an old woman we knew as Hake. Normally, the body would be thoroughly washed then wrapped carefully in a white sheet and placed directly into the ground in an opening six feet deep. The undertaker would place wooden slats at a slanting angle over the body then cover it with cornstalks to prevent dirt from falling through. For this reason, Grandmother's final request was unusual and not in keeping with Muslim observances. Uncle Emin's son, Sami, came over to the house to comply with her last wish. He found some suitable lumber around our house, and we made a coffin for her.

Sadly, there were very few people who came to Grandmother Aishe's funeral. She had been an influential member of our village for many years and was loved and respected by the townspeople, but they could not come to pay their last respects out of fear for what might happen if they were seen associating with my family. We buried Grandmother Aishe without any fanfare and with only a handful of family members to say goodbye to an ancient old lady born long before communism mattered to any of us.

The anticipation of winter filled us with dread. Soon, the heavy fall rains gave way to winter snow, and the temperature dropped lower and lower. I had to make another trip to the village of Progri to try and secure more rations for us, but this time, the trip proved disastrous. The plan I'd used before led to a brutal beating. The Communists tending the rations clubbed me and kicked me and left me on the roadside to die. For a long several minutes, all I could see was the red of my own blood. My breathing was shallow and labored. I felt dry from the inside out.

I don't know how long I lay there before I decided to try to move, but when I did attempt to lift myself to my feet, it was a fool's errand. My ankles were too swollen to stand. Somehow, I managed to crawl to my donkey and wrench myself onto his back, but I have little recollection of the trip home. What I do recall is being so filled with hate that there was almost no room left for my will to survive.

Fortunately, I still had my faith, which has always been a driving force for me. As I approached the cemetery, I decided to go to the holy prayerhouse where Grandfather Ramo was buried to spend some time in prayer and meditation before continuing home. Even with all the pain I was suffering, I felt that I had to pray.

I was just opening the door to enter the prayer house when I saw Gezim about twenty yards away. He was engaged in a verbal confrontation with four boys from our village. My legs had stopped throbbing, so I closed the door and limped toward him to investigate the problem. Before I could get there, all four boys jumped on Gezim and began beating him with wooden clubs. They were older than him and greater in number. Gezim was completely helpless.

All concept of reason had left me. The frustration and abuse we had been enduring for so long, combined with the beating I had suffered in Progri, caused me to think of nothing but killing all four of these boys if they didn't leave Gezim alone.

"I'm giving you one chance," I called out to them. "Let him go and we'll forget this happened. Do that or I swear on my brother's grave I'll kill every last one of you!"

The boys didn't hesitate to leave Gezim alone and turn their clubs on me. I can't remember feeling anything. I only remember snatching the club from their leader's hand, and as the other boys were pounding on me, I drew back as far as I could and swung for the leader's head, busting it wide open. Then I turned on the other boys. They were so full of fear that they wasted not one second as they fled the scene, leaving the leader of the group lying on the ground. He was losing a lot of blood and breathing heavily. I knew he needed a doctor.

That was the first time I had ever lost my temper and physically hurt someone. I didn't know I was even capable of violence to that degree. I felt badly that it happened, but I loved my family and would protect them at any cost.

At the same time, I knew of the boy's father and believed him to be a party member. If his son died, he would avenge his death by killing me. So as I watched my enemy bleed, I knew I couldn't stay in Pilur. The only choice I had was to leave, if only until the heat died down. I told Gezim to go home and tell Lumka and Myrset what happened. Then without looking back, I began limping toward Dishnice.

Aunt Idajet had remarried a few years after Uncle Nevrus was executed. Her husband was a kind, gentle man named Xhevit. Xhevit's wife had been killed by the Germans during World War II, leaving him a widower with five children. Suleman was the oldest son, about twenty-five. Vait was his second son of about seventeen. Then he had three daughters who were already married and living in another village.

As soon as I arrived, Aunt Idajet seemed to sense something was wrong. I'm sure it had something to do with my appearance, but she wasted no time in breathlessly asking me what had happened. I explained the beatings and how I had overcome Gezim's attackers. They immediately offered that I stay with them for as long as necessary.

"First, we'll need to get some information on the boy you clubbed," Xhevit said with a solemn nod.

Aunt Idajet agreed, and so it was decided that we would ask around to see if anyone had information about what had happened to the boy I clocked.

In the time I stayed with them, I came to know and care for this honorable family very much. I was treated with love and kindness, with dignity and respect—not only by them but also by the people of Dishnice. It was so different there compared to my village. Most of the people in Pilur had lost their will to fight, but here, there were still many people unwilling to cave in to the regime.

Eventually, we received word from Pilur that the boy had spent quite a while in the hospital but had healed from the gash I'd put in his head and was released. I felt relieved to know that he had suffered no permanent damage. I also learned that the father of the three other boys was caught collaborating with the freedom fighters and imprisoned.

This was enough for me to believe it safe to return home to Pilur. I was saddened by the thought of leaving Dishnice but also felt a sense of pride and excitement at the prospect of reuniting with my family.

On my trip home, I passed through Zemblak, where I noticed the Sigurim had completely surrounded the village. I was curious, so I asked a villager what had happened. He told me that a group of freedom fighters had come to Albania from Yugoslavia and had been detected by the Communist soldiers. Fighting broke out, with heavy gunfire coming from both sides. Even though the freedom fighters were heavily outnumbered, they fought bravely but decided to retreat rather than lose more of their men in an unevenly matched battle. They crossed the border back to Yugoslavia but sadly left behind the bodies of Reshat Kuller, their leader, and Sami Lico, another key freedom fighter.

With all the attention on rooting out more of the resistance, I couldn't stay a minute longer, so I quickly passed through town and headed for home.

*****

By winter, our life was beginning to look completely hopeless. There was an adequate supply of firewood on hand, and the old cooking stove did a good enough job of warming the house to keep us from freezing, but we had hit bottom in terms of food. It had been almost two weeks since we had last eaten. We wore death like a shroud. In our innocence, we began to laugh and talk about dying. Somehow, it seemed funny. Yllke was the youngest. She was about eight years old by then, and she was the weakest of us all. We knew that she probably would be the first to go, and so we teased her about it.

Eventually, our brash talk of death angered Lumka.

"Quit that sort of talk this instant!" she hollered. "Do you hear? Why are we talking about dying? We're not going to die. We're going to bow our heads and pray for guidance and courage."

I'll always remember what happened next. After the prayer and out of the blue sky, Lumka said, "We're going to get a letter from America."

We all looked at her in surprise. I thought she must be hallucinating from the extreme hunger.

"Oh yes, it will happen," she insisted. "You'll see. And I'll tell you something else. There will be a check in the letter for one hundred and fifty dollars. When we get this money, we won't have to worry for a while. We'll be able to buy enough food to make ourselves good and fat."

Even though we really didn't believe Lumka, we jokingly discussed the luxurious food we would buy with that sort of money. The girls giggled as they planned all the different meals they would cook. We knew it was all in our imagination, but somehow, the laughter seemed to ease my hunger pangs, and it put an end to the talk of dying.

I will never be convinced that God does not perform miracles because that day, we experienced one.

The wind was roaring, and the blistery weather caused our house to creak and groan at every hinge. All we had was the warmth from our stove now, so we stayed huddled near it, weak from hunger.

Suddenly, there was a loud knock on the window. At first, we mistook it for a noise caused by the storm, but then we heard it again, much louder this time. When it sounded a third time, I began to stir but found that I couldn't rise. I was so weak from hunger that I could hardly move. The others were no better.

Then to my surprise, there he stood in the room. I recognized his short stature and his hunched back. It was Sefedin, the mailman, and he was holding a letter.

Myrset took it from him and stared at the envelope. "It's from America," she mumbled quietly.

The news caused a surge of adrenaline within me, and immediately, I found myself on my feet. The others joined me, staggering upright, one by one. We all pawed at the envelope, all of us wanting to open it at the same time.

I don't know about the others, but I so firmly believed in Lumka's prescience in that moment that I didn't care about whom the letter was from or what it might say. I just wanted confirmation that it contained the money she claimed it would.

And there it was: a check for one hundred and fifty American dollars.

The mailman, who had visited us enough times to witness our desperate circumstances, softly whispered, "Thank you, God, the merciful and compassionate." We looked at each other in total amazement.

"Are we dreaming?" I asked. "Is this really happening?"

Then with all the strength we could muster up, we began to jump and sing with joy.

Many years later, I learned from my father the details of this miracle. Uncle Arif and Father were in Greece after their escape (and remember we had no knowledge of their location at the time of this incident). One night while in Greece, Uncle Arif had a very distressful dream about our family. In the dream, we had appeared to him standing on the edge of a muddy river. We stood there helpless, dressed in ragged clothes and a muddy wave of water was heading toward us. The fear of the dream caused Uncle Arif to suddenly awaken and sit straight up. This strange dream had disturbed him so much that after he told my father about it, he wrote a letter to Amit Fazo, a close Albanian friend of his that had been in the United States since before the Second World war, and lived in Waterbury, Connecticut. In the letter, Uncle Arif asked him if it would be at all possible to send one hundred fifty dollars to us in Albania. He promised to pay the money back to Amit at the first opportunity. This good family friend immediately sent the money directly to us in Pilur.

We wasted no time getting ready. Myrset and I went to a bank in Korca, which was the closest place we knew of where they would cash a check from America. There, instead of regular money, we were given Volute, a type of currency that could only be obtained with American dollars. We left the bank quickly and went to the store. We picked up necessary food items: flour, some fruits, potatoes, and a few items of clothing. After we had the supplies we needed, we made our way to the front of the store where I quickly added a soccer ball to our wares. Myrset was upset at first, but I explained that I had a plan to use it to our advantage back home.

"This soccer ball will be the only one in the entire village," I said. "And I'm sure all the kids in Pilur would gladly trade some beans or grain to be able to play with it. This ball may very well be what keeps food in our stomachs after the money runs out."

Once back in Pilur, word began to spread among the kids in the village that I had a real soccer ball. We created several teams and began organizing the games. My friend Haki Spaho was about seventeen years old, so he took charge in setting up the teams. He was liked and respected by most of the teenagers in the area, so he was a perfect candidate for the job. He also wasn't afraid to speak openly with me about how much he hated the Communists, even though his father was at one time one of the high officials in the village.

One day, after a friendly game of soccer, I took Haki aside and told him of my idea. "You know how much my family has been suffering. I was thinking of charging the players a small ration of beans and corn for the use of my soccer ball. This will help us through this crisis. What do you think?"

"That's a great idea, Pertef," he said. "But let me be the one to make the suggestion to them. This way, it'll seem like it was my idea and not yours."

The plan worked even better than I thought it would. I was putting food on the table for my family every day.

The soccer ball remained with me always until the day I went to visit my grandparents on my mother's side. Before I left, I gave it to my cousin Selami and told him to guard it with his life.

"This is my pot of gold, Selami," I told him. "Don't let it out of your sight."

Mother's parents were living with their oldest son Seit (Dervish) at the time. Recently, the government had released him from prison after a five-year sentence. Having experienced the horrors of a Communist prison, he had become so paranoid that he trusted no one. He forbade all his family members, including his father, from ever speaking about politics or religion. "One wrong word," he would tell them, "and I'll be back behind bars. And it'll be a life sentence next time."

His brother Hysen was already serving such a sentence, so no one could blame him for his worry.

Grandmother Fatiko was glad to see me but then quickly turned to scolding me for not visiting more often. Then she suddenly burst into tears.

"Grandmother, what's wrong?" I asked, my voice quavering at the sight of her sadness.

She shuddered through a sob before collecting herself enough to speak. "What about my beloved daughter?" she asked in a solemn voice. "Have you heard any news from her?"

"We did receive one letter from her," I said. "She mostly complained that she hadn't received any mail from us. But we've been sending her letters, Grandmother. I fear they're just not getting through to her. I'm sure we're not receiving most of hers either. The stinking government is keeping us in the dark!"

Grandmother Fatiko seemed to notice the concern in my voice. "We'll pray that she's returned to us safely and as soon as possible."

My attention was suddenly drawn to the door, where my Aunt Reshide stood. My beloved aunt was around forty-five years old with black hair and dark brown eyes. She was a beautiful, gentle, and goodhearted woman. We called her "the American Lady" since she had once lived in that country about which she spoke so highly. Even with all the suffering my family had endured, I felt sorry for her, for she had lost two sons and a daughter, and her husband Hysen was serving a life sentence. To any outsider, it would have seemed as if she had nothing to live for, but I knew she was a courageous and determined woman, and she often spoke about the hope she carried. She hoped that someday her husband would be free and they would be able to return to America.

When she saw me, Aunt Reshide buried me in hugs and kisses. "I thought you had forgotten us," she said happily. "It has been such a long time since I have seen you. Come, tell me how the family is!"

We left the house and went into the orchards. Our conversation seemed to shatter the quietness of this placid paradise, so we chose our words carefully on the slim chance we could be overheard. We talked for a while.

As the sun dropped down behind the mountains, my cousin Zhuleta interrupted us.

"Grandfather just woke and wants to see you," she said.

"Shall we go in?" Aunt Reshide asked.

I nodded and so we headed back for the house. There, I greeted Grandfather with a hug and a kiss. He asked how everyone was doing and then complained about the Communist government and how they would not let his son Hysen and daughter Resmije out of prison.

"The Albanian people have been taken over by the devil," he said. "This so-called government is not only an enemy of the people but also an enemy of God. They're atheists, and they're trying to turn us into atheists too!"

The talk was upsetting him, and I knew it was making my uncle nervous, so I changed the conversation to Mother and how much we both missed her. When he grew too tired to continue, Grandfather got up and started toward his room. He hugged me and whispered in my ear, "I will pray for all of you when I go to my room. I would like to tell you that things will get better, but I think our situation will get much worse in the years to come as these gangsters gain more power and control."

I spent much of the rest of the day asking Aunt Reshide about America because every time someone began talking about freedom and democracy, the United States always entered the conversation.

"Auntie," I said to her, "the Communists are saying that in America, people are starving and there isn't enough work to go around. They say that in America, the streets are full of unemployed workers and the people are protesting every day because there is a shortage of food. Is that true?"

She laughed. "Don't you believe a word of that, Pertef! It's nonsense—nothing but propaganda! The Communists want you to believe that so you'll think their idea of government is better. They want to convince you that when they rob and steal from us and torture us, it's for the good of the Albanian people."

"So it's not true what they say about the poverty in America?"

"The United States is the richest country on the face of the earth. Of course, there's plenty of food for everybody. When your uncle and I went to the grocery store to buy food, he bought chicken by the case, all cut up and ready to put into the oven."

My mouth started watering as Aunt Reshide began telling me about the abundance of meats and breads available in America. It all sounded so surreal that I had to keep asking her if she was really telling the truth. I could not even imagine a country where the people had plenty of food and work and never wanted for anything.

The way Aunt Reshide talked to me about America that day caused the ideals of that country to be drilled into my head. She had given me the motivation I needed. From that day forward, it seemed as if I thought of nothing else but going to America. I grew to love the United States long before I ever stood on its soil. I loved America because of what she represented: freedom. And I loved her because she presented our only real hope to escape the bondage of communism. The seed had been planted. I was determined to one day make my home in America.

The last night of my visit came, and I said my goodbyes with a heavy heart. I promised Aunt Reshide that I would visit again soon. The next morning, I awoke before dawn and started walking toward home.

When I arrived at Pilur, Selami told me that some of the boys had stolen the soccer ball from him and thrown it into a dry well. The news devastated me, but I was determined not to lose my family's meal ticket. So I took Selami and my trusted friend Haki with me just to be sure this wasn't a trick of some kind. Over the years, I had heard many horror stories about this particular well. One such story was about a man that raised goats. When one of his goats accidentally fell into the well, the man tied a rope around his waist and had his friends lower him down to retrieve his lost livestock. But after his friends pulled him up with the goat, the man found that he was deaf and mute. As the story goes, he would live that way to the end of his days.

The adults had encouraged the telling of this story when we were children, and I'm sure it was just a measure to keep us from playing near the well, but I have to admit a certain reluctance to go after my soccer ball. The power of myth is strong. Ultimately, I knew I had no choice. I couldn't count on any more mysterious letters from the United States; I had to either go after that ball or starve to death.

So with a long, heavy rope in tow, Haki, Selami, and I edged toward the well. I tied the rope securely around my waist, and they began lowering me into the dark depths of what seemed to be a bottomless pit. I was a young boy of fourteen with a very short childhood. I had been given a man's responsibilities at an early age, and most of my years had been a fight for survival. I was a man in a boy's body. To me, death and fear were just words. I feared nothing—except, of course, snakes.

And as I was soon to learn, there were plenty of rattlesnakes at the bottom of the well. Their rattling and hissing grew louder the closer I came to the bottom. I knew it was an impossible number, but to my terrified ear, it sounded like there were thousands of them.

I was glad that I had chosen two good friends to hold the rope, and lucky for me, they were managing to lower me slowly. When I was finally in a position to make out the outline of the soccer ball, I could see that it was lying right on top of the nest of rattlesnakes. Thanking God all the while for his mercy, I extended my feet slowly and carefully until my toes felt the ball. Then I carefully slid a foot down each side of the ball until I could get a firm clutch on it. I was pouring sweat and could hardly keep my eyes open, I was so afraid.

When I had the ball, I immediately signaled for them to pull me up. Bless them, they did it quickly.

The moment I was safely out of the well, I fell to the ground, knees weak and needing to change my clothes. That incident would stick with me in bad dreams for years to come, but the outcome was positive. I put my rescued ball back to work immediately. Haki scheduled games throughout that day, and I was relieved to see that the food bank was once again open for us. I decided I would not let the soccer ball out of my possession again. It was too valuable—it meant life or death for my family.

Of course, over the years to come, it would be just one of many elements on which our lives hinged.

Chapter 7

One evening after playing soccer in our vacant field, I arrived home to find that Medi had returned from the job that had kept him away for so long. We stayed up until midnight that night, talking and laughing. We were all so uplifted to see him again.

It couldn't have been more than an hour after we went to sleep when a startling crash from the front of the house wrenched me out of bed. I went into the hallway with Medi. From there, we could see that three men had broken through the front door and were standing in the house. I recognized one of them as Shaban Tale, a trouble-maker from our area, and the other two as officers of the Sigurim.

"Don't move!" one of them shouted. "We have you surrounded!"

I was frozen with fear and confusion. I had no idea what they wanted or why they had come.

One of the officers looked up the stairs and spotted us. "Which one of you is Medi?" he demanded.

"I am," my brother replied.

I had never heard my brother speak with such a strong voice. He sounded fearless. It seemed that Medi had grown up during the time he was away and had become his own man.

"What do you want with me?" he asked of our intruders.

"In the name of the party, you are under arrest. We advise you not to move if you want to live."

"I'm not going anywhere until I get my pants on," Medi replied as he turned for the bedroom.

The officer was upstairs in a flash, escorting Medi at gunpoint.

I waited nervously as Medi put on his pants, tucked in his shirt, and returned to the hallway, where we all stood and stared at each other for a while. The officers kept their pistols drawn and pointed at Medi's head while Shaban Tale used a piece of wire to tie my brother's hands behind his back. Shaban twisted the wire so tightly that Medi yelled out in pain—so tightly that I could see blood coming from his forearm where the flesh had been cut. Shaban had a reputation for brutality. He had been given so much authority that he could kill you on the spot, no questions asked.

When Lumka and Myrset saw how Medi was being treated, they both cried out to Shaban, telling him it wasn't necessary to be so cruel.

He laughed loudly. "The two of you shut your mouths," he said with a sneer. "Or next time will be your time!"

Once Medi's hands were tied, Shaban kicked him toward the door, causing him to stumble and fall to the floor. Shaban then grabbed him by his clothes and dragged him away. That was the last time I saw or talked to my brother Medi until the fall of communism in Albania, thirty-eight years later.

We eventually learned that Medi and his friend Kujtim Demiraj were both accused of plotting an escape to Greece. They were taken for interrogation at the prison headquarters in Korca. The building was known all over Albania as one of the worst places to be taken upon arrest. Word had it that anyone able to survive imprisonment there would be extremely lucky to ever be normal again.

A week passed with no word about my brother, so I decided to go to the prison to visit him and take him some clean clothes. When I asked to see Medi, the guard at the main gate took the clothes from me and told me to wait. I waited for quite some time, hoping that I would have a chance to speak with my brother, but eventually, it became clear that they would never allow me in, so I left for home.

I made it back to Pilur by dusk, only to find Lumka and Myrset moving our few belongings out of the house.

"What's going on?" I asked.

"Our home has been taken from us," Lumka said, fighting back tears.

"It's going to another party member," Myrset said.

"We're moving back to the store."

"The Palace," Myrset quipped darkly.

The tears spilled over Lumka's cheeks.

Given that I had just spent the day at the hellhole where the Communists were keeping my brother, I felt my patience wearing thin. My hatred was building up inside, and I just wasn't sure how much more we could take from these bastards.

"No way are we moving there again," I said and refused to move from the spot I was standing on. I was ready to make my stand right then and there. "These filthy scumbags have played with us for the last time!"

Lumka and Myrset began to cry in earnest. They begged me to calm down.

"They'll kill you if you refuse to move," Lumka said. "What will we do then? We'll starve to death! Please, Pertef, let it go. It'll be all right."

They were right. We had no choice. So we moved, along with our donkey and nanny, who had just given birth to two baby goats. We tried to clean the old store once again, but the floor was nothing more than exposed ground, and try as we might, we could hardly make it into a home. The girls did their best to keep a positive attitude. When the donkey and goats were in a good mood, it wasn't quiet. We had plenty of music. I guess you could say we all lived in harmony.

I would get food whenever I could, but because of the cold from the approaching winter, the soccer games were few. We were not only hungry but also cold from the blustery winds and icy rains. Most nights, we huddled together, trying to stay warm enough so that we could get a little sleep.

It didn't take us long to guess the reason for the party's mad behavior. They were making our lives as miserable as they could, leaving us homeless, robbing us of opportunity for food or work, and causing us humiliation and rejection from the people we once called friends. We were old enough now to be sent to one of their hard labor camps, but they didn't want to arrest us—not yet anyway. They were using us as bait for Father and Uncle Arif. The party must have figured that when the men got word about our inhumane treatment, they would be forced to return from Greece and take us to safety. They wanted nothing more than to capture and execute Father and Uncle Arif. They were on the top of the most wanted list most likely because they had outsmarted them and made them look foolish. It was for this reason that we had remained under the Communists' surveillance and the party's thumb for the almost four years since Father and Uncle Arif's escape.

There was an empty field as big as a soccer pitch that belonged to our store where we were now living. It was in that field where Gezim and I were playing some one-on-one soccer when I noticed about ten boys from the ages of fourteen to eighteen coming toward us. As soon as I got a good look at them, I knew they had been sent to cause trouble.

The leader was Shaban Tale's younger brother Kadri. They surrounded Gezim and me and told us they were going to hang us. I knew I was the focus of their hostility more than Gezim, so I asked them to let my younger brother go.

"Fine," Kadri said. "Let's see the baby run."

"Go inside, Gezim," I said sternly. "Stay in the store no matter what. Do you hear me?"

With wide, frightened eyes, he nodded and took off. I was certain that he would seek out Lumka and Myrset immediately to tell them what was happening and just as certain that they would try to intervene.

Sure enough, a few moments later, my sister and cousin rounded the corner from behind the store and started toward me.

"Get back inside," I yelled. "Just wait for me." Reluctantly, they did as I told them.

I could see that Kadri had a piece of wire in his hands. He was fashioning it into a noose. He and five of the other boys had surrounded me by then, but the rest were standing off to the side, looking less than enthusiastic about this encounter. One among this latter group I recognized as someone I was friends with when I was allowed to go to school. I had helped him out a few times when he was in fights, so I figured that he owed me and that he might just be my one chance to escape this confrontation with my life.

So I inched my way over to him and asked if he would give me the club he was carrying. He looked first at me and then at the other boys, clearly contemplating his decision and also making sure he would not be seen. Then he reluctantly passed the club to me.

I knew I couldn't hesitate to act. My only chance was a surprise attack on the leader of this mob. The deck was stacked against me, ten to one, but I had learned already that crushing the leader had a way of evening the odds. So with club in hand, I charged toward Kadri. By the time he realized what was happening, I was on top of him. I brought the club down on his head hard and so fast that before he hit the ground, I had clubbed him multiple times. The other boys looked stunned by my sudden rebellion. Kadri was on the ground with his head busted open, and his gang could only stare down at him in disbelief.

This gave me an opportunity and only a split second to make a dash toward our store. When my family saw me coming with the gang of boys behind me, they picked up knives, sticks, and clubs—anything they could get their hands on—and stood ready to fight back. As I ran for the protection of the store, I pictured the place where I kept my axe. I found it quickly. Then raising the axe over my shoulder, I took my place beside Gezim, Lumka, Yllke, and Myrset. Together, we made our stand against our tormenters, who suddenly looked quite a lot more hesitant in the face of all our sharp, glinting weapons.

"If any of you think you're brave enough to hang me now," I cried, "come in here and get me! We'll kill you filthy scum one by one!"

Rather than charge us, the boys threw rocks and insults for over an hour. They flashed more aggressive action from time to time, but it was clear they were too afraid to breach our line, too concerned that I would make good on my promise to kill them. Finally, they gave up and skulked away, carrying the bloodied Kadri with them. I never did hear what happened to him after the damage I'd done to his head.

*****

Despite our squalor, Myrset became engaged to Shefqet Mulla, who came from a family we had known for quite some time. After a short engagement of just a few weeks, we all agreed that it would be better if they went ahead and married. At least she would be able to move from the rat hole we were calling home.

It was a happy few days for us because we knew that Myrset's life would improve dramatically with a roof over her head and a husband to care for her. But the joy would be short-lived. When the government found out about their engagement, they were both arrested and sent to a labor camp. It would be almost forty years before I would see or talk to Myrset and her husband again.

At the time of their arrest, none of us could have foreseen that we would face the same fate before the week was out. But then it happened. In the wee hours of the morning, a pod of Sigurim crashed through our door and arrested Gezim, Lumka, Yllke, and me. With little fanfare and even less explanation of the charges, we were shoved into a truck and taken away, our destination unknown.

Our faith as a family couldn't have been any stronger than it was at that time. Even though our predicament seemed hopeless, we remained positive that something good would prevail. God was always there to help us when it seemed all hope was lost, so together, we prayed that if we were going to be put in a labor camp, to please let it be the one that would reunite us with our mother. It had been four years since we last had seen her and about two years since we received the letter from her acknowledging Fejzi's death and letting us know she was at Kamze. We had received no other word about her whereabouts or even if she was still alive.

We arrived at a camp early the next morning. Our assignment was to Gjaze. Almost immediately, I realized that our prayers had been answered once again.

As soon as I stepped down from the truck, I spotted them. Mother, Aunt Sibe, and Feruze were all running toward us, crying and beaming with excitement and relief. It is impossible to describe the joy I felt when I saw my mother that day. Lumka and Gezim ran ahead to meet them, and I stayed behind to help Yllke, who was eight, from the back of the truck.

"Is that Mother?" Yllke asked.

It broke my heart when I realized that as young as she was, Yllke didn't have any remaining memory of what Mother or Father looked like. "That's her," I said with a smile. "Shall we go see her?"

With an excited grin, Yllke trotted ahead of me. When Yllke and I arrived at the reunion, we all greeted each other with hugs and kisses, time and again. None of us had any words, for the tears of joy were too strong to overcome.

That night, Mother proudly introduced us to all the friends she had made in the camp. We traded stories from the four years we were apart. That was when we learned of Uncle Qani's death. He had died at Tepelena, well known as the worst labor camp in Albania, a place where more than three hundred children died from starvation. Mother told us that she checked every day when the trucks arrived with new arrestees searching for family members or anyone that had information about her children. She never gave up hope that we would be together again. Then Mother told us the story of how she had learned about Fejzi's cruel fate.

"I guess it was several days after Fejzi's death," she said, her gaze dark and distant. "I was summoned to the commander's office at the camp of Kamze. They considered my son's death a victory for their regime and were eager to share the news with me."

She gave a bitter look and continued with the story. "'I've called you here today to inform you of the death of your son,' the commander told me. 'It was a known fact that he was a traitor, working with American imperialists to overthrow our government. It gives me much joy to tell you that earlier this week, the People's Army fought bravely against your son and killed him.'"

I scoffed when I heard this. The Communist side of the story always had a strange flavor.

"I doubted the details too, Pertef," Mother said. Then she shook her head. "The commander told me that Fejzi Bylykbashi would no longer be an opposition for their government. 'I might add,' he said, 'that it's only a matter of time before your husband and the others are captured, and I can assure you that they'll meet the same fate. Your future is here for the rest of your life.'" She clenched her teeth as her eyes began to water. "Then he said the most ludicrous thing. He said, 'But if you'll openly denounce your husband and family, the authorities may show some leniency toward you and your younger children. If you refuse to do this, life for you will become more difficult to endure than hellfire itself.'"

Mother shifted her weight and looked toward the horizon. Somehow, I could sense that she was thinking about Father.

"I had already heard talk in the camp of my dear son's death," she said. "So I knew the true details. The respect the other people in camp showed me and Fejzi made me proud. But when I heard that ruthless butcher of a commander speak of his memory in such a disrespectful way, it ripped my heart apart. I clenched my teeth and refused to give him the satisfaction of seeing me shed a single tear." Mother seemed to steel up as she spoke. "All the worry and fear I'd felt for so many years vanished and was instantly replaced with energy and courage. At that moment, I became fearless. I was determined to say my peace at any cost."

She clenched her hands into fists and rose, chin up, to demonstrate how she had stood before her enemy. "I stared straight into his eyes, and with a voice that was sure and unshaking, I told him, 'In my wildest dreams, I could never imagine an Albanian mother giving birth to such a monster as you. Let us be truthful here. My courageous son would not give your soldiers the satisfaction of killing him. He courageously took that pleasure from them and did it himself.'

"The commander ordered me silent, but I could no longer be silent. 'My courageous son has given all of us hope,' I told him. 'And we know there's a light at the end of this dark, treacherous tunnel. My beloved Fejzi has planted the seed of freedom with his life, and now the Albanian people will nourish that seed until it's fully grown.

"And as far as me denouncing my husband or any of my family, I love each of them and support everything they stand for. And I will continue to support them until the day I die even if it is only with the prayers I whisper in my mind every day.'

"By then, the commander had called the guards to drag me outside and shut me up. I was beaten severely, a tactic used all too often by those animals, as a show of power. But the beating I received was a small price to pay for the words I was able to speak for my beloved son Fejzi."

I often think about my mother and how for thirty-two years in captivity, she received endless physical and verbal abuse—and through all that, they could never break her spirit, could never make her renounce her love for her husband and family. She never lost her hope for freedom and remained devoted to her husband and his cause until her death in 1982.

As for the rest of us, it's hard to imagine how someone could be happy after being placed into a labor camp, but happy we were. For the first time in many years, most of our family was together.

The following morning, we went outside for roll call. After they had accounted for everyone, the daily routine began. The camp officials led the men and women into the fields to dig ditches. It was heart-wrenching to see Mother and the others marching out of the camp with picks and shovels slung over their shoulders, but it was better to be able to see them than to know we would have to spend another day apart.

November was the rainy season for that region, and the weather created terrible working conditions for the prisoners. The ground was nothing but mud, and most of them had inadequate footwear. I could see that it was only by God's grace that Mother had been able to survive so many years of working from sunrise to sunset, rain or shine, with very little food rations or clothing. The work they were required to do would be considered backbreaking for the strongest and healthiest of men, yet these men and women, as frail as they were, would work all day long, day in and day out, with their clothes soaked and their feet wet and muddy.

That first day, they left me and the rest of the children at camp with nothing to do because our work detail had not yet been assigned. So we waited idly for thirteen hours while the adults worked in the fields. When they returned that evening, we received only a bowl of cabbage soup and a piece of stale cornbread to eat.

Mealtime gave us a chance to visit with some of the people in the barracks, including Uncle Shaban, whom we had not seen since our arrival. Prior to communism, Uncle Shaban had been an elected official in our region and had always prided himself for his discipline and structure. This made him a natural target for imprisonment by the regime and also made him a popular man at the camp.

It was apparent that Mother was a much-respected and popular figure at Gjaze as well. Both young and old prisoners held her in high regard. By the second night, we had met most of her friends, including a young man named Faik Agastra, from Baban in Southern Albania. Faik was twenty-two years old, handsome, confident, well-mannered, and pleasantly respectful. It was obvious from the moment I met him that he was well-bred. I learned that he had helped Mother through many difficult times, and so they had become trusting friends.

Faik kept us up most of that second night, telling us about the many novels he had read. He was an avid reader, and the way he told the stories made it seem as if he had written them himself. It was obvious why Mother liked this young man so much. She—and just about everyone else in the compound—was fascinated by Faik. We too fell in love with him after knowing him for just one night. For some of us, the love was more noticeable than others. I noticed early in the evening that Faik had an eye for Lumka, and it wasn't long before I caught her sending glances his way.

We stayed in Gjaze for only three months. Then all of us were transferred to Saver, which was not far by caravan. As we were climbing down from the trucks, Faik came over to assist us. It seemed like a nice gesture at the time, but it wasn't until much later that I realized Faik had ulterior motives. He had loved Lumka from the night they first met, and there was nothing he wouldn't do for her. Unfortunately for their burgeoning romance, Faik would be with us at Saver for only a few months before he and fifty other prisoners received transfer orders to another camp.

The quarters I was assigned was shared with seven other family members. The room was the size of a small bedroom, about ten feet by ten feet, and it had a concrete floor. The only water available was located in the middle of the compound, and it was shared by everyone in the camp. There were no toilet facilities, so we made our own by digging a hole in the ground and erecting makeshift privacy walls with sticks and old cornstalks.

Roll call was every morning at six o'clock, and when it was finished, we were divided into groups. Feruze and I received the same work assignment, and I was thankful for that because it would give us a chance to catch up after such a long time apart. Also with us were Zydi Hysolli and his sister Ismet, Agim and his sister Vexhide, and two young men named Paul and Vebi Collaku, who—because of their size and strength—drew the task of digging. The rest of us would take the mud that Paul and Vebi dug and form it into bricks. Every day, we would stomp in the mud from seven o'clock in the morning until six in the evening. It was difficult work, but I had no choice but to do it. This was my assignment now, my future.

So I stomped the mud and straw, my legs burning until they became numb and I could feel nothing at all. With each passing day, I felt more strongly that death would be better than a life that had nothing to offer beyond muddy days and sleepless nights. I had started to succumb to the sense that I would be a slave to communism for the rest of my life.

What kept me from going completely insane was my faith in God, the memory of Aunt Reshide's stories of America, and hope—the hope that someday America would be my home. Whenever I was whiling away the hours in the mud, I would close my eyes and, over and over in my mind, repeat Aunt Reshide's words of praise about America.

Once a week, the camp officials would distribute mail to anyone lucky enough to receive it. I never missed mail call, always hoping I would get a letter from Aunt Reshide, always staying until the very last letter found its recipient, but nothing ever came for me. One day, the name of the family that stayed in the barracks next to ours had their names called, but they were not present. I offered to deliver the mail to them, and when I received the letter, I saw that it was from Faik. Out of curiosity and excitement to hear how he was doing, I opened the letter and began to read. I was shocked to find that he had written the letter to my sister Lumka, expressing his feelings for her.

The strong courtship traditions of the Albanian people would not allow for this kind of behavior. Most marriages were arranged by the elders, and it was absolutely forbidden to express any romantic feelings without first asking permission from the family to whom the desired person belonged. I was so outraged by what I had read that I took the letter directly to Mother. She and Uncle Shaban were having a bowl of soup, and after I gave them the necessary greetings, I told them about what I carried. All the while, I was clenching the letter tightly in my fist.

Mother's reaction was both of anger and surprise. "I never expected something like this to happen," she said. "I'm disappointed in them both but especially Faik. He is a man and should know better. This is not the way we do things."

"I agree, Mother," I said dutifully.

"Why didn't he come to us and ask for her hand in marriage? That would have been the traditional way, and we would have agreed." Mother's cheeks reddened. "What he has done brings shame to our family, and we have to do something about it! He leaves us no alternative but to refuse him the right to marry my daughter."

When she was finished, Uncle Shaban raised a hand as if asking for calm. "Resmije, you're getting too upset. Maybe this is nothing. Let's talk to Lumka about it first."

A few minutes later, Lumka walked in and greeted each of us with a kiss. I couldn't resist waving the letter in front of her face.

"What's this?" she asked.

"You know exactly what this is!" I said smugly.

"I'm only going to ask you once," Mother said. "And I want the truth. Why did he send this letter to you? And how long has this been going on behind our backs?"

Lumka's face lost its color as she denied everything. I could tell she was lying.

"You listen to me," I said as Mother nodded her approval. "You're going to get a pencil and piece of paper and write exactly what I tell you." She wrote as I dictated:

> Faik,
>   Please stop writing letters to me. I no longer
> want to have anything to do with you. You have
> upset my family and me.
>
>   Lumka

After she finished, I put the letter in an envelope and mailed it myself. We did not dislike Faik; we just didn't like the way he went about courting my sister. In truth, I thought they were a perfect match for each other, and I would have given them permission to marry had they approached it by our customs. Mother praised me for my actions, and we congratulated ourselves for ending the problem. But we would soon learn that we hadn't done anything of the sort. Even in the most adverse conditions, when two people are in love, they will find a way to communicate. We had no idea that Lumka had secretly written another letter to Faik, explaining what had happened and telling him to disregard the first letter. Their love affair secretly continued through letters for another six months until Faik was transferred back to our camp.

The first time I saw them together, I could tell they were in love just by the looks they were exchanging. We put pressure on Lumka to break the relationship and stop caring so much for Faik, but their feelings for each other seemed stronger than any Albanian tradition.

I kept a watchful eye on them. They never had a moment alone—never a chance to touch or hold hands or even to have a conversation in private. What they did have was a love that burned inside, and it was growing stronger with every passing day.

In order to bring peace to the family, Mother gave in to them, but I didn't agree with the match and refused to accept Mother's decision. I wanted to go by the traditions my family had honored for generations.

I carried this anger with me for a long time—right up until Mother became ill. Her weakened state grew worse each day. A few days passed without any improvement. I tried talking to her, but she was so weak that she could barely respond. I kissed her and held her hand, telling her how much we loved her and needed her. When she didn't reply, I made a promise to myself that I would do whatever was necessary to restore peace and harmony in our family for Mother's sake.

"Yllke really needs her mother," I said in a pleading tone. "She's still so young and fragile. Please don't leave us, Mother. Please." No reply.

I sighed. "Okay, Mother. Then I have to tell you that I've given Lumka and Faik my permission and blessing to become engaged. We're just waiting for you to get well so we can celebrate." This, of course was a lie, but I could see that Mother needed a reason to get better—something to live for beyond more days of digging in the mud and more days of disharmony among her children.

To my surprise, a weak smile crossed Mother's lips. Her eyes remained closed, but I could see that she was uplifted when she heard about the plans for Lumka's engagement. As if to acknowledge that she understood, she squeezed my hand and held it for a moment. I could see that she needed to rest, so I gently kissed her cheek and told her that I would be back very soon to check on her.

I knew that I had to talk to Lumka next, so I could mend the problems regarding her relationship with Faik. It had been a long while since I had really spoken to her, so I couldn't begrudge her the look of shock she assumed when I addressed her with kindness in my voice.

"Do we still have the bottle of raki Uncle Seit gave to us?" I asked.

She furrowed her brow. "Why do you need the raki? Why don't you wait until Mother gets better and open it then?" Then she cocked her head to one side. "Besides, you don't even drink."

"Stop arguing with me and bring me the bottle," I said, my tone cheerful. "If today isn't the day for a celebration, then when?" When I winked at her, I nearly broke into laughter at the confusion it seemed to cause her.

Even so, as she turned to fetch the bottle, I caught a glimpse of a sparkle in her eyes. It was clear that she was happy to be talking with me at all, given how much we had drifted apart.

I opened the bottle and poured two shots, handing one to her.

"I don't drink," she said.

"You will drink this," I replied with a grin.

"Okay, but what are we drinking for?"

"First, for our mother, whom we will pray has a speedy recovery, and then for you, my sister, for I am granting you permission to become engaged to Faik." I raised my drink. "I congratulate you!" She beamed.

"I'm very sorry for all the terrible names I've called you," I said, "and for the times our arguments got out of control. I just want you to know that I was only doing what our traditions called for. You do understand, don't you?"

By now, Lumka was in tears. At first, I thought I had saddened her, but when she leapt into my arms to hug me, I could see that they were tears of joy. For me, it was the first time in my life that I had enough drinks to feel drunk. We had a marvelous time talking and laughing, and as the night progressed, our conversation made less and less sense. I had never seen Lumka that happy.

With each passing day, Mother's health improved. She praised me on the decision to honor the engagement between Lumka and Faik and thanked me for restoring peace and harmony in the family.

When we weren't celebrating unions and reunions, life in the camp was becoming more difficult. The authorities were cracking the whip, claiming that we were not fulfilling our daily quota of responsibilities. We were working harder and longer hours with very little food to put in our stomachs.

Through it all, I began to think about what I would do with my life. I had a wonderful support system of family and friends—people with high moral character from whom I was drawing knowledge and wisdom each day. The only thing standing in our way was a common enemy called communism.

Chapter 8

The year 1956 found us still in Saver. Little had changed, apart from my work detail. Now I was sent to clear rocks from an abandoned airstrip reportedly built by the Italian army during World War II. The labor would be backbreaking, but it pleased me to learn that I would be teamed up with a friend named Sinan Ajdari.

Sinan stood slightly taller than me, was thin in frame, and always kept a serious demeanor. His face was weathered from the outside work, and on his left ear, he wore an earring. This latter point was because, prior to Sinan's birth, his mother had gone through a miscarriage. There was an old wives' tale in Albania claiming that the first surviving child following a miscarriage, no matter what the gender, would need to have an earring placed in the left earlobe if he was to survive. The superstition seemed a bit odd to me, but our society had accepted and embraced the tradition.

Sinan's father and uncle had escaped Albania just before World War II ended; and soon after, Sinan, his mother, two sisters, and two brothers were arrested and placed in the labor camp. I had only known my friend for a short time, but we had grown close quickly, and now that we were working together, I looked forward to sharing a few laughs now and then.

Sinan and I were on our work detail when we heard the first reports of the Hungarian Revolution. It renewed our hope that a revolution similar to this could happen in our country. There were only two newspapers in Albania, and they were owned and operated by the government. The articles reporting the uprising blamed the American imperialists, saying that they were the agitators of this revolution, and were responsible for trying to poison the minds of our Hungarian brothers and sisters. The reporter wrote that, with the help of Russian allies, the revolution would be crushed and the Hungarian people would be free again.

What a stupid thing to report, I thought. *Why would anyone revolt if they were already free?*

The Communists feared that Albania would follow Hungary's lead, so they began sending commissioners throughout the towns, villages, prisons, and labor camps to give speeches and lectures on imperialism. The idiots were talking nonsense, trying to convince us that communism was protecting the Albanian people. Of course not all Albanians believed their propaganda, including us. We knew they were pathological liars that could not be trusted. Often, I sensed fear and uncertainty in the voices of the men warning us about the consequences if anyone was caught plotting against the government.

It was Esma, Sinan's mother, who decided to speak up about it during one of these lectures.

"What's happened, Comrade?" she said in a mocking tone. "Have you started to fear us now?"

"What did you say?" the speaker asked incredulously.

Esma continued, undaunted. "We know the day of freedom is getting closer and closer. Maybe today, tomorrow, or the next day, our husbands, sons, fathers, and brothers will come by the thousands to free us from bondage and from the excruciating suffering you have put us through."

"Comrade, sit down," the speaker tried to interject.

My friend's mother kept on. "Just remember, *Comrade*, the winds are changing in our favor, and the same rope that you have used on many of us will probably end up around your neck! When that happens, I won't even let your *tongue* hang free. I'll recommend they tear it out."

Everyone present seemed on edge. I stood in disbelief and fear for Esma, for we all knew that such defiance would never be tolerated by the Communists. But to our surprise, even though the police dragged her out of the barracks, no harm was done to her. With their failure to punish Esma, this made us certain that they were fearful of their government being overthrown.

The first week of November, we heard that the bloodthirsty Russian Communist government had ordered their heavily armed soldiers and tanks to move into Hungary. The capital of Budapest was attacked shortly after. In this siege, the Communists massacred thousands of innocent men, women, and children. My heart was full of sadness for the people of Hungary, and my hope of freedom was shattered.

A few weeks later, new prisoners were transferred to Saver from other labor camps, and I went directly to the barracks to meet them. My attention was drawn to a man in his midtwenties who was whistling as he put his belongings in his assigned area of the barracks. I walked over to him, and we exchanged introductions. His name was Xhemil Jazxhi.

"How did you come to be here, Xhemil?" I asked.

"Well, my young friend," he said cheerfully, "while I was serving in the army, my family crossed the border to Greece and escaped to freedom. When my time in the service was up, because of my family's actions, instead of receiving a medallion, I was rewarded with a lifetime of hard labor." He wore a sarcastic grin on his face as he told the story.

I liked him immediately and knew he was a person of character. It made me proud to hear him speak of our family.

"I've heard of your courageous brother Fejzi," he said, "and how he met his fate. Such bravery is seldom found." I thanked him.

"You were too young to remember," he added, "but our families knew each other."

Xhemil and I became trusted friends. We talked together whenever we had a chance. The more our trust grew, the more serious our talks became. We began discussing politics, along with our plan to escape from the camp. This was risky conversation, but we knew that secrets would remain safe between us.

One Sunday morning, I went to see Xhemil in his barracks, and as soon as I arrived, he said he had a surprise for me. My first thought was that he had changed the plan and we were going to escape that very day.

"I love surprises," I said, "and I'm ready whenever you are!"

"No, no," he said. "I have some news on that front, but the timing is not quite right yet."

I grew anxious. "Well then, what kind of surprise do you have for me?"

He smiled. "I have a friend who has some connections outside the camp. He has promised to arrange our escape. Do not worry, my friend! This is our lucky year, and our future couldn't look brighter. Very soon, we'll say goodbye to this hell on earth."

Evening came, and rather than sleeping, I found myself analyzing every word that Xhemil had said during our conversation. I was disappointed that he had been so careless with giving out information about our escape. We all knew the government planted informers everywhere, both inside and outside the prisons and labor camps. I couldn't put my finger on it, but for some reason, I had a bad feeling about going through with our plan.

The next time Xhemil and I met, we talked about specifics of the escape, but this time, I demanded that he reveal his source since not only his life but also my life would be on the line.

He gave me a half-smile that did little to reassure me. "Pertef," he said, "do you know the accountant, Sabri?"

"Yes," I replied. When I heard this name, I felt a cold sweat come over my body.

"He has agreed to secure transportation and drive us close to the Greek border. From there, we'll cross into Greece by foot."

"You're falling into a trap," I told him. "I know for certain that the accountant is a Communist and works as a spy for the government."

Xhemil wouldn't listen to anything I was saying. He trusted the accountant and tried to convince me to do the same. I didn't agree about Sabri's trustworthiness but ultimately decided that if he was indeed an informant, the damage had already been done. I asked Xhemil to give me his word that he would not mention my name to the accountant until the time came for our escape. He assured me he would say nothing, and we left it at that.

As I expected, the accountant notified the authorities, and Xhemil was taken to the Interrogation Headquarters in Tirana. When I heard this, I was consumed with fear. Now my future and my life were in his hands. I had faith in my trusted friend, but brutal torture could make even the strongest of men talk. If he implicated me during his interrogation, my fate would be sealed. All I could do now was wait.

*****

The winter passed, giving way to spring. I was assigned to a new detail of planting corn, a relatively easy job compared to my previous work. I was the only man in a group of girls ranging from seventeen to twenty-five years of age. They were innocent, beautiful women who, prior to communism, were the daughters of Albania's elite. Being the only male, I found myself acting as a big brother to them. I would have protected them with my life in any case.

Our bond began during the first week of the new detail. On the first day, we were being transported to the cornfields when suddenly our truck came to an abrupt halt. Just ahead, I spotted a group of two hundred or more prisoners working on the road. For some reason, the prison guard came to the back of the truck, took a quick inventory of who was in the back, then told me to get out and walk. I walked nearly a kilometer to the location where he said the truck would be waiting to pick me up. To this day, I don't understand why I was given this order, but at the time, I was terrified at the notion that my friend had finally given me up and I was about to be taken in for interrogation.

The second day, they did the same thing. On the third day, as we were loaded into the back of the truck, I noticed that one of the girls, Nika, looked very pale. I asked her if she was okay.

"I'm afraid I don't feel too well," she said.

I assured her that I would think of something to get her out of work. Then I heard my name mentioned as the girls were talking among themselves. Curiosity got the better of me, and I asked them what they were planning. They said they had an idea that would keep me from having to walk past the prison detail, and before I realized what was happening, they tied a scarf to my head and stuffed my shirt with material to make it look like I had breasts. With just a little creativity, they had transformed me into one of the girls.

Soon, the truck came to a stop, and the guard climbed into the back, where we were sitting. He was so close to me that his nose almost touched my face. "Where is the man that was on the truck yesterday?" The guard was asking me directly.

I had no choice but to answer him quickly and in a high feminine tone. "He was sick today and had to remain at the camp."

The guard jumped from the truck and told the driver to go. We began to laugh uncontrollably as we congratulated each other on the success of our scheme.

Tractors were used in the cornfields to turn the soil and make the rows for seed. These tractors would pull a planter that would drop the right amount of corn seed into each row. Two of us would stand on each side of the seed planter, and when the tractor would reach the end of the row, our job was to pull the lever and raise the cylinders. Once the tractor completed the turn and started on the next row, we would drop the lever and lower the cylinders to the ground.

Nika and I were teamed together for the day, and just before we began work, I pulled her to the side and gave her instructions. "When the tractor starts its turn, rather than lifting the blades and cylinders, we'll leave them down. If we do this, they'll become clogged with underbrush and dirt. It'll take the technicians most of the day to find and fix the problem, and this will give you a chance to rest."

She did exactly as I said, and my plan worked. Within an hour, a technician took notice that our machine was clogged. He yelled for the driver to stop and began screaming at me, but I kept my mouth shut. He grabbed my arm with one hand and my shirt with the other then harshly threw me to the ground, knocking the breath completely out of my body.

When I was able to stand on my own, Nika and I headed for the shade of a nearby tree while the technician worked on the machine. We sat down and just looked at each other for a moment, both of us enjoying the satisfaction that came from outsmarting the technicians.

"Pertef," she said, "you went to a lot of trouble for me today. I hope you're not badly hurt."

Her words were gentle and sincere, and for the first time in my life, I had feelings running through my body that I couldn't quite explain. The sun blazed down, warming the ground, and a soft morning breeze cooled the air. Suddenly, many thoughts were racing in my mind. *What is wrong with me?* I thought. *These girls are like sisters to me. So why am I having these feelings?* Then I steeled up my brow. *I can't allow this to happen. I have to stay focused on my future. After all, my main priority is to execute my escape plan and make my way to freedom.*

I knew I had to clear my mind and body of the feelings stirring inside, but I simply couldn't. My heart began to pound, and blood rushed through my veins like a raging river during a flood. In an attempt to regain composure, I sat up but was very careful not to look in Nika's direction.

"Are you okay, Pertef?" she asked.

My mind was telling me that I wasn't okay, but I heard myself saying, "Yes, I'm fine. Just very thirsty."

Eager to please me, she smiled softly then raced off like a rabbit across the field. She returned a few minutes later with a canteen of water. The cold water was just what I needed to refresh my parched mouth and throat. When I finished my drink and lowered the canteen, Nika smiled.

"Thanks for everything you've done for me," she replied. "Pertef, you knew I was sick, and you took care of me today."

Both the silence and the mood were broken when we heard the rest of the girls, led by Christina and her sister Cilistina (Markagjoni), coming toward us. As they came closer, I could hear Cilistina mumbling to the others. "This is a life of misery," she was saying. "We are nothing more than slaves. How long do they expect us to endure this suffering?"

She and Christina were devout Roman Catholics, but they wisely kept their prayers and their religion secret from the Communists and their atheist agenda. Punishment for honoring God was always severe, but Albanians knew that God was bigger than any government and, just like Christina and Cilistina, quickly learned to worship quietly and independently. Most of us believed that God would be our strength and, in time, our Redeemer.

After the roll call that evening, one of the camp officials ordered me to report to Lieutenant Sulo Sterneci, the commandant-in-charge of the labor camp. I did as I was told, and when I arrived, the lieutenant told me I was being restricted from work detail the next day.

"Why?" I asked, scratching my head nervously.

"You are not to question the orders I give you," the bulldog of a man barked at me.

A chilly wave of fear rippled through me as it occurred to me that this could be related to what I'd been fearing since Xhemil's arrest. Word had spread that Xhemil still remained at the interrogation headquarters, and even for someone suspected of planning an escape, that was a long time to be held for interrogation and subjected to torture.

Before I could show any fear in my expression, I quickly excused myself and returned to my room at the barracks. *I have to get everything in perspective*, I thought. *I need to come up with a plan to counter their plan, whatever that plan may be.* I could imagine the brutal torture my friend had endured, and it seemed to me a certainty that I was next in line. Even though we were close, how long can a man possibly endure pain before he starts naming names?

Since I was sitting alone on the floor and mumbling to myself, I guess Mother realized that I was in some kind of trouble.

"What's wrong, Pertef?" she asked. "You look troubled."

"Nothing's wrong," I lied. "Everything is okay."

But the more I thought about my predicament, the angrier I became with myself. I had known something like this would happen. If I'd had any sense, then I would have attempted escape the first chance I got after they took Xhemil from the camp.

"I know what to do!" I said under my breath.

"What did you say?" Mother asked.

"Oh, nothing," I replied too quickly. "I was just talking to myself."

Two of my most trusted friends, Syrja Frasheri and Emnor Kaleci, were assigned to a barracks not far from ours. I valued their opinions highly, so since I felt in need of advice, I paid them a visit.

When I entered their barracks, both men stood and greeted me.

"I thought you'd forgotten us," Syrja joked.

"It's been over a week since we've seen you," Emnor agreed.

They both looked as though they could sense I was troubled.

"What is it, my friend?" Syrja said softly.

I gave a long, cathartic sigh. "The lieutenant ordered me to remain at camp tomorrow. I'm to miss work detail, and I fear it may have something to do with my friend Xhemil." I looked around to be sure that no one else was listening. "I can tell you this now. Xhemil and I were planning an escape. We were betrayed by Sabri, the accountant, and Xhemil was taken to the Interrogation Headquarters in Tirana."

"Say no more," Emnor said, raising his hand for silence.

My friends exchanged a knowing look.

"This is my advice to you," Syrja said. "More than likely, your friend has implicated you. So when you are questioned by the authorities, answer with the truth, ask forgiveness, then quietly ask God to have mercy on you."

This was not the advice I had expected from two middle-aged men I once knew to be courageous and steadfast against communism. For the first time, I could see that their courage, along with their spirits, had been broken.

"What's wrong with you?" I asked.

They both looked straight at me, their eyes filled with fear.

"Listen to me, Pertef," Emnor said. "You have no idea what they'll do to you if you don't tell the truth. They have methods of getting the truth out of stubborn people like you."

It was disappointing to see them act in what I thought was such a cowardly way, so I had difficulty hiding the look of disgust that crossed my face. "Just forget you've even seen me tonight," I said balefully. "I'm sorry I came to you for advice because your kind of advice could jeopardize my friend Xhemil's life."

"Think about it, Pertef," Syrja said. "By now, he has already confessed, or else you would not have been summoned for questioning."

"I haven't been summoned," I snapped. "They've just ordered me to remain behind tomorrow."

Emnor gave a dark chuckle. "Don't play at naiveté. They already know you were involved in the escape plan."

A part of me knew that what they said made sense and was probably true. Still it angered me to know that they were more concerned about incriminating themselves than they were about the outcome for Xhemil and me.

As I said goodbye to them, their eyes filled with tears. My anger softened because I could see that in their hearts, they wanted to help me. But now it was out of their hands.

There was nothing anyone could do for me.

Chapter 9

It was a sleepless night, full of uncertainty. On more than one occasion, I fought back the urge to flee the barracks and make a break for it. Escaping without a plan was akin to suicide, I had to remind myself.

When morning arrived, I washed up and went to the lieutenant's office. Out of the corner of my eye, I could see a military jeep parked at the side of the building with a soldier behind the wheel. Sabri, the accountant, was seated behind him. A guard stopped me at the door to the lieutenant's office and ordered me into the jeep.

No one said anything as I climbed into the back beside Sabri. Another officer got into the front seat, and we left the camp with no explanation of our destination. We rode for fifteen minutes or so before Sabri finally broke the silence.

"I hope we're not in serious trouble," he said as if trying to start a conversation.

"Why should we be?" I asked.

He didn't answer me verbally, instead shaking his head as if to say, "I don't know."

"Well then," I said, "we haven't anything to worry about, have we?" This time, he ignored me completely.

We rode for more than an hour, traveling along the beaches and shorelines of Albania. Waves broke over the rocks, and the morning sun danced over the clear water and warmed the sandy beaches. I had always loved the ocean, and even now as we drove toward my dire fate, it filled me with a hollow sort of joy. It was like I was seeing the beauty of these beaches for the very first time and possibly the last time. I had no idea where we were going or even whether I would be alive tomorrow. It was a harrowing feeling.

When we arrived at the capitol, it was late morning. This was my first time in Tirana, and even under such adverse circumstances, I was awestruck by its beauty. But even that beauty had been spoiled by the regime, as the main boulevard was darkened by a statue of Stalin, the butcher of Eastern Europe.

We made a few turns through the historic city center, passing over wide, straight, tree-lined streets and beside long high-rises taller than any building I had ever seen. Then the jeep came to a stop in front of a heavily guarded iron gate. The driver handed some documents to the guards who made a call. Within a few minutes, an officer arrived and ordered the gate opened.

"I'm Major Stafa," the officer said. "These traitors are under my jurisdiction, and I will take custody."

We exited the jeep. Then the major pulled Sabri off to the side for a brief conversation. There was no doubt now that he was an informer. I acted as indifferent as I could, wanting to appear unafraid and make them think I had no idea why I was there.

Then Major Stafa called me over. "What is your name?"

"Comrade," I said, raising an eyebrow, "do you mean to say that I was brought here from miles away and you do not know my name?"

My reply seemed to anger him. "When I ask a question, I expect an answer." Half a heartbeat later, I felt his fist connect with my face, followed by a strong knee to the stomach. "Kelyshi Imperializmit American!" (The cubs of American Imperialism!) he shouted.

A gut-wrenching pain ran through my body, but with as clear a voice as I could muster, I replied, "Does that make you feel better?"

The major stood silent for a few seconds. He straightened his jacket and stuck out his surprisingly weak chin. "I want to be sure you understand," he said in a condescending tone. "As of today, your life is in my hands." He drew himself close to me—close enough that I could smell his sour breath. "I assure you that the time will come when you'll wish you hadn't been born." He shoved me hard. "Now get out of my sight before I get really mad and beat you to death."

I took a step back. "Where do I go?"

He pointed wildly over my shoulder. "Go over there and wait inside."

When I turned, I saw that he must have meant to indicate a building about fifty yards away. The place was guarded by a single soldier, and when he opened the door, I could see that it was solid and heavy.

Once inside, I saw my friend Xhemil sitting in a chair on the right side of the room. He was handcuffed, and his face was swollen and covered with dried blood. He looked thin and weak. They had beaten him so severely that had I not known him so well, I probably wouldn't have recognized him. On the far wall in front of him was a platform with four desks and chairs. I assumed that was where the court officials sat during trials. There was little else in the room.

"Xhemil," I said. "How are you doing?"

With the remaining humor he could muster, he replied, "Si muti ne shi." (Like crap in rain).

One of the guards in the room cut in. "Shut up," he shouted, "or I'll empty my gun on the both of you!"

The other guard looked at his comrade in disbelief. "Let them talk. Our orders are only to shoot them should they make any attempt to escape."

With that, Xhemil and I were able to have a short conversation. "How are they treating you?" I asked.

"Oh, they're treating me beautifully," he said sarcastically as he pointed to his swollen face with his chained hand. "I once thought Saver was hell on earth, but it was only a rest stop compared to this."

A few minutes later, the authorities began to enter. They were all plump and dressed in finely pressed uniforms that hugged them and made them look like fat sausages. Just as I had expected, four of the men took places behind the desks. I was seated in the middle of the room with two guards dressed in civilian clothes on either side of me. There was a long silence as a few of the officials murmured back and forth in voices I couldn't quite hear.

Then one of the officers stood and walked toward me. "Depending on your statement today," he said in a booming, gravely serious tone, "we will consider your release and send you back to the labor camp. That will depend on whether you tell us the truth or choose to lie." He buried his chin, causing a shadow to cast over his face. "But know this: if you lie to this court, we will show no mercy, and you will receive the same punishment given to the traitor who sits behind you."

The officer relaxed his posture and took a step away from my chair. From the way he was looking at me, I could sense that he felt he had broken me already. These men were clearly unaware of the Bylykbashi spirit.

After a moment of thought, I shrugged. "I'd like to tell the court one thing, if I may."

With a reluctant nod, the officer bade me to continue.

"If you torture me," I said, "I'll tell you anything you want to hear, even if it isn't the truth. But if I'm treated right, then I will tell you the truth."

The other officials grumbled as if they had never heard such an outrageous suggestion. It seemed to ruffle my interrogator for a moment, but then he straightened up and stepped toward me with his eyes in a fixed glare.

"Did you, Pertef Bylykbashi, have any connection with Xhemil Jazxhi?"

"No, Comrade," I said without hesitation. "I did not."

"You are lying to us!" one of the officials shouted. My interrogator grinned hungrily. "You have one minute to think the question over, and if you continue to lie, your punishment will be severe."

Casually, I leaned back in my chair. "I don't need to think it over. I had no dealings with this man." Then I stood as if preparing to leave.

"Sit down, you fool!" my interrogator screamed. "We're not finished with you yet." His eyes bore holes through me for a moment before he finally turned them on Xhemil. "Xhemil Jazxhi," he hissed, "did Pertef Bylykbashi plan to escape with you?"

"Yes," Xhemil squeaked. Then he seemed to regain his composure. That old, courageous light returned to his eyes. "But I would like to take full blame. Pertef is very young and was only following my lead. I was the agitator."

"Shut your mouth, you filth," the interrogator snapped. "Or I'll rip your tongue out. We want no more than a yes or no from you. Do you understand?" Xhemil nodded slowly.

"In our government," another of the officials said haughtily, "everyone pays for their own mistakes."

From there, my interrogator returned to his table, and the officials took turns asking question after question. There was no format to their line of questioning, but one thing became abundantly clear: the charges were all fabricated. We had not committed any real crime, but Xhemil had confessed to an escape attempt, and all they wanted now was to implicate me.

When they were finished, they told me to rise. My knees felt weak as I climbed to my feet.

"Pertef Bylykbashi," my interrogator said, "you have lied to your government. Stand up and confess. Tell us who you are trying to protect and how many people are in your group."

What I wanted to say was, "This is *not* my government. This is *your* rotten government," but I found myself unable to speak. It wasn't from a loss of courage but rather a divine intervention that kept me silent. Then suddenly, I knew what to do. I began to laugh."

"Stop your laughing right now," one of the officers shouted. "Or I'll come over there and make your back softer than your stomach."

"Oh, God," I mumbled under my breath.

"What did you say?" the interrogator questioned. "Did you say God? Who is he?"

He gave a sardonic look to the others. "God can't help you. No one can help you now."

I waited for their indignation to cool before speaking again. "I'm not laughing at you, Comrades," I said with a defiant smile. "It's just that I've only just now realized why you brought me here. I wasn't concerned before, but now I see how serious this matter has become. I can assure you, there has been a big misunderstanding—a lot of trouble over what is really nothing." I motioned to Xhemil. "My friend here is right. I *did* want to escape, but I only wanted to flee the labor camp so I could settle in our beautiful capital Tirana. Here, I had planned to find a job, and by the time the authorities found out where I was, they would realize I was no threat to the government and would let me remain here. I'm young, you see, and I don't want to spend the rest of my life in a labor camp."

The room fell silent. I could tell that the officials were actually listening this time and that there might be some part of them that believed the ruse.

"Are you afraid of me becoming a free man?" I asked. "I've not done anything against your government. In fact, I was only a small boy when the Communists liberated Albania from the Italian occupation. What could I have possibly done to the country as a child?"

The officers exchanged wide-eyed glances. One of them cleared his throat. "Do you know where your father is?" he asked, his tone much gentler now.

"I don't," I said. The truth was that I did know where my father had gone, but I had no intention of giving my captors that information. So instead, I answered with a question. "Do *you* know where my father is?"

"Yes," my interrogator said. "He is in Greece."

With disdain in my voice, I replied, "Then go pick him up and bring him here. I want to ask him why he would leave his wife and children behind to toil in your labor camps."

My interrogator looked hot under the collar as he drew a breath to speak. "Your father is a traitor to our country, and we know he's working with American imperialists to overthrow our government."

"Excuse me, Comrade," I said. "Are you trying me based on my father's beliefs? Didn't you say just a moment ago that in this government, everyone pays for their own mistakes?"

No one spoke.

I sighed as if exasperated. "If that's true, then why are you trying to punish me for my father's actions?"

The officers began whispering among themselves. Finally, one of them turned to Xhemil. "Did you tell this man that you were going to escape to Tirana?"

Xhemil was quick to respond. "I told you before that Pertef is very young and probably thought we were going to Tirana, even though my intention was to escape to the West and to freedom."

My heart leapt when I saw that my friend had returned to himself and was doing the right thing. The questioning continued through the afternoon. Then the guards received orders to escort me outside while the court continued with Xhemil's sentencing.

As I waited in the compound's yard, an officer approached me and introduced himself, saying he was from the southern part of Albania. He told me he knew my parents well and even used their familiar names when he spoke of them. He seemed polite enough, so I let my guard down for a moment, and that turned out to be a mistake.

"Your name is Pertef, right?" he said.

"Yes, it is," I said. Then I smiled wearily. "It's nice to meet someone who knows my family. I'm glad to meet you, Comrade."

"So am I," he said. "So am I." He motioned for me to follow him. "Please come into my office where we can talk."

As it turned out, all the talk of knowing my parents was a lie designed to help him gain my trust. He removed his hat then sat down and propped his feet up on his desk. In the blink of an eye, both the tone of his voice and his personality changed. He became like a wild animal.

"Now, you filthy scum!" he screamed as his spit flew through the air. "I want you to look at the top of my head and tell me exactly what you see!" He leaned over the desk, and I could see a very small spot of discoloration on the top of his baldhead.

Since this had nothing to do with me, I chose not to answer.

"Answer my question, or you'll curse the day your mother gave birth to you," he barked.

I could see that he had no intention of letting up, so I decided to play along. "I don't see much there. What do you want me to say?"

He raised his head and glared at me. "Look at the spot on my head—the burn spot. Your uncle did that to me."

I knew this wasn't true, and I just couldn't allow him to continue with his lies. "It doesn't look like a burn spot to me," I said with a shrug. "Anyway, I'm sure you didn't bring me here to discuss your head. I don't know who did this to you, but I know it wasn't me."

He jumped from his chair and charged toward me like a maniac. He kicked and beat me for what felt like hours but in reality was only about five minutes. When he stopped to catch his breath, I thought he was finally going to end this madness and let me go, but I was wrong. He pulled his pistol out of the holster, cocked it, and shoved the barrel in my mouth.

"If you don't describe my head," he hissed, "then I'll empty this gun into yours!"

The barrel in my mouth would have made it difficult to speak even if I'd wanted to.

"You *will* tell me what I want to hear," he added, "or I'll finish you off."

I really thought I was a dead man. I had run out of ideas for survival, and my fear escalated when I saw the look in his eyes. When he pulled the gun from my mouth, I did my best to tell him what he wanted to hear. He holstered his pistol, but after I'd finished, the beating started all over again. He kicked me with such force that my feet left the floor and I crashed into the wall.

It was then that I'd had enough. I could see him coming toward me with his fist drawn back, ready to punch me in the face. The moment he swung, I bent down, and rather than hitting me, his fist went through the wall.

He screamed out, just like the coward he was. "Look what you did to me! You made me break my hand. I'll kill you and every member of your family." His eyes were as crazed as his voice, so I knew he meant what he said.

Thankfully, an unexpected knock came at the door, distracting his attention. The trial was over. Later, I heard that Xhemil had been sentenced to fifteen years in prison.

Ultimately, my statement must have convinced the court, but for whatever reason, they made the decision to send me back to camp. Sabri and I were driven back to Saver. The whole way back, I never gave him an indication that I knew he was an informant for the government.

When I arrived at the camp, Mother, Gezim, and my sisters were waiting for me.

They were so happy to see me, and I was equally as happy to see them.

From that day on, I kept a low profile, trusting no one but myself. It proved a sound strategy but not quite sound enough to remove me from the role of the party's next political target. Three weeks after Xhemil's trial, during morning roll call, I received a summons to the commandant's headquarters. When I arrived, Lieutenant Sterneci was waiting. He excused my escort, asking him to close the door on his way out. When the two of us were alone, he pointed to a chair in front of his desk as a gesture for me to sit.

"Pertef," he said in an oddly pleasant tone, "I have some good news. I believe that today is your lucky day. What do you say to that?"

I didn't hesitate. "The only way I would say that this is a lucky day would be if you're about to tell me that my family and I can get the hell out of this rat hole and be free. And I'm pretty sure that's not the case today."

He chuckled in a good-natured fashion. It didn't suit him. "Well, that's true. You'll not be free to leave here, but if you're willing to work with me, I *will* make it very easy for you and your family while you *are* here."

I knew exactly where the conversation was going but made him believe I didn't understand him. "I'm already working day and night. I don't think there are enough hours left in a day for me to work any harder."

"I know that you work very hard," he said with a slow nod. "And I have to compliment you on that. But hard, manual labor and physical work is not what I'm referring to." He leaned forward and clasped his hands on the desk and gave me a sly smile. "How would you like to be an observer? You'd be my eyes and ears, and I would repay you with many favors. Life would be much easier for you and your family, especially your mother." Now I clearly understood why the decision was made at Interrogation Headquarters to return me to the labor camp rather than send me to prison.

The smirk on my face came from the satisfaction of knowing that I was much smarter than the lieutenant thought I was. Still since

I didn't get many opportunities for entertainment, I played dumb. "If I understand you correctly, you want me to be an informer. Is that what you're trying to say, Comrade Lieutenant?"

"That's not at all what I'm trying to say to you," he said, his eyes going soft and placating. "What I'm saying is that we all must do such things to protect the state's property, watch for saboteurs, and to out people who might be against our beloved Communist government."

I pretended to ponder the offer for a moment. From the way he watched me breathlessly, I could tell he was anxious to bring me into the fold.

"Now I understand what you want from me, Comrade," I said, pressing my finger to my lips contemplatively. "But before I give you my answer, let's change our position and pretend that you are me and that I'm you."

"By all means," he said, motioning for me to continue.

"Okay." I gave a long sigh. "Now what do you suppose I would think of you if you turned against your mother, your sisters, your brother, and all your friends just so you could help in a cause that you truly do not believe in? Do you think I would have any trust or respect for you?"

Commandant Sterneci furrowed his brow as if contemplating my response. "I can't figure you out," he said after a time. "You're either a very stupid person or a very courageous one."

I shrugged. "I guess I'm a little of both."

"One thing is for sure, though." He shook his head in a way that said he was either perplexed or in awe of me. "The way you are reminds me of myself when I was young. I believed in communism with all my heart. In fact, I was ready to give my life for the cause." He looked up then pointed briefly toward the ceiling. "Pertef, do you have any idea why there are hooks on this ceiling?"

I looked up then answered, "Yes, I know. Those hooks are for the butchers. When animals are slaughtered for the winter, the butchers hang the meat up there to dry."

My host gave me another placating smile. "I'm glad to hear that you know the answer. Now I'm going to suggest something for you, and this must not be known to anyone else but you and me. If a word of this conversation leaves this room, I'll have no option but to bring you to my office and personally hang you on one of these hooks until there is no breath left in your body. Do you understand?" I didn't reply.

He straightened up in his chair and gave me a haughty look. "I'm suggesting to you that you should open that door and look to the west." He pointed to the door. "Because for you, son, the days are numbered. And in all honesty, you must do it as soon as possible."

I was stunned. The words came as such a surprise to me that it took me a while to reason out what he was saying. In truth, he was speaking in a thinly veiled code. I couldn't believe what I was hearing. This man that I had thought to be the most immediate threat to me and my family was telling me to escape the labor camp before the gallows came calling. I looked him straight in his eyes, seeking confirmation that I had heard him correctly. When he gave me a barely perceptible nod, I steeled up and gave him a grateful gaze.

I went to the door and opened it. Before I departed, I turned to him one last time. "I won't forget this gift you've given me as long as I'm on this earth," I said in a voice just above a whisper. "And you, sir, will be in my prayers."

The next morning, during the roll call for work, I noticed some new faces. One of them was a man in his early twenties. I introduced myself. "You're new here, aren't you?" I asked.

"Yes," he said plainly. "As a matter of fact, I was brought here last night. My name is Zarif Spaho. My brother escaped from the country, and my family and I were arrested and brought here."

"How is life on the outside?"

He shook his head sadly. "Even out there, life is rough."

I talked with Zarif for only a few minutes, but a few days later, our paths crossed again while working in the fields. That day, I learned that Zarif was from the southern part of Albania and was very familiar with the region because he was a shepherd by trade. I was thrilled to hear this wonderful news because I knew that this would give him tremendous insight into the geography surrounding the southern Albanian border that connected with Greece.

Not wanting to arouse his suspicions about my intentions, I commented that he must be a very courageous man, being alone with a herd of sheep in the mountains. "I've heard there are many wild animals in the mountains," I said, pretending to be terrified of the wilderness. "Especially *wolves*."

He puffed out his chest proudly. "I'm not afraid of anything."

"Do you miss being a shepherd?"

"Of course, I do."

Now I raised an eyebrow. I knew I had to be careful with this next question, so I gave a look back over my shoulder. "Have you ever been close to the border?"

His ego seemed to build even more. "Are you kidding? I was right at the barbed wire."

I tried to hide my excitement at learning a detail I could use. "That was the border then?"

"Yes."

My brother Gezim was with us, and he seemed to understand exactly why I was asking so many questions. He was less tactful in his approach than I was trying to be.

"Can you draw a map of the beautiful mountain ranges?"

I gave him a look that said he should slow down or he would arouse suspicion.

Quickly, he gave a friendly chuckle. "You see, I'm from that part of the region. My family and I were brought here when I was very young, and I miss the mountains. It would be nice to have something to help me visualize it again."

I rolled my eyes at him. Surely, our new friend wouldn't buy such a lame excuse.

"Sure," I heard Zarif saying pleasantly.

To my astonishment, he began to draw a map in the dirt as he explained every detail. I studied it with great interest and for a long time—long enough for it to embed in my mind. When we finished, I nonchalantly kicked some dirt over the map to hide it from any prying eyes. I couldn't believe how blessed I was to have something like this drop in my lap.

That evening, when we returned to camp, I found Mother trying to console one of her inmate friends who was crying uncontrollably. The authorities had told Mother's friend that her brother had been killed by the border guards while trying to infiltrate Albania from Greece.

"He got what he deserved," they had told her. "He was a criminal and a traitor who joined forces with other deserters to overthrow our regime."

It didn't matter whether the story was true, I still couldn't bear to see this poor woman suffer. I assured Mother and her friend that it was likely only propaganda. "If these pigs had killed or captured your brother," I said confidently, "his body would have been here within twenty-four hours to be used as. an example for the entire camp. Think about it. Have you ever known these filthy bastards to miss an opportunity to terrorize us all with a dead body?"

That seemed to calm Mother's friend.

"Don't believe their lies," I urged her. "And don't worry. Someday, I'll find your brother."

Mother was an extraordinary woman—dedicated to the cause of freedom and the well-being of our people. Even though she was the only parent we had with us, she was determined to teach us to be honest and fair. There was never a doubt where Mother stood on virtues like honesty, and she had taught all of us well in the lesson that it was better to die than betray the cause of freedom. That night, Mother and I had a lengthy conversation. I told her about the talk with the Commandant and his warning about my days being numbered at the camp. We exchanged ideas, both of us saying that my only choice was to try and escape.

"I'll be careful," I assured her. "And when the time comes, I'll escape alone."

"You can't tell anyone else about this," she said.

"No one will know of my plan or when it'll take place. I promise."

She nodded, a tear carving a line through the dirt caked on her cheek.

"We have to remember one thing," I said, taking her hand in mine.

She gave me a hopeful look.

"There's a strong possibility I won't succeed," I said. "And we both know that if I'm captured, I won't be coming back alive."

With a sorrowful nod, she agreed. The incident with Xhemil was a lesson learned for both of us, so we never had any delusions about what would happen to me. I would face the firing squad just as soon as they could assemble enough guns to get the job done.

"I mean it, Pertef," she said, squeezing my hand. "You can't tell anyone about your plan. I don't even want you to tell *me* any of the details."

"You're right," I said. "I should keep it to myself. If they think you had anything to do with it, they'll torture you."

She looked away, quivering.

"When the time's right," I said, "I'll just go."

The night before I left, we talked about many things—the old days when our family was together, my memories of being a young boy, and the love I had for my mother, both then and now. I wanted to say so much to her, but most importantly, I wanted to let her know that she should remain strong.

"Mother, never worry about me," I said, "because I'll be okay. You need to stay strong for yourself to endure the days ahead. You'll hear rumors about me being killed or captured. Don't believe them. My will to live is much more powerful than their hatred is for us, and I promise that if I go, you *will* see me again. I will come for you."

As promised, I didn't tell her I had planned my escape for the next day, but I had the sense that we both knew this would be our last time together.

"My dearest son," Mother said quietly, "you have no idea how heavy my heart is at this moment. Go with my blessing, Pertef, and may God guide you and keep you safe. Go and tell your father of my love and devotion to him. Tell him and the others not to forget us."

That evening, I must have slept only a couple of hours, but in those few hours, I had my usual dreams. As always, I flew like a hawk high above in the sky. That night, accompanying me in the dream was a beautiful white stallion that ran along below my path. Any time I felt tired, I would swoop down and mount this beautiful creature, and we would fly over the green meadows and high mountains.

As soon as I awoke, I tried to interpret the meaning of the dream, as I remembered Grandmother Aishe doing when I was a child. Quickly, I deduced that it meant I would be successful in my escape and that very soon, I would be a free man.

Chapter 10

The stage was set for my escape. The only tools I had on hand included: a sketch of the mountain range etched in my mind that I had briefly seen drawn in the dirt with a stick, the driving force of freedom running through my veins, and God to guide each step I took.

On a crisp morning in September 1957, our work detail was digging trenches for the planting of olive trees. I knew this would be the day to execute my plan. I had always taken pride in being a hard worker, but on that day, I did not work at my usual pace, for I knew I would need stamina and strength for what lay ahead. We worked until sunset and the blow of the whistle to signal the end of the workday. As usual, everyone began heading to the trucks—everyone but me. I fell to the ground and slowly inched my way to the area where we had been digging. Then I crawled into one of the trenches and remained hidden until all the trucks were gone.

After I heard the last engine roar away, I waited twenty minutes or so to make sure I was truly alone. It began to rain, softly at first, but then it pounded hard enough to wash the freshly turned soil on top of me. I waited a little longer then began furiously digging myself out of the muck and mire. Once I had freed my legs from the trench, I jumped up and ran as fast as I could toward the thickness of the trees and bushes and continued running until I felt like there was no breath left in me. Then I stopped to gain my bearings. I knew that if I had to walk the entire distance, it would take at least fifteen days to reach the Greek border, so I decided to keep a comfortable, steady pace in the hopes of conserving energy.

After walking for a few hours, I thought it would be safe enough to go to the main road and try my luck at getting some kind of transportation. It was a risky proposition, trying to hitch a ride, but I wanted to be as far away from the camp as possible before the authorities realized I was missing. That would give me until the next morning at roll call.

Soon, I reached the road, and before long, I spotted a truck coming toward me. I lifted my hand to signal the driver to stop. I can't explain why, but somehow, I knew he would give me a ride. The truck stopped beside me, and the driver didn't bother asking me any questions, save for the important one.

"Where are you going?" he asked.

I had no definite itinerary. I just knew my ultimate destination was Greece and that my final destination would be America. At the same time, I didn't want to tell him to take me all the way to the border for fear that it would arouse suspicion. So I told him I was heading to a town called Elbasan, which was about the halfway point. The driver acknowledged with a nod and, of all things, told me he too was heading to Elbasan.

When we reached the destination, I got off the truck, thanked the driver, and once again began walking.

That night, I slept for a few hours under a bush, hidden from sight, but not too far from the main road. I had chosen that spot near the main road with the thinking that before dawn, I could possibly get another ride to the town of Korca. I was somewhat familiar with the terrain in that area, and so I knew that once I made it to Korca, I would be within eight hours' walking distance from the border and freedom. I also knew that it would be the longest and possibly the most dangerous eight hours of my life.

I did what I could to keep from thinking too far ahead. As far as I was concerned, my focus was only productive if it remained on the here and now. The plan was the thing, and as long as I didn't deviate, I would be fine. Everything had gone smoothly so far after all. Fear would be the only thing that could threaten my chances at success.

That night under the bushes, I dreamed again about flying freely over the mountains and valleys with my white stallion galloping below. That dream seemed to relieve some of the stress and worry the dangerous trip had evoked in me. I slept fitfully, but each time I would wake from the dream, I would feel a deeper sense of hope for my ultimate freedom.

Morning came, and I sat for a moment, collecting my thoughts. My mind soon filled with thoughts of my mother. Would I ever see her again? Did we say our last words yesterday as I left the labor camp for my work detail? If I could only have told her that I would not return that day. Had I hugged and kissed her for the last time? And what of my sisters and brother? They depended on me for so many things. Would they be able to survive now that I was not there to watch over them?

You have to stop this, Pertef, I told myself. The more I brooded, the clearer it became that my mind was my biggest threat and worst enemy. But then I cleared all the anxiety away with a single thought: *One thing is for certain—I'll be a free man in a few days.* Then I sighed. *Or a dead man.* I rose to my feet.

"Well, I guess one way or another, at least it'll be settled," I said to myself.

The truth was that even a quick death on the road seemed preferable to more time at the camp. Had I remained in my bonds, I would've had only one fate: a torturous death at the hands of the enemy. Escape was the only way to break free, whether in life or in death.

During my flight to freedom, I learned that my willpower was strong, as was my determination to live my life as a free man. God was ever present in my mind and heart. I found myself talking to him all the way through my escape. Any time I noticed my mind playing its dangerous tricks with me, I would call on him to give me the strength to press forward and the knowledge to make good decisions. Every time I prayed, the doubt and fear left immediately, and I would be filled with a warm inner peace that even now is indescribable. I asked God for help and got it. I asked for courage and got it. I asked for guidance, and God led me in the right direction.

When I set out that morning, I had walked less than half a mile before I heard a vehicle coming toward me from behind. Again, I made the decision to flag the vehicle for a ride, and again, I found that my driver was piloting a truck. This time, however, was different. When the truck slowly came to a stop beside me, the sight of the truck's passengers numbed me with fear. The cab and the truck bed were both chock full of soldiers. Terror ran up my spine. A few seconds passed before I regained my senses.

God is on my side, I told myself, trying to find calm. *God is on my side.*

My mind was screaming to tell the driver to forget it, to take off without me. *This can't be happening to me*, I thought. *Soldiers never stop to pick up civilians! So why did they stop for me? They must know who I am! I can't believe I came all this way just to be captured by a truckload of soldiers that I flagged down myself!*

But my better sense won out. After all, once the truck had pulled to a stop, I had no choice but to get in; otherwise, I would be suspect for certain.

With the soldiers occupying the side benches in the back of the truck, I climbed in and sat on the floor. From their conversation, I quickly realized that they were border patrol guards.

"Where are you going, boy?" one of them asked. He had close-cropped brown hair, and I noticed that he wore the uniform of a sergeant.

"I'm going to the town of Bilisht," I said.

"Is that right," he said, rocking his head back.

For a moment, I thought he had made me for an escapee.

But then he smiled. "We're going through that town on our way to the border. We can drop you there." Then he reached into a large bag and took out a few loaves of bread and some cheese, passing it to the soldiers and offering me a ration, which I gratefully accepted.

There was a sudden, loud pounding on the driver's side of the cabin. "Sergeant!" the driver yelled. "There's a road block ahead. The Sigurim have stopped a couple of busses and trucks and are checking them."

An icy chill washed over me. I knew my journey had ended.

"Don't stop behind the busses," the sergeant said. "Go around them. We're late enough as it is."

In all my life, I had never known relief to feel so good.

"Something big must have happened," one of the other soldiers said.

"Maybe they're chasing saboteurs or someone who's escaped from prison," said another.

As quickly as it had gone, my fear returned tenfold. I could hardly breathe from the worry by the time the driver pulled in front of the busses. The secret police, armed with their automatic rifles around their necks, were screaming and creating chaos. I heard a loud voice say, "We got them! We got them both!"

I watched as the Sigurim dragged two men out of the busses and brutally beat them.

When it came to be our turn to approach the roadblock, I decided to lie down on the bed of the truck and pretend I was asleep. Opening my eyes a slit, I saw a Sigurim officer approach the truck.

"Comrade Captain," the sergeant said, "is everything okay? We'd like to give you a hand, but we're already late."

"Everything's fine," the officer said. "We were looking for two escaped prisoners, but we've just captured them. The situation is under control."

The sergeant then ordered the driver to move on, and I was safe once again—at least for the time being. I battled against the urge to shiver for much of the rest of the trip. There I had been, the hunted in the company of my hunters. On top of that, the border patrol had their fox right under their nose and didn't know it.

The closer we came to my stated destination, the more I regretted telling them to take me to Bilisht. *How stupid of me!* I thought. *Bilisht is too close to the border. If they begin asking questions, I could very well botch it up and jeopardize myself.*

We were about thirty minutes from a little village called Dishnice, and I asked the sergeant if I could be dropped there instead.

"My mother's sister lives here," I said, which was true, although I had no intention of visiting my aunt.

The sergeant nodded in approval.

After that, the soldiers started passing the time by exchanging stories of their captures and arrests of spies and escapees. By this point in my life, I thought I had been introduced to every level of fear known to man, and I had become almost fearless. But my next half hour in the truck, listening to the soldiers' talk of captures and escape attempts, let me know that I had plenty of fear left to learn. I could taste freedom, but it still seemed so far away. I kept myself steady by thinking the most unexpected thought. This would be my only chance for escape, and if it was to go poorly, then I was not going to be taken alive. There's a strange sense of comfort to be found in that kind of conviction. When you have decided that you would rather live one day as a free man than the rest of your life like an animal in captivity, that is when you first learn to be truly free.

"Young fellow?" came the voice of the sergeant, breaking my thoughts. "I believe this is where you want to go. Dishnice, right?"

I stepped down from the back, thanked them, then watched as the truck disappeared from sight. As I walked, my knees still shaking, I couldn't help but think about the irony of it all. Today, these soldiers had given me a ride, but tomorrow, they might well be the ones to capture or kill me.

For the next few hours, I walked until I came to another village called Cangonj. My grandparents on my mother's side were from this village, so I decided to stop there for the night. They were astonished when they saw me. They thought I had been released from the labor camp, and I chose not to tell them differently, thinking it would be less worrisome for them if they didn't know the details surrounding my visit. Grandmother could not get enough of me. She was kissing and hugging me, her tears dripping on her frail cheeks.

"Pertef," she said desperately, "where are the rest of my grandchildren? Where is my daughter? Is she okay?"

I assured her that Mother was doing fine and that soon they all would be set free. I felt a twinge of guilt about lying, but then I reminded myself that news like this would renew her hope of being with her family. Hope was the most important commodity available to those of us suffering under the heel of communism. It was all we had now.

I was surprised and happy to see that Uncle Hysen had received his release from prison and he and Aunt Reshide were finally together again. I quickly decided to ask them to escape with me. I knew my aunt would not hesitate, but I was unsure of Uncle Hysen, thinking he might still be harboring the kind of fear one picks up in prison.

To my astonishment, I didn't have to convince either of them. They were both so ready to return to America that I didn't have to argue. Both had lost their American freedom when they returned to Albania just before the outset of World War II. A border closing had prevented them from ever getting more than just a taste of the life they had so adored. Now they wanted it again and would stop at nothing to seize the opportunity.

We kept the conversation between the three of us. This way, no one else would ever have to try to hide knowledge of our escape from our tormentors.

Under the cover of night, we left through the back door of Uncle Hysen's house and went to the orchard. I asked my uncle if he had any idea of the direction we should go. His answer was not very satisfying.

"I'm not," he said, trailing off as he looked in all directions in search of the answer.

I always knew him to be gutsy, but it was clear that prison had taken a toll on my uncle. It suddenly occurred to me that he might not be mentally and physically capable to handle what lay ahead for us. I wanted to help them escape to freedom, but if we were caught, it would mean death for them. I couldn't bear the thought, for I loved these two people so much. To me, they stood for everything that made the bond between a man and a woman sacred. Through their long history, their love had been tested many times and had always proven true. Their devotion to each other was without measure.

My decision to escape was mine. No one pushed me to do so. So now I was feeling guilty for involving them in the danger. I took tally of the situation and realized the best way for all of us would be for me to keep to my original plan and escape alone. "Please just let me go alone," I told them.

Their expressions were strange. At first, they looked disappointed, but then that quickly evaporated. It was as if both of them had been having the same thoughts that had so suddenly roared through my mind.

It was Aunt Reshide who first showed some measure of protest. "But, Pertef, we—"

"It's too dangerous," I interrupted. "If I am caught, I will not go to one of their prisons nor will I return to camp. I can accept that decision for myself. But if I were responsible for you being caught—" I couldn't bear to finish the thought.

My aunt drew another breath as if to argue, but Uncle Hysen calmed her by taking her hand. "Perhaps we're not meant to return to America just yet," he said softly.

For a time, they spoke to one another in voices just above a whisper. I couldn't hear what they were saying, but the more Uncle Hysen spoke, the more relaxed Aunt Reshide's posture became. She nodded several times before he finished then steeled herself up to face me.

"You're right," she said. "One can escape more easily than three."

My gaze was unwavering as I looked into her eyes and promised her that I would return for them. "I'll go to Greece," I explained, "then return to Albania for you and for everyone else in the family. You all deserve your freedom, and I'll do whatever it takes to secure it."

Uncle Hysen reached out a shaky hand and placed it on my shoulder. It was shocking to me how weak his grasp seemed. It was as if prison had turned him into a much older man. "Go carefully, son," he said, his eyes dewy. "And send word when you can."

"Find your father," Aunt Reshide said. "Between the two of you, anything is possible. I'm sure of it."

I assured her that I would find Father, but it was difficult to hide my sorrow. I found strength in the expressions of resolve I saw in my aunt and uncle. Parting can be difficult, but for an Albanian— and particularly for my family—strength conquers all.

I said my goodbye and turned from them, and the last thing Aunt Reshide said to me was, "Please, Pertef, do not forget about us." It would not be until after the fall of communism, thirty-five years later that Aunt Reshide and I would be reunited.

Alone again, I decided to walk along the main road, thinking that it would be less suspicious if I didn't appear to be hiding from passersby. Each time I passed someone on the road, I would begin to sing or whistle as though I didn't have a care in the world. Usually, they would give greetings or a nod of approval. Two of the villagers I passed even complimented me on my singing voice.

I walked a few hours before I reached the outskirts of Bilisht. Now I began to go over the map I had etched in my mind, remembering each detail Zarif had drawn for me in the dirt. I was looking for a large orchard that was supposed to be to my left. When I spotted it, I felt the relief that came with knowing I was heading in the right direction. I passed through the orchard and then into the forest, where the relative darkness served as a welcome cloak. It was a beautiful night, but not ideal for an escape, given the bright full moon. Even the stars lit up the heavens like a Christmas tree. To avoid being seen, I stopped just long enough to camouflage myself by sticking tree branches in my clothes.

With no watch to estimate time, I walked through the forest along the mountains for what felt like two hours. I was tired and thirsty, but my stubbornness, determination, and hatred for communism gave me the energy to keep going. The uphill terrain was treacherous and full of slippery rocks, which made for a difficult climb. The downhill walk was much easier, but I tried not to fall victim to the desire to make up for lost time by striding too quickly. One false step on a loose rock could make a quick end of me.

Having no water was making the journey more difficult. My throat and lips were dry. Just when it seemed I could take no more, I spotted a little brook with clear, cold, rippling water making its way over the rocks and down the mountain. For the first time, I rushed. I stumbled a few times on the way to the brook, but I made it without incident. I didn't hesitate to put my lips on the cold water and begin to drink. It was the most delicious water I had ever tasted. I wanted to drink the brook dry.

When I'd had my fill, I found a seat on the rocks, thinking I would rest awhile, but within a few minutes, I began to hear noises then voices. I carefully went down on my stomach and crawled to a clump of bushes, where I could observe and listen. From my perch, I spotted a border guardhouse about fifty yards down the mountain. It was close enough that I could hear the guards talking and laughing. More importantly, it was close enough that they would surely hear me if I made any noise.

The wind was blowing from up the mountain as I turned on hands and knees and began crawling away from the guardhouse. I'm not sure how far I crawled, but my knees ached by the time I felt like it was safe to stand and walk again.

With the way blocked, I knew I had to find another route. This presented my next obstacle: another mountain, this one much steeper than the others I had already traversed. The climb took every ounce of my strength, but it was enough to reach the top. I fell to my knees then toppled down on my hands to rest for a while and catch my breath. I was so grateful to be finished with the climb that it took me a long while to see it. But then I looked up, and there it stood, right in front of my face: a barbed wire fence that appeared to be about ten feet high. In most circumstances, a sight like this would have filled me with dread, but as an escapee looking to cross the border, this fence looked like my salvation.

Can it be true? I thought. *Have I really made it?*

Surely, this fence had to represent the border. This meant that I was about fifteen feet from becoming a free man. As exhausted as I was, that fifteen feet might as well have been fifteen miles.

Still there is something about the promise of freedom to imbue strength and courage in a man. Not wanting to waste another second, I quickly removed the branches I had used for camouflage, threw them to the ground, and ran to the fence. Adrenaline rushed through my veins as I climbed. The barbs were cutting into my hands, arms, and legs, but I felt no pain. In a matter of seconds, I reached the top of the fence, threw my legs over, and dropped to the other side. When I landed, my leg twisted under the weight of my body. The pain was excruciating, but I knew I had to move quickly and get out of sight.

I didn't make it more than a single step before pain lanced through my leg, and I collapsed. Had I been anywhere else, I would have screamed, but here along the border with my oppressors, all I could do was clench my teeth and pray that my leg wasn't broken. Huffing air through my teeth, I carefully examined the damage. I could see that my ankle was twisted and badly bruised, but I could see no sign of a break.

What now? I thought. Zarif had only given me the information I needed to get me to the border. He didn't know what was on the other side, and neither did I. In many ways, this was the first time on my journey to freedom when I was truly alone. I had no tools, no map, and no longtime friends to provide guidance and advice. I couldn't ever remember feeling like my mind was so blank.

There was only one thing I could think to do. I lifted my head and asked God to help me make the right decision. I spoke to him as if he was sitting right there beside me.

"God, I need your help," I said. "I don't know where to go. Could you point the way?"

Suddenly, I was struck with the notion that I had the answer I sought. But when I stood up to try walking again, I found that I couldn't and not because of my twisted ankle. There was another force holding me back. No matter how I tried, my feet would not move. A chill rippled through me, followed by a feeling more powerful than anything I had ever experienced. I couldn't understand what was happening, but strangely, I wasn't frightened.

Then a voice came into my mind. It was as if it were right beside me, right in front of me, and right behind me all at once. I will never forget that beautiful voice. It still haunts me to this day.

"Climb the fence," it said softly. "Go back to the other side."

For a moment, I stood mesmerized, unable to believe what I had just heard in my mind, or maybe in my subconscious, and unwilling to agree with the counsel. My first thought was that my imagination was playing tricks on me, but no matter how I tried, I couldn't ignore how certain I felt that I had heard a voice telling me to, "Go back! Go back!"

Again, I tried to take a step forward but found that I couldn't move. It was as if my feet were glued to the ground. *Going back doesn't make any sense*, I thought. *Returning to Communist territory would be suicide!* But I couldn't shake that gentle and yet powerful voice from my head. I had to obey.

When I turned to start back, my legs moved with no hesitation and no pain. It took me much longer to climb the fence on the way back, but I made it without further injury to myself. I was back on the other side of the border. Despite being alone, I felt like an idiot. Here I was, going back and forth over the border fence as if I couldn't decide whether I wanted to be free.

Since I had no idea what I was supposed to do now that I was back on the other side, I sarcastically asked in a low voice, "Okay, what now? What do you want me to do?"

To my surprise, that same gentle voice returned to my mind. "Pick up the branches you used for camouflage and hide them away."

Now I understood why I had to return. The voice in my head was telling me that I had to do a better job of covering my tracks. So I quickly hid the branches and then climbed the fence to the other side yet again. By now, I was so exhausted that I had no choice but to sit and rest.

My respite wouldn't last long. The sweet, firm voice returned, telling me to get up and run. My legs ached from exhaustion, but when I stood up, a burst of energy came to me suddenly. I felt instantly recharged. I ran faster and surer than I had ever run.

About five hundred yards later, I encountered another barbed wire fence, this one with its wire arranged in coils that made it clear there was no way for me to climb. I knew instantly that the only way to get to the other side was to dig under the fence with my bare hands.

I found a place where the ground appeared soft. There I began to dig as quickly as I could. It took a long time. Dawn was closing in on me, as was the fear that I wouldn't make it under the barbed wire and out of sight before the light of day betrayed me. The closer it came to daybreak, the faster I would dig. Just before the sun peaked over the horizon, I had made it to the other side.

From the other side of the wire, I finally felt safe enough to examine my injuries. My body and my clothes were caked with dirt and dried blood, and my ankle had swollen to twice its normal size. The pain returned to me all at once, and it became immediately clear that I had cuts and scrapes on just about every surface of my body.

Still I walked, wincing with each step and watching for any sign that I had in fact made it into Greece. I also searched for water to wash myself and quench my intense thirst. It wasn't long before I found the sign I had been desperate to see. It came in the unlikeliest of forms. It was an empty pack of cigarettes, its brand written in Greek. As elated as I was to see this, I wasn't completely convinced but was at least confident enough to continue limping in the same direction and for as far as my legs would take me.

Death didn't frighten me. My fear was the thought of returning to captivity under the Communists. If they caught me, I would surely live like a rat in their prisons for the rest of my life. I would have to endure hideous torture, degradation, and shame. For me, death would be much sweeter.

By now, the sun had risen enough to allow me to see about a mile in the distance. Somewhere far off, I heard the faint sound of bells that I recognized as a herd of grazing sheep. When I strained my eyes, I could see the outline of a person wandering through the grass in the valley ahead. His heavy black wool poncho and rifle revealed him to be a shepherd.

When I came closer, I could hear that he was yelling something out to me, but I couldn't make out what he was saying. He repeated it a few times before I realized that he was speaking in a different language. He started toward me, repeating himself. Now I could hear him. "Ela etho! Ela etho, Pethy mu!" (Come here! Come here, boy!)

"Go away and leave me alone," I replied in Albanian. I was hungry, sleep deprived, and completely exhausted. This physical anguish ensured that nothing made sense to me. I knew that there was no way I could endure another crisis in that moment, so feebly, I tried to turn the crisis away.

I changed my direction and attempted to run away from the man. I could hear him shouting from behind me, but I just kept on. Over the next hill, I spotted a company of soldiers in a sprawling valley. My heart leapt, and I quickly changed my direction, but I was too tired, and it was too late. They had spotted me.

It's over, I thought, slumping down. *I can't run anymore.*

After a time, three of the soldiers approached me. It wasn't until much later when someone explained it to me that I learned what they were saying. "Do not worry," they had said in Greek. "You are in Greece."

Since they spoke in a language I couldn't understand and because my mind was so far gone from the exhaustion, I was afraid that they were the Albanian border patrol soldiers trying to trick me.

I didn't bother resisting when they helped me to my feet. They took me to their headquarters and fed me breakfast. I ate ravenously. When I finished, a guard escorted me to the barracks. He sat on one of the bunk beds and pointed for me to sit on the bed across from him. Then he mimed that I should sleep. I was so exhausted and confused that I fell asleep the moment my head hit the pillow.

I'm not sure how long I slept, but when I opened my eyes and looked across the room, the same soldier that had delivered me to these barracks was still sitting on the same bunk bed. When he saw that I was ready to get up, he motioned for me to follow him. He led me to a water spring. There, I washed up a bit before he motioned for me to follow him back to the headquarters. When we reached a long hallway with many doors, he held up his hand as if telling me to wait, which I did. I watched as he opened one of the doors and went into what looked like an office. A quick glimpse inside was enough for me to see that the place was Spartan but clearly official. There were file folders along each wall, and at the center stood a simple wooden desk with a table lamp and a telephone.

The sight made me so nervous that I began pacing. I was still afraid and confused enough to believe it possible that I had somehow gotten mixed up and dug my way from Albania and into Albania. For all I knew, this was all an elaborate ruse by the border patrol to get me to rat out anyone who may have helped me along the way.

As I paced in the hallway, I noticed two big portraits in ornate, gold-leaf frames on the wall. One portrait depicted a man dressed in military officer attire, and the other was of a woman dressed in a fine gown, a glittering crown on her head. At the time, I had no idea who they were, but later, I learned that they were King Paul and Queen Frederika of Greece.

A short while later, my escort returned and beckoned for me to follow him into the office. Now I saw that there was a short, stocky man with a balding head sitting behind the desk. He appeared to be about forty-five years old and was dressed in civilian clothes.

"Sit down," he said and my heart skipped to hear my native language. In my view, the fact that he spoke Albanian confirmed my worst fears. I thought for sure that I had been captured.

My body went limp. I fell back into the chair, my mind numbed by the thought that my life was over.

"What is your name?" the man asked.

I was so stunned and devastated that I couldn't answer him beyond a blank stare.

"What is your name?" he repeated.

"My name is Pertef Bylykbashi," I said, throwing in a sarcastic question in reply.

"What is your name?"

The man told me his name. Since I hadn't expected a reply—and especially one delivered in a civil tone—his answer caught me off guard. For a brief moment, I allowed myself a shred of hope that I was in fact in Greece. But I couldn't hold onto that faint hope. It seemed too good to be true. The man rose from his desk and went to a file cabinet. He quickly thumbed through some folders then pulled a few from their slots before returning to his seat.

"Arif Bylykbashi," he read from one of the folders then from another, "Zenel Bylykbashi, Fejzi Bylykbashi," and then the names of my three cousins. When he had finished, he looked up at me. "How are you related to these men, son?"

As I explained my relationship to each of them, I guess he must have read the look of confusion on my face. I was so sure that I had been captured, but at the same time, this man's behavior was clearly different from the Communist pigs infesting my country.

"Are you okay?" he asked, raising an eyebrow.

I didn't know how to answer. All I could do was stare at him.

He shrugged and leaned back into his chair. "Hey, young fellow, we're almost through here. And then you can go back to the barracks and get some rest. I only have a few more questions for you." Then he gave a soft smile. "And by the way, welcome to Greece."

I don't know what it was about the way the man said the words, but for the first time since I had encountered those soldiers in the valley, I believed it to be true. I was a free man. In enemy troop transports, along busy roads full of traitorous eyes, through mountains and forests and over barbed wire fences, I had gained my freedom. Even as I write about it, I feel a tingling sensation in my veins.

"I really made it, huh?" I said, finally relaxing.

His smile grew. "Yes, you fooled them all."

I pointed at my chair. "Is it okay if I get up?"

The question seemed to amuse him. "By all means."

I stood and stepped around his desk, standing beside him and offering my hand. When he shook it, I thanked him. Then I grabbed his head in my hands, leaned down, and kissed him right on the top of his head. I was so excited that I didn't know what to do. As he laughed, I raised my hands up and cried out, "I am *free*! Free from those Communist bastards!"

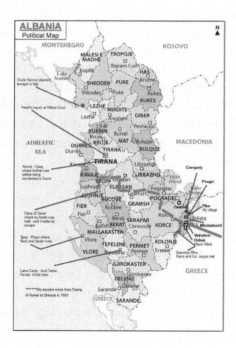

Chapter 11

I spent the rest of that first day and night of freedom with the soldiers in the barracks. Everyone treated me well. It was a strange thing to deal with, having spent years fearing soldiers only to be rescued by them.

The next morning, the Greek secret service drove me to a small village named Maniaki. The local officials had made preparations for my arrival, including setting up a large tent for me on the outskirts of the village. My stay in the tent would last two weeks while the officials decided what to do with me.

My gratefulness knew no bounds, but it didn't take long for me to get a little stir crazy. They had given me shelter and food, but I had nothing to do. After the first few days, the boredom began to set in. By the end of the first week, my mind was so idle that doubt began to creep back to me. I had no idea what was in store, and that lack of knowledge made me something of a prisoner in my own mind.

Have I merely escaped to a different kind of prison? I wondered. *Does anyone care about me at all? Have the authorities forgotten about me?*

These were the kinds of questions that raced through my mind—the kinds of questions with no immediate or apparent answer. I had no one to consult with on these matters since the only time I was able to interact with anyone was when a soldier brought me a meal three times each day. The soldier was always cordial and polite, but he didn't speak Albanian, so conversation wasn't possible. Fortunately, the food was wonderful. I ate like a horse.

Around the beginning of the second week, a young man of average height, blue eyes, and a head full of dark brown hair came to my tent. He looked to be in his early twenties and was neatly dressed in a Greek army uniform. He spoke in Greek, and I replied to him in my native Albanian.

"I don't speak Greek," I said. "I can't understand a word you're saying."

He just smiled and placed a bag of sweets and a few packs of cigarettes on the floor. He seemed nervous. He kept looking out from the door of the tent as if he were watching for someone. Then he turned toward me, gave me another smile, and left. I couldn't have been more confused. The man seemed to know what he was doing, but I couldn't guess who he had been watching for, who he was afraid of, and why. His demeanor made me suspicious. I had been told that in the border area, there were many Communist sympathizers and that I should be very careful about whom I associated with. With his simple gift, perhaps this coy soldier was merely trying to win my heart and mind to a cause that otherwise made my blood boil.

The soldier who usually brought my food arrived the next morning with breakfast. This time, he stayed with me for a while, and we tried to communicate. He understood when I motioned to him that I wanted to take a walk. Cordially, he led the way. It felt good to leave the confines of my assigned space, if only for a little while. The sun was warm, the morning dewy, and the rolling hills of the borderlands were lush with fall colors of green and gold.

When we returned to the tent, we found two men waiting for us, one in an officer's uniform and the other in civilian clothes. The civilian was likely in his forties while the officer was younger. Both wore kind smiles.

"How are you, son?" the officer asked in Greek. "Have you been treated well?" Meanwhile, the man in civilian attire translated the words into Albanian.

"I've been treated very well, thank you," I replied. The moment the translator finished conveying the message, I complimented him for speaking Albanian so well. "Are you Albanian?" I asked.

"Of course, I'm Albanian," he said, puffing out his chest with pride. "By the way, this is Captain Dimitrios, and my name is Taqi."

We shook hands. It felt good to be speaking with someone, especially with someone as polite as these two men seemed to be.

"Tell me, Mr. Taqi," I said, "how long will I be in this tent? And what's going to happen to me? I've been here for ten days, and I'm going out of my mind."

"Don't worry, Pertef," he said. "We'll take good care of you. You can count on it."

"It would be our pleasure to show you around the village," the officer added.

The three of us took a walk around the quaint village nestled on the hillside. Then we went to the army's mess hall for lunch. From the size of Taqi, I had sensed that he was a rather large fan of food, and as we sat down to eat, I could see that I was right. I enjoyed my own food but couldn't help but marvel at how much and how rapidly my company consumed.

After we finished, Taqi took me to the tailor to be fitted for a suit. I could hardly believe it when he told me what we were doing, for this was the first time in my life I would own a store-bought suit. As the tailor took my measurements, he asked what color I wanted.

"Color isn't too important to me," I said. "I'll just be glad to have something nice to wear for once."

"What about a nice pair of shoes?" Taqi asked.

I nodded gratefully.

We left the tailor and stopped at a shoe store. I worried that I wouldn't be able to find my size, but to my delight, I found the perfect fit. It is difficult to describe what a joy it can be to have a new pair of shoes after many years of strapping scraps to your feet.

After a day of shopping, we returned to my tent in the late afternoon. As Taqi turned to leave, I thanked him.

"I'll see you tomorrow," he said with a wave.

I sighed and smiled at the thought of how uplifting the day had been. Captain Dimitrios and Taqi had done so much more than shake me from my boredom and buy me new clothes to wear. They also had given me the assurance I needed to start building some confidence in my situation and in my future. Before that experience, my tent had felt like purgatory. Now I could see that it was only meant to be a staging ground. Light and hope was gathering in the distance.

I didn't have long to revel in these thoughts because the soldier that had brought me candies and cigarettes was suddenly standing at the door to my tent. It struck me as odd that he would choose this exact moment to show up. It was almost as if he had been watching my tent and waiting for my return. I had just picked up the matches and lit a cigarette when he poked his head in. So there I was smoking one of his gifts at the moment he arrived.

In his hands, he held more cigarettes and another bag of chocolates and other candies. I could see that he wanted to talk, but there was no way to do so. Again, he looked nervously over his shoulder before setting his gift on the floor and departing. It left me every bit as confused as the first time.

When I woke the next morning, Taqi had already arrived. "You must have slept well," he said. "I've been sitting here for ten minutes."

"Why didn't you wake me up?" I asked.

He shrugged. "I thought you were tired. If you still want to sleep, I'll come back later."

"No, that's okay. I'm going crazy in this tent. Having someone to talk to is nice."

"All right then. Get dressed and we'll go for some breakfast." I started to rise from my bed when he added, "You know what? When you were sleeping, you reminded me of your brother Fejzi."

My heart leapt into my throat. "What?" I said breathlessly. "You knew my brother?"

"Oh yes. I knew him." He sighed. "He was a courageous man and was dedicated to the cause of freedom. We were told of his bravery and of his courage. We heard about how he used his last bullet to end his life rather than allowing himself to be captured."

To hear my new friend speak so highly of my beloved brother caused my vision to blur with tears. His story and his memory will always be sensitive subjects for me. Still I wanted to learn every detail Taqi could share about my brother.

"He was much taller than you," Taqi said with a smile, "but the resemblance is uncanny."

He was giving me a compliment I didn't deserve. Fejzi was far better looking than me, and in fact, we looked almost nothing alike. Hearing him say this reminded me of something my mother had told us many years earlier: "When someone compliments you on something about yourself that you know not to be true, be cautious. That person wants something from you."

Now it all came clear. The various kindnesses, the pleasantries, the gifts—this wasn't a sympathetic nation showing support for a refugee. Taqi and the officers he served merely wanted to recruit me as an infiltrator between Albania and Greece. They wanted to turn me into a freedom fighter. They were being cautious about it, I supposed, but there was no reason for it. They had no idea how much I wanted to take up the fight where my brother had left off.

On the way to the mess hall, I thought of Fejzi—the way he died and the cause for which he died. The more I pondered it, the more I brooded in resentment. From the day of Fejzi's death, I had carried around a picture in my mind. It was a picture of the informers that had led him to his death. I believed in the cause of freeing Albania, but I owed my desire to become a freedom fighter just as much to my yearning to return to the village of Baban, find Eshref Mancka and Tako Gjalpi, scoop their eyeballs out, and take them back with me to Greece. I also had promises to keep—the promises to free my mother and the rest of my family from Albania.

We got our food and took a seat at one of the tables. Across from our table, I spotted the young man that had brought cigarettes and sweets to my tent. He caught my gaze at the same time but quickly looked away as if he didn't see me—a gesture that made me even more suspicious.

My handlers had already planned my day for me. After breakfast, Taqi and I went to the captain's office at the intelligence headquarters, where the captain and two other officers awaited us. They spoke highly of Fejzi, making me proud. Using Taqi as the translator, the captain officially asked if for the good of Albania and its people, I would like to join the Greek intelligence service.

"Before I give you my answer," I said, "I'd like to know if the American CIA is part of this mission." I had been pondering this question for some time and figured that if the Americans were involved, I was ready and willing to accept the mission.

"The United States is involved, yes," the captain said guardedly.

I beamed. "Then nothing would give me more pleasure than to fight for the freedom of my country."

"Well then," one of the officers said through Taqi's translation, "the preparations for your training will start soon. Mr. Taqi will take you to your new quarters. We'll notify you when we're ready for you to begin training."

Taqi and I left the office and walked directly to my newly assigned quarters: a well-appointed first-floor apartment. After two weeks in a tent, the place felt like a palace. A few officers kept rooms on the second floor. It wasn't long before I learned that among them was the young man who so often brought smokes and sweets for me. I wasn't sure how I felt about that.

One day shortly after I moved in, Taqi arrived to ask if the apartment was suitable. "Yes," I said. "It's been very nice."

The one thing I didn't care for was the fact that they insisted on keeping a soldier in the room to watch over me. The idea of being guarded was infuriating.

How can I work for an organization that has no trust in me? I thought.

I chose to wait for a more appropriate time to speak my mind. At the next scheduled meeting with the captain and Taqi, I let them know that I didn't appreciate the guard posted at my apartment.

"If you feel like house arrest is necessary for me," I said, "then I'm just going to have to reconsider my decision to join your mission. I mean, if you don't trust me, how can I trust you?"

Both Taqi and the captain became wide-eyed and defensive.

"We only assigned that soldier for your benefit," the captain said through Taqi's frantic translation.

"He'll only be staying with you until you're comfortable with the local customs and the surrounding area," Taqi explained.

I didn't really like the explanation, but I could at least understand it. "Fine," I said dismissively. "But if those are the terms, then it's time I learned Greek." I figured if I learned the local language, then I could pick up these customs and traditions that seemed so important and could even intermingle with the villagers and maybe make a friend or two.

The soldier assigned to me was an easygoing man named Kosta. Given that he was my constant companion from that point forward, we quickly became friends. On our morning and afternoon walks, he would help me as I practiced my Greek words. One of my favorite places to walk was along the river. The banks were full of chestnut trees, and on some days, we would sit and eat chestnuts while I practiced my Greek.

One day, Kosta wasn't feeling well and asked if we could go back so he could lie down. As we were walking back to the apartment, we passed the man who had been mysteriously showing up at my tent unannounced. For the first time since he had started making these appearances, he was bold enough to speak. He quickly pulled me aside from my obviously ailing escort and whispered in my ear. I was startled to understand the words as Albanian.

"Pertef," he said, "when you have a chance, I have something very important to discuss with you. See if you can come alone, and I'll meet you by the river later this afternoon."

"Yes," I said as he pulled away. "I'll try."

When we got back to the apartment, Kosta lay down on his bunk and immediately fell asleep. As soon as I was sure he was in a deep sleep, I quietly left the apartment and headed to the river. I found the mysterious man waiting there for me. I greeted him guardedly.

"Hello, Pertef," he replied.

"What is your name?" I asked.

He gave another of those conspiratorial looks from side to side. "My name isn't important right now, but what I'm going to tell you is extremely important. You must promise to keep this conversation between us."

I shrugged. "I'm listening." I raised a finger to halt him. "But before I give a promise, I want to hear what you have to say."

"I know your family's background," he said with a sigh. "So I guess you have the right to know about me and my family. My name is Gani Mardeda, and I've been in Greece for over two years. I'm from the northern part of Albania. My father was killed when I was very young. I was serving in the Albanian army when I decided to cross the border to Greece." He shook his head sadly. "I have no idea what happened to my family."

"I'm sorry," I said, meaning it despite the distaste I felt for him. "I know how you feel."

"When I came to Greece two years and some months ago," he continued, "I joined their secret service mission. I've gone back and forth between Albania and Greece many times. But I've decided to give this mission up. The situation is very dangerous there, and for me, even more than ever, now that I'm considered a double agent. You have no idea how dangerous that is."

The more he talked, the more I disliked him. By that point, I was having trouble hiding it. "What are you saying? You're actually working for the Communists? You're working for those same devils that destroyed both our families and the whole country?" I spat. "That makes me sick!"

He waved his hands. "Pertef, calm down and let me explain."

"I don't want any explanation. The whole thing makes no sense."

"You must listen to me!" he snapped. The way his face had gone red with fury gave me pause. But then the expression faded into one of genuine embarrassment. He calmed himself before continuing. "The first year of my trips into Albania were fine, but then something went very wrong. I had a connection through an informant living in Albania. He was the one giving me the information to take to the authorities in Greece. The last time I went to visit him, it was a stormy night. I have thanked God over and over again for the rain that night. Otherwise, I wouldn't be here talking to you right now. I'd be dead or, *worse*, rotting in one of those Communist prisons."

He shuddered as he appeared to ponder such a fate. I wanted to tell him that I had spent time in exactly that kind of prison and also had endured years in a labor camp, but he returned to his story before I could speak.

"As soon as I entered the house, I felt that something wasn't right. The informant looked worried. His face was pale. It was night-time, so I couldn't see much through the window as I looked out at his yard. Suddenly, a bolt of lightning struck a tree in the front yard, causing the sky to light up as if it was daytime. What I saw made my heart stop beating for a moment. The house was surrounded by Sigurim."

He shook his head in a solemn, regretting sort of way. He seemed to think that his story was building sympathy from me, but so far, I was having trouble understanding why I should sympathize. We had all been through many of these same events. Why that should give him the right to join up with our oppressors was beyond me.

"That was when I knew my informant had betrayed me," Gani said, his eyes glazing over with tears. "I had only seconds to come up with an idea. I turned to the informant and told him the reason for my coming this time into Albania was not to get information but to surrender to the authorities. 'I want to work for the Albanian government,' I told him. I saw the relief on his face. 'I came to your house to give you the opportunity to receive the credit for this decision. Please go and tell the authorities that I am here and am ready to surrender.'

"He praised my action. Then he asked if I was sure of my decision. I assured him that I had been thinking on this and planning for a long while. He left the house, not returning for another thirty minutes. He didn't know that I had seen how the Sigurim had gathered in his yard and wanted me to believe that it took him that long to get in touch with the authorities."

A strong breeze kicked up over the river, nearly knocking Gani's hat from his head. It brought with it the odor of dead fish, giving me an excuse to crinkle up my nose without it being so obvious that this story disgusted me.

"I felt certain that they had no suspicions and completely believed my story," Gani continued. "The informant entered the living room first, and behind him was the Sigurim captain. He gave me the usual greeting, and I returned it. We sat down for a cup of coffee and a brief conversation. Then I turned my pistol over to him and was taken to a facility in a town called Kavaja, close to the capital of Tirana."

"I know where Kavaja is," I interrupted, my patience thinning. "Keep talking."

"I was kept there for three weeks. After a very intensive interrogation, they were convinced that I was telling the truth and would now work for the Communist Party as their informant. They didn't waste any time. Within a few weeks, the Communist pigs sent me on a mission into Greece. They ensured that I went back on precisely the date that I was supposed to be back. This way, no one would be suspicious that I had been flipped."

I raised an eyebrow to show my skepticism. "What did you do then?"

"Well, what the hell do you think I did? When I got back, I reported all this! That's what I'm trying to tell you. The CIA here in Greece knows the whole story, but now the Albanian authorities are aware that I lied to them and have decided to quit. If they catch me in Albania again, I'll be hanged. Pertef, believe me. I'm telling you this because I don't want you to die like your brother did."

Again, he gave one of those nervous looks to make sure we weren't being overheard. Then he continued, "I've heard that the U.S. government established a refugee camp here in Greece in a town call Lavrio. Let's hope that we end up there. Then we can take a good look at our situation and figure out a better way to help our families and our country. I know for a fact that the captain and Taqi want to recruit you. Tell them you're too young, and you want to go to the U.S. where your father is."

For the first time, I saw something of sense in what Gani was saying. If what he said was true, then along with the story of my brother's death, it did suggest a certain sense of doom when it came to this espionage project. "I don't know why you're doing this for me," I said softly. "And besides, why should I believe you? You owe me nothing. I don't even know you."

"Pertef, I respect your family, and yes, I think you deserve a chance to work for Albania's freedom. But the cause doesn't need another martyr like your brother. The cause needs someone to do good work from the *outside*. Turn down the captain and find another way."

With a profound nod, I thanked him but made no promises to take his advice.

"Well," he said with a shrug, "I did my best. It's up to you to decide if you want to trust what I've told you. But please think about it. I have to go now. I have some business to take care of in town."

As I watched him depart the clearing, I tried to process all the information and events that had taken place since my escape. The more I thought on it, the more confused I became. One thing was clear: even though I had escaped to a free country, my life still depended on a well-designed plan and perfect follow-through. I couldn't afford to make even one wrong decision. I could see that Gani was trying to help me, but then I couldn't be sure how far gone he was. How could I know if he even *knew* what the truth was anymore?

I can't trust him just because he told me some sad story, I thought. *I'm on my own now, and my life depends on every move I make.*

Later that day, I saw Gani leaving the building with a few of his officer friends. As soon as he was out of sight, I went to his room. I wanted to search for anything that would prove his story to be true or even that he was Albanian. I found an ID card with his name on it, and it was indeed from my home country. Still needing more proof, I continued my search. I came across another ID with his picture but with a different name. There was a report that he had filled out when he returned from the last trip he made to Albania. It seemed he had spent two weeks in the militia and the other two weeks in the capital.

Breaking into his room was exciting but also entirely scary. After reading everything I could find, I put it all back in order and left the room just the way I had found it. I returned to my room and lay on my bed. *It's my decision now*, I thought. *Now that I know there is at least some truth to his story, do I trust him or not? Is he telling me the truth or trying to set me up for information to take back to the Communists?*

As much as it pained me to think about giving up the mission I so desperately wanted to perform, ultimately, I concluded that Gani's story was true and that I should trust him.

That night, I had the most horrible nightmare I had ever had or have ever had since. In the dream, everywhere I went, I encountered border patrol soldiers chasing after me. No matter where I ran, they were right on my heels. I continued to run but wasn't getting anywhere. When I woke, my body was soaked in sweat. I lit a cigarette, trying to calm my nerves, and realized that this was a nightmare—and unlike a dream, it wasn't open to interpretation. It was merely my fears manifesting themselves in my subconscious mind.

The next morning, I asked Taqi if it would be all right for me to write to my father who lived in the United States. "I want to let him know that I'm okay," I told him.

Taqi seemed stunned. "Do you have your father's address?"

I nodded. "It's like I said. He's in the United States."

"Yes, I know that," Taqi said with a smile. "But the United States is a big place. We'll need a specific address."

"I have it."

"But when you first came in, we checked you and your pockets. You had no identification at all—no addresses, nothing."

"I don't have it on paper, but it's right here." I pointed to my head.

Now the smile left Taqi's face, and he became serious again. "I'm glad you asked before you wrote to him. This is a delicate situation. I'm afraid we can't allow you to write to your father." When he saw the disappointed look on my face, he started to scramble. "If he knows that you're working with us as an agent, he may tell his friends. Word of your whereabouts may find its way into the wrong hands, and your safety will be jeopardized. Then your chances of a successful mission diminish. We can't afford to take that chance."

I furrowed my brow. "Yes, I understand," I said in a placating tone. "How stupid of me not to think of that."

As if he could sense how frustrated the news made me, he quickly added, "From now on, you can go anywhere you want in the village without a soldier to accompany you."

I thanked him.

"Later on today," he said, "I'll introduce you to another young fellow. His name is Gani."

My heart leapt when he spoke the name.

Taqi performed that back-and-forth look over his shoulders that I had seen so many times from Gani himself. "But whatever we talk about here, you must not mention to him or anyone else. You should be very careful not to share any information with anyone. It'll be much safer for you. Keep your conversations on a friendly note and stay away from personal or business issues."

As we talked, I could see that Gani was walking toward us. Taqi called him over and introduced us, having no idea of our earlier meetings or conversations. Both Gani and I went through the motions of pretending to meet each other officially for the first time.

Already, I felt like a double agent.

There were very few people in this camp that I believed I could fully trust, but now that I was permitted to travel without escort, I felt utterly free for the first time in years. The people in this beautiful village were friendly, respectful, and caring. Their passion and sorrow for my family and me and for our country's plight was evident. I never refused their gifts because doing so would be an insult to such compassionate people, but their outward gestures of kindness made me feel a bit uncomfortable. Greeks and Albanians carry similar traditions. If you are their guest, they will go to the extreme to make sure you feel welcome and at home. There I was as a political refugee in Greece, and so everyone in the village thought of me as their guest. This made for many uncomfortable moments of accepting gifts I didn't need or want, but it also led to many fast friendships and fond memories.

What I did learn about the people in Greece during my time there was that they enjoy every second of life and genuinely know how to have a good time.

Chapter 12

Despite its roots of distrust, my friendship with Gani grew stronger by the day. It got to where he started inviting me along to various social gatherings in the area. In Maniaki, he had a friend named Petros. A few years older than Gani, he was extremely talented at both the accordion and the guitar and was well-known and well-liked. Petros's cousin was getting married, and Gani managed to land us an invitation to attend the affair.

Upon our arrival at the wedding and reception site, I was amazed at the detail the planners had given to the occasion. The tables were decorated with bottles of wine, Ouzo, and Metaxa. A host of servers wandered through the party, serving delicious Greek hors d'oeuvres. They had reserved a special table for Gani and his friends, including me.

Everyone was drinking, dancing, and having a grand time.

After a few drinks, two girls came to the table and tried to get Gani on the dance floor. He graciously refused their offer, then one of the girls pulled me by the arm, and I reluctantly joined the dancing circle. I had no idea what I was doing, but that only seemed to add to the charm of the moment. Eventually, I ended up with a handkerchief in my hand, which signified that I, of all people, was the one leading the dance. Eventually, Gani and the rest of his friends joined in, and in following the local custom, the guests began throwing money over our heads as we danced. There was money scattered everywhere. When the dance ended, the crowd roared happily and applauded us for joining them in their native dances and customs.

The wedding continued until three in the morning. I told Gani that I would be okay to walk to my apartment alone, so he left with

Maria. I soon realized that in fact, I couldn't remember how to get to my apartment. I'd had enough to drink that night that I never really remembered how I finally managed to find my bed, but I do know that I slept like the dead.

The next morning, I was having coffee when Gani came downstairs to the kitchen. Sophia, the housekeeper's daughter, arrived shortly after and immediately started talking and laughing with Gani. I was able to speak a few words in Greek by then, but I couldn't understand whole sentences, so I wasn't quite able to follow the conversation.

"What are you two talking about?" I asked.

Gani smiled. "She said that she liked you a lot and that it would be nice to kiss your eyes."

It was surprising to hear such a forward comment. In my culture, such a thing would've drawn scorn.

"Do you have any more clothes that need to be washed?" she asked demurely.

I gave her my dirty clothes. Then Gani and I went outside, where he immediately began putting ideas into my head about Sophia and me.

"Why are you telling me these things about her?" I asked.

"I don't know," he said. "She just seems nice is all. The two of you would make sense together."

"Why don't you take her for yourself if all the wonderful things you say about her are true?"

Gani shrugged. "She really likes you, Pertef," he said. "And besides, I have Maria."

Up to that point in my life, I had never had physical contact with a woman. Gani didn't know that, of course, because whenever we had discussions on the subject, I made it sound as if I was a Casanova and had been with many girls. Now that the prospect for an actual relationship was on the table, I felt like a blushing bride.

Later that week, Gani again assured me that Sophia was attracted to me. Since I had no idea about women and intimacy, I proceeded with Gani's advice. I decided to respond to Sophia's advances—or at least to what Gani told me were advances. One beautiful afternoon,

Sophia was pressing my suit with a coal iron on a low table. When she bent down to press my pants, I went close to her, and like an idiot, I grabbed her on her bottom.

She jumped up and screamed, "Do you want this hot iron on your face?" I was humiliated. The only thing left for me to do was apologize.

When she saw how badly she had frightened me, she tried to comfort me by talking softly and even apologized to me for her behavior. This only confused me further. Even if she had spoken to me in my language or if I had been fluent in her language, I wouldn't have understood what had just happened or what she meant. Through it all, I couldn't concentrate on parsing out the meaning of the exchange because I was so busy focusing on how to get even with Gani for setting me up.

I met Gani later that day and told him what had happened with Sophia. "I don't appreciate what you did to me," I said scornfully.

Gani was laughing hysterically, and the more he laughed, the angrier I became. Of course, that only made him laugh harder. Eventually, he was doubled over, and I guess the sight of it was enough to break the dam of anger I had constructed. Soon, my own laughter was spilling over. After all, it wasn't Gani who told me to grab Sophia—it was my own stupidity and ignorance.

"I'm sorry," he said after he had calmed down, "but you should've approached her in a different way. You must've scared her to death. Look, I know she likes you. She just needs a gentler approach."

"You've given me enough problems to last me for the rest of my life," I said. "I think it's Sophia that needs help. One moment, she was ready to roast my face with an iron, and the next moment, she was apologetic and soft like a kitten with me."

Again, Gani roared with laughter. "What did you expect her to do? Just brain you and walk away? That's not how women work, Pertef."

"I think I've had enough lessons on women for a while," I said. "If you think you know so much about them, you go ahead and try your hand with her."

Like a schoolboy, he giggled. "You've already showed me the danger of trying hands with her." Then he calmed himself and looked at me seriously for the first time. "Hey, Pertef?"

"Yeah?"

His smirk returned. "She really scared the hell out of you, didn't she?" I chuffed. "Wouldn't you have been scared if you were in my shoes?"

*****

A few weeks later, I was called to the captain's office. Taqi was there already by the time I arrived. Through Taqi's interpretation, the captain told me that it was time to begin preparing for my mission.

"I'm glad you brought this subject up, Captain," I said, "because I've been thinking about this and have decided it would be nothing but a suicide mission for me." Both Taqi and the captain visibly slumped.

I didn't let it deter me. My mind was made up. "Albania won't become free because of the actions of one or two people," I explained. "We need all the Albanians in Greece, plus more, in order to free the country. We don't need a secret passed here or a piece of information there. We need a coordinated assault to retake my homeland." I paused for a moment, searching my mind for just the right words. "So I guess what I'm trying to tell you is that I've changed my mind and will not be going on this mission. I want to go to America and make my life there. I hope that you will honor my decision." By that point, the captain's face was a deep red. He began shouting in Greek as Taqi furiously tried to keep up with the translation. When it became clear that the captain was trying to strong-arm me, I too became angry to the point that I didn't give a damn what either of them was saying.

"Are you going to force me to do this even if I don't want to?" I said. "What is this? I thought I was a free man. There's no way you'll ever make me go back into Albania now. No one will take my freedom from me ever again!"

At that, the captain calmed down, and the room fell silent. Taqi asked me to step out of the office, so I left and returned to my apartment. I spent the rest of that week going back and forth to the captain's office, enduring session after session of pleading and coercing. It was a week from hell. They used every method imaginable to scare me back into service, but my decision was firm, especially now that I knew they were trying to force me to do something against my will. They finally realized that the effort was hopeless. A month passed, and they carted me off to the police station and locked me up.

I couldn't believe it. That day, the guards brought me a cup of soup and a glass of water and nothing more. It felt like I was back home at the labor camp.

The next morning, an officer arrived at my cell. He was tall and wiry, narrow of shoulder and wide of hip. He wore a thick black mustache in the Mussolini style with the eyebrows to match. "How long have you been in Greece?" he asked me gruffly and without greeting.

"I've been here three months," I answered in his native Greek.

"You are a lying pig," he said smugly. I had been taking insults like this from the Communists since I was a child, so by now, I was used to the verbal abuse. But I was so disgusted with my situation I no longer felt I should hold myself accountable for the words that spilled out in reply.

"I am *not* a liar," I hissed, "and I am not a pig. But you, sir, are a pig yourself! You have my documents. Go ahead and check them. You'll see that I didn't lie!"

With a scoff, the officer closed the door and left me there. An hour later, he came back to my cell and let me out.

"I checked your record and found out that you've told me the truth," he said. "I have to say that I didn't believe you at first because you learned to speak the Greek language in such a short time. You must like our country very much."

I assured him that I did like Greece. "The people are fantastic, but I'm still a little unsure about government procedure."

He gave a knowing nod. "This can be a complicated place."

They kept me in the police station a few more days before taking me across the country to a beautiful city called Thessalonica. On the ride there, I had hoped that this would be my transfer to a place where I would finally be truly free to make my own decisions, but that hope was short-lived. Not five minutes after our arrival in that lovely city, they locked me up again.

The containment area in Thessalonica resided on the edge of the city, a few miles from the beach—close enough to smell the sea salt air. Its two large rooms housed about ten refugees each. When we reached my cell, the officer escorting me turned on the lights, and the inmates woke and rose from their beds.

"This young man is going to be in your cell block," the officer said. "And by the way, he's from Albania."

In the cell block were Albanians, Bulgarians, and Yugoslavians who had escaped their countries. I quickly learned that these men had been here for a month and were to be transferred to the camp in Lavrio that very morning. Upon hearing that I was Albanian, two of the men came to my bunk. I introduced myself, but they didn't give me their names.

"How have they been treating you?" I asked of them, but rather than answering my questions directly, one of them explained what I could expect while I was there.

"You'll be here about a month, and then you'll be transferred to Lavrio, like us."

"You must be patient here," the other said.

"Do you have any money?" asked the first.

I patted at my pockets. "I don't have a penny with me."

The first man—a man whose name I would later learn to be Bariq Talo—reached into his pocket, pulled out his wallet, and stuffed a few paper bills into my hand. "Here you would starve to death without money. They'll only feed you enough to barely keep you alive."

The other man looked back over his shoulder to make sure the officer who had escorted me had gone. "You see, in this place, the entire police department is corrupt. All the money allocated by the United States government for the immigrants goes into the pockets of these crooks."

I looked to Bariq, who had taken a seat on the bunk beside me. "How long have you been in Greece?"

"I've been here a little more than three years. I escaped in 1954."

At the mention of that year, I thought of my brother Medi, who was arrested and thrown into prison around that same year. He was only seventeen years old at the time. Then my thoughts changed to Mother's friend, to whom I had made a promise to find her brother, if he were still alive.

"I think you left the country about the same time a friend of my family did," I said to Bariq. "His name was Ymbri Jazxhi. Do you know of him?"

Bariq's eyebrows raised. "How do you know this name?"

"My family was in a labor camp with his sister. She and my mother know each other. The Communists told her that Ymbri was killed by the border patrol, but I didn't believe that."

The other man smiled. "Well, you were right," he said triumphantly. "Because I'm still alive and kicking."

"So you're Ymbri?" I asked with astonishment. I wasn't surprised that he was alive because I knew the Communists had lied to his sister. I just couldn't believe the coincidence.

We stayed up and talked all night. I was happy to meet these men and to get a better idea of what I should and shouldn't expect here in Thessalonica. Sometime during the conversation, it occurred to me that if my transfer had been delayed just one more day, our paths might never have crossed.

Bariq and Ymbri had worked for the Greek Intelligence Service for over three years. One month after they decided to call it quits, the Greek government discarded them like garbage and brought them here. Now Gani's advice began to make sense. It seemed like everyone was quitting the organization—so many people that their desperation for new recruits had caused them to use pressure tactics or containment as a form of coercion. I wondered aloud whether any of these bureaucrats saw the irony in the situation. None of us found any humor in the observation.

The more I spoke to these men, the gladder I became that Gani had taken a chance and talked with me. Now I felt sure that all my decisions since my escape had been good ones.

Around six o'clock the next morning, a truck arrived to pick up the men who had been there for a month. Shortly after, another truck followed, this one loaded with fresh refugees to drop off. I was the only one left behind with the new arrivals. One of the new immigrants was an Albanian who had escaped by way of Yugoslavia. Within a couple of days, he and I had developed a friendship. His name was Bardhyl Kombarci, and he was a trustful and honest young man from the town of Dibra in the northern part of Albania.

One day, during a heated conversation, a fight broke out between Bardhyl and one of the men from Yugoslavia. Blows were exchanged, and I rushed in to separate them.

During the scuffle, I shoved them both backward in an effort to break up the fight. When I shoved them apart, the young man from Yugoslavia tripped and hit his head on the wall.

The guards heard the commotion and rushed in to put an end to the fight.

"Who hit this man?" one of the guards asked when he saw the Yugoslavian lying on the ground.

"I did it," I said quickly. Despite my attempt to explain that it was an accident in my effort to break up the fight, I was put in solitary confinement for three days.

My friend Bardhyl was devastated that I had to pay for his actions. When I returned from the cell, he apologized to me on and on.

He kept insisting that he should have been the one to bear the punishment. He wouldn't let up, and I finally said, "Well, I think I have a solution. I think that maybe you should start another fight. You have my word that I won't step in and try to break it up. That way, you'll get three days solitary confinement, and I'll be free of your guilt."

Bardhyl gave a knowing smile. "No, Pertef," he said, his voice dripping with sarcasm, "I don't think I could bear the thought of being away from you for another three days."

At that, we both laughed aloud. This was the beginning of a friendship that would last a lifetime.

*****

A month later, the Greek officials transferred us to the camp in Lavrio. Since it was a place built specifically for immigrants in my situation, the conditions were much better there than I'd gotten used to. It also helped that while the camp fell under the administrative authority of the Greek government, the American government served as financiers. This meant that the United States kept a close watch, making sure that we received proper food and clothes, and even the option to advance our educations at the technical school they had funded.

Unlike at previous stops, my fellow refugees and I were allowed to travel freely around the town of Lavrio. With special permission, we could also travel to the beautiful ancient city of Athens.

I met many Albanians at the camp and was always proud to share company with brave men who had escaped the Communists. It was disappointing, however, when I began to realize that there was no leadership or unity among them. The Albanians had divided themselves into small groups, each group its own entity with its own agenda. Among the five hundred of us, there must have been at least a half-dozen political parties. In many instances, these parties fought hard against each other, making it difficult for us to decide on any one course of action to improve our situations. It was frustrating and disheartening at first, but the more I sat in on these unproductive meetings, the more it began to feel like betrayal.

At least at the labor camp we were united, I thought darkly. And it was true. The men, women, and children at that camp loved one another and thought of themselves as belonging to one family. We helped each other under any circumstances and were all fighting for the same cause. Whereas these party-line debaters thought of opposing parties as enemies, at the labor camp in Saver, we had one and only one enemy: the Communist regime.

That was a strangely comforting viewpoint to have at the time, but now that I was becoming more exposed to news from the outside world, I could see how naïve it was. Hate and bitterness had spread to our free Albanian brothers. The true irony was that while the rest of us toiled away in chains and waited for our escaped fathers and brothers to return and free us, those same escaped fathers and brothers were arguing among themselves over who would have the right to rule the free Albania. It reminded me of an Albanian proverb "Peshku Nedet Tigani Nezjar." As the story goes, there was once a family that fought among themselves because they couldn't agree on which way the fish would be cooked. The trouble for this family was that they were arguing about something totally irrelevant because they didn't yet even *have* the fish to cook. The fish were still in the ocean, hundreds of miles away.

It had been over a month since I had seen Gani, but one day, I heard through the grapevine that he had quit the intelligence mission program and was sent to a prison on the Greek island of Syros. While there, he bribed a guard to allow him to place a call to Mr. Andrews, an agent with the American CIA in Greece. Mr. Andrews wasted no time traveling to Syros himself to retrieve Gani and deliver him to Lavrio. The moment I heard the news, I went in search of my friend in the camp.

That day was a happy one for me. Not only did I reunite with my friend, but I also received a letter from my father. In the letter, he explained how he had spent five years at the camp in Lavrio before being allowed to emigrate to America. He expressed how happy he was to learn that I had escaped but also how concerned he was about the rest of the family members that remained in prisons and labor camps. Enclosed in the letter was a check for two hundred American dollars. That was a lot of money at that time. To me, it felt more like a million dollars.

In closing, he told me not to worry because he had gone to the immigration office, where he learned that, within four months, I would receive my approval to enter the United States. After reading the words my father had written by his own hand, I couldn't imagine anything that could make me happier.

Chapter 13

About a week after I received the letter and money from my father, a delegation from the American Embassy came to the camp in Lavrio and offered an opportunity to join the United States Army. This offer, made possible by the Lodge Act passed in 1950, allowed for a number of non-citizen Eastern Europeans to enlist in the United States military. We would all be vetted, of course, but anyone with an anti-Communist background and the ability to pass the examination was eligible. The required enlistment period was five years.

The more the delegates from the embassy spoke, the more excited I became. To me, it was a dream realized. For a boy who had spent much of his childhood in a labor camp, an opportunity of this nature couldn't come more than once in a lifetime. So it wasn't so much a question of whether I would be willing to join the greatest army on earth. The question was whether I would be lucky enough to be accepted.

I rushed to see if Bardhyl knew of this fantastic news and to see if I could convince him to join me in my decision to enlist. As it turned out, Bardhyl needed no convincing. We both put our names on the list. Gani was difficult to track down, and since I thought I knew him well, I put his name on the list too even without consulting him. I just didn't want his absence to cause him to miss out on such a golden opportunity.

That afternoon, I finally found Gani and spoke to him about the Lodge Act and all the good news it had afforded us. I tried to explain in detail what it would mean to join the U.S. Army, but he refused to listen.

"What are you thinking, Pertef?" he said, interrupting my pitch.

"What do you mean?" I asked him, deflating.

"Don't do this to yourself and especially to your father. He's waiting for you in America already, and you know that within a few months you'll be going there to be reunited with him."

"But, Gani, this guarantees us the training we'll need to fight for our families' freedom," I insisted.

My friend sighed. "You're young."

I shrugged. "So what?"

"You don't know how difficult it is to be a soldier. I served one full year in the Albanian army, and let me tell you, it wasn't fun. It was torture."

"Don't compare the United States Army with that ridiculous Communist army," I snapped. "You're not making any sense."

"So you're willing to give up yet another five years of your life?"

"Sure," I said dismissively. "But more importantly, I'll also be spending five years training with a military that can properly prepare me to fight those Communist bastards. They can't do that here. You've seen it yourself. If we want to bring the fight to our enemies and free our families, the United States gives us the best chance."

"He's right, you know," Bardyl said as he stepped into Gani's rather austere room.

The color of frustration seemed to drain from Gani's cheeks as he realized he was outnumbered.

Bardyl continued, "The chance to train was exactly what convinced me. That was the reason I put my name on the list."

"You mean the great Bardyl signed for it too?" Gani said sardonically.

"Yes, I did," Bardyl said. "And without hesitation."

"I also want to continue my education, if possible," I added. "And the only way for me to do that is by being in the service. Besides that, I don't know how you guys feel, but I love America and what that country stands for. I plan on making my home there, and I would feel honored to wear the uniform of an American soldier."

Gani shook his head.

"My decision is made," I said, looking Gani square in the eyes. "And no one will be able to change it. For the sake of my family and for the sake of my country, I pray to God that my dream will come true and they'll accept me into the army. That's all I have to say."

"Well, I love America too," Gani said. "But I'm never committing to another army as long as I live."

I was disheartened by my friend's decision but knew I had to honor it. We were free now, and that also meant freedom to turn our backs on chances of a lifetime.

Two weeks later, four people from the American Embassy arrived in Lavrio with the list of individuals approved to take the IQ test required for enlistment. I had seen the final signup list of fifty names, so it came as a surprise to me that only twenty-five of us were allowed to take the test.

The head recruiter was a strikingly tall man named Mr. John Anderson. In his thirties, his frame of six and a half feet and his blonde hair leant him a decidedly Nordic look. He was fluent in Albanian but had an accent so heavy that it was often difficult to understand him. We all loved that he spoke our native language, but we couldn't help but laugh at the way he mispronounced some of the words. The foible was apparent from the moment he began reading the names from his list. He read through names of new friends like Sazan Dema, Limani Sokoli, and Myzafer Karameta, and even my own name, but when Gani heard his name called, I knew I was in trouble. He pulled me aside after it was all over.

"Look here, Pertef," he hissed. "I've got my life, and you've got yours. Don't make my life any more complicated than it already is."

I don't know what came over me, but all my frustration at Gani's decision came bubbling over at once. "Don't act stupid, Gani. If you don't want to go, no one will force you to do so. Seems to me you've gotten used to this place. You've become stagnant." I waved a hand dismissively. "So go ahead and stay here for the rest of your life." He shook his head, his face reddening.

"I think I know what's wrong," I added, my tone dripping with sarcasm. "You're afraid you won't pass the test."

He furrowed his heavy brow. "I can pass that test with my eyes closed."

At the time, I couldn't figure out what it was that had done it—I had either shamed Gani or convinced him that I was right about the value of joining the U.S. military—but whatever the case, he agreed to take the test. Out of the twenty-five, only fifteen of us passed the exam, and Gani scored the highest grade. Whether it was pride or an opening of his eyes, I'll never know, but upon hearing the news, Gani decided to enlist.

When he was finished doling out the grades, Mr. Anderson used our native Albanian language to welcome those of us who had passed. "Tomorrow," he said, "you will all come to Athens. From there, we'll leave for Frankfurt, Germany, where your processing begins."

My chest swelled with pride, and my mind reeled with excitement.

"Good luck, gentlemen," Mr. Anderson said. "I'll see you tomorrow."

Now that Gani was riding the high of his score, he was like an entirely different person. "Listen," he said to me and Bardhyl. "This adventure isn't going to be all fun and games. It won't be easy. You'll have to work harder than you've ever worked."

"Years in a labor camp," I said, pointing at my chest. "I'm sure I can take it."

We stayed up all night that night, talking with our friends and saying our long goodbyes. I made promises to several of them that as soon as I got my first paycheck in the army, I would send them some money.

Our stop in Athens lasted only a few days. There, we received our vaccinations and submitted to physicals from the army doctors. Then I boarded the plane for the first flight of my life, and we were on our way to Germany.

When we touched down, it was quite late by local Frankfurt time. Groggy-eyed, I followed Mr. Anderson and his team to a square-shouldered military barracks lined with fifteen bunk beds. It was good to have Mr. Anderson there to translate, as otherwise, many of us would have faced a significant language barrier.

We received our wake-up call the next morning at five o'clock sharp. I showered quickly and got in line to be fitted for a uniform. After dressing in my new fatigues, I marched with the others to the mess hall. There are few times in my life that I've been prouder than I was as I stood in line with the American servicemen. At the same time, my mind roiled with the darkness of my past—the torture, the degradation, and the humiliation my family and I had endured over the years—all the darkness that I hoped this uniform would help me wipe from the earth. My heart was ready to jump out of my chest.

I wonder what the Communists would say if they saw me in an American uniform, I thought. *Would they have the guts to treat me like they did before?* In my view, the answer was clear. It was an entirely different ball game now. I now stood shoulder to shoulder with the full might of the U.S. Army. I had escaped communism as a boy fleeing to freedom, and whatever happened, I would return two million times stronger than I was when I left. *One for all, and all for one,* I thought. *If those Communist bastards were here right now, my new friends and I would kill them all.*

When I reached the front of the chow line, I saw more food than I had ever seen at one time. My fellow enlistees and I looked in awe at the cornucopia then at each other.

"Man!" someone said. "This isn't the army. This is paradise!"

"This mess hall must be for the millionaires' sons," Sazan said ruefully. "We're not supposed to be here."

"Millionaires' sons or not, let's grab some of this food before the authorities figure out the mistake," Sokoli replied.

Onto my shiny metal tray, I piled up enough food to last me a week. My friends did the same. Then we sat down, four to a table. Each of us had grabbed a quart of milk in a carton, but we looked to one another with wide eyes for some sign that anyone knew how to open them. None of us had a clue. Ultimately, it was Trevdo Todorov one of our Bulgarian friends who was brave enough to be the first to try. His attempt involved slicing into the carton with a knife, but he must have cut too far down because the milk spilled over the table, onto his uniform, and dripped to the floor.

We all burst into laughter.

Todorov was so embarrassed that he didn't bother to finish his breakfast. Instead, he stomped over to our table and tossed an unopened carton at us. "Here, you jackasses!" he snapped. "If you Albanians think you're so smart, let's see if one of you can open it." Most of us cowed to his point, but one or two kept laughing.

"Don't you see?" Todorov said, more quietly this time. "You guys are just as ignorant as I am, so you're really laughing at yourself." He looked around to make sure none of the Americans were watching. "We all have a lot to learn here. So let's try to help one another."

Then we were all nodding because it was clear Todorov was right. We had a long, hard road ahead of us.

After breakfast, we returned to our quarters, where Mr. Anderson began the process of trying to educate us with enough information so that we could function on our own. In the beginning, I don't think he realized how far removed we would be from the traditions of army regulations and American culture. To make it more difficult, not one of us could understand or speak a word of English. It's difficult for me to imagine even a team of counselors and psychologists able to meet such a challenge, but Mr. Anderson would soon prove that he was more than capable. He worked hard to understand every one of us on an individual level. He shared in our pain and frustration and also took part in our joys. To us, he was like our unofficial general, our supreme leader from the very beginning. He had earned our trust and respect—so much so that we would follow him wherever he told us to go.

The other trouble Mr. Anderson faced was a short timetable. He had only two weeks to get us psychologically ready to endure the tough times ahead of us. During this time, he also had to prepare us to take the oath that would make us official members of the United States Army.

The work began with Mr. Anderson making two schedules for us. One was a time schedule that listed the times for things like morning roll call, meals, and lights out. The second schedule featured one column with our names and another column assigning daily tasks to each of us.

"Now that you fellas know your way around," he told us after we returned from breakfast, "make sure you report to the mess hall promptly for each meal. Otherwise, you won't be eating. You're also required to check the bulletin board for your daily duties."

The following day, some of the men were supposed to work in the kitchen, but they didn't read the bulletin board and didn't show up. When Mr. Anderson received word of this, it was the first time we had ever seen him angry.

"I've been told that you men have been acting like a bunch of animals," he said. "I'm trying to help you, but I don't think you want to help yourselves." He let that sink in for a time before squaring his broad shoulders and continuing. "You're in the U.S. Army now, gentlemen, and you must obey the orders of that army. Do you understand?" We said that we understood.

He seemed to calm some. "If you're having any problems with your assignments, just let me know, and we'll see what we can do. But if you don't bother to show up, you may end up in serious trouble."

"But, Mr. Anderson," Ramolli started to say before our leader interrupted him.

"You!" Mr. Anderson cut in. "Ramolli, isn't it?"

Ramolli nodded innocently.

"I heard you jumped out of one of the windows so you wouldn't have to work in the kitchen. What do you have to say for yourself?" Some of us started to chuckle.

"Sir, I didn't jump from the window," Ramolli said.

"Why should I believe you?"

Ramolli shrugged. "Because I believe in following orders, sir. In fact, if I ever intentionally disobeyed an order, I would hope the army would hang me."

Mr. Anderson let loose with an exasperated chuckle. "Son, we don't hang people in the U.S. Army. But if you men continue to screw up, we can and will make your life miserable."

From his perch on one of the bunk beds, Sokoli raised his hand. "Mr. Anderson, sir?"

Our leader pointed to him and acknowledged that he could speak.

"If that jackass wants to be hanged," Sokoli said, "why don't we do it right here and right now?" He hopped down from the bed. "We can use my belt. I think it's strong enough to hold him."

Slowly, we all realized that Sokoli was telling another joke—his forte, to be certain. The room rippled with laughter. Mr. Anderson shook his head as if we were all crazy. But then he could hold it no longer and joined in the laughter.

From that point on, we tried to shape up and listen to Mr. Anderson. We felt comfortable and trusted him. We also had high respect for him and didn't want to displease him. He spoke our language, he knew about our traditions, and—most importantly—he believed in us enough to recruit us in the first place. We knew he wouldn't be staying with us long, so we wanted to make him proud of the job he had done in mentoring us and preparing us for the grueling days ahead.

The hard work paid off. On April 5, 1958, all fifteen of us were sworn in to the greatest army on the planet. It was a happy day for me and for my fellow enlistees. Mr. Anderson congratulated each of us individually and wished us the best. One by one, we hugged and thanked him. I would be sorry to part with him, as he was a great leader and a comforting spirit.

I wouldn't have much time to ponder that regret, however, because a few days later, we boarded a military plane bound for New York City. The joy of it was difficult for me to fathom at the time, but I was on my way to America.

Chapter 14

When we arrived at the airport in New York, there was a sergeant waiting for us. He didn't speak our language and spoke to us only in English. Every time he would say something, we tried to translate the words with the pocket dictionaries that Mr. Anderson had given us before we left Germany. It was disastrously difficult to keep up with him.

We boarded a bus at the airport, and about an hour later, we arrived at Grand Central Station. I had never been more awed by the beauty of any building. The place was crowded with people rushing in every direction trying to catch their trains. Through all the confusion and excitement, the sergeant was having a difficult time keeping us all together. We tried to keep up with him but couldn't help but wander off from time to time. We were just so transfixed by this beautiful place.

Aunt Reshide had told me many stories about New York City, but nothing could have prepared me for this. In my wildest imagination, I never could have described the feeling of that first panoramic view of this inspiring city. Seeing it with my own eyes—all those millions of people scrumming back and forth like honeybees—was overwhelming, to say the least. I had never seen so many people at one time and in one place, and I had never seen buildings so tall or grand as these.

We could sense the sergeant's concern, so eventually, we started walking closer together and keeping watch on each other. Within a few hours, our train had arrived. We boarded, bound for Fort Jackson, South Carolina, with our duffle bags thrown over our shoulders. Altogether, we were twenty soldiers assigned to the same company, twelve of us Albanians, four Bulgarians, two Greeks with Albanian origin, one Turk, and one Azerbaijani. Once on the base, we were each assigned an American soldier to watch over us until someone determined that we could handle ourselves on our own.

When I think about those most difficult days of training, one vision in particular sticks out to me. I recall looking on as a company of soldiers marched past, their uniforms crisp and their boots shining brightly. They were so disciplined, so precise in their rhythmic march, and in such great physical shape. I was enamored with the notion that I would soon be like these men that it made the hair stand up on the back of my neck.

"Those guys escaped from Hungary during the revolution," the American who was assigned to me said. I didn't pick up the full meaning right away, but between his hand signals and my dictionary, we got it sorted out. I was awestruck by the thought that these men weren't just American soldiers; they were men who had fled their country and the oppression of the Russian Communists, just like me. Most of them had lost their parents, brothers, and sisters in that terrible revolution, just like me. It made me happy to know that they were safe now and so clearly proud to be marching shoulder to shoulder with their American allies. I wanted desperately to feel that same way and as soon as possible.

First, however, I would have to learn English and as quickly as possible. It took three days for us to settle in to our quarters, gather our army-issued supplies, sort out our work details, and figure out how to navigate the base. Then it was off to school.

In the beginning, we had it easy. The only thing we had to worry about was learning the language, and most everyone treated us as if we were a cut above the rest of the enlisted soldiers. Anytime someone tried to assign any of us to a duty we didn't want to perform, the excuse was, "Me no speak English." For a little while, "Me no speak English" worked like a charm. But as time passed, gradually and psychologically, the army molded us to their standard.

One day, I had just returned from school with a few of my friends, and as we entered the barracks, we found our first sergeant waiting for us. I had never seen anyone more capable of communicating anger with nothing more than a harsh contortion of his facial muscles. He was an expressive man, and those expressions always had a way of cutting to the core of me. Part of it was because at forty-five years old, he had plenty of practice in the art of scaring the life out of his enlistees.

The other part of it was that at maybe five feet eight inches tall and weighing in at three hundred pounds, those expressive facial muscles were about the only toned part of his body. That rotund frame made them look practically chiseled by comparison.

"Is this a barn or an army barracks?" he said as soon as we walked in.

I was so taken aback by the sudden assault on our decency that it took me a moment to realize that I'd learned enough in class to understand him already.

"Gentlemen, you're a disgrace to the United States Army," he continued. "You have only two hours to bring this place to army standards, or I'll court-martial every last one of you. Is that understood?"

"Yes, Sergeant," we answered in unison.

Then we stood around blinking at each other about how it was true. We did understand him, and that was remarkable.

From that day forward, it was clear that the noose was getting tighter and that if we wanted to succeed in this outfit, we had to start taking responsibility for ourselves and cut out all the lax standards and horseplay. So with the help of our supervisors, we buffed the floor like it had never been buffed before. We made our beds and hung our uniforms. We shined what needed shining and tucked what needed tucking. By the time we were finished, our barracks looked more pristine than any I had ever seen.

In exactly two hours, the sergeant returned, this time bringing the company commander along with him. The two of them conducted a thorough inspection, ultimately finding the place to meet with their satisfaction. Sergeant Morgan even went so far as to compliment us.

Similar inspections continued the next morning when we reported for revelry. As it turned out, Gani, Sokoli, and my Bulgarian friend Todorov were the only men on hand who had managed to meet the uniform code in full.

"Since you're the only men that look like soldiers," Sergeant Morgan said as he gave the rest of the line the stink eye, "I'm giving each of you a three-day pass." This meant they would be free to leave the base each night for three full days. Then the sergeant turned his full attention on us. "As for the rest of you pigs, get your asses back to your barracks and get cleaned up."

We bolted so quickly that he had to call after us.

"If you look as decent as these three," he yelled, "I may give you some reward too."

The sergeant had earned such a reaction from us because he had found the perfect ingredients to motivate us. The first was to call an Albanian a pig. In Albania, that was the worst insult you could possibly give a man. So my fellow Albanians and I worked hard not to give him any opportunity to use that word on us again. The second motivation was the offer of the three-day pass. It wasn't so much that I wanted to receive the same accolades as the other three men who had already been granted the reward, although that helped. Really, all I wanted was a chance to get out and see some American girls. That was all any of us wanted to do, in fact. As far as we were concerned, American girls were the prettiest we had ever seen.

I did my best to shine up my shoes quickly and set my uniform to looking right, but ultimately, there would be no further reward that day. I was determined not to fail my sergeant again, however; so after classes that afternoon, I headed straight back to the barracks and spent the rest of the day and into the evening putting a spit shine on my boots, pressing my uniform, and helping the others clean the bathrooms.

The next morning, we looked sharp, alert, and as polished as any other soldier on the base. While we waited for inspection, we talked among ourselves about what we were going to do on our first three-day pass. Sergeant Morgan arrived and called us to attention. He looked us over from head to toe, and when he was done, he ordered my platoon to face him.

We turned, still standing at attention. The sergeant took a deep breath and held it for a second. I thought he was having chest pains or maybe even a heart attack, but then he released the breath he was holding and commanded us to stand at ease.

"It looks like I finally got through to you soldiers," he said. "Now you know what I expect. I want you to look sharp every day. I want your barracks clean. And from now on, you will *not* be excluded from any duties. You'll pull your own load like everyone else. Is that clear?"

"Yes, sir!" we replied.

"Oh," he said, holding a finger up. "One more thing. I don't ever want to hear that 'Me don't speak English' crap again, is that clear?"

Again, we replied with a resounding, "Yes, sir!"

The teachers at the English school were tremendous, and many of us were making great progress with the language. But in hindsight, it would've gone a whole lot quicker if we hadn't all stuck together like a pack of wolves. The twenty of us were like one big support group, not a native English speaker in sight.

One Saturday morning just after breakfast, many of that same support group were sitting around under a shady tree, just talking, laughing, and taking it easy. Weekends were times of relaxation from drills, inspections, and the daily rigors of military life, and all of us took full advantage. That day, however, would be somewhat less than relaxing.

It all started when my Albanian friend Sazan spotted a soldier marching past us. The moment he saw his face, he jumped up and started screaming at the top of his lungs. Before I could figure out what he was so upset about, he started running for a group of soldiers just up the street. In his native Albanian, he was screaming bloody murder.

The rest of us jumped up and ran after Sazan, trying to catch him as he screamed like a madman. Finally, someone got their arms over his shoulders and pulled him to a stop. We all circled him and tried to calm him down. When he caught his breath, he explained himself.

"That man I saw was a Sigurim officer," he insisted.

"How can you be sure?" I asked him.

He went rigid. "That was the same soldier who tortured me for months while I was in solitary confinement at the prison back home."

"Are you sure, Sazan?" Gani asked as he looked back over his shoulder as if to check the veracity of his friend's claim.

"Yeah," I said. "Maybe it was just someone who looks like him. Why would the army enlist someone from the Albanian Sigurim anyway?"

Sazan took one more look at the soldier and seemed to calm. But then all his rage returned at once, and he charged toward the soldier, screaming about how he was going to kill him.

I reached out to try to stop him—to try to keep him from making the kind of mistake that would get him tossed from the army and sent back to Greece—but it was too late. He lunged at the soldier, tackling him from behind. By the time the rest of us got to him, he had already flung the soldier around and punched him square in the face.

"Oh, Nene!" (Oh, Mother!) the soldier cried out, bringing us all to a halt.

It was then that we realized Sazan had the right man. The recognition washed over us each in turn. And in an instant, all hell had broken loose. The accused soldier had an Albanian soldier friend with him, and the two of them fought back, turning it into an all-out street brawl. From a distance, it couldn't possibly have been clear who was fighting whom because all of us wanted a piece of that Communist bastard, no matter the consequences.

It couldn't have been more than a minute or two before the military police showed up and broke up the fight. It was chaos as the MPs separated us, but to their credit, they picked through our broken English to figure out that we were in the right and that the man we had assaulted had been a member of a party that had committed countless crimes against the Albanian people.

The MPs hauled away Sazan's torturer, and that was the last we ever saw of him. I never heard what happened to the wolf in sheep's clothing, but I can't imagine it was pleasant.

That left us standing alongside the other Albanian soldier who had helped the accused fight against us. It seemed as if he hadn't been aware of his friend's background, but still it made for an awkward moment.

"I'm Benjamin Piri," he said, introducing himself sheepishly. "I'm from the southern part of Albania from the town of Bilisht. I'm so sorry about this. Please believe me when I tell you that I had no idea he was a member of the Sigurim."

Albanian people are stubborn as hell. Even though Benjamin had told us he was oblivious to his friend's history, in his rage, Gani took another swing at him. I reached in to break it up, calling for Gani to stop.

"Wait!" I said. "I have heard this name—Piri."

Gani backed away and seethed, but he kept his angry eyes on Benjamin.

"You said you're from Bilisht?" I said, panting.

He nodded.

"Well, Benjamin Piri from Bilisht," I said with a steady gaze, "I know your father and brother. They were in the labor camp at Saver with my family."

When everyone calmed down, we were able to reintroduce ourselves and accept our new comrade as a true friend.

"But what I don't understand," Gani said, "is how could a Communist spy infiltrate the U.S. Army without the CIA knowing about it?"

Benjamin shrugged his broad shoulders as if to say, "Maybe they do."

Sokoli elbowed Sazan and smirked. "How does it feel to foil an American espionage operation?"

Sazan's face grew red, but quickly, the tension diffused into laughter.

Chapter 15

When the day finally came, the day that I received my first paycheck from the United States Army, I couldn't have been more excited. My friends shared similar opinions on the matter. We agreed that we would send a portion of our hard-earned money to our friends still stuck in Greece, as we had promised. Then for six of us at least, we would pool the rest of our money together and purchase a car. I still can't imagine why we thought we needed one so badly, but the decision was quickly made and seemed like a logical one at the time.

The day after payday, we all dressed up in our uniforms and took the bus to downtown Columbia, South Carolina, where we soon found ourselves in the parking lot of a used car dealer. The way we were aimlessly examining cars we knew nothing at all about, we must have looked like a bunch of brainless Albanians. And we were in a way. Not one of us had ever owned a car, driven a car, or even had a driver's license.

I was the one to spot the 1951 Buick, its shiny black paint and polished chrome calling out to me. We all agreed that it looked very nice.

"How much for this car?" I asked the salesman, who couldn't have showed up at a more opportune time to make a quick sale to six foreigners speaking extremely broken English.

The salesman gave a plastic grin. "Two hundred fifty dollars and you can take it home today."

Without a moment of haggling, I handed him the money. The salesman looked like he couldn't believe what was happening. He put together the papers and handed them to Gani. Then he jangled the keys over to my friend Vangjeli.

"Well, good luck, gentlemen," the salesman said, counting the money as he strolled away whistling.

I remember that moment of elation at the thought that I was at least one-sixth owner of such a beautiful car. That moment lasted about three heartbeats before it dissipated into a cloud of reality. We had a car, but now we also had a little problem. None of us had any idea how to start the thing, let alone drive it. So we all stood there, just looking in through the driver's side window, trying to figure out who would be brave or stupid enough to get behind the wheel.

"Do any of you guys know anything about driving a car?" I asked.

"Not me," Gani said, waving the papers in the air.

"I don't think any of us have ever driven," Sokoli said. Then he pointed to Vangjeli. "Why don't we make this little fly bite holding the keys do the driving?"

High-strung and on the nervous side, Vangjeli didn't take to the suggestion immediately. The green face he made caused us all to break out in laughter. He steeled up his face. "I am *not* a fly bite," he snapped. Then he clenched the keys in his fist and held them up for us to see. "I'll show you how this works. Come on, everybody. Get in the car!"

We were not ones to argue. One after the other, we climbed into our new-used Buick, following the lead of a driver who had never driven in his life and had the lack of license to prove it. Gani and I sat in the front with Vangeli while Sokoli, Sazan, and Bardhyl took their positions in the back.

The truth was that I wasn't really worried until the moment I saw Vangjeli struggling to find the ignition. He fiddled around for a while, stabbing at the dash with the key, until eventually our collective insight managed to find the slot. Sweat breaking over his brow, he turned the key and the engine started. But then instead of putting the car in drive, he threw it into reverse and stepped on the gas. The car peeled backward. We all roared with fear and laughter.

The salesman was standing behind the car at the time, I guess thinking he would watch us drive off, but when he saw the car coming at him in reverse at full speed, he leaped out of the way, careening onto the hood of the car just beside him.

We couldn't have missed him by more than a hair's breadth.

It wasn't until we came right up against the line of parked cars for sale that Vangjeli finally found the brakes. After I caught my breath and looked back ahead, the first thing I saw was the terrified salesman sliding down from the hood where he had taken refuge. His legs were like Jell-O, so wobbly he had to lean against his safety car for support. Despite the thirty feet and the windshield between us, I could hear that he was swearing profanely. I hadn't been in America long enough to understand the full meaning of what he was saying, but I had heard several of the more colorful words plenty of times to get the gist of their meaning. The bottom line of his tirade was this:

"You idiots must be drunk! Get out of that car before you kill someone!"

By this time, Vangjeli already had the car in drive and was heading out of the lot toward Main Street and downtown Columbia. I could practically feel the heat off the salesman's forehead as we blew past.

We made it about five hundred feet out of the lot when as if we didn't already have enough problems, it began to rain heavily. I took a look at Vangjeli and saw that he was covered with sweat.

His uniform was soaked, and he was desperately trying to loosen his necktie, but the knot was too tight. Finally, he gave up on the tie and began looking for the windshield wipers. The moment he switched them on, we encountered another problem. The moisture outside met with the nervous body heat from the six of us inside the car, and the windows quickly fogged up.

"There's a defroster," someone said. How he knew this information, I have no idea, and how Vangjeli found the defroster so quickly, I will also never know.

However, we soon learned that the defroster in our new-used Buick didn't work. Still Vangjeli kept on. He reached forward and tried to wipe the condensation off a portion of the glass, but I was sure he couldn't see a thing.

"Pull the car off the road right now," I told him, "or we're all gonna die!"

Instead, he made a sharp right turn at what I guessed was the next intersection. Car horns were blaring at us from every direction as we pulled—safely and miraculously—into a gas station parking lot.

We all just sat there and breathed for a while. I took stock of the fact that I was still somehow in one piece. I'm sure the others did the same.

Once the rain subsided, Vangeli headed back onto Main Street. Now we learned the hard way that traffic signals are more than mere suggestion. Left and right, oncoming cars had to slam on their brakes to avoid hitting us. Miraculously, we made it through the busy part of town and found ourselves on open highway. It seemed to me that Vangjeli was building confidence in his driving skills because he started going faster and faster. Before long, we were passing every car we encountered.

Now that we had survived the first few obstacles and had found open road, we all started to loosen up.

"This was a good idea," Gani said.

We all agreed. It was a very good investment, it seemed.

"Other than the defroster not working," someone said, "this baby's in perfect shape."

"And we'll figure out how to drive it," Sokoli insisted. "Someday."

We traveled for two or three more miles, talking, laughing, and listening to an Elvis song on the radio. Since we had the radio on so loud, it was the police cruiser's lights that caught our attention long before the siren. Sazan was first to notice them.

"What would the police want with us?" Vangjeli asked naively as he roared past another car in the right lane.

The cruiser was on us now, bearing within a few feet, plenty apparent with its lights blazing and its siren blaring.

"Maybe we should stop and ask him," Sazan suggested.

Vangjeli made an aggressive slide to the side of the road. Then all six of us climbed out of the car and whipped out our pocket dictionaries so we could engage with the officers. As they approached, the state troopers looked on in obvious amazement at the six guys in uniform who clearly couldn't command their language with the greatest of ease.

It was Bardhyl who explained the situation to the befuddled troopers. "We can't speak English too well," he said, raising an eyebrow. Then in choppy sentences abbreviated by glances at his dictionary, he informed the officers that we were just taking our new car to find a lake so we could go swimming.

This came as news to me, but I didn't say anything.

"Do you have a license?" one of the officers said to Vangjeli.

"No, sir," our driver said clearly. Then he struggled to add, "I don't have a license."

"Officer," Sokoli said, his sardonic tone evident, "this misfit doesn't have a license. We all feared for our lives while he was driving. Why don't you pull him by his ears and lock him up because he's a very dangerous driver."

We all took a good look at Vangjeli and burst out laughing. The officers didn't share in the revelry.

I elbowed Sokoli. "C'mon, man," I whispered in Albanian. "For once in your life, be serious. This is a critical situation."

"Shut up," Sokoli replied in our native tongue. "Or I'll—" then he trailed off.

"Or what?" I said. "Just because you're taller than me, you think I'm afraid of you?"

"You'd better be afraid of me."

I assessed him with a cockeyed gaze. "Are you serious?"

"I'm dead serious."

"First let's get out of this mess that we put ourselves in," I said, shaking my head. "And when we get back to the barracks, you and I will fight. But the fight is going to be American style. Is that fair?"

Sokoli seemed to shrink. "I was only joking."

"What's wrong now, Sokoli? Are you a man or a mouse? Do we have a fight or not?"

The faces of the officers were painted with what looked like bemused expressions. They followed our conversation with their eyes, but they couldn't have had any idea what we were talking about.

Our friends, meanwhile, looked surprised that I had challenged Sokoli and even more surprised about how Sokoli was trying to back down from the fight. Sokoli thought about it for a moment longer before accepting my challenge.

"Listen," one of the troopers interjected. "You fellas are gonna have to get this car all the way off the road."

We flipped through our dictionaries and seemed to come to the same conclusion all at once. Together, five of us got behind the Buick while Gani worked the wheel and we managed to get the car completely off the pavement and onto the shoulder. While we were doing this, one of the troopers called for additional cruisers.

Two arrived and took all six of us to the nearby lake.

"What time do you need to be back to the base?" our new driver asked as he dropped us off.

We told him, and he said he would be back to get us.

"What's going to happen with the car?" I asked him before he could take off.

He nodded. "We'll take care of it." Then he left.

I wasn't sure what he meant, but the way he said it made it sound like all would be well. *This America is even better than I'd imagined*, I thought. *The police drive you wherever you want to go!*

That day, we had a blast talking with civilians and meeting many beautiful American girls. Then at 4:00 p.m. sharp, two police cruisers returned and drove us back to the base. We were raucously excited the whole way, but that mood died the moment we learned that the company commander wanted to see us immediately. That could only mean trouble.

As we approached our date with punishment, we decided that we would explain exactly what had happened without any lies or hedges. But before we reached the door, Sazan somehow managed to convince us that if we let him do the talking, he could get us out of trouble. We agreed.

"Don't worry," Sazan said. "I know the captain well. Many times, I have been in his office for casual conversations. He speaks several languages, so we converse in Bulgarian. Just let me handle it and everything will be fine."

Again, we promised not to utter a word.

We entered the office and saluted Captain Borowski, who returned the salute in a hangdog sort of way. Then he asked us to tell our side of the story. At the beginning, Sazan did well, telling the entire story exactly the way it happened. But then I guess to win favor from the captain, he started talking about his family and their ill fate under the boot of the Communist regime.

"My father was a high-ranking elected official in Albania prior to the Communist takeover," he said. "This meant persecution for my family."

The captain appeared sympathetic. He directed his response to Sazan. "It's unfortunate what happened to your father and your family. I'm very sorry about that and about what is taking place in that beautiful country of yours." Then the captain gave a smile. "And I would like to add that I'm thrilled and honored to have the pleasure of meeting all of you, especially the elite one." He pointed his finger at Sazan.

We all looked at one another proudly, convinced that Sazan had saved our butts. But it wasn't as easy as we thought.

The captain abruptly stood from his chair, and the first thing I noticed was that the smile had gone. "Now listen here, you bunch of undisciplined, disgusting soldiers," he began and a chill ran up my spine. "I don't give a damn what titles you or your family had or have in Albania. Right now, you are in the United States Army, and my job is to make soldiers out of you. Do you understand me?"

"Yes, sir!" we all said.

At that exact second, Sokoli elbowed me and rolled his eyes. I don't know why, but it caused me to laugh aloud. Then Sokoli began to laugh.

This made the captain furious. "You two ignorant asses stay here. The rest of you, get out of my office and back to your barracks."

Sokoli and I were ordered to work after hours filling bags of sand for three straight days. The last day of our punishment was a hot one. We were both soaking with sweat, but since it was the last day for us, we figured if we worked as hard as we could, we might somehow merit reward.

Sokoli, however, was never able to do anything without turning around a few jokes. While I was bending over to tie a bag of sand, he dumped a shovel full on the back of my neck. The sand was hot, and since I was so wet with sweat, it burned like hell. I swore at him in English and Albanian, every bad word I could think of. Sokoli merely laughed in reply.

"Okay, that's it," I said. "As soon as we finish here, you and I have some issues to settle. I have to give you a lesson so in the future you can show some respect to me and others."

My clownish friend clammed up.

After our shift of sandbagging was over, we headed to the supply room and signed out for boxing gloves. Word had spread that Sokoli and I were going to fight, so the entire company gathered around to watch the event.

For a little while, we traded a nearly even number of punches. Then Sokoli, with his long arms, got me with a few jabs. I knew that if I didn't force the fight, I would lose, which would've been disastrous for my reputation. Time seemed to slow down for me. The cheers from our friends delivered in a deeper tone. I could see every bead of sweat on Sokoli's face with crystalline clarity. The ring formed by soldiers seemed to close in and grow smaller, hemming my opponent in to me. I had entered that trancelike state that caused me to do no wrong.

Then I saw it. Sokoli made the mistake of dropping his left hand. In a flash, I came in with an uppercut from my right hand. The hit was direct and fierce. Sokoli went down like a wet sack of sand. Our friends roared.

Without hesitation, Gani moved in and raised my hand. Everyone declared me the winner. I extended my hand to Sokoli and pulled him up. He nodded as if ready to accept defeat. But then as soon as I turned my back on him and started talking to Bardhyl, my opponent came from behind and hit me on the back of the head, knocking me down.

Everyone booed him, but Sokoli waved it off. He came to me then, a strange smile pressed on his face, and extended his hand to help me up. At first, I was angry with him about the cheap shot, but then I realized that Sokoli would always be Sokoli. He would never take anything seriously, and that included the rules of a boxing match.

"Okay," he said. "Now we're even. We both went down." I let him think I was seething for a moment.

He furrowed his brow. "Are we still friends, Pertef?"

Then I brightened up. "Until death!" I said with a smile.

We shook hands and bear hugged, and all the soldiers standing around us applauded.

Chapter 16

I had been in the army for over two months, and I still hadn't received contact from my father. At first, I thought maybe he was waiting to come visit me in person, but then I started to wonder if maybe the letter I sent him had been addressed incorrectly.

One day, the letter was returned to me marked "Undeliverable." So that evening, I decided to try calling him from the communal phone at Fort Jackson. From our correspondence while I was in Greece, I knew that he worked at a place called Lyndi's Restaurant in Waterbury, Connecticut, so I dialed the operator and asked for the business listing. The operator quickly found the number and connected me to the restaurant.

"Lyndi's Restaurant," the man on the other end of the line said.

I asked to speak with Mr. Zenel or Arif Bylykbashi.

"They aren't in today," he told me.

I slumped. "Well, would it be possible for you to arrange for them to be there at two o'clock tomorrow afternoon?" I asked. "It's very important that I speak with them."

It took the man a long moment to reply. I guess he was trying to assess what I wanted with them. Finally, he agreed that he would pass word on to the men I sought.

I wished I had left him my name.

The next day, I called back, and the same man answered the phone. "May I speak to Mr. Zenel Bylykbashi please?"

"Just one minute," came the reply.

I had not seen my father, nor heard his voice, since I was twelve years old. But then I heard it. "Hello," he said and the voice was unmistakably his.

My heart raced. "Hello, Father," I answered, too excited to think of anything else to say.

There was a long silent pause on the other end of the phone, followed with, "Pertef, my son, is this really you?"

I couldn't help the smile that reached my lips. "Yes, Father, it's really me."

"Where are you calling from? Are you in New York City?"

"No, not in New York," I said. I knew that since he had not received my letter, I would still have to explain my decision to join the army. "I'm in the United States, but in the state called South Carolina. Have you heard of it?"

"No," he replied quickly. "What are you doing there?"

"I joined the United States Army," I said in an eager tone.

There was another long pause.

"Hello?" I said. "Are you still there?"

"Yes, I am still here." From his tone, I could tell that he disapproved of the decision.

"I will write to you and explain the whole thing," I said. "So don't you worry." Father then handed the phone to Uncle Arif.

"Pertef, my boy!" he said enthusiastically. "So good to hear from you. How are you? And *where* are you?"

The connection wasn't pristine, and the way we were both choking up with emotion didn't help, so we had a hard time hearing each other. My eyes filled with tears.

"How is my wife?" my uncle asked. "And your mother and the rest of the family?"

"As good as one can be in prison, my uncle." Quickly, it occurred to me that my reply might have been too harsh. "I assure you that everyone is alive and their spirits high. But their will for freedom is even higher."

"That is good to know."

"You take care of yourself, Pertef. I hope to see you soon." He handed the phone to my father once again.

"Give me your address, and I'll visit you," Father said.

Surprised at the notion that he would be able to travel such a distance, I gave him the address at Fort Jackson. Then I told him I loved him before ending the call.

A few days passed. Then one morning around seven o'clock, a soldier in my platoon came to my barracks. "The company commander wants to see you in his office," he said.

I quickly made my way to the office.

"You have some visitors," the captain said.

Confused, I looked through the doorway that led into the adjoining room. There were four men all dressed in suits. I stared at them for a minute, wondering who they could be. Then suddenly, I realized. It was my father. It shocked me to see that he had traveled all this way in such a short time and on such short notice.

As I approached him, we locked eyes and held that gaze for a long while. It had been so many years, and I suppose I had grown up considerably since the last time he had seen me. I wasn't sure whether he recognized me at first, so I hugged him, and we both tumbled into overwhelming, tearful joy. We cried for all the years we had missed being together, cried for the rest of the family still rotting in prison, and cried because we knew we might never see them again.

I looked over my father's shoulder to see who had joined him. I was disappointed to learn that for health reasons, Uncle Arif hadn't come along on the journey. Instead, two of my father's nephews, my cousins Sybi and Nazmi, accompanied him. We all started talking at once, trying to cover the events of eight years in five minutes. Then Sybi introduced me to the fourth man. "This is Besim," he said. "Besim, this is Pertef."

"A pleasure to meet you," I said.

"Do you know Myzafer Karameta?" Besim asked. "He is my brother-in-law."

"Oh yes," I said with a smile. "I thought I recognized your name. Myzafer has talked to me about you, and since you're related to him, I consider you my family as well."

We shook hands again. By now, word had spread about Father's visit, and everyone was rushing to the office to meet them, including Myzafer. I introduced Gani and the rest of my friends to my relatives.

After a time, the captain entered to ask my father about how long he planned on staying with us at Fort Jackson.

Without hesitation, Sybi answered for him in English. "We're staying a week."

"Well then," the captain said, his eyes fluttering with surprise. "I welcome you as guests of the United States Army for as long as you wish to stay. I'll prepare quarters for all of you so you can be together and have more privacy to talk about your families and your old country."

The captain, in a show of incredible kindness, granted all the Albanians in my platoon a week off. We were astounded. These were certainly extraordinary circumstances, but I had never expected the army to show such generosity. It made me feel even more honored to be a soldier and even more willing to give my life for my adoptive country America.

When I look back at my life, I always note that the week with my father is earmarked as one of the greatest I've ever experienced. Father and the other three men slept in the same barracks with us and were even allowed to eat with us in the mess hall.

On the second day, we received another surprise: the company commander assigned a bus for us to use on a sightseeing tour.

Whenever Father and I had a chance to speak in private, he would raise the subject of his wife and children still stuck in Albania. He seemed uncertain about whether they would ever make it out of that labor camp and prison alive. I could sense guilt in his heart, for he had tried many different ways to achieve their freedom through diplomatic means, but there was only so much one man can do.

"If you had to do it over again, Father," I said, "would you do anything differently?"

"Yes," he answered immediately. "I had no choice but to escape from Albania when I did, but as dangerous as it would have been, I would have chanced taking my wife and children with me." As he spoke, the tears returned, dripping down his cheeks. He paused for a moment, regaining his composure, and then continued, "I am very thankful and humble to God that at last he brought one of my children to me. But I hurt for the rest of my family and my beloved

Resmije. If it could have been possible, I would have exchanged my life for them so they could be free."

This struck me as a remarkable sentiment because it was almost the same answer my mother had given me when I was twelve years old and my family was transported to prison. I asked her if she blamed my father for the suffering and humiliation that we were having to endure.

"Your father had no other choice but to escape to save his life," she had told me. "It would have been great if we had a chance for all of us to escape together, but that didn't happen. If your father hadn't escaped when he did, he would've been executed along with his brother. So you see, my son, even if he had stayed, he would've been taken away from us. This way, at least we know that he is alive and well."

I could see that Father was hurting for his family, but at the time, I had no idea how deep that hurt could run. I wasn't yet a father, and now that I am, I realize how strong my own father was. If I had been in his shoes, I'd have died rather than be separated from my children. But his decision was to escape, thinking that he could and would return for the rest of us. I guess Fejzi's death opened his eyes to the shortcomings in this plan. He had lost one son to the effort to retake Albania. He didn't wish to lose any more.

This notion was at least part of why Father had initially objected to my joining the army. But now that he had spent several days with us on the base, it was clear that he had changed his mind. The way the company commander was treating us was more than enough to convince him that I had found the right place to join the fight to free my family.

Before he left for Connecticut, he gave me his blessing, which meant more to me than I can say. We made plans to meet up again soon, but I knew it would be quite a while before I had finished my basic training and could find the kind of time it would take to travel to Connecticut. In some ways, it felt like we were parting indefinitely once more. In other ways, it was like a hole in my heart had been refilled.

*****

Even though many years have passed, I will never forget the day I went to see the company commander to ask him for a day off to celebrate Albanian Independence Day. Sazan and Sokoli went with me to the captain's office while the rest of our group waited outside, their breath surely baited. When he heard my request, the captain flashed that broad smile of his. "What date did Albania officially win their independence, soldier?"

I puffed out my chest. "I'm proud to say, sir, that we won our independence from the Turkish Empire on November 28, 1912. And I would like to add, sir, that during that particular time, our country was less than a million in population. We Albanians are very proud of this day."

"Does every one of the Albanian soldiers feel the way you do, soldier Bylykbashi?"

I furrowed my brow. "I would say yes, sir."

The captain leaned back in his chair. "Well then, I'll say yes to your request. I'm granting all the Albanians on the base a two-day pass to celebrate your Independence Day." Then his expression became serious. "I want you all to have a good time but make sure to stay out of trouble. Is that clear?"

"Yes, sir!" we said eagerly as we gave a firm, upright salute. Then Sokoli, Sazan, and I turned to leave, all of us carrying huge smiles.

The other men waiting outside brightened up the moment they saw our faces, as it was clear our request had been granted. That night, as we packed for our leave, we all agreed that the American people were different from any other compatriots. They were kind to their very souls, understanding, and more compassionate than anyone we could imagine.

The next morning, on November 28, we made a reservation at a hotel in Columbia. We celebrated the day with a large meal and a few drinks, and then we sang the American and Albanian national anthems in turn. Following that, Sazan made a speech on the importance of the day.

"It was the help of Americans that made it possible to win our independence from the Ottoman Empire in 1912," he said. "And with America's help and help from God, soon, we will see Albania freed from the grips of communism!"

We all cheered. He held up a hand to signal that he had more to say.

"We should never forget that Albanian and American people are old friends. We now have a chance to show our gratitude by being the best soldiers we can be!"

Now we cheered even louder. We all agreed that it was a time for us to meet our responsibilities and measure up to the army's expectations.

Chapter 17

When the language school came to a close, all of us had passed with good marks. This meant basic training could begin. We embarked on that venture in the same battalion, but most of us wound up in different companies.

Vangjeli and I were the only Albanians assigned to our company. When we reported, we had to wait an hour or so for our new sergeant to arrive to give us the details. Sergeant Tracey turned out to be a gruff, upright, hard-nosed man entirely fond of the intimidating effects of pacing.

"Fall in and stand at attention," he barked as he paced. "You all look like a bunch of ladies! You don't deserve to wear that patch on your sleeve. I'm Sergeant Tracey, and when I question you, I want you to answer with 'Yes, sir!' or 'No, sir!' and nothing else. By the time I finish with you, you'll either be soldiers, or you'll be cursing your mother for giving birth to you."

Sergeant Tracey's voice carried its own authority. He was as mean as they come. He was in his midthirties and looked to be in great physical shape. He kept a large cigar in his mouth, most of the time unlit. Whenever he spoke, he would bite the end of the cigar off and spit it out. Apart from this rather unsettling habit, he was all class and clean. He dressed sharp, his fatigues always crisp, and his mustache rendered him a distinguished and yet tough-as-nails Teddy Roosevelt air. When he spoke, he was firm and to the point. He was also the first black officer under whom I ever served. In fact, until I enlisted in the army, I had never seen a black person before.

"All of you that are Americans, go to your barracks," he said, the spittle and cigar chunks flying from his lips. "And when I call you, I want you here immediately. If you're not here immediately, I'll tear your insides out. Is that clear?"

"Yes, sir," we said.

"I can't hear you," the sergeant yelled.

"Yes, sir!" we bellowed.

He would make us say this over and over until the volume satisfied him. After the Americans returned to the barracks, there were about a dozen soldiers remaining that most people like Sergeant Tracey referred to as the "Lodge Act personnel."

"I want you to form a single line," the drill sergeant barked.

We did as ordered, and I wound up at the end of the line with Vangjeli and everyone else to my right. Sergeant Tracey went to the opposite end of the line and tried to provoke us all one by one. He was cursing us with every dirty word he could think of, and the whole time, his face couldn't have been more than an eighth of an inch away from whatever face he happened to be berating.

"Would you like to fight me, Private?" he kept asking everyone.

"No, sir!" was the consistent reply.

To my surprise, all the other soldiers kept their cool. I didn't like this kind of treatment, especially when he was using vulgar language about our mothers and sisters. My mind turned to thoughts of my mother, my sisters, and my brothers. Knowing what kind of life they had to endure made it difficult for me to stand there and let this man belittle them.

As the sergeant made his way down the line of soldiers toward me, I quietly asked Vangjeli if he would let the sergeant humiliate his family the way he was doing to the other soldiers.

"No way is he going to talk to me like that," Vangjeli said. "I'll tell him so too."

Moments later, Sergeant Tracey stood nose to nose with Vangjeli, who proved to be much smarter than I was because he stood there with his mouth shut, just like the rest of the soldiers. I gave him a dirty look that Sergeant Tracey noticed.

"What are you looking at, you Mongolian-eyed bastard?" the sergeant said as he turned to me. He made a move to grab me, but I swatted his hands away.

"Keep your hands off me," I snapped. "And for your information, I am *not* Mongolian. I am Albanian. I'll spell it for you if you don't know how. I'm a soldier, and I expect to be treated like one. I'll show you respect and obey your orders, but I will *not* let you humiliate me or my family."

A little smirk sprouted on Sergeant Tracey's face. He bit off the end of his cigar and spit it out. He performed a hefty cough that I would learn to be something of a trademark for him. Then he ordered me to relax. "All the rest of you stooges, go to the barracks." Then he pointed at me. "Except for the Alphabet here." He was referring to my last name. "Alphabet, you follow me."

"What a way to start training," I mumbled to myself.

I followed the sergeant, no idea what was in store for me. From the back, I could tell that this man was a real soldier. He walked with finesse and yet toughness.

We arrived at his quarters, and he held the door for me to enter.

"How do you like my place, Soldier Bylykbashi?" he asked.

The room was spotless, everything in its right place, every line pristine.

"It's very nice, sir," I replied.

"Well now, tell me exactly what is bothering you, soldier. Are you tough, stupid, or a mama's boy?"

"Little bit of all them, sir." The quip seemed to relax him some, so I continued, "Sir, you should know that in my country, if you don't protect the honor of your family, then you are nothing. And in my case, right at this very moment, sir, my mother, brothers, and sisters are prisoners in a Communist labor camp. Only God knows their future and what their fates will be. The kind of language you used on us, it's unacceptable to any Albanian but least of all to me. I don't take these kinds of insults lightly."

It took a while for Sergeant Tracey to form a reply. When finally he spoke, his face gave no hint of whether he meant to be friendly or rigid. "I like you, Soldier Bylykbashi. You're one hell of a tough guy. But I want to make one thing very clear. Don't look for any special treatment from me while you're in basic training. I'm going to work you harder than anyone else, and I promise to make you the best soldier in this battalion. As far as insulting you, I apologize, but you must understand that I am an instructor. And before I start training my men, I want to know each one of them—what they eat, when they sleep, the way they think, the way they act, and what kind of clay they're made of. It's my job to turn my soldier students into fighting machines. By the time I'm through with you guys, some of you will probably hate my guts, but someday, my training may save your asses."

We kept eye contact for a while before I looked down into a nod.

"You understand what I'm saying to you, don't you, soldier?" he asked.

"I understand you very well, sir," I said. "I also want to thank you, sir, for trying to understand me."

I liked the sergeant. He was sincere. It also seemed like he understood my situation and sympathized with my family's plight. He reached into his cabinet and pulled out a bottle of whiskey and two glasses. "Come, let's have a drink," he said. "I think you and I will get along just fine."

"I'm sorry, sir," I said. "I can't drink because I'm still on duty. It's against army rules and regulations."

He broke into a wide, satisfied smile. "You learn fast, soldier. I like that. I think I'll keep you around so you can teach me a thing or two."

From that day on, Sergeant Tracey and I built a good relationship with each other. He put us through hell and back during our basic training, but when it was over, every one of us was mentally and physically in shape to perform any duties asked of us.

At the testing ceremony that concluded basic training, I wound up getting the highest marks, and I felt I owed it all to Sergeant Tracey, especially after he stood up for me during a confrontation in which some of the ranking officers accused me and Vanjgeli of cheating during the sit-up competition. I had managed to finish the mandated eighty-five sit-ups in just under a minute and a half, which few people believed possible. After Sergeant Tracey stood up for me, everyone agreed that I should do the exercise again to prove myself.

Those last five sit-ups of the second round felt like a knife stabbing into my back, but I completed them in large part because of Sergeant Tracey's support and the support of my whole battalion standing over me chanting along with the count. I completed the second set of eighty-five in under ninety seconds as well, an act that helped earn me the highest marks and a trophy at the end of the ceremony.

After basic training was over, I used my two weeks of leave to visit my father and Uncle Arif in Waterbury, Connecticut. It was a nice, relaxing visit that allowed us to catch up on all those things said and unsaid when they had come down to South Carolina. I could see that my father had made a nice home for himself but that a part of his heart was missing. Every day, he knew the pain of loss and frustration at not being able to rescue his family.

When I returned to my unit, my orders were waiting for me. Sergeant Tracey told me that I was assigned to paratrooper school. I thanked him for his support and understanding and told him that I knew he had gone above and beyond what the army required of him to ensure that we were trained not only in the ways of the army but also in the American way. We parted as friends.

My orders took me to the Eighty-second Airborne Division in Fort Bragg, North Carolina, where I would subject myself to even more intensive training. When my father learned about my assignment, he wrote to me with his adamant disapproval. His letter explained the fear and the heavy burden I had placed on him by accepting a role with such a high risk of actual wartime conflict. He emphasized the impact Fejzi's death had on the family and explained that if anything happened to me, his life wouldn't be worth living. He had been so happy and relieved when I escaped Albania and made it to America and couldn't bear the thought of losing me because of such a hazardous assignment.

This caused me to stop and analyze my decision. I knew that Father's heart had ached for years due to the separation from his family, and I couldn't bear to know that I had added to his heartache. So I decided to respect his wishes and ask for a transfer to the infantry division. My request was granted, and I was sipped to Fort Benning, Georgia. Gani, Sazan, and Sokoli had already taken up residence on bases in Germany while Bardhyl and most of the others in our group had gone on to assignments in South Korea. Only a few of my friends were lucky enough to spend their service time in the United States.

When I arrived at Fort Benning, I met two Hungarians, Kovacs and Dennis.

They had defected during the 1956 Hungarian Revolution and joined the army as I did.

We became good friends and spent most of our free time together.

One day, while we were having a conversation about our company commander, they told me that he seemed to have biases toward foreigners.

"How do you know this?" I asked Kovacs.

He explained that he and Dennis had asked the captain for his permission to register for a few of the continuing education courses offered to the American soldiers. The captain was very disrespectful and rude, Kovacs said.

"He actually told us to get out of his office."

"Did he give you any explanation?" I asked.

"No, not at all. He just yelled and told us we weren't in the category of people allowed to attend the classes."

I thought about it for a while. Then an idea occurred to me. "I think I have a solution to the problem, and it will land all three of us in a classroom. Just give me a few days to work on it."

By the afternoon, I had already found out that two sergeants from our company were attending school to obtain their GED. When I learned that good news, I was certain that the company commander could not refuse us the same privilege. How could he after all? We needed the education just as much as the sergeants, if not more because of our poor skills with English. The more I thought about it, the less convincing Kovacs and Dennis's claims seemed.

After getting permission from my platoon sergeant, the next morning, I made my way to the first sergeant's office and told him I wanted to see the company commander.

"He's in his office," the first sergeant said. "Wait here a few minutes, and I'll tell him."

After the first sergeant had a talk with the commander, he granted my permission to enter the office.

Once inside, I saluted. "Private Bylykbashi reporting as directed, sir."

He returned my salute and asked if I had permission from my platoon sergeant to be there. I assured him that I had gone through the proper channels.

He kept his head down as if to make me think he was reading something.

"What can I do for you, soldier?"

"Captain, sir, I heard that there is a continuing education program on the base. I would like very much to be able to register and attend this school. This way, sir, I can become more efficient and useful to the United States Army, sir."

He sighed. "Soldier, right now, I'm very busy. You're wasting my time. I'm going to order you to about-face and get out of this office. You're a soldier, not a student. Is that understood?"

Now I could see that my Hungarian friends had been right. This officer clearly held strong racial biases. For a moment, I thought about protesting, but then I decided against pressing the issue because I could see there would be no swaying him from his distorted way of thinking.

"I would like permission to see my battalion commander, sir," I said instead.

"Permission denied, soldier," he snapped. "And I told you to get out of here or I'll court-martial you for disobeying an order!"

"Well, sir, you may have to do that because I'm going to see my battalion commander anyway." Then I saluted him and left the office.

I probably should have kept my mouth shut, but that was never a strong suit of mine, especially when it came to the principles of right and wrong.

The next morning, I put on my best uniform and went to the battalion headquarters. There, I met face-to-face with the sergeant major. "What are you doing here, soldier?" he asked.

"I've come to see the battalion commander, sir."

He looked at his scheduling chart for the day. "I don't understand. Your name isn't on the roster. Did the battalion commander send for you?"

"No, sir. The colonel doesn't know anything about this. I'm sorry, Sergeant Major, sir, but I came here on my own and for a personal reason."

The door to the battalion commander's office was open, allowing him to overhear our conversation. Shortly, he stepped out to join us. "What's going on here?" he asked the sergeant major.

"Sir, this soldier here says he wants to see you."

"Well, send him in."

When I entered, I tried to report to him, but he interrupted, "That's okay, soldier. What can I do for you today?"

"I am going to speak slowly," I said, "because I do not speak the language too—"

The battalion commander interrupted me again, "You speak very well, son. I understand you loud and clear."

"Sir, I know that you are a very busy man, so I will get right to the point. I would like to continue my education like some of the other soldiers. You see, sir, in my country, the Communist regime considered me and my family enemies of the people. So I was permitted only four years of formal education."

"Did you ask permission from your company commander, soldier?"

"I asked my company commander, but he did not grant me his permission, sir."

"Then, soldier, you better go back to your company. You know the army rules and regulations."

I straightened up. "I do not think that is a good idea, sir. If I go back to my company, I know that I'm going to be court-martialed for disobeying my commanding officer anyway. So the best thing for me to do is to let you do the honors. And besides that, sir, the love and respect that I have for the United States Army, I would not let anyone put me in stockade in my uniform."

As I was talking, I removed my jacket and began unbuckling the belt to my pants.

"I've been in prison from the age of twelve, and it's starting to look like prison is my destiny no matter what I do."

The commander stopped me from continuing to undress. "How do you pronounce your name, soldier?"

I pronounced my name for him.

"Do you speak Russian?"

"No, sir. When I think or hear anything about Russia, it gives me goose bumps. I feel sorry for the Russian people because they are under dictatorship the way my country is. And let me tell you, sir, that is not the kind of life you wish even on your enemy."

"What nationality are you, Soldier Bylykbashi?"

"I am from Albania, sir."

"Is your family here in the United States with you?"

"Unfortunately not, sir. My family is still in a labor camp in Albania."

The battalion commander stood and walked around from behind his desk.

"Okay, soldier. Buckle your belt and put your jacket on. You've convinced me. I think you deserve—probably more than anyone else—the chance at an education. I'll grant your request. But I expect you to do well." He bent down, picked up my jacket, and held it out for me. "Come, put it on."

I was astonished by his politeness. "Sir, I hope you're not kidding with me, for you know very well that the captain is waiting to get his hands on me."

He smiled. "You let me worry about that, soldier. Tomorrow morning, I want you to register for classes. Is that understood?"

"Yes, sir," I said excitedly. "Thank you very much, sir. I will do my best to be a good soldier and a good student." Then I remembered the other reason I had come.

"One more thing, sir," I added.

"What is it, soldier?"

"Sir, in my company, there are two more soldiers that escaped during the Hungarian Revolution. They also want to continue their education but have been denied."

"Okay, give me their names."

I gave the names of my friends Kovacs and Dennis. Then I saluted the commander, thanked him, and left the office. I was not a stranger to resistance. I had to fight it all my life, but I learned at an early age to choose my battles and to fight with wit and cunning rather than fists and force. More often than not, I would walk away with a victory.

I couldn't have been happier to be allowed to continue my education. The Communists had stolen my childhood education away from me, and I had carried that pain with me for years. School was always part of my dream, and now it would serve as a major component to my own personal American Dream. Thanks to the United States Army, my blessings were abundant.

At the end of the school year, Kovacs, Dennis, and I received a certificate from the Department of the Army Education Center. The certificate designated that we had completed the eighth grade. That piece of paper made me feel like someone had just handed me the world. I wouldn't have exchanged that certificate for any amount of money. That was merely the first step for me. Thanks to the army, I am proud to say that I now hold an associate's degree in specialized business. None of it would have been possible if not for that miracle that allowed me to start back on the path of learning.

*****

Not long after receiving my education certificate, the members of my regiment chose me as their representative in an intensive gymnastics training course that would lead to my participation in a competition against soldiers from the air force, navy, and marines. I was thrilled to be one of only five men chosen to represent the army, but soon, my excitement would be overshadowed by some bad news from Connecticut.

A week before the military competition, I was summoned to the chaplain's office, where I learned that my cousin Sybi, Uncle Arif's son, had died from cancer at the age of only twenty-seven. The chaplain offered his condolences and explained that he had already made arrangements for a sergeant to accompany me on the trip to Connecticut.

We arrived at Bradley Airport in Hartford around three o'clock that afternoon. Our family friends Idajet Bushka (who escaped with father) and his brother Myfit were waiting for us at the airport.

I thanked the sergeant and assured him that I would be with family from here on and that he could return to the base.

In Waterbury, I found Father and Uncle Arif in mourning. It was heartbreaking to see the two of them in such agony and confusion. They sat close together, arm in arm, as they battled the pain of losing another family member. These brothers had shared the same heartaches over the years—so much so that their lives had become mirror images of each other. Both had wives and children in the labor camps in Albania, and now both knew the grief of losing a son—one to an enemy called communism and one to an enemy called cancer. The only difference was that Uncle Arif's son was buried under proper religious ceremony, whereas to this day, we have never learned where the Communists took Fejzi's body.

The room was full of friends that had immigrated from the old country, and many new friends from America that we had come to know and love. I talked to as many as I could, personally thanking them for all their support during Sybi's illness. At the ceremony the next day, I gave the eulogy. I stayed in Waterbury for two weeks after to provide comfort and support to Father and Uncle Arif.

Sybi's death was difficult for me to accept. Try as I might, I couldn't help but question the reasons God would allow Sybi to free himself from the Communists, only to have his young life taken away by cancer. My grief continued for many months. Even as I returned to life at Fort Benning, I just couldn't shake the question of why God would allow such a terrible thing to happen to such a good person.

My feelings of disillusionment were only reinforced one day when I went to town with a friend of mine we called Gambler. It was supposed to be a day of leisure, but when a nice leather jacket hanging in the window of a men's clothing store caught our attention, I had my eyes opened by the seedier side of American culture in the late 1950s.

"Let's go try that jacket on," I said. But as I opened the door to go in, Gambler didn't follow.

"I'll wait out here for you," he said.

I let go of the door and walked back outside to see if maybe I had offended him somehow. I stood in absolute amazement as he explained to me that because he was a black man, he couldn't enter a privately-owned store designated for white people. What he was saying was so bizarre that at first, I thought he was playing a trick on me.

"You're kidding," I said with a laugh. I grabbed him by his arm and dragged him toward the door then shoved him inside. "I'll be your protector," I said. "No one is going to hurt my friend. We're American soldiers, and we'll stick together to the end."

As we were walking down the aisle, I noticed the store owner standing behind the counter. His eyes went wide at the sight of us. Then without hesitating, he bent down and gathered a baseball bat from behind the counter. He charged toward us, screaming obscenities and racial slurs I've never been able to forget, no matter how I try.

My blood ran cold. It was as if upon entering this store, I had wandered back into Albania. The only difference was that now, instead of me being the target, I had to watch as my friend Gambler faced verbal torture, physical threat, and abuse to his character.

"Don't you move, Gambler," I said, stepping between them. "And don't be afraid because I'm going to beat the hell out of this bastard."

I leveled my gaze on the owner and then snatched the bat from his hand and drew it back with the intent of splitting his head open. But just as I was ready to swing, Gambler grabbed the end of the bat and stopped me.

"Let the scumbag go, Pertef," he said. "He's not worth the trouble!"

In a flash, I saw that Gambler was right. I let go of the bat then turned a glare on the storeowner. What's wrong with you? "You should thank my friend," I said.

"Not only may he one day have to give his life fighting for your freedom, but he just saved your life today. Otherwise, I would've beaten you to death with your own bat, you ignorant pig." I put my arm over Gambler's shoulder. "Come on, my friend. Let's get the hell out of here. I can't stand looking at this filth another minute."

When we returned to the base, I went to the barracks and lay down on my bunk. My mind was reeling, and my heart was hurting from the events of the day. I hurt for my friend Gambler, but I hurt for America as a whole. I hadn't known that people faced such torment just because of their color. The notion seemed more ridiculous than the ideology of communism.

This is America, I thought. *Everyone in America is supposed to be free.*

All that week, I felt like I had been kicked in the stomach. Now I could see how some of the other things I had encountered made more sense in this context. The reason Sergeant Tracey had been so compassionate and understanding with me was because he had experienced firsthand the pain of personal degradation and humiliation. I recalled how, back when I was under his command, there was an evening when some of my black friends planned a trip to town to have a few beers. I asked them if it would be okay for me to join them.

"Probably not," one of them said.

"What?" I said with disbelief. "Why?"

Someone explained that being seen with me would cause the kind of tension that could be dangerous for them and for me as well. At the time, without the context I had learned that day at the store with Gambler, I didn't know what they were talking about. Instead, I figured they were making up an excuse because they didn't want me out with them. Now I understood that I was wrong to have felt slighted that day. Those men were merely trying to protect themselves and me from bigots.

Eventually, I came to accept that racism was a reality in America and that no matter how it bothered me, it was just something I would have to learn to live with. Everyone else had learned this lesson already, it seemed. Now I just had to recognize that although American prejudices were disappointing, the love for my new country soared above it all. I had seen firsthand the magnitude of American kindness. So I knew that someday, with God's help, the American people would find common ground for peace.

Chapter 18

In November 1959, I received orders to leave my beloved America for an assignment overseas. It was bittersweet for me when my transfer orders came through. The bitter part I owed to the fact that I would be trading in my home on American soil for one with the army rifle battalion, Thirty-sixth Infantry Division, about thirty kilometers from Frankfurt, Germany, near a little town called Friedberg. The sweet part was because the post would allow me the opportunity to travel through Europe during my extended leaves but also mostly because it would reunite me with my friend Gani, who had been stationed there for over a year and a half already.

Gani's skills had placed him in charge of field target training. As a special duty assignment, the job was five days a week, which gave him every weekend off. More importantly, it allowed him the wildly desirable privilege of a permanent pass.

At the time, I couldn't imagine a more beautiful dream. So my first order of business was to figure out just how to get a permanent pass of my own.

The long, hard search would end in short order. The day I reported to my new assignment, I encountered the kind of happy coincidence that only a charmed fate can provide. From the start, my new first sergeant clearly didn't like what he saw. My hair had gotten too long for army standards. The journey had worn me out besides, and my ears were still ringing from the heavy pressure put on them during the long flight. I said as much to the first sergeant when he asked me to explain my disheveled appearance.

"Let me ask you something, soldier," he said, his voice dripping with sarcasm. "Where's your violin?"

Tired as I was, to me, it sounded like he had said, "Where's your field jacket?"

"I left it at the cleaners, sir," I replied.

He cocked his head to one side and flashed a disgusted expression. "You left your violin at the cleaners?" It looked as if he thought I was a little slow in the head.

This was a difficult position for me. I was tired and more than a little on edge, and I especially didn't want to get into a confrontation with my first sergeant on the very first day. I'd been in the army for almost two years by then, so I had already learned my share of valuable lessons—most of them the hard way. One of those lessons was to always make a positive first impression with any new commanding officer. Now here I stood with a choice to make: either suck it up and apologize or do something that suggested I'd never learned that valuable lesson in the first place.

Throughout my life, many people have told me that I've had a guardian angel watching over me. I've always agreed with the observation, and this particular situation would provide plenty of evidence on its own. At that very moment when I was about to let my crankiness get the better of me and smart off to my new first sergeant, my guardian angel strolled into the room. The angel had taken the form of my old friend and former drill sergeant, Sergeant Tracey.

It had been almost a year since I had seen Sergeant Tracey, but when I caught sight of him, all anger was immediately flushed from me. My mouth fell open in disbelief. My first instinct was to take a step in his direction so I could pull him into a bear hug, but I held my ground because I didn't want to ignore my new first sergeant or embarrass him in front of his fellow sergeant.

But my old friend didn't share the same level of restraint. Happy as he was to see me, he immediately grabbed me and hugged me tight.

"Sergeant Tracey," my first sergeant said, beside himself, "do you know this soldier?"

"He took his basic training under me at Fort Jackson," Tracey said as he pulled away and fought off excited laughter. "If it's all the same to you, I'd like to assign him to my platoon."

The moment the other officer nodded reluctantly, I started to question how it was that I could be so lucky. The army had bases all over the world. Even if I had set out in *search* of Sergeant Tracey, my chances of finding him would've been slim. And here I found him right on time to save me from insulting the very man who could make my life in Germany miserable.

That was how I wound up in one of the best platoons on the base and also how I managed to secure a cushy special duty assignment of my own.

"The base is in need of a carpenter," Sergeant Tracey told me one day. "It's a special assignment, so it'll get you out of guard duty. And there'll be a few other perks. Would you be interested in the job?"

I knew very well what those other perks would be, so I was quick to reply in the affirmative.

Now Sergeant Tracey took on a conspiratorial tone. "Okay then. Tomorrow at revelry, when I ask who wants the position, I want you to raise your hand. Do that and you'll be the one chosen for this assignment."

Suddenly, I felt lighter from the excitement, but then a troubling thought skipped through my head. "Does this mean I won't be in your platoon anymore?"

"No, no," he said. "You'll stay in the same company. You'll just be working for the battalion. Also you'll be excluded from guard duty and will be issued a permanent pass."

I could hardly speak; I was so giddy and grateful.

The next morning at revelry, just as Sergeant Tracey said it would happen, he stood up and asked if anyone was a carpenter by trade and would like to work on special assignment. Every last man in the company raised his hand. With a chuckle, Sergeant Tracey scanned the crowd and found me.

"What about you, Alphabet?" he said.

Everyone started laughing when they heard my nickname.

Sergeant Tracey called for me to stand out of the line. "Okay, soldier. Go to your room and lock your wall locker and footlocker. We are having an inspection today so make sure that you leave a sign stating that you've gone to work for S-4 and report immediately to the person in charge at the repair and utility service unit."

Quickly, I went to my room, locked up all my belongings, and then headed to my new job. There, I met Sergeant Pierson, who would serve as my supervisor. He was the kind of man who always seemed to keep his eyes narrowed as if he was either deep in thought or deeply suspicious.

"PFC Bylykbashi reporting for the carpenter position, sir," I said.

Pierson looked confused. "Soldier, I don't know what's going on in your company, but my request was for a plumber, not a carpenter."

My desire to get that permanent pass was so strong that I managed to think of a lie quickly enough to avoid having my face fall and give me away. "Well, Sergeant," I said, sounding as earnest as I could, "I guess we're both having a lucky day today because in my country, I worked as a plumber. That's actually my true profession."

In truth, I had no idea what it would take to pass as a professional plumber. In fact, I didn't even know what the word *plumber* meant. To me, these were minor details. What mattered was that I clearly understood "no guard duty" and "permanent pass." I was willing to do whatever it took to keep this special assignment.

I'd have given just about anything to have my dictionary with me that day. But as it was, I would have to sort of feel out what it meant to be a plumber. Even as I made small talk with Sergeant Pierson, my mind was racing for a way to pass as a craftsman in a craft I didn't even know how to define. Then an idea came to me. *If I can see what kinds of tools a plumber uses, then I can probably figure out the meaning of this unknown profession.*

"Hey, Sergeant," I said coolly. "I'm going to get a cup of coffee. How do you take yours?"

"I drink it black," Sergeant Pierson said. "But I'm buying the coffee today."

"No way! Today, the coffee is on me!" Since I could see my diversion was falling flat, I quickly changed gears before the sergeant could get suspicious. "I bet you lose a lot of your tools around here, huh?"

He kept his eyes narrowed, but from the way his lips parted, I could see he was impressed. "You hit the nail on the head, soldier." He shook his head. "Every month, it costs us thousands of dollars to replace lost tools. I have some good soldiers here, but as far as the tools are concerned, they leave them all over the place and lose them. They just don't take care of them like they would their own."

I held a finger aloft. "I have a great idea to share with you if you're interested in something that would save the army lots of money."

"Oh yeah?" he said, crossing his arms and nodding his head back. "What's that?"

"You should have all the soldiers sign their tools in and out."

"Hey, that just might work."

"You can start this new procedure with me," I said quickly. "While I'm getting the coffee, if you'll put all my tools together in a box, then when I get back, I'll sign for them. This way, I'll be responsible for any tools that are missing when I return them."

The sergeant's face lit up at the idea. "You know, soldier, you and I are going to get along just fine. You've been here five minutes and have already solved one of my biggest problems and made my job easier."

Our shop was in the basement of a retail complex. Above us was the coffee shop where all the soldiers would hang out. When I went upstairs to get the coffee and some donuts, I purposely spent far more time than I needed to spend on the task. This way, I figured I could be certain that the sergeant would have enough time to gather up all my tools. When I returned with the coffee, I saw the toolbox he had prepared for me. It was full of wrenches, washers, screwdrivers, and sink handles. Up to now, everything was going according to plan.

"Soldier," Sergeant Pierson said, still beaming from the suggestion I'd given him, "it's about time they sent me someone with some horse sense in this damn place! I not only placed your tools in the box for you, but I'm going to recommend you for a promotion."

I couldn't have been more thrilled with this information. When I first entered this assignment, I was just hoping I could pass as a carpenter at least long enough to avoid being busted back to guard duty. But now I not only had convinced the sergeant that I was a plumber by trade, but for some reason, I'd landed a promotion as well.

Not bad for a couple minutes' work, I thought.

I signed for my tools, and after inspecting them, I now at least had a vague idea of what my job was. Still I knew absolutely nothing about how to do the actual *plumbing* part of the job.

You'll be fine as long as no one calls with a plumbing emergency, I thought, trying to reassure myself.

The next day, at eleven o'clock in the morning, the phone rang in the shop. The sergeant answered, but the voice on the other end of the line was so frantic that I could hear it even though I stood six feet away.

"We need a plumber here on the double," the voice said. "The pipes in the shower room are broken, and none of us have any idea were the shutoffs are."

Sergeant Pierson assured the caller that he would send someone over right away. Then he hung up and turned to me. "Okay, Private. Now's the time to show these idiots your professional ability." He smirked.

My dread was such that I felt as if someone had hit me in the head with a sledgehammer. I had hoped to spend at least another day or two of picking up the lingo before someone called me in on an emergency. I was so nervous about how I would get myself out of this one that I left the shop without the toolbox.

"Soldier, you forgot your tools!" Pierson called after me.

I tried to look nonchalant when I returned through the door.

"What do you think you're going to do, fix it with your bare hands?"

"No, no," I said quickly. "I'm just going to use the bathroom real quick since I don't know if any of the heads will be in working order at the site."

The sergeant nodded and sent me off. I stayed in the bathroom for a few minutes, trying to figure a way out of this predicament. In the end, no matter how I looked at it, I realized I had no choice but to at least go to the job site to see if I could fake my way through it.

I went back to the office, picked up my toolbox, and left for my first plumbing work order. As I approached my assignment, I kept a prayer on my lips, but I wasn't sure that even that would help me. The only thing that I could imagine saving me now would be a strong wind whipping through and totally leveling the building. "What in Christ's name do I do now?" I said to myself.

In the shower room, I found the showerheads all hissing with hot water. I counted myself lucky that the steam was so thick as to hide from the other soldiers the utter panic written on my face. I could see immediately that there wasn't a chance in hell that I'd ever be able to fix these showers. I was a plumber who knew nothing about plumbing, and the thought was making me more and more nervous.

Okay, Pertef, I thought. *Calm down. If you just take a logical approach to it, you'll be able to figure out the problem.*

The problem was that I didn't know a thing about main shut-off valves. So I took a wrench from my toolbox and headed for the showers, thinking I could maybe tighten the handles and prevent the steam from escaping. I gave the wrench a hefty turn to the right, and in an instant, the pipe broke. Steam and hot water pumped into the room with force now. The scalding hot water soaked me from head to toe. I was screaming from the burn and spewing every Albanian and English curse word I could think of.

When I'd calmed, I gazed through the fog at the mess I had helped create. Then very calmly, I left the shower room to find the nearest telephone. I figured there was no escaping the matter now: my promotion and my special assignment were probably lost forever, not to mention my permanent pass.

"Sergeant Pierson," I said into the phone. Then I paused, brightening up when the lie came to me suddenly. "This job is too big for one man to handle. We're going to be in at least three feet of water if we don't take care of this problem right away."

"Oh, I forgot to tell you!" he said. "If the job is too large for us to take care of, we have access to an outside crew of civilians. So call this number, and they'll come to repair it."

I called the number right away and told them to send a crew over as soon as possible. About twenty inches of pouring water later, three professional plumbers arrived to clean up my mess. I watched closely as they shut off the main valve then replaced the pipe, handles, and all the showerheads. There couldn't have been a better sequence for me to watch as a crash course in plumbing repair. Later that day, when I signed off on the work order, I proudly noted that not one of the showerheads leaked any longer. As it turned out, Mr. Pierson would soon complete his army obligation. I was surprised to learn that he not only recommended me for a promotion to Corporal, but he also recommended that I be put in charge of the parts and utility department, where I remained until my tour of duty was over.

After six months on the job and some leave time that took me and an army buddy of mine named Paul Sadesky to Switzerland and Italy, I found myself back on the base and roped in to a double date alongside a friend named Danny. He had been too shy to personally ask out Anna, a beautiful local shoe store clerk, so I'd done it for him. The night of the date, a fortuitous series of events led to Danny and me getting invited back to Anna's house for drinks and dancing. That's where I met her younger sister Inga. She was young and beautiful and witty and whip smart, and I was in love from the moment we danced.

Anna and Danny didn't last as a couple, but from that day on, Inga and I saw each other almost every day. On the day of her seventeenth birthday, Inga and I decided that we would get married the following month. We had a small wedding, inviting seven of my closest service friends, all whom attended in full dress uniform. Inga's whole family was there, along with a few of her classmates and other friends. I wore a black tuxedo, a white shirt, a bowtie, and gloves. Inga dressed in a beautiful white wedding gown that made her look absolutely stunning.

After a small reception, we went to Inga's house, changed clothes, and left for our honeymoon in the beautiful country of Holland. When we returned home a few weeks later, I found a small but cozy apartment in the town of Badenheim. It was about six kilometers from the army base and close to her childhood home, which made the commute convenient for both of us.

Our marriage imbued in me a new kind of intensity. I had been raised on the steadfast notion that family must always come first, and by then, I had spent years unable to do exactly that. Every day, I did what I could to become a better soldier, and every night, I burned with frustration and anguish at the thought that I was still no closer to freeing my family from the grip of communism. In many ways, this led me to be even more passionate in my dealings with Inga than I might have been otherwise.

In March 1963, I received orders to return to the United States. My five-year voluntary service obligation to the U.S. Army was coming to an end. This was a proud day for me, but also a solemn one, as it reminded me just how long it had been since I had left my family behind. I took heart in the knowledge that as a proper U.S. citizen, I might be in a better position to lobby the kinds of people who could make a difference for my family and everyone else suffering in Albania, but I still couldn't reconcile with the thought of how long my mother and siblings had suffered.

My final orders with the army were to report to the states to receive my honorable discharge. Inga and I arrived at Maguire Airport then took a taxi to 127 Troutman Street in Brooklyn, New York, where my first cousin Zyfer Pasholli lived.

Inga was clearly nervous about all the changes taking place, and I must admit that I couldn't blame her because I had no idea what to do next now that my time with the army was over. I had no trade, knew very little about the American way of life, and now had a responsibility to take care of and provide for another person.

This led to quite a lot of tension between Inga and me on that first day in the United States. It didn't take us long to have our very first argument as a married couple. We were still in the taxi on our way to Brooklyn when the fight broke out, in fact.

"You're forgetting the promise you made me before we were married," she insisted.

"And what promise was that?" I asked flippantly.

"You promised that as soon as you were discharged, we would return to Germany and live there."

With all the stress of trying to figure out how we were going to get through the next day, let alone the next years of our lives, the taxi cab immediately after touchdown felt like the worst possible place and time to remind me of a promise I'd made. "Couldn't you have at least waited until I actually *received* my discharge papers to bring all this up?" I snapped. "Why do you have to try and spoil our very first day in America?"

She steeled up as if trying not to cry.

I should have taken the hint that it was time for cooler heads to prevail, but I just couldn't let the argument go. "Inga, I've been looking forward to this day since I was twelve years old. Please don't spoil this for me. Besides, this is not the time or place to discuss our future!"

She burst into tears and began apologizing. I felt terrible for raising my voice at her, so I quickly began apologizing too.

When we arrived at Zyfer's, the driver got out of his cab and pointed out the house for us. I paid him the cab fare then held out a tip for him, but he shook his head, refusing to accept it.

"Some other time, soldier," he said. "This one's on me. I wish you and your bride the best. Good luck to you!"

I thanked him, and he drove away.

The only luggage we had was my duffle bag and a small suitcase for Inga. The army was to ship the rest of our clothes and furniture to New York within thirty days. I had no idea what we would do with it all once it arrived, let alone how we would get it back to Germany if Inga ever did manage to win our running argument.

We walked up to the front of the house and stood there for a moment, trying to decide which bell to ring. One bell was for the first floor and the other for the second.

Since I didn't know which floor my cousin lived on, I decided to ring both. Quickly, the door opened, and Zyfer's wife Violet was standing there with her mother beside her.

"It's Pertef!" Violet said, her face lit with surprise.

After hugs and greetings, I introduced Inga. Then Violet led us to the first-floor apartment where her parents lived. Inga and I stayed with Violet's parents and their two sons, Atlas and Lek, in the downstairs apartment. Since they had an extra bedroom, they told us we could stay as long as we liked. In the few months we lived with them, I came to love this old-fashioned and genuine Albanian family. They treated us like royalty—far better than we ever could have expected.

On April 5, 1963, I received an honorable discharge from the United States Army. As the clerk was preparing the discharge papers, he noticed that I had been processed into the army in Frankfurt. He told me that according to army regulation, I was entitled to a free trip back to Germany—a trip that I could use any time I wanted.

I was glad that Inga hadn't been there to learn this fact, or I'd have never heard the end of it. By then, I had already made up my mind. As far as I was concerned, I had worked too hard to become an American citizen only to turn my back on this country that I so loved and return to Germany. She would just have to learn to love America as much as I did.

Within a month, I found a job in a meat factory. The job was tough, but the pay was good. Sometime after our furniture arrived from Germany, Inga and I leased a small apartment on the same street where Zyfer and his family lived. Here, we got down to the business of trying to make a normal and happy life for ourselves despite the pall of Inga's homesickness and my resultant guilt hanging over us.

That was part of why I was so grateful to have such a significant distraction one Saturday afternoon. Gani surprised me with a visit. It had been over two years since I'd last seen him, so it was a happy reunion. Our orders might have taken us to different bases by the end of our careers, but since we had joined up at the same time, Gani and Bardhyl had received their discharges on the same day I had. They had both settled in New York City as well.

It wasn't all good news, however. I was struck with grief when Gani informed me that Sokoli had been killed in a jeep accident while on a tour of duty in Alaska. The news struck a major blow, for Sokoli and I had been good friends who had endured some tough but memorable times together.

Sensing that I needed a change of subject, Gani put on a happier face and tried to redirect the conversation. "I was surprised when I heard you were settling in Brooklyn," he said. "I figured you would wind up in Connecticut with your father."

I shrugged. "I thought it would be easier to find work in Brooklyn since it's so much larger than Waterbury."

We shared a few drinks and laughed about the old days. When the hour grew late, I asked if he wanted to stay over, but he said he couldn't because of a job interview the following morning. So instead, we exchanged phone numbers and promised to stay in touch.

The following day, I was so melancholy about my conversation with Gani that I decided to call in sick for work. My mind raced with myriad thoughts, but none of them made sense. Gani's questioning of my decision to remain in New York, coupled with the tragic news about Sokoli, was making me feel uncertain about the course I was taking in life.

Perhaps sensing that I was feeling more fragile than usual, Inga spent the day putting pressure on me to make good on my promise to return to Germany. The whole day was nothing but argument, but by the evening, she had managed to convince me that I had to sit down and put everything about my life into perspective. It was time for some careful analysis—not just about what we would do next to survive but rather about what would be best for both of us.

After sleeping on it that night, I had come to a decision that I felt was clear but would be very difficult to explain to my young bride. Her resistance was plain on her face as I told her that, even though I had made the promise to live in Germany, I felt it would be best for us to make our home in America.

"But why do you want to stay here?" she replied. "You were happy in Germany. I just don't understand why you would want to start all over in this new place."

"You're asking me why I would want to stay here?" I said with wide eyes. "I'll tell you why—because I'm an American and a proud one. I worked hard for my citizenship. I love this beautiful country and its people."

When the realization that I had made my final decision set in, Inga's face dropped. Then a strange sort of defiance I had never seen from her before started to creep into her expression. It was clear what she was thinking: *You have made your decision, and I have made mine.*

I wanted to lash out, but the truth was that I couldn't blame her. Inga was very young and had never been separated from her family by such distance and for such a long time. In many ways, I could relate to her homesickness. I had lost my family home many times in my youth and had lost much of my family to Communist oppression. I had even lost my home country to that infernal struggle. The difference was that I had come to America voluntarily while Inga had come as a bride. I knew firsthand that homesickness is one of the worst illnesses a person can contract, particularly when you're forced into the circumstances that cause it.

We left the discussion unresolved, and in that fact, I realized that our marriage was in serious trouble. Even so, I still thought that time would repair the breach. Then one day when I came home from work, I found a note from Inga. She wrote that she had purchased a plane ticket and returned to Germany. It made me angry to read the words, but at the same time, it didn't come as a surprise. A part of me had been expecting her to flee.

I waited a few months to cool off before I decided to call her to see how she felt about getting back together. She suggested that I come to Germany so we could talk about our future. I missed her. Plus, a vacation sounded like a good idea, and I still had that free trip from the army. So I requested some time off work then called the army and made my travel arrangements.

It was wonderful to be with Inga again. The first few days together were perfect, but a strange uneasiness hung over us because we both knew that sooner or later the subject of our living arrangement would boil to the surface. "We could have a wonderful life together here, Pertef," she said on the third day. "Look how beautiful these few days have been for us."

I sat quietly until she had finished making her case. Then I gave a deep sigh.

"Inga, it's not just about my wanting to remain in America. Life here would be easier for you because you would be closer to your family, but for us as a couple, it would be very difficult. To get any kind of job, I'll have to learn German, and it'll take me at least three to four years to become fluent enough to get the kind of job that can provide us with a decent living. That means we'd be struggling financially for quite a few years. And yes, it would bother me to sacrifice an opportunity to live in the United States."

"You use that word *sacrifice*," she said with furrowed brow. "You're not really sacrificing anything by coming here to live with me. Germany is a free country with just as much opportunity as they offer in the U.S. But if you refuse to live here with me, then you'll be sacrificing our love and marriage."

I nodded through the pain that the observation caused me.

"If you truly love me," she said with tragic hope in her voice, "you can show me by making your home here with me. You do love me, don't you?"

I could see that she already had made up her mind to remain in Germany with or without me. "I love you, Inga, but we have a huge problem here. You should know me by now. I love America and will never give up my home there."

"Well, I can't leave my mother and little brother behind," she said sadly.

"What would happen to them if I left them alone?"

Inga's dog was barking by the door, wanting to go out, so we decided to take him for a walk. It was snowing hard that day, which felt like a bad omen. We walked around Inga's little village several times, speaking at length about our lives. Every time we endured this conversation before that day, I would get loud and angry, but this time, I remained calm. It was just so clear to me that the decision had already been made that it didn't seem right to argue any longer.

That day, we came to realize that our marriage wouldn't work. If we decided to try to maintain the relationship over the distance between us, it would take a small miracle for it to last even a short while. We both had strong ties and obligations to our families. She had her mother and little brother to care for, just as I had Father and

Uncle Arif in America. If I made the decision to live in Germany, it would devastate them.

The last day Inga and I were together was beautiful and painful, even though we both knew we were making the right decision and that we would probably never see each other again. We parted on pleasant terms, both of us having accepted the notion that fate was leading us in different directions.

I spent that night in Frankfurt and the next day took a flight to New York City. During the nine-hour flight home, I noted that it wasn't sadness I felt, but instead, a certain sense of relief from a responsibility that would never be fulfilling for either of us. Had there been children involved, I'm sure we would have made a different decision to keep the family together, but as it stood, I would never be able to make Inga happy.

Chapter 19

The day after I arrived home from Germany, I called a moving company and made arrangements to have my furniture hauled to Waterbury, Connecticut. There, I found a nice four-bedroom apartment with a large kitchen, bathroom, and living room. I needed the extra bedrooms because Father and Uncle Arif would be moving in with me, along with my cousin Nazmi, who was like a son to the elder men in the family. The three of them had lived together from the very first day of their escape from Albania, so their bond had become too tight to sever. Like the others, he too had to leave behind his wife Kike and child Ibrije when he escaped. I had no complaints because Nazmi was great company.

Waterbury was a pleasant town. I enjoyed living there for a couple of reasons. First, there were several hundred Albanians living in the community. The bulk of my five years in the army had kept me from immersing myself in my culture and spending time with masses of my countrymen. Now that I was able to spend time with so many of these honorable and beautiful people, I realized just how much I missed and needed them.

My best friend among the lot of them was Fiqiri Agolli, who like me at that time was single. He showed me around the city, always careful to point out the best weekend hangouts. He was a smart, nice-looking fellow who was only a few years older than I was. Most importantly, he was thoughtful and caring and always a big help to the Albanian people in the community. Most of the Albanian men living in Waterbury were just like my father—older men who had fled their native country to seek political refuge. As such, few of them spoke English. As a fluent speaker with a kind heart, Fiqiri assisted these men in finding jobs, scheduling doctor appointments, and acting as a translator for whatever their needs happened to be. He even provided transportation for those who couldn't get themselves around town.

For Fiqiri, volunteering in this way was the least he could do. He felt the same pain these men felt. He understood the sorrow that comes from separation from loved ones and the frustration about not being able to change it. After all, he too had family back home in the labor camps.

My arrival in Waterbury allowed me to team up with Fiqiri and take some of the load from his shoulders. It was easy for me at first because I hadn't yet found employment and had the days free.

One night during supper, Uncle Arif asked me to do a favor for a friend of the family. "Our friend Ymer Mancelli has engaged his son with a girl from Turkey," he said.

"What does that have to do with me?" I asked as I picked at my food. Then I set down my fork and chuckled. "Don't tell me I have to go to Turkey and bring the matching bride directly to the groom!"

"No, son," Uncle Arif said with an eye roll. "That job would be too easy for you. And anyway, who would be crazy enough to trust you with a beautiful eighteen-year-old girl?"

I pointed at my chest and feigned surprise.

"You have a good heart, son," Uncle Arif said with a wry smile. "But as far as women are concerned, our Albanian friends think you are a ladies' man. They call you Casanova!"

"Is that so?" I wasn't quite sure whether my uncle meant the comment as insult or compliment, but I had to admit I did love women.

"But, Uncle," I said after a time, "I thought Ymer's son was in his forties. How can his bride be eighteen?" I winked at Father. "I mean, you think he can handle her?"

Father's look of disapproval said he didn't share my humor in the matter. So I steeled up and got serious.

"What I'm trying to tell you is this," Uncle Arif cut in. "We need someone to hold down Ymer's son's job. That way, when he returns from Turkey with his bride, his job will still be here for him."

"So you're asking me to work his job for him while he's gone?"

He shrugged. "As you know, his son doesn't speak English at all. So it would be very difficult for him to find another job if he lost the one he has."

"And what's the job he has?"

"Dishwasher."

My lips parted in surprise. "So you're asking me to go wash dishes for him while he's gone?"

They spoke no words, but their gravely serious stares said it all.

"I don't know about this, Uncle," I said. "How long would I have the honors of working such a privileged position?"

"No more than a month," Uncle Arif said quickly. "I'm almost certain."

My father had been silent all this time, but now he spoke and with that same authority I remembered from my youth. "I wouldn't put a time limit on what we ask, Arif. And besides that, we're not asking Pertef. This is something he *will* do. He has no alternative but to respect our decision, so this conversation is over." He batted a dismissive hand. "Now let's talk about something else."

I laughed to myself when I realized that this wasn't a matter of a son respecting his father's wishes. Rather, it was a matter of family honor. Clearly, my father and Uncle Arif had already told Mr. Ymer that I would take his son's job for him. So I really didn't have any choice but to accept. For the next month or so, even though I was fluent in Albanian and English and trained by the best army in the world, I would serve the community as a professional dishwasher at an upscale downtown restaurant called The FrontPage.

The next morning, I shaved, showered, and—without thinking—put on my suit like I always did. By the time I made it halfway to the stairs, I realized how silly I looked going to wash dishes in a suit. But with the start of my shift only a few minutes away, I didn't have enough time to change into something more comfortable.

When I entered the dining room at The FrontPage, I came face-to-face with the hostess, a pretty, middle-aged woman with a nametag that read Hanna. "How many are in your party for lunch today?" Hanna said.

I shook my head. "I'm here to see the owner. Is he here yet?"

"Yes, Mr. Martin is in the kitchen. Just go straight ahead through the swinging doors."

The swinging doors had signs on them labelled "In" and "Out." Despite taking the correct door, the moment I entered the kitchen, I bumped into Mr. Martin. He was an elderly man with stooped shoulders, so the blow nearly knocked him over.

"Take it easy, young man," he said. "It seems to me that if this kitchen of mine doesn't kill me, *you* will."

We exchanged an awkward smile.

"What can I do for you?" he asked.

"I'm here to secure the dishwashing job for Ymer's son while he is gone," I replied.

"Are you Albanian?"

"Yes, I am."

Mr. Martin seemed surprised to see a younger Albanian, as most of my fellow countrymen living in the town were older. "Well, young man, come here behind the galley. And forget about washing dishes. I need someone to give me a hand in the kitchen. As far as the dishes are concerned, Ymer can handle that. He's a very experienced dish-washer, so I'm sure he can manage the work by himself until his son returns." He paused, looking back with his brow furrowed. "Would you please try and explain that to him for me?"

Ymer was loading the dishwasher when I approached him and told him in Albanian what Mr. Martin had just related to me. Ymer smiled and nodded to Mr. Martin. "Okay," he said, using the only English word he knew.

"Mr. Martin," I said, "I'm afraid I won't be much help to you in the kitchen. I assure you, sir, that I don't even know how to cook an egg."

"Let me worry about that," he replied with a shrug. "I'm a seventy-five-year-old man, and I know what I'm talking about. You seem like a smart kid, so I'm pretty sure I can teach you if you want to learn."

It didn't take me long to start liking my new profession. Mr. Martin was a good teacher and also an excellent chef. *Once again, luck is with me*, I thought. *I'm being taught a profession while getting paid at the same time!*

One Monday around eight o'clock in the evening, I was preparing the last dinner orders of my shift when something strange happened. It wasn't unusual that I would pass the time with thoughts of my poor, departed friend Sokoli, but on this night, I was struck with the odd notion that he would pay me a visit soon. *That's impossible,* I thought. *Sokoli is dead.*

I stopped for a moment, wanting to shake off this morbid feeling, but I just couldn't rid myself of the thought. It wasn't the first time I'd had this premonition over the past few weeks either. In fact, I'd been having a recurring dream about Sokoli riding to meet me on a beautiful white stallion. In the dream, he always brought an identical horse for me as a present. As I wrapped up my work, I tried to connect the dream with the premonition I was having but couldn't come up with a satisfying interpretation. So I tried to take my mind off Sokoli completely.

I was stacking the clean dishes from the dishwasher on the counter when I heard someone call out my last name. It was strange to hear because Sokoli was the only person who had ever referred to me that way. A chill caused me to shiver. *It can't be!* I thought. But when I turned around, I couldn't believe who stood there. It was Sokoli in the living flesh! I froze, that sensation that I was seeing a ghost creeping up my spine. The stack of dishes dropped from my hands and hit the floor, shattering into pieces.

He smiled.

"You son of a bitch, Sokoli!" I hollered. "All this time, I thought you were dead. Gani told me you died in a Jeep accident in Alaska."

Sokoli gave a casual shrug. "You heard right about my accident, my friend, but I'm afraid he was wrong about my death." He patted his chest. "Sokoli doesn't die."

"But *how?*"

"I jumped twenty feet high, landed on my feet, and told death to kiss my ass!" We both laughed as we hugged each other.

Our reunion was a raucous one, as Sokoli was always a likeable and funny man. Father and Uncle Arif professed that my friend fit into our family perfectly.

The next morning, I called Gani in Washington, DC. He was working as head waiter in an exclusive hotel, so it was tough to get him on the phone at first. But when I told him about Sokoli, he immediately dropped everything and drove his beautiful Thunderbird from Washington. It was wonderful to have two of my best friends in the same place again if only for a few days.

I worked at The FrontPage full time for over six months. With each day that passed, my confidence grew stronger. Eventually, I thought I might benefit from expanding my repertoire by working in a different restaurant. So the next morning, I picked up the Help Wanted section in the local newspaper. The ad at the top of the page called out to me: "New in Town—Hager's Steak and Seafood House—Cook Wanted." It seemed perfect for me, so I applied for the position of first cook.

Maybe it was my confidence and general know-it-all attitude, but for some reason, Hager's hired me. Little did I realize at the time that this whim of a decision to branch out as a cook would change my life forever.

I had been working at Hager's for less than two months when I met her. It was a Thursday afternoon when the general manager's wife came through the swinging doors into the kitchen with a new waitress in tow.

"And now let me introduce you to our Casanova," the GM's wife said.

The girl she introduced me to had jet-black hair she had pulled back into a French twist. The look accentuated just how pretty she was. In truth, I was a little awestruck by her sublime beauty. She had big eyes and soft features, and the way her lips curled into a shy smile made my heart skip.

"Hello, Casanova," she said in a voice just above a whisper.

"Hi, honey," I said, feeling much more disarmed than I sounded. "How are you?"

She held her head high in a display of uncommonly classy confidence. Then without a word, she turned sharply and walked away.

Wow! I thought. *She's as beautiful from the back as she is from the front.* I knew from the moment she proved willing to ignore me that I had to get to know this woman as quickly as possible.

In that effort, fate would help us along. In fact, she found reason to visit me in the kitchen as soon as she placed her very first order. She came rushing in, looking somewhat flummoxed already. Even in her anxiety, she was beautiful.

"Pertef," she said and I noted that she remembered my name, "I need to place an order, and I could sure use your help."

"Sure, baby," I said, trying to sound smooth. "I'll give you anything you want."

Her eyes narrowed into a glare that did nothing to dim the beauty of her features. "Your help with the order is all I'll need, thank you."

I tried not to look too floored by her moxie. "Well, in that case, sweetheart, you can place the order from right where you are, and I'll get to it when I can." My false bravado was dripping off me. "And another thing, you better make sure you're here when it's ready to pick up because I won't take the blame for a cold steak!"

"Yes, sir," she replied curtly as she handed in her order. With that, she returned to the dining room.

That was the longest night I'd ever spent in that kitchen because I found myself keeping one eye on the steaks that were on the broiler and the other on the swinging door to the dining room.

Toward the end of the evening, as the supper crowd began to dwindle, she came to pick up some shrimp cocktails.

"How'd it go for you tonight, Nancy?" I asked.

"It was a rat race in the beginning, but I felt more comfortable as the night went on." She rolled her eyes playfully. "At least I know where the coffee cups are now."

By now, I had come out from behind the counter and was standing beside her. I gently placed my hand on her back. "Well, you're looking good, honey!"

She spun around, her dark eyes flashing with anger. "Listen, buddy," she said. "If you ever lay a hand on me again, I'll cut your arm off and make Hungarian goulash out of it!"

I backed away a few steps, holding my hands up in feigned fright. "You can cut my arm off but not for Hungarian goulash. These arms are only good for Albanian stew."

"Same difference," she snapped as her almond-shaped brown eyes burned holes in me. "Just stay out of my way."

For the first time in my life, a woman I fancied had me tongue-tied. Then finally, I found my head. "You better treat me nice now because I think someday you'll be my wife."

She scoffed as she turned to leave the kitchen. "Over my dead body!"

We spent the remainder of the evening casting dirty looks at each other. It had been a long time since I'd been turned down so hard by a woman. *Just who the hell does she think she is?* I thought. After stewing on it for a while, I decided to give her a dose of her own medicine. From then on, she wouldn't find it so easy to work with me.

The next day passed in polite coldness. Nancy certainly knew how to respond to my pointed remarks. It didn't take me long to recognize that she had a quick wit and a sharp sense of humor. All my coworkers thought she was a terrific person, which really irritated me. Worse yet, I hardly knew this girl, and yet she was all I could think about. I had the sense that I had fallen in love with a girl who, by all appearances, hated my guts.

When a week of treating her coldly didn't work, I turned to kindness. To my delight, she accepted my change of mood with a pleasant one of her own. It seemed to me that she had begun to return my affection.

The next time I looked at the staff schedule, I saw that Nancy was the opening waitress for the coming Friday morning, so I requested to take the opening shift for that day as well. This meant that she and I would be the only ones working until lunchtime. I figured this meant that we would have plenty of time to talk and flirt and maybe build on this nice new rapport we carried for each other. But my plan was foiled when the lunch rush started early that day. For three full hours, we were absolutely slammed.

After the last of the lunch customers had gone, Nancy and I were the first to take a break. I brought an extra cup of coffee into the banquet room for her. I found her leaning against the wall as if trying to catch her breath. I handed her the coffee. She thanked me wordlessly and set it down beside her. She slid her cigarettes from her pocket, took one out of the pack, and put it in her mouth. Before she could open the matchbook cover, I held a light up for her.

"Thanks," she said and I noted not for the first time that her voice was one of the sexiest I had ever heard. "I felt like a building fell on me."

I don't know why, but this seemed like the best opportunity I was ever going to get. "Look," I said, trying to catch her gaze, "I'm a nice guy. I swear. Just give me a break, and I swear I'll prove it to you."

"I can't give you a break, Pertef. I can't give you anything for that matter. I'm married and have two sons."

My heart fell to my knees. I was so wounded that I had to flail to cover my tracks. "So what? Does the fact that you're married mean that you can't be friendly toward the people you work with?"

She blew a long stream of smoke. "Not your kind of *friendly*, Pertef." She smiled softly.

"Look, Nancy, I certainly don't want to break up a marriage, and I'm not looking for a readymade family. I just wanted to be your friend. Honest!"

"So we'll be friends. You know my terms. I'll expect you to be a gentleman and adhere to them."

I smiled impishly. "Well, friend, how about going out for a drink tonight?" She frowned.

"Only kidding!"

I enjoyed Nancy's laughter as much as anything I had ever enjoyed in my life.

Back then, I couldn't explain why I felt so strongly about her. But with the benefit of hindsight, I realize that my attraction to her set the stage for the rest of my life—a stage on which Nancy would play a central role.

Chapter 20

Nancy and I managed to keep our friendship casual for the next few weeks, but I still couldn't manage to temper my attraction to her. When she arrived one morning with a new hairdo, I lost all control.

"How do you like the new me?" she asked, motioning to her hair.

"The old you wasn't that bad," I quipped.

"Well, you certainly know how to brighten a girl's day," she said sarcastically.

"Baby, I'd love to brighten all your days." I don't know what made me say it, but I just couldn't hold back my true feelings any longer. "And I'm going to do just that."

She scrunched up her nose in the most adorable way. "What do you mean?"

"I'm going to marry you one of these days. Just wait and see."

She stood quietly for a moment before sighing. "Pertef, we talked about this. Hell will freeze over before I'd marry you. Even if I wasn't married already, I'd never consider the offer."

This charade that we called a casual friendship was eating away my insides, so I just had to share my true feelings. "Let's stop playing games. I want to put my cards on the table. I'm in love with you, and I'm going to make you my wife someday. I don't know when or how, but you'll see—one day, we'll be married."

She glared at me for a moment, but I guess something in my expression must have given her the impression that I was joking because she doubled up with laughter and playfully tapped me on the arm. "Oh, Pertef. You're too much."

So for the next several days, I reluctantly went back to behaving like a caring friend. When she told me that she was taking a two-week vacation to Atlanta to visit her family, I couldn't bear the thought of being apart from her for such a long time. It was that feeling that made me realize I had to find a way to get over this dangerous love. Nancy was a driven and dedicated woman, and even if she did have feelings for me, she would never jeopardize her family. Her husband and children had to come first.

Since I knew that she would be with her family on vacation, I felt that it was time to lick my wounds, to heal, and then to move on with my life. She gave me a wink then hugged me goodbye. The frustration I felt was almost more than I could bear. As much as I wanted to give her a piece of my mind about how she had toyed with me long enough, my love for her forced me to keep it to myself, return her embrace, and wish her a safe trip.

I started missing her before she was even gone, but I also knew that I couldn't go on playing this game with a married woman. Somehow, I would have to forget about Nancy—*somehow*.

As it happened, Sokoli and I had been planning a trip to Canada to coincide with Nancy's vacation. So when my old friend called from Washington to see if I was still in on the idea, I quickly told him to pick me up in Waterbury. He arrived in a brand new fire-engine-red Chevy convertible with all the bells and whistles. As we headed north, we laughed about all those hilarious times and old friends we'd shared.

It was just the medicine I needed to begin my healing process from a broken heart.

"Forget about her, Pertef," Sokoli kept telling me whenever I brought up Nancy. "A situation like that will mean nothing but trouble for you from beginning to end."

I tried to convince him that he was wrong—that not every situation like this one was so cut and dried—but my heart just wasn't in it. After all, at that very minute, she was on her way to Georgia on a family vacation, and I was on my way to Canada with Sokoli. The situation spoke for itself: hopeless and helpless.

We stopped for the night outside Montreal. After finding a motel, we began looking for a good place to eat. Sokoli suggested that after dinner, we visit a few night spots and possibly meet some girls. I agreed, thinking what better time than right now to get on with my life.

After a dinner where Sokoli spent lavishly as always and received the reciprocal level of attention from our waitress, we stopped by several lounges until we found a dimly lit, cozy joint with a surplus of unattached females. Within five minutes, we had met two girls and invited them to our table. We spent the remainder of the evening ordering drinks, dancing, and turning on our charm. Maybe it was because I was still drowning my sorrows about Nancy, but I drank so much that I don't even recall the ride back to the motel that night.

I woke the next morning with a roaring headache. "Oh, Sokoli," I groaned. "Why did you let me drink so much?"

"That was all on you, my friend."

"I don't even remember the end of the night." I gave him a bleary-eyed stare.

"Did we have a good time?"

"We had a great time," he said with a shrug. "Too bad you don't remember. I got those girls' telephone numbers before they left. If you're still too in love to want your girl's number, I'd be happy to keep them both." He laughed.

I could only groan again in reply.

"I'll go get some coffee while you get your shower," he said, sounding entirely too chipper for a man who'd been out all night drinking. "Then we'll be on our way."

In Toronto, we visited some old army buddies and fellow Albanians. We enjoyed the week with our friends, did some sightseeing, and had some wonderful food. Even so, try as I might, I couldn't get Nancy out of my head. I found myself counting the days until we started for home and I could see her again.

When finally we returned, Sokoli dropped me off at my apartment, and I ran in to shower and dress before heading for the restaurant. I still had two vacation days left, but I was anxious to find out if

Nancy had returned. I casually walked into the banquet room amidst screams of welcome and asked directly if Nancy was back.

Betsy, another of the waitresses, told me that they had received postcards from Nancy.

"Actually, I think there's a postcard addressed to you in the office," she said casually.

I tried not to look too much like I was bolting for the office, but that's essentially what I did. It was a scenic postcard from Virginia with a little note on the back reminding me to be good. "I'll be returning with my sister," it read. "I think you'll like her." I ignored the implied meaning behind the words and instead focused on the date of Nancy's return. It looked as if she would be back to work the next day.

My heart leapt, and my longing burned once more.

The next morning, Nancy came bouncing into the restaurant. She looked tanned and rested. I smiled a warm welcome to her as she made the rounds, filling everyone in on her vacation. She stopped when she got to me and whispered a soft greeting. "My sister can't wait to meet you this afternoon," she said with a wink.

"I don't know," I said hesitantly.

"You'll love her, Pertef. I promise. Her name is Sherry, and she is almost exactly like me."

"No one could be almost exactly like you." My tone was mournful, so Nancy gave a playful roll of her eyes and told me to perk up.

"It'll be great," she insisted. "I'm going to bring her in after my shift to talk to Mr. Lemkin about working part time as a cashier on weekends."

I stayed after work that afternoon and kept a faithful watch on the swinging doors to the banquet room. Finally, when Nancy strolled in with Sherry in tow, I felt like someone had punched me in the gut. What a knockout! From head to toe, she was as flawlessly beautiful as her sister. The only difference was where Nancy had more elegant features that showed maturity, Sherry's was the carefree gaze of youth. Nancy's hair was jet black, and Sherry's was dark brown. Nancy was more slender and busty, but Sherry had a face like an angel. Their devastating smiles, however, were the same.

"Pertef," Nancy said as she cordially extended a hand toward her sister, "this is my sister Sherry I've been telling you about." She smiled probably because it was clear that I was awed by Sherry's beauty. I knew immediately that no matter how pretty I found her, she would never replace my adoration for her older sister. Still I decided to play alon since setting the two of us up was clearly what Nancy wanted.

"Well, you certainly weren't exaggerating," I said. "She's beautiful." Sherry gave a shy smile that I returned with a wink.

At Nancy's urging, I invited Sherry to join me for a Greek wedding the next weekend before she started work at the restaurant. I still knew that I loved Nancy, but our situation had my thinking so distorted that I thought going out with Sherry would cure me of my love or, barring that, would at least give me an excuse to be closer to her during our free time.

In the end, despite the forced distraction and despite how wonderful Sherry proved to be during the wedding and the few innocent weeks we spent time together thereafter, my love for Nancy never waned. I felt badly for Sherry, who eventually developed a sort of puppy love for me, but I just couldn't shake my feelings for her sister.

Nearly every night, I would toss and turn about how to overcome this powerful love that was eating me alive. Eventually, Nancy began to think that I was using her sister to make her jealous, and in some ways, that was true. But when she reacted to the situation with fury, all it did was convince me further that my feelings for Nancy were requited. If she didn't care for me in the same way I cared for her, then she would have been happy at the idea that Sherry was falling for me.

Whatever the case, I knew that I had to do something about this strange love triangle as soon as possible. Nancy was too angry for me to just call her up and arrange a meeting, and she was giving me the cold shoulder at work. So I decided that the only thing to do would be to wait until she reached out to me.

I spent the next few days thinking about how terrible all this made me feel and how doomed the whole thing probably was anyway. Even if I could somehow get Nancy to see that we were meant to be together, there were my father and uncle and the Albanian culture to contend with. I was reminded of this one day after my shift at work. I had gone to the local coffeehouse, where a group of older Albanians gathered daily to rehash the political issues that kept their homeland captive and to share news and gossip from their meager letters from home. They all shouted out greetings as I entered.

I had high respect for these men, and they all seemed to hold me in high regard.

At least they enjoyed hearing my stories, which always made them laugh. Even when the stories were about chasing beautiful women, the common theme from these men was always that I would one day find a nice Albanian woman to marry when I was ready to settle down.

"Pertef, Pertef!" one of the men said. "Sit down and tell us what has been going on in your life."

With all the smiles looking back at me, I felt my heart sink. *Pertef, you're absolutely out of your mind!* I thought. *Even if you manage to convince Nancy that your love is true, you'll never convince your Albanian circle of family and friends to accept her.*

That heavy thought caused me to sigh. "Nothing much to report," I told them.

They groaned playfully in reply. Then to my relief, they got back to passing the time with politics. I listened as they barked their political opinions and laughed with each other for another ten minutes or so before I saw something out of the corner of my eye.

It was the owner of the coffeehouse, a man named Tefik Lindraku. I knew his family from when I was in the labor camp, so Tefik and I often talked at length about how they were faring. When Tefik motioned that I had a call, I jumped from the table and ran to the phone. The shop owner went back to his work before I arrived, so I found the receiver dangling on the hook.

"Hello, this is Pertef."

"Pertef, this is Nancy," came the familiar voice.

My chest felt suddenly tight. "What can I do for you, Nan?"

There was a long, uncomfortable pause. "I want to meet with you tonight. We really need to discuss some things."

"Where?"

"Do you know the pizza house across the bridge in Watertown?" I had been there before, so I told her I would meet her there that evening.

"I'll let you buy me a cup of coffee," she said wryly.

It was good to hear her since of humor return. "It'll be my pleasure. See you tonight."

*****

When I arrived at the pizza shop, Nancy's car was nowhere to be found, so I waited in the car and smoked a cigarette, glancing nervously at every car that passed. Finally, I spotted her slowing down to make the turn into the parking lot. I walked to her car to open the door.

"Come on," I said firmly. "I'll get you that coffee."

She nodded as I reached for her arm to help her from the car. She kept silent as I made the first move and gave her a hug. Then we walked quietly into the restaurant.

Inside, I was pleased to see that the place wasn't busy. At last, we would be able to have an uninterrupted conversation and some privacy to discuss whatever Nancy came to say.

"Are you hungry?" I asked.

"Not really," she replied, feigning disgust. "Anyway, is it safe to eat here?"

I laughed. The place was a little dumpy, but the pizza smelled delicious. "Let's take our chances."

She stared down at her hands as if pondering something deeply. The tension was thick enough to cut with a knife. Not knowing what else to do, I reached across the table for her hand. She didn't resist. I'm not sure why, but I could sense that now was the time I had been waiting for since the moment I met her.

"I love you," I said. "Truly. You know that, don't you?"

Her eyes filled with tears.

I tried to gently reach across the table and wipe them away. "Hey, that's not any reason to cry, is it?"

Finally, she looked up at me. "It's every reason to cry, Pertef. I'm doing everything in my power to fight this. There are too many people in our lives that will be hurt if this goes any further." Her gaze was pleading as if she didn't have the power to end this herself and she expected me to do it for her. She tried desperately to explain to me all the reasons our feelings for each other should stop, but they were just words to me—words I had already pondered and didn't want to hear.

"Believe me when I say that I've fought with this since the first day I saw you," I said. "I've tried to get you out of my head. Even when I agreed to go out with Sherry, I tried to convince myself that if I dated her, she would eventually replace the feelings I have for you. Now I know what I really wanted was a way to stay near you and, in some small way, to be a part of your life. I quickly realized that it was a mistake. No one will ever take your place in my heart or in my mind."

"But, Pertef—"

"I have feelings too," I interrupted before she could object again. "I've loved you from the moment we met. This is our destiny. I know it! I don't know how, but we will spend our lives together. One day, we will be a family. You're asking me to change the way I feel, but I can't change destiny."

"But I have a family—" the way she trailed off said that she had her doubts about her family situation.

"I'll wait for you," I said. "It doesn't matter how long as long as I know that someday we can be together."

She sighed and looked away, shaking her head distantly for a long time. "I know how you feel. You've been very clear about that. And now you know that I'm also struggling with my emotions. But I think of my boys—the Christmas mornings they've shared with their mommy and daddy, the vacations we've taken as a family, all the things that children make their childhood memories from."

"You don't think we can be that happy together as a family?" I asked.

"That's not what I'm saying." She looked down at her hands again, her lips quivering before she returned her gaze to me. "If I pursue that happiness, it will destroy my children's lives as they know them."

"But what about *your* life? What about *your* feelings and emotions?"

"Regardless of the feelings between me and my husband, the boys love their father, and he loves them. I have the power to keep my family together or to destroy it. It's all up to me, and I don't know how to deal with it."

I took deep and sincere pause at the notion that this meant she was seriously considering being with me.

"I have a lot of soul searching to do, and I need some time to set my mind straight," she said.

"I'll do whatever it takes," I said. "I'll make it as easy on you as I can."

"Thank you, Pertef. I know you mean that." She reached out and placed her hand over mine. She tried to force a smile, but it quickly faded. "Please know that you're not the cause of this situation. This is something I have to work out on my own. There must be a reason that I could be swayed away from my family obligations so easily. I need to find out what's in my heart and my head in relation to my situation at home. Then maybe I can make a sensible decision."

My heart soaring from the possibility of it all, Nancy and I tried to calm ourselves and enjoy our coffee over forced small talk. When the waitress returned to take our food order, we gave each other one look and declined, preferring instead to part ways and be alone with our thoughts.

I paid the small bill and walked Nancy to her car, where we silently hugged for a long while. When we parted, Nancy said nothing. She just turned, got into her car, and pulled off.

We were both on the schedule for work the next morning. I clocked in first. Nancy showed up fifteen minutes later. I was anxiously waiting for her to acknowledge me with a smile or a good morning, but there was nothing. She simply said hello without any warmth, poured her coffee, and left.

Hurt and confused, I watched as she passed through the double doors from the kitchen. I quickly wiped my hands on my apron and headed to the banquet room after her.

"What's wrong with you this morning?" I demanded. "You've certainly changed your attitude from yesterday. Did something happen when you got home last night?"

"Yes, it did," she said. "I went home to my boys and husband and couldn't stand myself for the thoughts I was having."

I drew a breath to object, but she cut me off.

"Pertef, you don't understand. I'm not thinking about whether my husband and I love each other. I have wondered many times if there ever was any real love between Bob and me. But when it comes to marriage, you need so much more than love. Bob provides for us, and he loves his children. He isn't abusive or an alcoholic. He's done nothing that would give me a valid reason to leave him. The fact that it's just an existence rather than a relationship isn't grounds to destroy my family." Then with tears in her eyes, she added, "This has to end, here and now."

I stood before her, stunned at the words I was hearing. "How are we going to work in the same place and put an end to this?" I said with urgency. I half sat and half fell into the chair next to her, my ears ringing and my body completely numb.

"I've thought about that," she said. "I'm going to tell Bob that I want to quit and find another job. I'll think of a reason that will satisfy him."

I wasn't taking any of this well. I made a serious effort to get up from the chair but slumped back down. *It can't end like this*, I thought. *I have to convince her that our life together makes the risks worthwhile.* My eyes had misted over by the time I looked over at Nancy. I could tell that she was ready to break, so instead of speaking my mind, I quietly left her sitting at the banquet table to finish her coffee.

That night, I couldn't sleep from wondering if she was okay. I knew that Nancy and I could work through anything if we were together, but since that wasn't going to happen, I knew I had to do something. I couldn't let her hurt like this any longer. Having her in my life was the most important thing to me, but I had created too much pain for both of us. My heart ached more each time I saw the unhappiness on her face.

Then it hit me. If she was to be my destiny, it would happen whether I pursued her or not. In fact, it would happen whether I stayed in Connecticut or not. For some reason, I was struck with the overwhelming urge to move to California. The thought of leaving my father and uncle pained me but not nearly as much as the thought of living anywhere near the woman I loved without being able to do anything about it.

The next day, I returned to work and immediately sought out Nancy.

"Okay," I told her, the two of us having found our far corner of the banquet room where we could have a discussion beyond prying ears. "I'll leave you alone if that's what you want. I've been thinking about going to California. If I can't have you with me, then I need to be as far away from you as I can get. Maybe that's what we both need to begin the healing process and get on with our lives."

When she sighed, it was as if a great weight had left her shoulders. "That may be the best for everyone involved. I know it doesn't seem like it right now, but once the hurt has passed, life will go on for *both* of us."

"Nan, I know I'll never love anyone as much as I love you. But maybe you're right. Maybe this is the best way to see if we're meant to be together. If the way I've always felt about you is indeed our destiny, then God will make a way for it to happen."

We embraced tightly, knowing the days ahead would be difficult for both of us.

"You'll write to me, won't you?" she said. "I'll want to know that you made it to California okay."

"Sure, I'll write," I said, pulling back and forcing a wry smile. "But doesn't that seem a little ridiculous to you? I'm driving three thousand miles because we need to be separated from each other, and then you ask me to drop you a line when I get there so you'll know I'm okay?" She grinned in reply.

"I will write," I promised. "But I can't promise that I'll be able to control my feelings. Until you tell me you feel absolutely nothing at all for me, I'll always tell you how much I love you and want you in my life."

She seemed to swoon. "Just make sure to keep it clean in the letters, okay?" she joked.

Then we both seemed to feel the weight of what we had just decided. We were alone in the banquet room, and I could sense that this was the final scene of our saga.

"I'm so sorry, Pertef," she said.

"For what?" I asked breathlessly.

"For the unhappiness I've caused you. I should have never allowed myself to become emotionally attached, but it happened before I realized it. Now I have to try and undo what has happened."

"You don't need to apologize. I'm the one who should be sorry. And besides, this will all work out for the best. I'm sure of it."

Nancy left first, departing through the dining room directly instead of passing through the kitchen. I waited and watched the swinging doors until the motion stopped, all the while wondering if I really meant what I had said about it all working out for the best. Somehow, I never felt as positive about anything when she wasn't there beside me.

When I told them I was going to California, my father and Uncle Arif didn't take the news well. But when I explained to them that I felt like I just needed to get away for a while to clear my head and think about settling down, they perked up about the idea. They had been trying for a while to arrange a marriage for me and had even gone so far as to urge me to take a trip to Turkey to meet with the girl they believed to be the best candidate, so hearing that I was at least thinking about tying the knot seemed to appease them.

It was two weeks before I could find another cook to replace me. Then I spent another week showing him around the kitchen and helping him with the ordering and menus. Once I had made all the necessary arrangements for the trip, I felt the loneliness creeping over my body. Nancy tried to remain upbeat and reminded me regularly that we were doing the right thing for everyone concerned, but as usual, my heart wasn't listening. The last time we had a minute to talk alone at work, I promised her that we would spend some time together before I left.

The two of us knew that parting would be difficult, but we promised each other that our goodbyes wouldn't be tearful. On a Tuesday morning, I called Nancy and told her that I would be leaving the next day and wanted to see her before I left. She asked me to come by her house that evening after the children had gone to sleep.

Little did I know that she and her sister Sherry had planned a little going-away party for me. When I arrived, I only had time to ring the doorbell once before the door flew open and there was Nancy, tumbling into my arms.

"Pertef!" she said as she pressed her cheek to my chest. "I was so worried you wouldn't be able to come by tonight. I'm so glad you're here!"

Her eagerness to see me was as refreshing as it was confusing, so I gave her a smile. "Well, hello, baby," I said slyly. "I'm happy to be here. If I hadn't made it, the person that did ring the doorbell would've had a pleasant surprise." I laughed at her embarrassment. It felt good to put my arm around her waist as we walked into the house.

"Sherry, Pertef's here!" Nancy called on her way into the kitchen. Sherry ran past her in the opposite direction and threw her arms around my neck.

"I've got girls throwing themselves at me tonight," I said with a laugh. I tried to keep it light, but the truth was that their welcome left me completely confused and wondering if I was making the right decision to leave.

I caught her eyes across the room, and she smiled back as she gracefully set out the glasses for a toast. She looked stunning in her cocktail dress. She insisted that we set up around the coffee table in the living room, so I sat on the large sofa. Almost immediately, Nancy took a seat beside me. She leaned back against the cushions of the sofa with her head down. I reached over to pull her chin up and could see the tears in her eyes ready to spill down her cheeks.

"What's wrong?" I whispered.

"I really thought that I could pull this off tonight," she said. "But I don't think I can."

I sighed and gave Sherry a look that said she should leave us for a moment. She didn't hesitate.

"Listen," I said to Nancy as I tried to hold her gaze. "Regardless of what we've agreed on, you know I'll be back. I can't and won't stay away from you forever. So this isn't goodbye. It's just 'I'll see you later.' You understand?" She smiled and lovingly tapped me on the cheek.

We were both unaware that Sherry had returned and was standing in the doorway.

"Okay," Nancy said. "The sad goodbyes are over. So let's eat." She disappeared into the kitchen, returning with a platter of cold cuts and rolls, which she set on the coffee table before leaving again. When she returned, Sherry came with her.

Each of them carried a brightly wrapped package.

"For me?" I asked, trying not to show my embarrassment as I grabbed for the gifts. The first box contained a cardigan sweater. I held it up and gave them a look that said I approved. It fit me perfectly when I tried it on.

The other package was smaller. Nancy handed it over, and I pulled her in to sit next to me as I opened it. Inside was a beautiful watch. "Thank you, baby," I said. "I love it! I'll wear it and think of you."

"Whenever you look at it, I want you to remember the time we had together as friends."

I chuckled. "Not only that, but I'm going to use this watch to count the time until we can be together."

She rolled her eyes playfully.

"I'm going to make a few serious decisions while I'm away," I said. "And I hope that you do the same."

After we'd spent a few hours eating, drinking, and discussing my plans for California, I could sense that it was time to say our goodbyes. Sherry had left the room by then and was sitting at the kitchen table reading a book. Nancy and I walked into the kitchen, where I brushed Sherry's arm with my hand to let her know we were there. She stood up and hugged me.

"Take care of her for me, will you?" I said.

"You know I will, Pertef!"

I kissed her on the cheek and thanked her. "You're a beautiful girl," I said sincerely. "Inside and out."

"Oh, I know all that already," she quipped.

With a sad laugh, the three of us walked slowly to the front door for one last goodbye. There, I threw my arms around the two sisters and told them that I would be seeing them soon. Even as I let go, even as I walked down the steps, even as I slid into my new 1965 Chevy SS, and even as I drove away, I could feel them watching me. I stared back at them in the rearview until they were little more than specs in my rearview mirror.

California, here I come, I thought darkly.

Chapter 21

Gani had volunteered to help me make the drive to California. He arrived around three o'clock that morning, mere hours after I said goodbye to Nancy and hours before my father and Uncle Arif would awake. I didn't want to clash with them anymore over the decision to leave, so I decided to go while everyone was still asleep.

We loaded my car and left Connecticut. The trip took approximately one week. I was twenty-six years old and by that time had traveled most of Europe while in the army, but I had no idea how big and beautiful America was. Every state we passed through had its own character and beauty. For most of the trip, Gani and I spoke almost exclusively about either our love for the United States or my love for Nancy.

After arriving in Los Angeles, we went to stay with our friend Skender Kacani, who worked in an upscale Italian restaurant called Feoria de Italia. The place catered to the elite, so Gani and I were excited about the possibility of seeing a few movie stars. Immediately, I loved everything about California. The beaches were beautiful and the weather gorgeous. I could have easily made my home there. I loved it so much that the next time I called Father and Uncle Arif, I tried to persuade them to move to the West Coast. Predictably, they told me that they were too entrenched in Waterbury to leave. I couldn't blame them. They had made their home there, along with their many friends.

Gani and I stayed with Skender for four months before we decided to return to Connecticut. It is said that time is the best healer. By the back end of our trip, I still thought of Nancy often but decided to let everything work out as it was meant to be.

The drive home seemed to take far longer than the drive west. When we reached Waterbury, Gani decided that he would stay and visit with my family and the community for a week before returning to Washington. When it was time for him to leave, my heart was heavy. We'd formed an even stronger bond on that wonderful trip, and I knew I would miss him.

I allowed myself a few days to settle back in with my family before I stopped by Hagar's to say hello to everyone. I wasn't sure whether I wanted Nancy to be there or not but made up my mind the moment I saw her. She was every bit the vision I remembered leaving behind, only now she had nothing but smiles for me. Casually, she approached and hugged me around my neck. Her scent—one that I had not forgotten—was almost more than I could take. I knew right then that there was no way I could ever come back to work at this place. Besides, all the way back from California, I had been thinking about how it would be better to work for myself from now on. Since the only trade I truly knew was cooking, it seemed like it would make sense to own my own restaurant.

When I first moved to Waterbury, I'd met a Jewish man named Mr. Abraham. Back then, he had described himself as a businessman who owed his great success to buying and selling real estate. Figuring that he would be my best resource for questions about what it takes to own a business, I set up a meeting with him.

"Pertef," he said as our coffee cups steamed on the café table between us, "I'd rather see you sell pencils on the street than work for someone else. Owning your own business is the only way you can gain the experience and knowledge you need to be successful."

"I agree," I said. "I just don't know where to start."

"Well then, you came to the right place," he told me, proudly placing a hand on his chest. He was a short, stocky man with thinning hair that he kept longer on the sides. "There is a husband and wife in downtown Waterbury who have owned their restaurant for many years. They're old and business has dropped off considerably. The restaurant has become a burden for them, and they're ready to retire. So they're anxious to sell. Why don't you go by and talk to them?"

I didn't much like the idea at first since I was familiar with the area and knew that a friend of the family had a restaurant in the same vicinity. But something sent me to talk to the restaurant owner anyway. I had a mere eighteen hundred dollars to my name at the time, but I figured it was worth it to at least pursue the idea. After all, this was America. The American Dream assured that with enough hard work, I would succeed.

So I decided to visit the store. I sat down at the counter and ordered a cup of coffee. When the owner himself delivered the cup, I struck up a conversation.

"I heard from someone that you might be interested in selling your place," I said.

"Well, you heard right," he said slowly. He was an elderly man with a prominent nose, large ears, and hair far grayer than his eyebrows.

"How much?" I asked casually.

"Fifteen thousand dollars."

Since I knew that the place wasn't worth nearly that much, I figured he was just throwing numbers at me to get my reaction. I thought about it for a minute before countering. "Now I want to give you a price, but here's what I'm going to do instead. I have some money in my pocket, and I'm going to take it all out and lay it on the counter. Whatever amount is there, I will keep three hundred for cleaning the store, painting, and for startup."

I laid out the money and began counting it. From his eyes, I could see that the owner was counting the money with me.

When we had finished, he said in a shocked voice, "You only have eighteen hundred?"

"No," I replied with a shrug. "Fifteen hundred. Remember, I told you that I need to hold out three hundred to start the business."

His eyes were wide with disbelief. "You've got to be kidding me," he said, aghast.

I calmly began removing the money from the counter and putting it back in my pocket. Then I paid for my coffee, thanked him, and started for the door. As soon as I opened the door, he called after me.

"Wait a minute, young man," he said.

I turned and gave him a casual gaze.

He looked defeated but resigned to the value I had offered him. He gathered himself for a moment before responding. "You just bought yourself a restaurant."

To this day, I still don't know why he accepted my offer. It was so lowball that I had a hard time masking my surprise as we shook hands. I can only think about the lucky stars under which I must have been born.

When my excitement died down and reality set in, I knew I would need help to make this work—good, honest, dependable help. The first call I made was to Gani.

"I bought a restaurant in Waterbury," I told him. "And I want you to go into business with me."

"But I have a good job here, Pertef," he said. "I make a good living already."

Persistence has always been one of my strong suits, so I kept after him, refusing to take no for an answer. As any faithful friend would do, he eventually came around to the idea.

Gani arrived a few days later. We decided to have lunch at our friend's restaurant—the one near which my new restaurant would be situated. I guess I was expecting them to congratulate me for going into business for myself, but their reaction was just the opposite.

"What makes you think you can make a go of it, Pertef?" they asked, their expressions all eyebrows and pursed lips. "There's hardly enough customers to keep us in business. The last thing we need is another competitive restaurant in the area."

The negative response hurt me, and it seemed to put off Gani. My initial reaction was to think they were being selfish for believing that all the town's restaurant patrons should belong to them. At the same time, I respected these men, so I felt I should be honest in my reply.

"I respect you," I said calmly, "but now I'm going to tell you why you have no business. Your customers come in hungry, the portions are small, the prices are high, and they leave hungry. I'm going to give my customers more than what they pay for. They'll come back and bring friends with them. Like it or not, I have no doubt that my business will be a success."

So with Gani's help, the restaurant opened. We called it Pete's Luncheonette, and we specialized in New York-style deli sandwiches. Waterbury had yet to commit to its recent sprawl of strip malls and shopping centers. Back then, it was mostly individual stores lining the streets. Ours was merely another storefront tucked in among the many others.

I had heard that Nancy's younger sister Pam had moved to Connecticut and that both she and Sherry were living with Nancy. Since I needed some waitresses and since I knew it was still the best idea to avoid regular contact with Nancy, I asked the younger girls if they wanted to come work at Pete's Luncheonette. Both Pam and Sherry agreed.

This was a time when almost all restaurant waitresses wore white uniforms, so I dared to be different. The uniforms I chose for Pam and Sherry featured black skirts and red blouses, the colors of the Albanian flag. They really stood out and looked sharp. It helped that both girls had charming personalities and beautiful smiles. When we first opened, they would stand on the sidewalk outside the restaurant, inviting people in to try our lunch. The news quickly spread about the quality and quantity of our food, and soon, we were packed all the time. Pete's Luncheonette was a huge success.

The business grew much faster than we had expected. We were all running in a frenzy just to keep up with the daily crowd. The old saying proved true: God takes care of fools and babies.

During that time, as busy as we were, Gani and Pam somehow found the time to fall in love. They would elope shortly thereafter.

Sometime during that first year in business, my cousin Syrja and his brothers Fadil and Selman escaped Albania and settled in Waterbury. They wanted me to sell Pete's Luncheonette to them, and since I figured I could set up another restaurant fairly easily, I agreed. This way, they would be able to begin in an established business, which would make it easier for them to get by after their transition from captivity. The problem was that they were not fluent in English, so Gani worked with them for a year or so until they felt comfortable running the business alone.

Meanwhile, I was making plans to open a new restaurant with Gani and a Greek friend of mine named Billy Tsavolis. We found a nice place in a shopping center in New Haven, Connecticut. There, we opened Olympian Diner. We worked together for six months, but regardless of what we tried, Billy and Gani never seemed to get along. They would argue over anything and everything. Their disagreements escalated to the point of them arguing in front of customers. I wasn't' sure how to handle the problem, but I knew something had to be done. So I called them into the office.

"Billy," I began, trying not to sound too exasperated, "you and Gani are my friends. We all know that we can't work together like this. So I'm giving you first option to buy Olympia Diner."

I could see that Gani was a little upset by it, but I knew he would get over it when I explained that he and I would use the profit from the sale to open another business together.

Billy called his brother in Canada and asked if he would be interested in buying the restaurant. At first, he agreed, but then the deal fell through, and Billy simply left the business to us. Gani and I tried to make a go of the diner on our own, but it still wasn't working. The two of us were on our feet working eighteen hours a day, seven days a week. It was more than we could handle. I didn't mind the hard work, but whenever the end of the week came and there wasn't enough money to pay the bills or the vendors, it was discouraging, to say the least.

I didn't worry much about myself because I had no responsibilities at the time. I was single, and if I was short on cash, I could travel to Waterbury and stay with my father. I was more concerned for Gani. I had dragged him from a stable income in Washington and gotten him involved in what was turning out to be a wild goose chase. Pam had just given birth to a beautiful baby girl, Mileta, so my friend and business partner now had a family to provide for.

At some point, Gani suggested that he go to work as a waiter in Milford, Connecticut, at an upscale continental restaurant named Fagan's. He was a good waiter and knew that he could make substantial money there. I agreed with his suggestion, and he began working part time at Fagan's. This worked for a while.

During this time, I heard that Nancy and her husband had divorced. At any other time in my life, this would have filled me with more excitement than I could contain, but the truth was that I was so busy I hardly had time to think about it. As Gani started working more and more at Fagan's, nearly all the responsibility for running the restaurant fell to me. The first chance I got, I called Nancy to see if she and Sherry would be interested in coming to work with me. Bob had moved to California by then, and Nancy was alone, so she jumped at the opportunity.

Nancy and I quickly kindled a relationship, and I found an apartment for all five of us in New Haven, Connecticut. Now that we were together, my love for Nancy blossomed in exactly the way I had always imagined. We were crazy about each other, and our personalities seemed to mesh perfectly. Between that and the fact that we had already spent such a long time loving each other without being able to do anything about it, we quickly decided to get married.

The only thing left was to convince my family that I wouldn't be betraying their honor or my culture by marrying a non-Albanian. I also had to explain to Nancy that taking me as a husband meant taking on my father and uncle as proper family.

"They will be living with us," I explained to her. "And since you aren't Albanian, they might be cold to you, at least at first." None of this seemed to faze her.

"In time, I know they will love you just as I do," I said. "But before we make anything official, I just want to make sure you're aware of what you're getting into here."

She assured me that she would be up for the challenge. Over the next couple of weeks, I kept reminding her about my familial obligations, and she kept saying that she would be fine. So we visited the local justice of the peace with the intention of tying the knot. After we made our introductions with the officiant, I asked for some time.

"Can we give Nancy about thirty more minutes to think about this?" I asked. I checked my watch, noting that my favorite show was on television. "I'll watch Bonanza while she thinks it over. Then if she's still in, we'll go through with it."

The justice laughed. "Boy, this guy is really tough," he said to Nancy. "If I were you, I'd take my time and think this over carefully."

Nancy giggled and said that she didn't need any time.

After exchanging our vows, we returned to the restaurant. While we were away, Pam, Sherry, and Nancy's third sister Loretta had decorated the restaurant to host our reception. We had prepared the food for the buffet the previous day, and Nancy baked a cake. Everything was perfectly arranged, and she was a beautiful bride. She had pulled back her raven hair to show her features, and she wore a long, form-fitting blue gown that looked as if it were made just for her.

Gani was there, and Sokoli made a surprise visit as well. Along with Nancy's sisters, they approached for hugs and kisses as soon as they saw us enter the reception.

Father and Uncle Arif followed soon after.

The reception was a wonderful time, and it sparked more than just one new romance that evening. The moment he met Sherry, Sokoli was taken by her charm and beauty, and the feeling was reciprocated. Since she was nearly fourteen years younger than Sokoli at that point, I tried to explain to him that he should go slow and be careful. Lovestruck as he was, he didn't hear a word I said. Six months later, Sherry moved to Washington, where she and Sokoli were married.

This meant three sisters from Alabama married three good friends from Albania. I couldn't imagine a stranger and more perfect arrangement.

As it turned out, my concern about how my father and Uncle Arif would take to Nancy had been almost unfounded. Father would take some winning over, but Uncle Arif and Nancy bonded almost immediately.

"Don't worry about anything," she often told them. "I'm going to take care of you three boys for the rest of my life."

I couldn't imagine a thought that could possibly make me happier.

*****

The year that followed, Nancy and I worked hard to get the Olympia Diner profitable. We put our hearts, minds, and souls into that business, determined to make it a success. Eventually, the restaurant began to turn around and show a profit. Between that and the fact that we now had more time to visit Gani, Pam, and little Milleta more often, life was good.

Then I had a dream that changed everything. This was one of the strangest dreams I had ever experienced, but because I had learned how to interpret them from Grandmother Aishe, I knew exactly what it meant. The only trouble was that because of the serious message behind it, I wasn't sure whether I should tell Nancy. I didn't want her to think that I'd gone crazy.

I didn't account for the fact that Nancy could always read my expressions as though she had known me all my life. We had just arrived at the restaurant. It was around five o'clock in the morning, and we were sitting at one of the tables, having our coffee as we prepared for the early breakfast customers.

"Pertef," she said, wrinkling her nose, "are you okay this morning?"

"Yes, I'm okay," I said, trying to look casual. "Why are you asking?"

"You're very quiet. And when that happens, I know there's something going on in your head." I sighed.

"Don't tell me you've had another one of your dreams."

Now I leaned back in my chair, resigned to share the truth of it. "As a matter of fact, I did have another one of my dreams. But this one was very strange."

"Most of your dreams are strange, except, of course, for those ones you say you wish would continue forever."

We laughed because we both knew what she meant.

"Will you interpret your dream for me?" she asked.

I nodded gravely. "I'll tell you about it, but please don't laugh because it's going to sound completely crazy." I took a quick sip of my coffee, relishing the crisp scent and the warmth of the mug between my hands. "I dreamed that a beautiful cow approached me. As it came closer, I realized that the cow was mine. Right between us was a huge bucket. I picked up the bucket and began milking the cow until it was dry and the bucket was full. Then Billy appeared and asked me if I would give him the cow."

"Wait," she interrupted. "You mean the Billy that helped you open this restaurant?"

I nodded then got back to explaining the dream. "So Billy wanted the cow. I hesitated for a moment, but then I thought, *Why not? This cow doesn't have anything else to offer me.* So I agreed to let Billy have the cow. As he pulled the animal away, I could see that its udders were completely dry."

Nancy looked starry-eyed as she flashed a wistful smile. "What does it mean?"

I shrugged. "I think it means that Billy is going to buy our restaurant."

Now she gave a good-natured frown. "Would you please stop with these dreams? You haven't seen or heard from Billy for over a year!"

"I'm telling you," I insisted. "Billy is going to buy the restaurant." There was just no doubt in my mind.

My wife rose from the table and made her way toward the counter. "Well, you were right, Pertef. That dream was ridiculous. What does a cow have to do with selling the restaurant?"

"You will see. Mark my words, the dream will come true."

Before we opened for breakfast that morning, I heard a knock on the front door. I had been certain of my dream's prescience, but even I was surprised at how quickly it came to pass. There at the door stood Billy Tsavolis. Nancy looked like she had seen a ghost.

Billy and I sat down at the table while Nancy went to the kitchen to fix us breakfast.

"Do you know why I'm here?" my friend began.

"I do know, yes," I said. "You came here to buy my restaurant."

Billy looked surprised, so I began telling him about the dream I'd had the night before. He asked the price and readily agreed when I told him. There was no haggling and no questions. "The deal is done," he said simply.

"Don't you want to know how much business the restaurant does and the profit margin?" I asked.

"I already know about that. My father-in-law has been sitting outside your restaurant almost every day for the past year, watching the customers come and go." When Nancy and I sold the restaurant to Billy, it was a profitable venture, but after eight or nine months, business dropped off considerably and never recovered. A year later, Olympia Diner was closed. The translation of my dream could not have been more accurate.

From that day on, I am proud to say that Nancy paid a little more attention to my dreams.

The American Dream meanwhile was calling for us to expand into new territory as restaurateurs. We bought an International House of Pancakes franchise and moved from New Haven to New Britain, Connecticut. We found a nice apartment in Plainville, just a short distance from the restaurant and Ronnie and Robbie's new school.

Nancy and I worked together side by side in our new business venture. She couldn't have been more supportive and never once complained about all the hard work. In large part because of her workaholic nature, the business quickly became profitable. Life as business owners and as a family couldn't have been better.

Soon after, Nancy became pregnant. I was over the moon at the prospect of Nancy and me having our first child together and couldn't wait to see how the boys would be as older brothers. My excitement spurred me to join Nancy for all her doctor visits. After one such visit, the doctor gave us the happy news that we were going to have another boy. My pride at the thought of having a baby nearly overwhelmed me. I spent many nights wondering about which honorable man of my family we would name him after.

When the day came for Nancy to deliver, I took her to New Britain General Hospital. Since it was midday and we were short-staffed, I had no choice but to leave her at the hospital for a time so I could help with the lunch rush at the restaurant. At work, I tried to keep everything business as usual, but I don't think my feet touched the floor all day. I just kept imagining how wonderful it would be for the boys to hold their baby brother for the first time.

We had two friends from our apartment building, Hans and Marlis, who had agreed to watch the boys while I stayed with Nancy at the hospital.

Not long after I arrived home from work, the telephone rang. I quickly answered.

"Mr. Bylykbashi," came the voice from the other end of the line, "this is Dr. Kaplan. Your wife is doing fine." Then there was a long pause. "And your baby daughter is beautiful and healthy."

Baby daughter? I thought. *Did I hear him correctly?*

I was dumbstruck for a time. Finally, I spoke, "But you told us we were going to have a boy."

"Well," he said with a little chuckle, "it seems God wanted you to have a daughter, if that's okay with you."

I could hardly contain my excitement. "You're forgiven this time, Doctor. But make sure you get it right on the next one, or it'll cost you dearly."

We shared a hearty laugh. Then I thanked him for all he had done for my family.

Even though I rushed to the hospital, it felt like the drive took hours. All the while, I tried to picture my daughter's beautiful, delicate face. I wondered which of us she would look like most, Nancy or me. My heart was beating so fast that it felt ready to explode.

I remember as if it were yesterday, that feeling I had when I saw her for the first time. She was the most beautiful girl in the world. As I held my baby girl for the first time, I kissed her on both cheeks.

"Isn't she beautiful, Pertef?" Nancy said.

"Yes, my love," I replied. "She is beautiful—as beautiful as you."

Nancy winked and gave me a smile. "I named her Resmije after your mother. I thought that would be the perfect name for our daughter."

I thought so too. Although she was soon given the nickname of Mia, in my mind, she has always been Resmije.

As I held my beautiful Resmije, I felt pride swell in my heart but also pain, for I wondered what Mother was doing at the camp at that moment. I whispered a prayer in my mind that someday she would be free and could hold her beautiful namesake in her arms.

Soon after, thanks to the success of our franchise, I gained the financial confidence I needed to buy our first home. I was told that the place was once owned by a famous movie star and used as his summer home, so I would often joke with Nancy that I had taken her out of Anniston, Alabama, and made her famous.

We took a few days to settle in with the children. Then I went to Waterbury to fetch my father and uncle and move them in with us.

The main house had four bedrooms. Nancy and I took the master bedroom, and we kept little Resmije in the room with us. Father and Uncle Arif each had their own room, and Ronnie and Robbie shared the fourth bedroom. This arrangement seemed as if it would work well for everyone involved, but we soon learned that a mix of cultures and personalities living in one house can lead to tension at first. Some days, it felt like everyone was walking around on broken glass.

Mostly, the tension resided between my father and my wife. Nancy did everything in her power to please my father and my uncle, but sometimes, old Albanian men can be stubborn. Nancy and Uncle Arif hit it off right away, but Father was a prideful man and just couldn't admit that he had been completely wrong that his son would never be happy with a non-Albanian wife. So even as Nancy proved time and again that she was a wonderful person and caregiver, Father chose to stand firm on his original feelings about modernized American women. I think a part of him believed that if he could push Nancy to the point of breaking, he could claim victory on the subject.

This would go on for the next few years. Nancy and Uncle Arif formed a tight bond during that time, but the closer the rest of us became, the more ornery my father behaved. He never missed an opportunity to let me and everyone else in the family know his feelings about my decision to marry an American.

It was a blessing from God that Father never learned the English language and that I had only taught Nancy a few phrases in Albanian.

This allowed me to devise what I believed to be a brilliant plan at the time. The first thing I did was get rid of all the English-Albanian language books in the house. This way, I would be in complete control of all translations between my wife and my father.

When my father would say something mean about Nancy, her eyes would flare, and she would snap, "What did he say about me, Pertef?"

I would shrug and casually say, "He said you are trying very hard to make him and Uncle Arif comfortable and that he appreciates all you do." Nancy would usually roll her eyes.

Then Father would ask in Albanian, "What things did your woman tell about me?"

I would smile and reply in our native tongue, "She said, 'What can I do to make Father happy? He seems sad. I want him to know he is loved and this is his home and I will care for him and Uncle Arif for all their lives.'"

He would usually bat his hand dismissively.

No matter what my father would say to Nancy, she was always respectful to him. At some point, she decided that his behavior was merely owed to jealousy. She had developed such a close relationship with Uncle Arif after all. Maybe Father was just feeling left out. So she tried taking him with her everywhere she went. She would take him to the restaurant for lunch, to the movies, or sometimes just out for coffee.

When that didn't work, I tried reasoning with him, but that didn't work either.

One day, Nancy needed to do some grocery shopping and decided to take my father with her. They were gone for most of the morning, which made me think that they must have been buying half the store. But when they returned, Nancy carried only two bags of groceries into the house. I was a bit agitated over this, but I could tell that Nancy was agitated too, so I gently asked her where the rest of the groceries were.

"I thought we needed all kinds of things," I said. "What you have here wouldn't feed our family one meal."

With a half-hearted laugh, she replied, "Today, Baba and I played cat and mouse in the grocery store. I would put groceries in the cart, and whenever I turned my back, your father would take them out. I put them in, your father took them out. By the time I got to the register to pay, what you see is all that was left."

"Why would he do that?" I asked, furrowing my brow.

"He thinks we spend too much money for food." I sighed and shook my head, frustrated.

"I know this is as hard on you as it is me," she said. "But sooner or later, Baba will realize how much I care for him, and he will come around."

I laughed. "Well, let's hope it's sooner, or we'll all starve to death."

Nancy kept chipping away at the wall my father had erected between them, but old Baba stood there like a big oak tree, refusing to bend. I loved him, but I loved my wife also, and his stubbornness was threatening our happiness.

I have everything I could want, I thought. *I have a wonderful family. Our business is prospering. We just bought our first home. We're living the American Dream. So why is this such a nightmare?*

Even with all those great ingredients, I began to understand that if my home wasn't happy, it would all be for nothing.

Nancy never gave up. Just when I thought she would give in, it seemed like she would stand back, regroup, and go right back to the mission at hand. It was a challenging situation for her, even though we actually found most of Baba's antics rather humorous. But I knew that in the end, this was my problem—a problem that had gone on long enough.

Late on a Friday afternoon, I was sitting in the restaurant office doing payroll for my employees when the telephone rang. It was my cousin Zyfer calling from Brooklyn.

"Nancy and the children arrived at my house a few minutes ago," he explained. "She told me your father threw her out."

I was shocked, to say the least. "I can't believe Father would do such a thing! Put Nancy on the phone!"

Nancy sounded calm when she greeted me with a simple, "Hello, Pertef."

"What's going on, honey? Are you okay? Tell me exactly what happened."

"Baba and I had a bit of a problem today. I was in the kitchen, making us a pot of stew for dinner. I had just checked the stew and walked to the counter to cut the bread. Baba went to the stove and took the cover off the pot to stir the stew, all the while adding more salt. I told him that it had already been salted and did not need more. He continued to pour salt into the stew, and when he ignored my request again to not add more salt, I said, 'Baba, the kitchen needs only one cook. Either I cook or you cook but not both of us! Do you understand me, Baba? No more salt!'

"Your father became very angry and told me, 'Get out of the house! This is my son's house! You don't tell me what to do here!'"

I could hardly find the words to reply. "I'm sorry, Nancy," was all I could manage.

"I didn't know what to do, Pertef," my wife said. "I didn't want to make an already bad situation worse, so I picked the kids up from school and came to Zyfer's house."

For a moment, I was so frustrated that I was having a hard time thinking. But then all at once, the solution occurred to me. I told my wife to stay at Zyfer's for the night. "When you come back tomorrow," I said, "our lives will be happy once again."

I left work around nine o'clock that evening and hurried home. My father and uncle had no idea that I had talked to Nancy or even that I already knew what had happened. The only thing they knew was that Nancy had left that afternoon to get the kids from school and never returned.

The two of them were waiting by the driveway when I pulled in. I got out of the car and greeted them with a kiss on their cheeks as if nothing were wrong. It was almost comical to see their fearful faces. I could sense how upset they were, but they deserved it, so I let them continue believing that I thought nothing was amiss.

When we were inside the house, I waited for them to speak first. Casually, I walked to the television and started to turn it on.

That was when Uncle Arif finally broke the silence. "Pertef, my son, up to now, I have been keeping my distance. I have only been an observer of the situation between your father and your wife. But I have come to a conclusion that my brother has been acting like a spoiled child. He has been very wrong and unjust to Nancy." He fired a chiding look at my father. "I told my stubborn brother that she is trying to take care of the two old buzzards that we are."

I nodded, still pretending not to know about the situation.

"Now do you have any idea what this stubborn brother of mine did?" Uncle Arif continued, waggling a finger. "Well, I will tell you! He threw Nancy out of the house, and now she is gone! Because of his stubbornness, we have no one to prepare our supper!"

I could see tears dripping from Uncle Arif's eyes onto his cheeks. By now, his voice had become agitated, and he spoke louder. "And let me tell you, it is your father's fault! Nancy hasn't done anything wrong. Your father has messed up your marriage, not to mention our lives!" By this time, Uncle Arif was trembling. He turned to my father and shouted, "What are we going to do now? Who will feed us? Who is going to take care of us now that Nancy is gone?"

Even though I already knew the whole story, I asked Father what had happened. At first, he tried to justify the incident, but Uncle Arif made sure that he told the story exactly as it happened. I wanted to remain respectful, but I needed Father to tell me the story from his perspective if my idea was ever going to work. I knew he wanted Nancy back as much as Uncle Arif did and that he was worried because he had no idea where she was.

This was the chance I had been waiting for. So I made my move. "Here's what I'm going to do," I told him. "I'm going to sell the house and the restaurant, and you, my dear uncle, are coming with me. You and I are going to set up in California. Father, I love you very much. But I love my wife also, and I cannot choose between the two of you. As unbearable as I think life would be without you both, it has proven to be more unbearable with the two of you in it. So I'm going to take Uncle Arif and move to California and leave you and Nancy behind."

I didn't like to see my father so hurt, but he stewed in that pain for a few minutes before he finally worked up the nerve to apologize.

"Baba," I said, "when it comes to me, you don't have anything to apologize for. I just want all of us to live together and have a nice life and a happy home."

"No, son," he said. "Let me finish, please." He drew a deep, shuddering breath. "I know that I have been unjust to Nancy. It's just that I wanted you to marry an Albanian girl. But it didn't take long for me to realize that Nancy had qualities that are rare in a person. I have known that for quite a while, but my stubbornness wouldn't let me admit that I had judged her wrongly. I take full blame for my actions. And if you can find her and bring her back, I will apologize to her also."

Nancy returned the next day, and from that moment until my father took his last breath, the two of them were inseparable. Finally, our house had some peace.

*****

A friend of mine who owned an IHOP in Waterbury needed some help balancing his books one day, so Nancy and I made the trip to take a look at the numbers. We managed to solve the problem, but that wasn't what made this particular day so memorable. Before we headed back home, we decided to have some lunch and coffee. From where we were sitting, I watched an enterprising young man working hard as a cook on the other side of the food galley. I noticed that he looked and dressed sharply and that he was a determined cook who seemed to enjoy working his job. Even to this day, I'm not sure why, but I felt compelled to go speak to this man.

He introduced himself as William Giampetruzi, "Billy" to his friends. Despite the fact that I had only just met him, I made him an offer to become an equal partner in my restaurant business. His eyes went wide.

"But, Mr. Bylykbashi," he said, "I've only just finished community college. I don't have any money to invest in a business."

I assured him that he wouldn't need any money, so long as he worked as hard for me as I had seen him working that day. The eager young family man and aspiring restaurateur readily agreed to the arrangement.

Nancy was hesitant about the idea at first, but after we had a chance to formally meet with Billy and his wife Joanie, it was clear to both of us that he was the perfect man for a partnership. In addition to his work ethic and intellect, he came from a good Catholic family that instilled in him high morals and character. Over the years that followed, Billy and I developed a strong partnership and a close friendship based on honesty and trust. My offer allowed him to get a huge jumpstart on his dream, and his hard work allowed me to explore additional business ventures while also spending more time with my family.

*****

One rainy morning, as I was sitting in my office working on my inventory, I received a call from Washington, DC. It was Sokoli, who kept in touch with me from time to time.

"What's happening with you, Sokoli?" I asked. "You sound like you're doing okay. Why are you so happy?"

"My divorce with Sherry has just come through," Sokoli replied. "I'm a free man. I'm finally free! I'm coming to see you. I'll be there in about four hours. We're going to celebrate my divorce."

"Be careful, Sokoli. Sherry is working tables here in the restaurant, and you better not let her hear you talk like that about her."

Sokoli laughed and told me not to worry about it because he would think of something.

I hung up with a strange sense of dread and excitement warring in my heart.

After the lunch crowd began to slow down, I went back to the office to finish my work. At the same time, I was trying to figure out how to handle the situation between Sherry and Sokoli to avoid friction. Sherry wasn't just working in the restaurant but staying at our house as well. And now Sokoli would be there for a few days. I was worried that they wouldn't be able to get along together under the same roof.

By the time I finished in the office, I saw Sokoli walking in the front door to the restaurant. Sherry was at one end of the dining room, Sokoli at the other. I wanted to rush over to hide Sokoli, but when Sherry saw him, she yelled his name and began running toward him.

"Sherry!" Sokoli said, running to meet her halfway. They met in the middle of the dining room and began hugging and kissing as if they were lovers who had been separated for years.

The customers in the dining room who saw this display of affection started smiling and applauding but not me. All I could think was, *These kids are crazy.* Sokoli had come to celebrate his divorce, and now it looked like they were madly in love.

"What's going on with the two of you?" I asked. "Your divorce was just finalized yesterday, right?"

"Yeah," Sherry said. "We got divorced, but that doesn't mean we can't get married again."

"That makes no sense," I said. "Sokoli came here to celebrate the divorce. Am I going crazy?"

"You're not going crazy," Sokoli said, beaming as he still held Sherry in his arms.

"Well then, get it out of your system," I said. "But don't get married again. It won't work."

Sherry gave me a stern look. "You're wrong, Pertef. You just don't get it. It wasn't until we were divorced that I realized how much I really love Sokoli."

I shook my head, perplexed. I gave them another moment before pulling Sokoli aside. "Please stop and think for a moment," I told him. "You've only been divorced one day."

But no matter what I tried to tell them, I couldn't convince them otherwise. So Sokoli and Sherry remarried and moved to Maryland.

A few months later, they came to visit Nancy and me. After being at our house for a couple of days, Sokoli got up one morning and, over breakfast, told us he was going to get the tires on his car rotated and balanced. He said he would be back in a couple of hours.

We heard nothing from him until that evening. He called and I answered the phone. "Sokoli, where are you, man? We've been worried about you."

"I'm back in Maryland," he said. "You were right. We were stupid. We should have never married again. There's no way we can make it together. I can't live with her."

I handed the phone to Sherry. They talked for a few minutes before Sherry's voice started to get louder. "You can't do this," I heard her say. "We need to talk this over."

With that, Sherry went back to Maryland.

After another few months, we heard that Sherry had packed up the apartment and moved out. That was the end of the saga of Sokoli and Sherry.

Around that same time, Pam and Gani's marriage began to break down as well. They had two daughters, Mileta and Beth, and Pam had recently become pregnant again. The pressure of everyday family responsibilities had become stressful for Gani. So he left for Las Vegas, where he would stay without making contact with his family for over six months. This left Nancy and me to help take care of Pam during her pregnancy. On the day her son was born, she did me the great honor of naming him Pertef.

I couldn't have been prouder to have a namesake, but the situation with Pam and Gani had made life a little too hectic at home. Along with our three children and my father and my uncle, we now had Pam and her three children staying with us. As if that weren't enough, Nancy and I served as surrogate parents for two fifteen-year-old Albanian boys, Remzi and Esat. Nancy was a person full of compassion and understanding, but houses don't get much fuller than that.

Eventually, we had to take steps to make our lives less chaotic. I helped Remzi and Esat enroll in a night school that held language classes so they could have jobs and work at the restaurant during the day. I found a small apartment for them near the restaurant and their school, and from there, they got on the path to taking care of themselves.

Next, I turned my sights to Gani's family. I found a nice apartment for Pam and her children. It was close to us in Unionville, which meant that Nancy and I could look in once in a while and keep an eye on them until Gani figured out what he was going to do.

It would be six more months before I received the call from Gani that I had been waiting for. Finally, he had decided that he would return home to be with his family and try to right the wrongs with his wife. Nancy was furious with him—and for good reason—but eventually, we managed to smooth things over to the point where my friend could get his second chance.

During this same time, I was in the process of negotiating the purchase of another restaurant at Westfarms Mall in West Hartford, Connecticut. Gani's return seemed like a good omen to me. He always seemed to show up in my life just when I needed him most. So when Gani and my partner William "Bill" Giampetruzzi hit it off from the word go, I decided that the three of us would make a good team on this new venture. I made Gani the manager of the new Landham's Restaurant, which would open in a matter of weeks.

There are times in life as a business owner that one has to make tough choices and sacrifices. The grand opening of Landham's coincided with the wedding of King Leka of Albania. My status as a higher profile refugee led to an invitation from Queen Geraldine herself to attend the wedding in Spain. Not only was I honored to receive an invitation from a royal family that I believed capable of finally helping us overthrow the Communists, but also Nancy was overwhelmed with excitement about the prospect of traveling to Spain, her first trip out of the country. But then we saw the date of the wedding, and our hearts sank.

I apologized to Nancy, saying that I couldn't change the opening or we would risk losing traction on the investment. She was disappointed but ultimately understood. And besides, I jokingly promised to get her an audience with the king and queen if they ever traveled to the United States for a state visit.

Little did I know that such a visit to America would happen and that the queen would invite me and my family to attend a gala in their honor. Nancy was beside herself with excitement about the opportunity.

Over the years, my father, uncle, and I had remained relentlessly involved in political issues concerning Albania and the efforts to free our country and families. We never stopped writing letters, making phone calls, and attending meetings. This was what aligned us with the opportunity to speak with the Albanian royal family during their trip to New York.

I accepted the invitation for myself and Nancy as well as my father and uncle. I also called Sokoli and told him to make plans to attend the grand event.

In typical Sokoli fashion, the reply came as a torrent of jokes. "You know what I'm going to say to the king when I see him?" he asked. "I'm going to say, come over here, king. Let's talk, one mountain man to another."

"What the hell's wrong with you?" I said. "You can't talk to a king like that. Don't be crazy! If you're planning to embarrass me, then you can forget about coming with us."

Sokoli apologized and promised not to say anything too out of line. Knowing Sokoli, though, it was still in the back of my head that he would make an impression on the king one way or another. There was just no stopping him.

Meanwhile, Nancy was walking on air about the chance to hobnob with royalty. Suddenly, her political opinions about the situation in Albania were getting louder.

"King Leka is going about it completely wrong if he wants to free Albania," she would say. "It just can't be done by asking for volunteers to fight for Albania's freedom. What he needs is the backing of a powerful country like the United States." All this talk was making me nervous. I could imagine reaching the front of the line to speak to the king and queen, only to have Sokoli act like a crazy person while my wife tried to tell the king how to do his job. I was confident that Nancy wouldn't embarrass me—she was far too smart and self-aware—but Sokoli was a different story. I knew he would make an ass out of himself. I just wasn't sure how King Leka would take it.

The day finally arrived, and we all readied ourselves to meet with the king and his new wife, Queen Susan. Nancy had bought herself some beautiful formalwear and had her hair, nails, and makeup done. She looked so beautiful and so elegant that I had a feeling she would draw much of the room's attention away from the royalty.

Five or six hundred people came from Europe, Canada, Australia, and the United States to attend the event. The black tie affair was lovely and very tasteful, but everyone seemed to look forward most to personally meeting the king and queen. When the time came, I took Nancy's hand, and we made our way through the crowd to meet our hosts. Sokoli followed behind us.

I had met the king a few times before on his visits to New York, but this was the first time Nancy had met him. With a slight curtsy and a bow of the head, she introduced herself.

"I'm so honored and proud to meet you," she said cordially. "And we all appreciate your visit to America."

I was so proud of her courtesies, but I knew we weren't out of the woods yet.

And then it happened.

"Your Majesty," she said, "with all due respect, I feel compelled to tell you that the way you are trying to gain freedom for Albania isn't going to work. It can't be done with just a few honorable Albanian volunteers that join together to form a small army. To gain freedom for your country, you will need the support of our government and the American people. Then and only then will you be able to free Albania."

By the time she was finished, the king looked shocked. Then his shock melted into a kind of awed disbelief that he had finally met someone who not only disagreed with his ideas on how to free Albania but was confident enough to say so. As he thanked my wife for her counsel, it was clear that he admired her for what she had said.

Then it was my turn to speak, but I was still so full of pride about my wife that I didn't manage to say anything more impactful than to wish him luck on his ventures.

Then it was Sokoli standing at the head of the line. I tensed as I waited for him to speak. It shouldn't have surprised me that he did exactly as he told me he would do. He walked right up to King

Leka, who hailed from the same northern part of Albania as Sokoli, and said, "Give me your hand! From one mountain man to another, let's shake."

I couldn't believe it, but the king broke into a smile, grasped Sokoli's hand, and pulled him forward. "From one mountain man to another," the king said as he bear-hugged my friend.

The king couldn't have realized it at the time, but that single gesture is what won my heart and Nancy's heart that day. The act showed compassion and understanding—a sign that he knew exactly how we were suffering and that he would stand beside us in the fight. I knew right then that he deserved to be king to a small country suffering under a foreign-sponsored dictatorship.

But then after the hug had ended, I realized that Sokoli was still standing in front of the king. I was mortified when I heard what came from his mouth next.

"Your Majesty," he said, gesturing back at me, "you have two more soldiers right here. Pertef and I were trained well by the United States Army, and we're ready to fight to free our country any time you need us."

After thanking Sokoli, King Leka then extended his hand to Uncle Arif and pulled him closer in to greet him and ask how he fared. Father received the same gestures when his turn came. When it was over, both men beamed with pride and with more hope than I had seen from them in years.

Several speeches from the king and other members of his cabinet followed. Then we all took our seats for a lavish dinner. Throughout the meal, chants would rise up, chants like, "Long live the king!" and "Long live Albania," and "Down with communism!"

It was a beautiful evening. For the first time in a long time, I felt like we were making progress in our efforts to oust the Communist regime.

The second morning, we had breakfast with the royal family and spent the morning talking with representatives from other countries about mutual political interests. As lunchtime drew close, Nancy pulled me aside.

"I am king and queened out," she told me. "You know we have a long evening with them again tonight. Could we please go to a nice little deli somewhere for lunch?"

The suggestion was just right as far as I was concerned. We found a New York deli that looked rather busy, so Nancy and I figured it had to be a good choice based on the sheer number of customers. As we stood in line for almost twenty minutes, we talked and joked about the events of the night before—the impressions that she and Sokoli must have made on King Leka and how proud I was that she had the confidence to offer her ideas on how Albania should be freed.

Nancy laughed. "The old boy took it pretty good on the chin, huh?"

I agreed.

"I like him," she said. "He seems smart and down to earth, but in all honesty, I do believe he needs some American advisors to help him with his decisions."

As we talked, I turned around, and standing in line right behind me was Alex Haley, the famous novelist and author of *Roots*. The miniseries had just finished on television and was still the buzz on most talk shows. At first, I thought maybe it was someone that just looked like him, so I tapped Nancy on the shoulder.

"Is this guy behind us Alex Haley?" I whispered.

She looked back, and her eyes got wide. She assured me that it was indeed Alex Haley.

I couldn't help myself. "Mr. Haley," I said, offering my hand. "My name is Pertef Bylykbashi, and this is my wife, Nancy. My wife is an avid reader. She read your book and admires you very much. I did not read the book, but I did see the movie. It was fantastic! I could relate to your story because it mirrors my life story. They are very similar."

"It's a pleasure to meet you, Pertef," he said. "Where are you from?"

"I'm from Albania, and right at this moment, my family has to endure many of the hardships your ancestors experienced years ago."

The maître d' called our name for a table, and I invited Mr. Haley to sit with us for lunch. I was honored when he accepted the invitation. He began asking me questions about my family and about my story. I told him that one day, when my family was free, I hoped to put our story into a book so those who read it could understand how valuable freedom is and the price paid by so many unsung heroes.

He was a wonderful person, and I was proud to have the opportunity to share some of my history with him. Before we parted ways, Mr. Haley filled me with encouragement.

"No matter what you do, Pertef," he said, "never forget your roots. Write your book, and let the world know what was and is going on in Albania. Let the truth be known. Maybe it will take a little time, but someday, you'll see that you have made a difference."

I thanked him profusely and promised that I would do as he suggested.

"I hope and pray that someday you will see your family again," he said as he shook my hand. "And I hope that it will be under a flag of freedom." Then he wished me good luck and went on his way.

After lunch, Nancy and I returned to the hotel for the last night of the festivities with the royal family. The next morning, we checked out of the hotel and headed back to Connecticut with stories we would talk about for the rest of our lives.

Uncle Arif spent much of the ride home complaining about not feeling well. This wasn't like him, so Nancy and I took him to the doctor the next day. There, we received the sad news that Uncle Arif had developed prostate cancer.

They scheduled him for surgery immediately. We took him home after he had spent some time recovering at the hospital. The doctors wanted us to check him in to a convalescent facility, but our deep love for Uncle Arif wouldn't allow for something like that.

Nancy only reinforced the decision when I sat down with her and asked if she supported the idea of taking care of Uncle Arif on our own.

"I know it's been very difficult for you over the years," I told her. "It hasn't been easy caring for my father and uncle to say nothing of all these other people coming in and out of our home. Now we are faced with another challenge, and I know that when it comes to Uncle Arif's care, most of the burden would again fall on your shoulders. Maybe we could find someone to come in every day to tend to his personal needs. This way, you don't have to shoulder it alone."

Nancy listened silently as I finished what I had to say regarding the care of Uncle Arif. "Remember our wedding day?" she said.

I nodded.

"Well then, you remember that I gave you my word about your father and your uncle. I told you that I would care for them all their lives. I plan to honor that commitment."

"But, Nancy—"

She was adamant. "Even if you had agreed with the doctor to send your uncle to that old folks' home, I wouldn't have allowed it. You see, it's not just the Albanian people that have family values and traditions. I can't speak for the rest of America, but in the South, we honor, love, respect, and care for our elderly in the same way."

"It's going to be so much work," I reminded her.

She wouldn't hear anything of it. "I will be the one to care for Uncle Arif, not a convalescent home and not some stranger hired to come into our house every day. He needs us, and that is what he will have."

Before that day, I knew that my wife was committed to my family, but it was at that moment I realized how much she had come to love my father and uncle. I could not have asked for a more honorable and selfless woman to be my wife.

My uncle never recovered to good health. For many years, he was too ill to take care of himself alone. Nancy tended his every need, bathed him, fed him, and did more than I ever could have asked or dreamed that she would do for Uncle Arif. She cared for him much like a mother would do for a young child. My uncle would often smile and call Nancy his angel.

"God sent your wife to all of us," Uncle Arif told me one day as I sat in his room to talk with him. "He knew our situation and recognized our needs. I don't believe anyone on this earth would have cared for me the way Nancy has. And I'm not talking about obligation to family either." He gave a soft smile. "Nancy has no obligation to me. She cares for me purely out of love and compassion."

*****

Landham's Steakhouse was doing well under Gani's management, so I decided that it would be a good time to look for another restaurant. As it turned out, I didn't have to look very far because my next business venture came to me as a gift.

One Saturday night during the dinner rush, an old gentleman walked into Landham's. I was standing at the front door greeting customers when he entered. I took his coat and hat, along with his cane, and checked them into the coatroom. Rather than waiting for the hostess to seat him, I sat him myself at a nice table.

Right away, he introduced himself. "My name is Aldo DeDominicis, but just call me Aldo. Are you the maître d'?"

"I'm the maître d', cook, waiter, dishwasher, and anything I need to be when I'm here," I quipped. "I'm the owner, Pertef Bylykbashi."

I guessed Mr. Aldo's age at about eighty years. He was dressed to the nines and quickly proved himself to be quick and sharp-witted. I took an immediate liking to him. After a few exchanges of chuckles over small talk, he asked if I had time to sit with him while he had dinner.

"It would be my pleasure," I said.

I sat down with him, and we ordered.

He seemed intensely interested in my history in the restaurant business. I told him that I had been in this line of work since my discharge from the army. He listened attentively as I gave him a brief history of my family and the restaurants we had owned. Each time I would steer the conversation away from the business and try to find other topics, Mr. Aldo would come back to my background and my restaurant career.

"Do you think you could run another place?" he asked me eventually.

I shrugged and said I thought I could.

"I have a big restaurant that was leased to an individual," Mr. Aldo explained. "But some personal issues caused him to close his business. I would like to open it again, but it needs the right management if it's going to be a good business." Then he leaned back and nodded. "I think you're the person for the job."

This seemed like a good opportunity, especially since I already had been thinking of opening another restaurant. When I asked Mr. Aldo about the location, his reply stunned me because the place was one of the best locations in the area.

"You may know where it is," he said. "The name is Cook's Tavern." I listened excitedly as he provided the details.

"There is quite a history attached to this place. Did you know that Cook's Tavern is a historical landmark?"

"I didn't know that," I said.

"I was told that George Washington slept there back when it was an inn and tavern."

Upon hearing that, I was like a boy waiting on his first bicycle. I quickly tried to imagine owning a restaurant like this. It was something I could have only dreamed about.

"Mr. Aldo, I don't understand. You don't even know me, and you are offering me not only a new business but an American landmark?"

"I do this for good reason," Mr. Aldo said. "You treat people as they should be treated. With your attitude on life, your personality, and the way I have already seen you handle your business affairs, I know you will be successful."

Nothing would have thrilled me more to accept his offer right then and there, but I knew I would have to think about it all the same. "I don't know," I said with a sigh. "Can you give me a little time to think about it? It has only been a few years since I opened this place, and I want to give it a chance to get off the ground." Most of my funds were invested in Landham's, so it didn't seem like Cook's would be within reach financially.

Then as if the night had not been strange enough already, I was still in for the biggest surprise of my life.

"You might have noticed that I didn't say anything about money," he said with a smile. Then he paid his check and rose to head for the door.

That had me intrigued. I walked Mr. Aldo to his car, and as his chauffeur opened the door for him to get in, we agreed to meet the following day to discuss the details. We shook hands and said goodnight.

I was still in disbelief when one of the parking attendants stopped me as I was heading inside.

"How do you know Mr. DeDominicis?" he asked, looking impressed.

I told him that I had just met him that night.

"Do you know who he is?"

"No," I replied.

"Mr. DeDominicis is a multimillionaire. He owns large commercial properties as well as some radio and television stations."

Now I understood why he had not been concerned about the financial aspects of our deal or about me having available cash on hand. The next day, his chauffeur arrived to pick me up for our appointment. Mr. Aldo and I walked all around and through Cook's Tavern, and I immediately fell in love with it. It was beautiful, with its multiple fireplaces, multiple dining rooms, and banquet rooms. By that point, I knew that Mr. Aldo would be able to offer me assistance with the financing, but I still felt as if I would be in over my head. There would be some initial costs involved, and I didn't want to overextend myself.

"Thank you very much for thinking of me, Mr. Aldo," I said. "The place is beautiful. Anyone would give an arm and leg to have a business like this. But it's as I said, with the build-out costs and the mortgage, I'm afraid I would be overextended financially."

He shook his head. "Take the key, Pertef. Come over tomorrow and figure out what you think it will take for you to fix the place the way you want it. Then give me a call."

The next day, I took Gani and Bill to the restaurant to come up with some numbers. We decided that it would take about one hundred thousand dollars for all repairs and renovations, including the addition of a really nice cocktail lounge.

I called Mr. Aldo the next day and told him what I wanted to do and how much it would cost. Up to that point, I was already awestruck by how unlikely this all seemed—about how just a day or two after meeting this kindly old man, it appeared he was ready to go into business with me. Little did I know that my awe had yet to even come close to peaking.

"I want to give you this restaurant business as a gift," he said flatly. "And I also want to put up the money you need for remodeling."

"But, Mr. Aldo," I said breathlessly.

"I am old," he interjected. "And you would be making an old man very happy if you accept my gift."

I didn't know what to say.

"My chauffeur and I will pick you up tomorrow and take you to my attorney's office," he continued. "I'll have the business put in your name and give you a check for the money you need to remodel."

Once again, I could hardly believe how completely luck was on my side. Mr. Aldo signed the restaurant business over to me. We finished renovations quickly, and I opened Cook's Tavern in Plainville, Connecticut, just a few months later.

*****

One evening, while I was working at Landham's, I received a visit from my Greek friend Jim Kastellis and an Albanian man he had brought along with him. Over the years, I had often wondered what happened to the soldier that Sazan had identified as a Sigurim officer when we were based at Fort Jackson. Since then, it had occurred to me that there were probably more Communists just like him living among us in America. This was part of why I was so guarded when I first met anyone from Albania that I had not known personally.

"Pertef," Jim said, "this is a friend of mine I want you to meet. Arthur Laski."

We shook hands, and I invited them to sit down. "Are you the Mr. Laski that owns the cocktail lounge in Hartford? The Train Robbery, it's called, am I right?"

He nodded. The three of us made small talk, and at some point during the conversation, I learned that Mr. Laski was able to travel freely to and from Albania whenever he wanted. I assumed that this could only mean one of two things: he was either working for the American government, or he was working for the Communist government. How else could he visit and leave whenever he so chose? My first urge was to immediately say goodbye and make an exit, but

I quickly changed my mind when it occurred to me that this man might be in a unique position to give me information about what was really going on in Albania. I had received almost no news about my family since my escape, and perhaps he had the means to get it for me. So I decided that as much as I distrusted him, it would be worth the risk to stay in touch.

One evening, I received a call from Mr. Laski inviting me to his house for drinks. I accepted the invitation. Arthur and his wife were very hospitable, greeting me warmly when I arrived and treating me to food and drink. We were enjoying a round of raki when Arthur told me that he and his wife had just returned from Albania.

"Would you like to see the pictures we took during the visit?" he asked.

I eagerly accepted the offer. It had been many years since I had seen my native land. My excitement quickly turned to anger when I saw the first picture. It depicted the vicious dictator Enver Hoxha and his prime minister Mehmet Shehu with their wives. Sitting right beside them at the same banquet table was Arthur Laski and his wife.

I threw the pictures across the room. "Arthur, I wouldn't advertise that I had friends like these. These are not men. They are murderers and butchers!"

Arthur's wife was astonished by my outburst, but Arthur quickly told her that I had a right to be angry because my family was in prisons and labor camps in Albania, and some of my relatives had even been killed by the Communists.

When he focused his attention on me again, he affixed me with a level gaze. "Enver Hoxha—this man you call a butcher—he asked me if I knew you and also if I knew Idajet Bushka, Fari Barolli, and Rustem Demiraj. I told him I didn't know any of you."

I scoffed. "I don't believe you. You speak only lies. I don't want to have anything to do with you, so I'll see myself out."

Arthur apologized again, more vigorously this time. "Wait, Pertef! I want to be very clear to you that I am not a Communist. In fact, I know the Albanian government is out of control, and I also know there is a lot of conflict between Hoxha and his prime minister. They are battling each other, and one of them will eventually have to go."

I didn't believe a thing he told me that day, but to my surprise, much of what he had said came true. Not long after my visit to the Laski home, the prime minister and a group of generals were accused of treason and all of them executed. Even if I wasn't yet sure if I could trust him, I was now convinced that Laski indeed had access to inside information from the Albanian government. So I decided to make occasional calls to him just to keep that line of communication open.

A few years later, the Albanian-American Basketball Organization was having a convention in Canada. I enjoyed taking my children to events like these so they could make friends and spend time with other Albanian children. Nancy wasn't feeling well that weekend, but she told us to go along without her. We arrived early at the convention, and the first thing I noticed in the lobby of the banquet hall was a table by the entrance door filled with pamphlets, newsletters, and books written by Enver Hoxha in support of communism. The sight of them caused my blood to boil.

Who in the hell would have the nerve to distribute such propaganda? I thought. *I'll kill them with my bare hands!*

My daughter Resmije tried to calm me, but I couldn't let it go. I entered the banquet room, where I found a group of people standing near the podium.

"Who's in charge of this event?" I asked of them.

"I'm the person in charge," one of the men replied. "Do you realize that everything you have on the table out there is propaganda?" I barked. "Enver Hoxha is a mass murderer. Hanging would be too good for him! That literature you're promoting needs to be put where it belongs."

The man looked a little shocked by my outburst. "And where does it belong?"

"It belongs in the trash!" I spat.

I stormed off with Resmije right behind me, and we began gathering and discarding the literature. Soon, the group from the podium joined us. Together, we threw every shred of paper with Hoxha's name on it in the bathroom trash receptacle.

The next day, Nancy called to say that Arthur Laski was trying to reach me.

"He sounded upset, Pertef," she said. "Did something happen at the convention?"

I told her about the confrontation at the banquet hall, and the more I talked, the clearer it became that somehow Laski had already gotten word of the situation. When we finished talking it through, I gave him a call.

"Nancy said you've been trying to get hold of me," I said, doing my best to sound casual. "What do you need?"

Laski sounded tense. "Do you realize what you've done? You've probably condemned what family you have left in Albania to death."

I let him have his say about how the Communists have eyes and ears everywhere before I replied.

"Fine, Arthur, I listened to you, now you listen to me. I know my family a whole lot better than you do, so I can tell you that they would rather die than know that I allowed my fellow countrymen to support that monster for a single second. You give the party that message from me. And tell them they'll pay for the crimes they've committed on my family and the rest of the Albanian people."

The conversation ended on that contentious note, but from that day forward, I believed that Arthur Laski could very well be a Communist collaborator.

*****

We were saddened when we learned that Pam and Gani's marital problems had returned and they had decided to file for divorce. Gani moved to Texas, and Pam settled in Florida. She left the children with Nancy and me because she needed time to establish herself financially and heal from the breakup. It seemed that every time something happened to any of our friends or relatives, Nancy ended up with more people to care for. Now with Pam's three children, altogether, there were ten people living in our house.

Meanwhile, one of the ten was in rapidly declining health. It was apparent that Uncle Arif didn't have much time left. I could see that Nancy was overworked. As much as I wanted to help her, I had a similar problem with my three restaurants. I knew the only solution would be to give Nancy a vacation with our children while I stayed home to manage the household responsibilities for a while. When I told her about the plans I had made for her to take our kids to New Hampshire, she refused to go because she didn't want to leave Uncle Arif.

"Your uncle is dying, Pertef," she said. "I should be with him. I have been with him all through his illness, and I don't want to leave him alone for the last few days of his life. He needs me now more than ever."

In a firm and assuring voice, I said, "Uncle Arif isn't going any-where. So go on vacation and relax. You deserve it. I mean, if you have to stress yourself in this house any longer, you might just lose your marbles, and then we'd all be in big trouble."

She smiled but I could sense that she still didn't like the idea of leaving.

That afternoon, I kissed Nancy and the kids goodbye, and they left for vacation. Uncle Arif died the next day. I called Nancy, and she returned immediately. She was a wreck about the loss. We both were.

We made funeral arrangements at Bergen's Funeral Home in Waterbury. People, flowers, and condolences came from all over the United States and Canada. Even King Leka and the royal family sent their regrets, along with a beautiful arrangement of flowers. We were moved that such a great man had found time in his busy day to honor our uncle. The outpouring of sympathy for our family's loss was remarkable—a true testament to just how much Uncle Arif was loved and respected by everyone who knew him.

After a wake that lasted two days, we held the funeral on the third day. The imam performed the service and spoke the prayers, and I gave the eulogy. As we stood by the grave site, I couldn't help but notice how silent it was—almost as if the masses of grievers had stopped breathing. I found myself recounting my years with Uncle Arif and wishing that I could have made his life different in some way. He had witnessed so many horrors when he was a younger man resisting the Communists in Albania, and together, we had spent so many emotionally draining days and nights since our escapes and separation from our families.

"Uncle Arif and my wife and children came to think of each other as a nuclear family," I said. "But there could never be any substitution for the family he longed to reunite with all his life. The way this man strived to make things right for his homeland and for his suffering family was inspiring. And while the work he did might not have been enough to free Albania from tyranny, the work itself was something to celebrate."

As I spoke these words in honor of Uncle Arif, I had the thought that his coffin looked so common considering the greatness of the man. It faced the east in the custom of Islamic faith, and I couldn't help imagining him saying a hearty hello to Allah.

The imam stepped forward when I was finished. He offered some words of comfort to the family before leading several prayers in both Arabic and Albanian tongue. Then he ordered the coffin lowered to its final resting place.

One by one, those who had come to honor Uncle Arif filed by the open grave and dropped single flowers pulled from the floral arrangements atop his coffin as a final farewell gesture. As I dropped my flower, the tears in my eyes were for the regret at losing a man that my family and I loved so dearly but also for the sorrow I felt over the fact that Uncle Arif had spent the majority of his adult life burdened by unfulfilled hopes to reunite with his family. I tried to take comfort in the notion that he was at peace now. The mental and physical anguish he had suffered through during his five-year battle with cancer was at an end, and even though he had not seen his family again in this lifetime, he would certainly meet them in the next.

From the expressions of the elders among us, I could see that I wasn't the only one having these thoughts. They too cried for Uncle Arif's unfulfilled wishes. They knew them all too well themselves. I had great respect for these men, for through all the pain, frustration, and heartbreak they had endured while lobbying and even fighting to free their families, they had kept their faith in God and their hope for a brighter future. I wished desperately that not even one more of these honorable men would have to die without holding their loved ones in their arms again.

Chapter 22

Uncle Arif's death took a great toll on my family. Coupled with the timing of a few bad investments and the resultant financial strain, we were experiencing our first real tension at home in years. I tried desperately to keep the businesses going, but ultimately, it proved impossible. My debts had become too great to sustain. I didn't want to hang my head, for I had faith in myself and in Nancy. I had endured situations like this before, and Nancy was even stronger than I, so I knew we would make a comeback. The only thing left to figure out was how to do that in a way that was both productive professionally and healing for our family.

Nancy and I had a long talk about the best course of action. We agreed that I should take some time away to clear my thoughts and make plans for our future. It might seem a little unorthodox for the man of the house to leave his wife and children behind so he can pursue a new professional avenue, but Nancy insisted that it was the best way for us to achieve our goals. With her support, truly nothing was impossible.

So we closed the doors on Landham's Restaurant and sold Cook's Tavern. Then I followed a lead sent to me by Gani, who had been living in Texas for over six months.

He claimed that Dallas's economy was booming and that the city was primed for new restaurants. From the way he made it sound, opening a business downtown seemed like the quickest way to bounce back.

Our oldest son Ron was a junior in high school at the time. Even though it meant a relocation to a new school for him and potentially only a short-term relocation, for that matter, he quickly volunteered to go along with me and help with some of the legwork on prospecting for a new restaurant and opening new streams of income. Nancy and I agonized over the decision, but we eventually decided that if Ron wanted to join me, then we weren't going to stop him. His help would prove invaluable besides.

The drive took us three days. We kept in touch with Gani throughout. When we arrived, we found him waiting for us at Chateau I, an upscale restaurant in downtown Dallas. He ran toward the car the moment he spotted us. I noticed immediately that Gani had lost a shocking amount of weight. I knew that he was still struggling with his gambling addiction and figured he owed the weight loss to the ever-present stress of making ends meet.

The first order of business was to find a nice apartment the three of us could share on a monthly lease. Before I signed anything, I made Gani give me his word that he wouldn't be doing any more gambling.

"I'm through with it, Pertef," he said. "I'll never gamble again."

His answer was so satisfying that it made the trip feel like a success already. Even if we never managed to get our feet under us on a new business here in Dallas, at least Ron and I would have helped my good friend beat his dreadful addiction.

So we moved into a three-bedroom, fully-furnished apartment. Despite the low rent, the place was far nicer than I would have believed prior to seeing it with my own eyes. It even had an Olympic-size swimming pool in the center of the complex. Here, for a while at least, we could be comfortable while we tried to beat a new path for our families.

Ron started school and also a part-time job as a valet at Chateau I's sister restaurant, Chateau II, which had just opened and needed new hires. Gani also landed a job there as a headwaiter. Both of them quickly started making very good money.

That left me to focus more of my efforts on finding a new opportunity for myself.

Dallas is a beautiful city. If not for my father's needs and desire to stay in Connecticut, I might have more seriously considered a permanent move. But soon, the sheer weight of how much I missed my family made it clear that I had allowed my priorities to get out of order. I had come here to clear my head and search for opportunity, but my head would never be clear without the support and presence of my family, and I was no more likely to find a viable opportunity in Dallas than I would had I been back home. That was when I resolved to start clearing the books in Dallas, finalizing the process of getting Gani back on his feet, and returning home.

The only trouble was that Gani didn't keep his word. With all that money coming in, he began to gamble again. It got so bad that he started hosting high-stakes poker games in the apartment. At first, I did my best to try to move the games out of our space, but gambling can be as compelling as any drug.

Eventually, I started joining the games. I'm ashamed to admit it, but I was becoming addicted myself. I didn't like what was happening to me. I had to get back on the right track before it was too late.

I almost didn't make it.

One night, we had two high-stakes tables set up in the apartment. With all the local bigwigs we had at the table, there must have been hundreds of thousands of dollars in the room, and I was doing well on the night.

We had set up in the dining room. Ron was on the sofa in the living room, watching television. Gani had taken precautions to secure the door, but as we soon found out, he didn't go far enough. Suddenly and with one thrust, the door burst open, and I found myself staring into the barrel of a shotgun.

As my eyes widened with fear, my mind focused with laser intensity. The first thing I noticed was how quickly the other players managed to recover their money from the pots and slide it back into their pockets. One of the other players—I'll call him John—must have been wearing fifty thousand dollars in gold jewelry. In what seemed like one quick motion, he removed every piece of jewelry he was wearing and hid it without the armed robbers noticing anything at all. It was clear that these men had been through this before and even clearer that I was the only novice at the stickup game. I alone had frozen. I felt like an extra in a movie scene.

The man holding the gun on me wasn't masked, and neither were his two associates, both of them carrying shotguns of their own. I glanced over to the sofa, where Ron sat petrified. I didn't care an ounce whether these men took my money. I just wanted them to leave my son alone.

Then the gunman ordered something of me that rocketed me out of my head and right back to my homeland. The gunman now looked like the Communist officer from my youth—the one who had stolen my Butterfly.

"Give me your watch," he said through gritted teeth.

I looked down at the wristwatch that had belonged to Uncle Arif. I had worn that watch since the day he died. "C'mon, man," I said softly. "This watch belonged to my uncle who has recently passed away. It has no monetary value. It's only valuable to me. It's the only thing I have to remember him by."

The burglar sneered. "Well, now your uncle wants me to have the watch, so hand it over."

It was like I was watching my enemy mount my horse all over again. For a moment, I tensed, meaning to resist. But then all those bad memories of what happens to resisters came flooding back. I saw my brother die, my mother abused, my siblings and friends worked to the bone in the labor camps. All my life, I had wanted nothing more than for the Communists to leave my country so my family would be safe. Now here in this room, I wanted nothing more than these thugs to leave my house so my son could be safe.

I had no alternative but to hand over my priceless watch to those thieves. When Gani saw me remove my watch, he went crazy. "You better not touch my brother's watch!" he threatened. "You take that watch, and sooner or later, I'll find you! I recognize all of you. I'll find you and kill you all one by one!"

The robber pointed his shotgun at Gani. "You must have a good memory for faces. If you don't keep your mouth shut, I'll blow that memory away!"

Now I began to panic. The anxiety in the room was escalating. I knew Gani could be a crazy man if he was angry enough, but I couldn't believe my ears when I heard him tell the burglars that he recognized them.

I looked to Ron, who was now slumping on the couch, his expression icy from the fear and confusion. I had to do something.

"Hey, man," I said calmly. "We don't know any of you. So let's all just stay cool and keep our heads. Just get what you came for and nobody gets hurt. My friend doesn't know or recognize any of you. None of us recognize you. So please take whatever you want and leave."

Suddenly, a ruckus kicked up from outside the apartment. The thieves' faces changed from anger to fear. It looked as if they were frightened that someone might have called the police. Quickly, they grabbed up what they came for and ran away.

It took a long time for me to return to myself. Gani spent the next few minutes apologizing to his shaken but furious guests, then the rest of the night pacing the apartment and muttering about pay-back I knew he would never pursue.

Ron held up well. He was strong. He assured me that he was okay, but I could see that something about the situation had changed. He had been enjoying his new life, but on a night like that, every-thing can come crashing down.

To see him like that was a wake-up call for me. Life is too pre-cious a commodity to jeopardize. I swore right then that I would never put myself or my family in a position like that ever again and put an end to my games in the private arenas. I also resolved to make the move home as quickly as possible.

It seemed like it was a wake-up call for our friend Jim Ieremias as well because the incident made him decide that it was finally time to clear up his immigration status. He had come to the United States as an employee for a Greek cruiser and had jumped ship while the cruise liner was docked in New York Harbor. The department of immigrations had been chasing him for over ten years since. The incident forced Jim to realize that sooner or later he was going to get caught by the authorities. So he decided to return to Connecticut with Ron and me and give himself up. A surrender was the only alternative if he ever wanted to come back to America as a legal immigrant.

It would turn out to be the right choice for him, although it would be hard work. He would stay at our house for a few day and then turn himself over to the immigration authorities. He would be returned to Greece, where it would take him another ten years to legally return to America. The process was difficult for him, but it paid off because now he and his family live in Vermont, where he is the owner of Fair Haven Restaurant in Fair Haven.

The day before we left Dallas, I tried one last time to convince Gani to return to Connecticut with us. But for Gani, Dallas was just the right city—beautiful women and lots of gambling and drinking—so he decided to remain behind. The car was packed and ready to go when I asked Gani to step outside so we could be alone to talk, just the two of us.

"Gani," I said, "we've been working under the pretense that you're trying to make a life for yourself here so you can raise your children. But I know there's no way you could bring your kids into this kind of environment."

He slumped but it looked to me that the resignation on his face wasn't fresh.

He had known this truth for a long time.

"I want you to know that Nancy and I will raise your children," I said. "We'll do the best for them just as we do for ours—nothing more and nothing less. I promise you that I will give them all the love I can. And believe me, I have plenty of love in my soul for your children already. Nancy does too. She and I will care for them for as long as you need."

Gani sighed as if unburdened of a great weight. "You're like a brother to me, Pertef. I thank you from the bottom of my heart. I know I can count on you to care for my children, and I will be forever grateful."

I nodded. We stood in silence for a time, both of us staring at our shoes.

"Tell Nancy that I love her and hope that someday I will be able to make this up to her," he said finally.

I looked up just as he was breaking into a wistful smile.

"You are the luckiest guy in the world to have a wife like Nancy."

"You've got that right," I said with a chuckle. At the same time, I thought, *How could I ever forget that, even for an instant?* I felt like a fool.

"Please kiss each of my children for me," Gani said. "Tell them I love them. Tell them that I'll make all this up to them someday."

"The only thing we want is for you to get back on track," I said.

Tears rolled down his cheeks. We hugged each other and said our goodbyes.

Then I climbed into the car with Ron and Jim and headed home to Connecticut and a long overdue reunion with the family.

*****

Back home, after things had settled down, Nancy and I had a long talk about our future. We knew that we would have to work hard to recover our losses. The first thing we did was lay out a business plan for our recovery. We carefully organized every detail. Our liquid assets were minimal, but what we did have would be worth much more. We had experience and plenty of it. We also had drive and determination. I had been fighting to make it in this world since the day the Communists first fired upon our house. The fight in me had only grown stronger in the years since. As far as I was concerned, failure was not an option.

I found a rundown liquor store and bought the business and the building for pennies on the dollar. It took me about two weeks to get the place cleaned up and painted, but when I was done, the store looked beautiful. Most of the customers that came in after that would comment about how nice and clean the place had become.

This made me realize from the time it opened that the business would be a success.

With that in mind, I immediately began thinking about my next investment. My ambition would not let me stand still. So I enrolled in a real estate class and received a Connecticut real estate license. By this time, Nancy had a real-estate broker's license already. She had begun working in the sales department of a development company. Her people skills, personality, and—of course—her beautiful smile made her a top-notch saleswoman, and she soon parlayed that ability into a new job with a major mortgage company.

Nancy's insight gave me a leg up to quickly learn about the mortgage and banking industries, which led to my being hired by a local bank. My goal with this move was to get us one step closer to opening our own mortgage company. So by pulling our belts tighter, following a well-planned budget, and saving everything we could, within a few years, we did just that.

*****

Five years had passed, and everything was going according to the plan we had laid out. Gani was still in Dallas but had settled down and wanted his children back. The request saddened Nancy and me. They were his children, so we knew we had to comply, but at the same time, they had become like family to us. We had come to love these children as if they were our own.

The girls, who were old enough to have remembered their father before he left for Texas and had fond memories of him, wanted to make the move. But for little Pertef, my namesake, Nancy and I were the only parents he had ever known. After all, I was the one who brought him home from the hospital when he was just a few days old. We were with him when he took his first steps, when he spoke his first word, when he went to school for the first time. He had grown up with our children—Ron, Rob, and Resmije—as his brothers and sister. This was his home. Now suddenly, he was being asked to move to a strange town and live with a strange man who was supposed to be his father.

Little Pertef cried his eyes out when we gave him the news. Eventually, we managed to talk him into giving it a try just for a little while.

"It'll be just like a vacation," I said to him. "And who knows? Maybe you'll like it there."

Reluctantly, he agreed.

Now with Gani's three children gone, Ron and Rob being away at college in Florida and Georgia respectively, we had suddenly gone from a full house to a decidedly emptier nest. The only people left at home were Resmije, my father, and Nancy and me. Resmije had just begun her freshman year at Farmington High School.

Nancy and I weren't used to having such an empty house, so we decided to have one more child. She was forty-two, and I was forty-seven, but we both seemed healthy and loved children so much that we agreed this would be a good decision for us. Nancy suggested we go for a physical first, and if we were given a clean bill of health, we would add a new member to the Bylykbashi family. She made an appointment for both of us to see her doctor.

The appointment was for nine o'clock, and when we arrived, the doctor took me into the office first to check my blood pressure and draw blood. Once he finished with me, he went to the room where Nancy was waiting.

Her exam took much longer than I expected, and I began to worry. Soon, the nurse entered the waiting room, her face ashen.

"The doctor wants to talk with you," she said.

Immediately, I knew something wasn't right. Nancy put on her usual bright smile, but I knew her well enough to recognize that she was smiling only because she didn't want to upset me.

"Mr. Bylykbashi?" the doctor said.

"Please call me Pertef, Doctor."

He sighed. "Well, Pertef, I think Nancy may have some problems that might require surgery. But before we jump to any conclusions, we'll wait for the pap test and then address the issue. I'll call Nancy as soon as I get the lab report."

For a moment, the room felt as if it was spinning. I could hardly grasp everything the doctor had said, let alone process all that it would mean for Nancy and for our family.

Sensing my fear, Nancy grabbed my hand and pulled me toward her. "Pertef," she said, "do you believe in God?"

"Of course, I do," I said. "You of all people know that."

"Well then, if this is God's will, so be it. It is what it is. So let's go home."

Her words gave me courage. I steeled up and nodded. "You know, there's a passage in the Bible that says if you call on God, he'll hear your prayers and answer. So I'll pray that we get a good report when your test comes back."

Nancy looked at me with surprise. "I didn't know you read the Christian Bible!"

I cocked my head to one side. "For your information, I read the Bible, the Quran, and the Torah, and I think anyone that believes in God should read all these wonderful holy books. As far as I'm concerned, they're all readings of God's works." My wife gave me a smile of approval—that smile that any man would die for.

The moment we arrived back home, I did as I had promised. I fell to my knees and prayed for over an hour. I prayed to God through his Son Jesus. I prayed to God through the Prophet Mohammad. I prayed to God through the Prophet Moses. I was so desperate that I wanted to make sure I'd covered them all.

"God," I said, "please let my beautiful Nancy live long enough to see her grandchildren and both of us to enjoy them."

That night, I couldn't sleep. Inside my head, a battle raged between positive and negative thoughts. Each time a negative thought would enter my mind, I would immediately try to replace it with a positive thought. I just continued to think that Nancy would be okay. I began to think things like, *The Almighty God created the universe in seven days, so curing Nancy would be a very small task for him.*

By the next afternoon, Nancy and I had been waiting impatiently all day for her doctor's call. When the phone rang, my wife quickly answered.

"Hello, Doctor," she said, holding the phone so we could both hear.

"Nancy, I'm sorry," he said. "I wish I had some good news to tell you, but I'm afraid the lab reports confirm that you have cancer of the uterus. We need to schedule surgery as soon as possible."

When I heard that dreadful word *cancer*, my mind went blank. The doctor was explaining the procedures that Nancy would go through and confirming surgery schedules. Nancy hung up the phone after he was finished, and we looked at each other with blank stares. We just couldn't believe what was happening.

Then we collapsed into each other's arms and cried in silence. We stood together in this way for quite a while before Nancy broke the silence.

"I hope you won't forget me too quickly," she said.

"Why are you talking so crazy?" I replied. "Are you going somewhere I'm not aware of?"

She let her gaze fall as her eyes watered once more.

"Listen, Nancy. Look me straight in my eyes."

She did as I asked, though it was clearly difficult for her.

"I promise you that you aren't going anywhere," I vowed. "I have this feeling that God is going to reward us."

"Why?" she said with a whimper.

"For one simple reason. Just stand back and analyze things for a moment. What would be the possibility of us going for a checkup if we hadn't planned on bringing another baby into our lives?"

"If not for the baby, the possibility of us going to the doctor would have been zero."

"So why would we have made that unlikely decision to have a baby at our age in the first place?"

She looked down.

"I think it was God urging us to check on you before it was too late," I said. "I *know* that you're going to be all right. We won't be able to have another child, but we may have exchanged one life for another."

*****

Nancy's hysterectomy was successful, and the doctor sounded certain that we had caught the cancer in time. It was isolated in the uterus and hadn't spread elsewhere.

"If she hadn't come in for that checkup," he said, "it would've been too late." Then he clapped me on the shoulder and said something that shook me to my core. "This was God's work, Pertef. You both wanted a new life, and God gave you the life you have together—his gift to you. So the two of you should go home and enjoy the rest of your time."

I hugged the doctor and thanked him for giving Nancy such good care. "I told Nancy those exact words just yesterday. This is a gift from God. He answered our prayers."

With Nancy on the mend, our lives began to settle down once again. My wife and I were spending more time with each other and focusing more time and energy on our children and their education. Gani was having some problems with his son. Little Pertef had endured his trial period and wanted to come back to live with us in Connecticut. Gani was hurt by this and had tried to make little Pertef understand that he loved him and that their place was together as father and son, but eventually, it became clear that there was no convincing the boy.

Gani was talking a mile a minute when he called me as he tried to explain the difficulties with little Pertef. He seemed to think it was his fault for not being able to make his son happy. I felt sorry for Gani, as I couldn't imagine how I would feel if I were in his shoes. He apologized over and over for dropping his problems in my lap, but Gani had no idea how much Nancy and I had missed that child. We were more than happy to take him back into our home.

When Nancy had overheard enough of the conversation to realize what was happening, her face lit up. I nodded that she was correct in the assumption that little Pertef would be returning to us. She exploded into a broad, giddy smile.

I tried to ease Gani's pain by telling him that it would be better for Pertef to be where he was comfortable and that besides it would give Gani more time to focus on raising his two daughters, Mileta and Beth. Gani wanted to be a good parent, and he was definitely a hard worker, but he hadn't been able to overcome a few of the personal problems that were always chipping away at him a little at a time.

The next day, Gani put Little Pertef on the plane for Connecticut, and Nancy and I went to Bradley Airport to pick him up. We hadn't seen him for over a year. He had grown so tall, but he seemed a little thin. We were so happy to see him. He was a beautiful child, especially when he flashed his beautiful dimpled smile. I will never forget that precious moment when little Pertef ran toward us and Nancy bent down to pick him up. He was kissing her face all over, and Nancy was doing the same to him. Anyone could see the bond was still there, even though a year had passed.

Life and destiny can take strange turns. One minute, we were in the midst of a nightmare dealing with Nancy's cancer, and the next minute, it seemed like all our wishes and desires had been fulfilled. We had wanted another child in our home, and we had gotten one.

All my life, I have been amazed by how events have unfolded and marked my destiny. I knew then and know now that the best way to deal with life is to have faith and trust in God and let him do his work.

God's work visited us again shortly after when a fateful letter arrived. At the time, Sokoli had come from Washington to spend a few days with me and my family. He and Sherry had been divorced for quite some time, but our friendship remained intact, and Nancy didn't object to her sister's former husband visiting with me and the children. My kids loved him, and the feeling was mutual. They called him Uncle Steve, which seemed to make him happy.

One day during his visit, we had just finished lunch and were enjoying some coffee when Nancy said she was going out to pick up the mail. She returned a few minutes later with most of the mail tucked under her arm. In her right hand, she held a single letter.

"You have a letter from Albania," she said excitedly. "Here, open it and read it to your father." She was shaking with anticipation.

She knew that we were always anxious to receive news from Albania because the worry over our family was ever present in our minds. Over the course of more than thirty years, we had received no more than four or five letters from the labor camp holding our family, and all them had been censored.

This was why I hung my head when I saw that the letter was indeed from the camp. The Communists might have censored much of the material we had received before, but something told me this one would be clean. They would never miss an opportunity to let the bad news get through.

Nancy carefully handed the letter to me. I looked at my father, took a deep breath, and then opened it and began reading it to myself:

> Dear Father and Brother Pertef,
>
> With regrets and with our broken hearts, I am writing you this letter to let you know that our beloved mother, your loving wife Resmije, as of October 6, 1982, has departed from us and from this world, and we are certain that God will give her peace and tranquility in eternity. As we all know, my dear father and brother, our mother endured thirty-two years of humiliation and degradation—always hungry and tired after endless days of hard labor—and for all these years, she had no peace. But never once did she regret fighting for what she believed in, fighting for our freedom. Our mother, God rest her soul, has now found peace.
>
> We know that no one can hurt her anymore.
> Your Loving Son and Brother,
> Gezim

Tears dripped from my face onto the pages as I finished. Nancy, Sokoli, and my father just sat, not making a sound and hardly breathing. I could see that they were hoping I was crying tears of joy.

Nancy seemed to pick up on the truth of it first. "Pertef, what's going on? Is everything all right? What's in the letter?"

I got up from the chair and threw the letter on the table. "The Communists have killed my mother!" I screamed. "My mother is dead!"

My poor father sat there in confusion. He understood enough English to realize that Resmije, his wife of over fifty-four years, was dead. Tears ran down his bright red cheeks. I went to Father and put my arms around him. We tried without much success to console and comfort each other. I felt so bad for him. He seemed to be totally lost. He had lived his life with the hope of being reunited with his wife and children. There was never a day that he did not think of his beautiful Resmije and his sons and daughters.

As I embraced my father, I began to imagine how difficult it must be in Albania for my sisters and brothers. I was convinced that they would be next in line to die. I knew in my heart that the Communists would not stop until they wiped out every member of our family. I couldn't shake the feeling of helplessness, knowing I could do nothing to save them.

Nancy and Sokoli came from behind me. We all circled my father for several minutes and wept in silence and sorrow. I could feel the reverence in the room, the honor for my wonderful, brave, and loving mother.

"Baba," Nancy said to my father, "please don't cry. We should all be happy for Mama Resmije. She is safe and at peace now and can never be tortured or mistreated again. I hope and pray to God that someday they will answer for the crimes they've committed against your family and the Albanian people. I know that God will reward Mama Resmije."

She picked up a few tissues and gently wiped my father's tears then got some more to wipe her own. She put both of her hands on his cheeks and kissed him on his forehead. "Don't worry, Baba. We will be here for you." Then she turned to me. "Pertef, I am so sorry that I didn't have a chance to meet and know this great lady. I have listened to you tell of her sacrifices for the cause of freedom. I know her dream for over thirty years was to see her family reunited in a free Albania and to live without fear. The children and I feel cheated that we never had the opportunity to meet Mama Resmije. My prayers were always that we could meet her, if only for a few minutes, and she could hug her namesake, her granddaughter Resmije."

I took a moment to think back to when Resmije was born. It was Nancy who insisted she be named after my mother. I was against this in the beginning because in the Albanian tradition, the only time you name your child after a parent is when the parent is deceased. But Nancy would not listen to my reasoning.

"You don't understand," she had said. "I've already made up my mind. This time, you'll have to give in to my wishes and do this by the American tradition."

Now looking back, I was thrilled that Nancy had stood firm on her decision.

Even though they had never met, my mother's death took a toll on Nancy. We would often spend time in the evenings talking about my memories of her and of the mark she had made on her family. One night, we discussed the time when little Resmije was only six months old and Nancy wanted to send a picture of her to my mother.

"You're wasting your time trying to do that," I had told Nancy. "The Communists won't give Mother the satisfaction of receiving a letter from the family, especially one with a picture of her newborn granddaughter."

Having never lived through anything like it, Nancy often expressed disbelief at how iron was the fist of my country's oppressors. There was propaganda mongering and absolute control, and then there was robbing a prisoner of anything resembling basic human decency. Nancy wouldn't listen to any of that. She insisted on sending the photograph of little Resmije.

"What does her granddaughter's picture have to do with anyone's political point of view?" she asked. "That just doesn't make any sense to me. This is a baby we're talking about. For Christ's sake, she's only six months old!"

I shrugged. "The Communists don't use good judgment or logic. They dictate through force, torture, and fear."

Just as I had predicted, a few months later, both the letter and the picture were returned marked "Person Unknown." The envelope had been opened and taped shut as if someone on the receiving end had inspected it thoroughly.

On another night, I was having a harder time than usual dealing with the loss of my mother because guilt had started rearing its ugly head. Nancy, Father, and I were sitting around the table with our after-dinner coffee when I got so choked up that I felt I had to leave. I excused myself and went outside to be alone for a few minutes.

As I paced the grass in my backyard, my mind wandered back to the time I escaped from my homeland. I was sitting there in Greece again, pondering accepting the offer of a secret reconnaissance mission back into Albania. I could still see Gani offering me chocolate and cigarettes, could still hear him whispering not to take the deal.

Did Gani really save my life back then? I wondered not for the first time. *Or did my decision not to go condemn my mother to a lifetime of imprisonment and hard labor in the concentration camps?*

Over the years, I had convinced myself that there was nothing my meager reconnaissance could have done to help my family. The Greek operations had failed again and again after all. But now that my mother was gone, I couldn't help but blame myself. If I had gone on the mission to Albania, maybe I could have planned an escape for the rest of my family. Maybe I could have given my mother, my brothers, and my sisters the gift of freedom. How happy it would have made my father if I had been able to bring his wife and family home to the United States with me. And how proud it would have made me to be able to do this one thing for my family.

Then my mind drifted to other possibilities. What if my plan had failed and my mother and I had been captured or killed? In this version of history, I would have been directly responsible for her death. My family would have blamed me for her loss and thought me too brash and young and stupid. On top of that, I would have never made it to the United States, and my father and uncle wouldn't have had the help they needed to stop living in squalor and despair and start making a comfortable living and home for themselves in Connecticut as they tried to lobby for their families' freedom.

Ultimately, I cleared my mind that night with the reminder that we must do the very best we can in any situation and put everything else in God's hands.

*****

The next day, I placed a call to Gani and told him about the loss of my mother. Gani flew from Dallas to spend a few days with us. It was comforting to have my two good friends with me in my time of sorrow. Even though it was the unpleasant news of my mother's death that had brought us together, we enjoyed a pleasant visit by recapturing many old memories of our times in the army.

Little did we know then that this would be the last time the three of us would ever be together. Sokoli was always complaining about having high blood pressure, but I never really took him seriously. Given that he had the kind of sense of humor that seemed like it could never die, I never really believed that Sokoli could succumb to poor health. Plus, he was only forty-nine years old, in good shape, not overweight, and was always so full of life. If I'd had to guess which of my friends would die young, I would have guessed Gani, who, on top of his dangerous gambling habit, drank almost a case of Heineken every day.

In the end, I suspect that it was Sokoli's smoking that ended his life so young. Not long after he returned to Maryland, Nancy received a call from his landlady, who informed her that Sokoli had died from a heart attack during the night. The only reason the landlady had even known to call us was because she had checked Sokoli's telephone bill and discovered that he had called us every other day.

When Nancy called to tell me the news, I found it so unbelievable that I couldn't digest it. We talked for ten minutes or so, and I sat in chatty disbelief throughout. It wasn't until after I hung up that the idea of my good friend's death finally sank in. My eyes immediately filled with tears at the thought of how fleeting life could be. The years had passed too fast, and now the only thing left was his memory.

I pulled myself together and knew that I couldn't waste any time. Since Sokoli was Muslim, I assumed he would be buried in the Muslim tradition—before sunset of the day of his death. Of course, I wanted to make sure that any member of his family not laboring in the camps would be in attendance, but Sokoli's sister lived in Belgium, and I didn't have her phone number. It would probably be impossible to get her to the United States in time, but I knew that Sokoli also had a niece living in Hackensack, New Jersey. I found her number by calling the information line then slowly dialed as I tried to decide just how to break the sad news to them.

Sokoli's niece was a bright, cheery young woman named Dalife, who married one of our army buddies, Malik Lala. I had met her several times and had always found her so pleasant and positive.

It was a great weight to know that I would have to give her this unhappy news.

When she answered, I choked up for a moment.

"Hello?" she repeated, sounding as if she might be thinking the call had been placed in error.

"Dalife," I said finally, "this is Pertef." I paused for a moment. The words I had meant to speak flew from my head so quickly that I could think of nothing more to say.

"I can guess why you're calling," she said. Then she revealed that Sokoli's landlady had already given her the news. "And don't worry, Pertef. I'm already handling the funeral arrangements."

Relieved that I wouldn't have to be the one to give her the news, I listened as she explained that Sokoli would be buried by Muslim tradition, which meant he would be wrapped from head to toe in a white sheet and placed in the casket. There would be a wake all day that day.

While I knew that Sokoli was Muslim, some of this news was troubling to me because I also knew that he never cared for the white sheet part of the tradition. He had adopted many American traditions and embraced the American fashions. Often, you would find him dressed in a stylish suit and tie. He always loved it when someone complimented him on what he was wearing. His dashing good looks and debonair appearance offered up a complete package. I knew from both suspicion and past conversation that Sokoli would prefer to be buried in a suit rather than a sheet. This way, everyone could see him one last time and remember him looking just the way he lived.

When his niece told me that they would be forgoing tradition and not burying him by sunset, I figured it only made sense to honor what I knew my friend would want in terms of his burial dress. So even though I knew she would have the final say in anything, I felt compelled to speak up on the matter.

"Your uncle was a fine man, Dalife," I told her. "He was born into the Muslim faith, but he lived most of his life according to American ideals and traditions." I gave a sad little chuckle. "If anyone has ever adopted American life, it's Sokoli."

"I agree," Dalife allowed.

I tried to choose my words carefully as I continued. "He was very particular, is what I mean—especially in his dress."

"So what are you saying?" she asked, sounding somewhat defensive for the first time.

I sighed. "Here in Waterbury, the Albanian-American Muslim community buries our dead in a suit and tie and places them in a nice casket. I think Sokoli would have wanted that."

Dalife explained that she understood, but she understood what the family's wishes on the subject were as well. Ultimately, we all had to bow to the traditions of the generation that preceded us.

The next day, Nancy and I arrived at the funeral home in Maryland to pay our respects to my dear friend. Everything was just as Dalife had described it. Sokoli's body was completely wrapped in a white sheet, with only a small portion of his face showing. There were no flowers. The moment I first laid eyes on the scene, I was filled with grief. I don't think it had really sunk in until then that I had lost one of my dearest friends.

After the service was over and Sokoli was in the ground, I stood by the grave and pondered years past.

My days as a soldier in the U.S. Army never would have been the same were it not for Sokoli. Even though he had accepted the honor as a soldier and took his duties seriously, his outlandish sense of humor often had him stepping out of line. He was, more than anything, spontaneous in his tendency to joke. He would react before he realized what he was saying or doing. On one such occasion, during the crisis in Lebanon when President Eisenhower sent a large number of troops to help the Lebanese, Sokoli and I were coming out of the library when we heard the news about the conflict. The two of us wanted to be pilots, even from a very young age, so we decided to write a letter to President Eisenhower requesting that we be sent to support the cause in the Middle East. As we walked back to our company, we discussed our idea and what we would write into our letter.

Looking back, it seems so naïve to think that our letter to the president of the United States would ever be noticed, let alone returned, but we honestly believed that President Eisenhower would take the time to consider our request. I had always been one to believe that I could achieve any goal I set my mind to, and now that I was with the U.S. Army, I felt that I could nearly conquer the world singlehandedly.

We took our education seriously, and we were in the top of our language class, but we did not have enough confidence in ourselves to feel that our English was good enough to write a letter to the president. So Sokoli and I decided to call on our friend Billy Vangjeli to write the letter for us. He was more advanced in his studies. We explained to Billy that we wanted to volunteer our services to fight for the cause of freedom on behalf of Lebanon and its people and then added that when the conflict had come to an end and we returned to America, Sokoli and I would appreciate being put in flight school and be trained as helicopter pilots. We signed, sealed, and stamped the letter and put it in the mail.

To our surprise, we received a response within two weeks, which was far quicker than even our high hopes could have asked for it to come. The letter came directly from the desk of President Eisenhower:

> I thank you, and the American people thank you, for your dedication to America and to the cause of freedom. At this time, our soldiers are being deployed as whole units. Regarding Flight Training School, it will be necessary for you to receive the training and pass the required tests before you can be considered. Thank you for your readiness to serve our country. Good luck and best wishes.

And the letter was signed "Dwight Eisenhower, President of the United States of America." Even though our request was denied, Sokoli and I truly believed that Dwight Eisenhower personally received and read our letter then wrote and signed the response. We felt honored to have received a letter from the president of the United States.

Whenever we were with friends, we never missed an opportunity to tell them about the letter. One day, as we were telling our story, one of our army buddies jokingly said, "The reason your request was denied was because another soldier sent a letter to the president requesting to become a carpenter, and because only one request can be granted at a time, the carpenter's request was granted and yours was denied." The carpenter joke spread like wildfire through our company.

Sokoli heard of the rumor that was spreading and was telling me about it one day as we were replacing ceiling tiles in the mess hall. He was a little annoyed by the rumor and was almost convinced that it could possibly be true. He stood on the ladder as he was telling me and not paying attention to the job at hand. Suddenly, he swung the hammer hard, and instead of hitting the nail, he hit his thumb. He began screaming like a madman, and the hammer flew out of his hand and hit the floor. Our friend Myzafer Ramolli happened to be holding the ladder for him at the time. Half from the pain and half from anger at the situation, Sokoli barked at Ramoli for him to get the hammer. When Ramolli retrieved it, Sokoli started giving him the business.

"It was you who sent the letter to the president asking if you could be a carpenter, wasn't it?"

"No, sir!" Ramolli replied emphatically. "I wouldn't do something stupid like that!"

What Sokoli did next startled me but did not surprise me a bit. Without warning, he got a good grip on the hammer and hit Ramolli right on the top of his head.

Ramolli screamed from the pain. "Why did you do that? You're crazy! I told you I wasn't the one that sent the letter!"

"If you didn't send it, then who did?"

"I don't know, but it wasn't me. I think it was somebody joking around and it turned into a rumor."

Sokoli grumbled. "I know it wasn't you. I just wanted you to imagine what I would have done if it had been you or if you ever think of doing something like that." As much as I was enjoying the repartee, I couldn't stay quiet any longer.

"You're crazy, Sokoli," I said. "You're a sick man. You need to apologize to Ramolli for your stupidity and for hitting him."

Sokoli apologized to Ramolli as if the entire incident had been an accident or a terrible misunderstanding. That was Sokoli. I might have tried to change him, but he would never change.

As I stood by his grave, I recalled the occasion when Sokoli and I found ourselves in a boxing match against each other.

I was declared the winner, but Sokoli got in the last lick, hitting me when my back was turned. Grinning, he reached out a gloved hand to help me up.

"Are we still friends, Pertef?" he asked.

"Until death," I had said, beaming.

The memory caused my eyes to water. Suddenly, I remembered the words my friend had spoken nearly twenty years earlier when he had entered The FrontPage Restaurant and surprised us all with the news that he had survived the car accident that had supposedly killed him.

"Sokoli will never die!" he had said. "I jumped twenty feet high and told death to kiss my ass."

I looked down at his grave and smiled through the tears. "You were wrong, my dear friend Sokoli. Sooner or later, everyone dies."

Sokoli was gone from my life forever but never from my heart. Even today, as I write my life story, a smile comes to my face as I think of his wonderful personality, that wild way he always gestured when he spoke, his never-ending smile, and his pure, unadulterated zest for life. If more people lived and laughed like Sokoli, the world would be a far better place.

Chapter 23

For Nancy and me, the greatest joy was that our children were ensuring brighter futures for themselves. Not long after Rob left college, the two of us opened the first People's Choice Pizza restaurant in Unionville, Connecticut, and to date has grown to be a profitable business with twelve restaurants and offering franchises throughout the United States.

Meanwhile, Ron was excelling in college, and our daughter Resmije had met the love of her life in a charming young man named Sebastian DiTommaso. He had been the first boy I had allowed her to date, so it came as quite a shock to me when seven months into the relationship, Sebby had come to me to ask for my daughter's hand in marriage. I had given my permission reluctantly, though proudly, for I knew that the decision to raise Resmije under a strict moral code and high expectations had paid off for her.

"Babi," Resmije said to me one day, her lovely face alight with excitement, "I want to say something from the bottom of my heart. I have been very happy with my life and with the way I was raised. I know that sometimes I rebelled and gave you and Mom a hard time, but I want to thank you both for the values you have instilled in me."

Those are the words that every parent in this world waits to hear. When Resmije giggled and hugged my neck, I knew our daughter had grown up to be everything we had hoped for and more.

Nancy chose that moment to enter the room. The three of us talked for a while, sharing in the excitement of the wedding plans that needed to be made and passing ideas on who would make which arrangements and how.

After our daughter left, Nancy and I sat silently at the table for a few minutes, both of us overwhelmed by all we had just learned. I just couldn't believe how quickly our daughter had grown up.

Then at the exact same moment, we both broke into the same spontaneous reaction many successful parents would have after realizing they had completed a job well done—we stood, grinned, and slapped a well-deserved high five. All our children had grown to be responsible and successful, and our daughter was now beginning her own journey as a wife. Despite the struggles we had occasionally encountered with her, she had grown to be a perfect ten.

The date was set for October 20, 1990. Nancy and Resmije went quickly to work on ensuring that not one detail went undone. We would hold the ceremony at St. Patrick's Catholic Church in Farmington, Connecticut, and the reception would take place at a banquet hall in Windsor Locks. My only responsibility in any of the planning was to pay the bills and put down the deposits. For as long as I have lived, I have never been happier to spend money.

The original plan was to invite only our closest family and friends, but we had so many people that we held dear that it was difficult to keep the guest list to a reasonable size. Eventually, the number swelled to more than five hundred, but none of us ever had regrets about how massive the affair became. There was just no way to leave anyone out—particularly with all that was happening in Albania at the time.

The first piece of happy news related to my homeland came two weeks before Seby and Resmije were married. My brother Gezim had escaped the labor camps and was in Budapest with his wife Adile, his son Tani, and his daughter Jeta. Adile's father had escaped Albania in 1950 and immigrated to Peterborough, Canada. It had been over forty years since Ibrahim had seen his daughter. Adile called her father to tell him of their escape, and he immediately made arrangements to travel to Hungary and bring them back to Canada.

Three days before the wedding, Gezim and his family arrived in Canada. It had been thirty-three years since I had heard my brother's voice. So many of the events in my life cannot be measured in words, and this was merely another. It is impossible to describe the feeling that comes with speaking to a brother after thirty-three years. We tried to bring them from Canada to Connecticut for the wedding but didn't have enough time to make the necessary arrangements for the travel visa they would need.

Albania was in the news more often by then. The government was in constant turmoil. We all knew that the end of the Communist era was finally drawing near. As much as I tried to stay focused on Resmije's wedding, much of my attention stayed with the situation in Albania. Through all the upheaval, I feared that my family might be in danger. Regime changes were always bloody affairs, and it seemed clear that this was what was happening in my birth country.

Despite the worry and despair on my face through much of the otherwise beautiful wedding, Resmije never once complained. She would often take time away from her duties at the reception to give me words of encouragement, hope, and support. That's my daughter—she always puts everyone else's feelings before her own.

My mind was particularly focused on Albania because news had just started to pour in about people being released from the labor camps. Some close family friends from my homeland, Axhire Bushka and her son, had received their release from a camp where they had spent forty miserable years. They had just arrived in America and were in Waterbury, Connecticut, with the rest of her children. Sadly, Axhire's husband Alil had passed away a few years earlier, and they were never able to reunite. I was honored to invite Axhire and her family to my daughter's wedding, but only the children could make it.

I acknowledged the Bushkas's at the reception. As I introduced them to the hundreds of guests and shared a small piece of their story of survival, there were no dry eyes in the hall. When the speech was over, the Bushkas received a standing ovation. I felt happy for Axhire and her family, but there was an emptiness in my heart as I thought of my mother and how wonderful it would have been if she too could have escaped the bonds of communism. How happy it would have made us all if only she could have taken her place next to my father at her granddaughter's wedding.

It was Saturday, October 20, 1990. Despite all that was on my mind, it was still one of the most joyful days of my life. What a beautiful bride my Resmije was! I was overwhelmed with love and pride for my daughter, but at the same time, I battled with the pain of knowing that my little girl was moving on from her parents' care. On top of that, I was still so thankful for every day Nancy had been able to live following her battle with cancer. It was truly God's blessing that allowed Nancy to live and be a part of such a joyous occasion.

I left early the next morning for Canada to see my brother and his family. My father wanted to make the trip with me, but because of his age and health, we determined that it would be too difficult for him. I promised him that I would do everything in my power to ensure a quick reunion in the United States for him and Gezim.

Still today, after so many years have passed, tears fill my eyes as I write about the reunion with my brother. I arrived in Peterborough around four o'clock in the afternoon. When I rang the doorbell, the door swung open almost immediately. There stood Gezim. I hadn't seen him in decades, but there was no mistaking my brother. He had been waiting by the door, and on his face, he wore that old familiar ear-to-ear smile as tears flowed down his cheeks. The pain and heartache we had endured for so many years seemed to break through all at once.

As I pulled my brother into a bear hug, I couldn't control the tears. Through the hugs and kisses, there were no words—only silence. The unspoken words expressed our love for one another and our joy to be together again. It had been thirty-three long, agonizing years since I had last seen my brother. We had been no more than boys the last time we had spoken. But now it seemed as if time had stood still as if we had never been separated.

When finally we spoke, the conversation flowed easily. I couldn't help but marvel about how familiar he was to me even with all the time that had passed. Over the years, I had often tried to imagine what my mother, sisters, and brothers would look like after all that time, but the proper image had always proved elusive. Now that I had seen Gezim, I could envision my brother Medi as a grown man, and my sisters exactly as the ladies they had become.

Gezim's wife and children knew more about me than I had imagined they would know. After a lovely dinner, I suggested to Gezim that we go somewhere so we could spend some time speaking in private about our family and the situation in Albania. We packed a few things and checked into a room close by. We stayed awake through the night, exchanging stories. It was then that I finally learned the full truth about all that had happened following my escape.

"Five days after your escape," Gezim explained, "the authorities told Mother that you had been captured and executed at the border. Many of the prisoners at the camp came by to give condolences to Mother, even though there was doubt about the story of your execution being true. Stil they gave her words of encouragement and hope." My brother shook his head sadly. "We realized that the authorities were lying and that this was only their way to discourage anyone else from attempting escape. But still Mother didn't know for sure what had happened to you." He looked me square in the eyes to let me know how deeply this had affected my family. "She worried constantly about your well-being. We all felt so sorry for her. She never recovered from the death of Fejzi, and now the Communist bastards had told her they killed you." Gezim sighed. "As much as we tried, we couldn't convince her it was only propaganda. She wanted solid proof, and we couldn't give that to her."

Tears came to my eyes as I leaned forward in the uncomfortable lounge chair in the motel room. "Mother lived her whole life thinking I was dead?" I asked, choking up as I delivered the words.

"No, my brother," Gezim said with a twinkle in his eye. "You see, after you had been gone for three weeks, something unusual happened. Mother was walking about the camp when she was approached by the commander's wife. Do you remember her?"

"Are you talking about Commander Sterneci's wife?"

"Yes, that's the one. You should remember him. He was in charge of the camp when you were there."

I wanted to interrupt him and tell a story that he wouldn't believe, but I wanted to hear everything he had to say first. "His wife always seemed more sympathetic," I offered instead.

"That's right," Gezim said. "And she showed it on that day. To Mother, she whispered, 'This is not to be repeated to anyone, and forget who and where you heard it from, but the authorities lied to you about your son. His escape was successful, and he is alive. Go back to your barracks and rest your mind.'"

"Bless that woman."

"That's what Mother said," Gezim said as he lowered his head. "The only words Mother spoke in reply to the commander's wife were, 'Thank you and God bless you and your family!' Pertef, you just can't imagine how our mother felt that day. Even though she was still locked in a labor camp, she was the happiest and proudest human being on the face of this earth. Your escape gave all of us hope and courage and showed us that whenever there is a will strong enough, there is a way to make it happen."

"I am honored and happy to know that my escape brought her at least one day of joy," I said sadly.

"Oh, it brought her more than that, brother," Gezim insisted. "Every day, she thanked God that you had made it to safety, and every day, she and the rest of us prayed that we could find a way to follow you. And many did. A year after your escape, others made their attempts. Some were captured, but some made it."

"Anyone I would remember?"

"Yes. Our friend Rexhep Qose tried in 1958."

"I remember Rexhep. He was bold."

"And I went with him," Gezim added nonchalantly.

I froze, shocked. I knew my brother to be a brave boy the last time I had seen him, but I could hardly imagine him trying the escape so soon after I had gone. He would have still been so young back then.

"The odds were stacked heavily against us," Gezim said with an almost wistful expression on his face. "I suppose our plan was doomed from the start. The biggest obstacle was the weather. It was the winter of 1958, and as you know, the treacherous Albanian mountain terrain didn't make the season any less brutal. We encountered a blizzard almost immediately. We would take five steps forward and fall four steps back. On top of that, the skies were pitch black with zero visibility, which made it impossible to know exactly the right direction to walk. We quickly became disoriented. We were within ten yards of the Albanian and Greek border, but rather than crossing into Greece, we somehow got turned around and headed back into Albanian territory."

"Something similar happened to me when I escaped," I interjected. "That border is confusing even on a clear night."

"When the patrol guards passed by the border fence, they noticed footprints we had left in the newly fallen snow. They followed our tracks, and within thirty minutes, they had Rexhep and me in their sights. There was no reason to resist. We were surrounded."

"Oh, Gezim," I said softly. "The punishment for attempting escape—" I couldn't finish the thought, it was so terrible to bear.

"Yes, our lives were a hell on earth from that point on," Gezim said, his voice retreating into a mechanical kind of indifference. "We were kept in solitary confinement for six months, with a daily routine of torture and interrogation. After solitary confinement, I was given a fifteen-year prison sentence. Rexhep received ten years. Both of us served at a prison in Vlore.

"When we arrived at the prison, they separated Rexhep and me. They placed me in a cell with nineteen other prisoners, and even from the moment I laid eyes on them, it was clear that none of them were well. All I could think was that death would've been much kinder and sweeter than serving my term in such inhumane conditions.

"*This is how I will look one day*, I thought desperately. I would guess that the youngest prisoner was sixty years of age, and the oldest of the prisoners must have been closer to seventy." My brother paused for a long while then, looking like he was fighting back tears. "And the worst part was that if I did manage to live out my fifteen years in that hellhole, they would release me only to be returned to a labor camp. To think that I was just a few feet from freedom, and the next thing I knew, I was looking at fifteen years in prison."

I started doing the math in my head. "You were what? Seventeen years old at the time?"

"I was," he replied with a curt nod. "And those other men looked like they had been in that cell forever. The old men had been labeled political prisoners. Before communism, they were well-educated pillars of their communities. When they saw me—a young, scrawny boy who was tired, scared, and hungry—they all stared in disbelief at what the Communists were doing even to Albania's children. I could see that they wanted to help me and to offer solace, but none of them could." A tear escaped over Gezim's cheek. "Then one of the older prisoners put his arm around my shoulder and said, 'Don't be afraid, son. You're among friends here. There are two kinds of prisons in this world. One prison is for thieves and cutthroats, and the other prison is for people who are trying to make a difference—people like you and like us, people who are fighting not only for ourselves but for everyone that prays to God and yearns each day for freedom. For that, my son, I want to tell you that we're all proud that you're here among us.'

"This man was very much respected by the rest of the inmates," Gezim continued. "He was one of the older prisoners. He had a distinguished look about him, a look that made it clear he was this group's leader. This man had received a law degree at a university in Italy before World War II.

"Gentlemen," he said to the others, "I would like to suggest something if I may." Then he turned and looked down at me to explain. "In here, we have established criteria that whenever an inmate dies, gets executed, or is transferred, the column moves up and the last sleeping spot—the one next to that urinating vase you see in the corner—belongs to the newcomer." Then he addressed the others once more. "As we all know, this means that this young man's place is next to the urinating vases. But I would like to suggest that we all move one spot down and give him the place furthest away from the stench."

"When a murmur of disapproval rose up, he raised a hand for silence. 'We are old and some of us are sick,' he said. 'In all probability, many of us will never get out of here alive. But if this boy can someday be our voice, our eyes, and our ears, then he can tell the story of what went on inside these walls. And the world will know that Albania was run by a clan of criminals, cutthroats, and thieves.'"

Now Gezim smiled through his sorrow. "All nineteen men nodded in agreement. And then one by one, they moved their blankets one space down so that I would have the best place in the cell. I was as far away as they could place me from the urine vases. Still the stench was unbearable, but at least the kind gesture of the prisoners kept the spray of urine off me and my blanket. I was tired and confused, but I thanked the prisoners and took my place in the spot they had cleared for me. Even as I drifted off to sleep, I hoped that I would wake the next morning and find that it was all just a terrible nightmare."

My brother went on to tell me many stories that encompassed the full fifteen years he served in that filthy prison before he was returned to the labor camp and finally found his escape in 1990. Gezim was lucky. As he later explained, our older brother Medi and cousin Nijazi didn't share in his luck. They both served twenty-five years in similar prisons, and after they served their full sentences, they were returned to a labor camp, where they remained until the fall of communism in 1991.

It's amazing how resilient God created human beings to be. No matter how desperate the situation gets, we always seem to have hope. Hope is the most powerful weapon that God ever created for our survival. If we were not equipped with this remarkable ability to hope—to hope for freedom, to hope for the day that our family would once again be together, to hope for survival—all of us would have lain down and died. Survival derives from other factors, of course. There is also love, determination, and one's own values that are instilled at an early age. But hope and BESA, those were the main components that held my family together and alive long enough to finally find their freedom.

Each one of us was condemned to serve a life sentence in captivity under Communist rule, never knowing when we awoke each day if it would be our last. But hope and BESA gave us the courage to stand up for what was right, gave us the strength and determination to make the best of every day.

At some point while Gezim was telling me about my family's lives after my escape, I could see that he needed to take a break to regain his composure. The stories still seemed fresh on his mind and were affecting him deeply as if he were reliving them all over again. So when he paused for a moment, I interjected with my own story of escape.

"It was actually Commander Sterneci that convinced me my only hope for survival would be to attempt an escape," I explained.

As I told my story, Gezim was wide-eyed, looking as if he couldn't believe what he was hearing. We talked about the commander for a time before we both agreed that in any vicious regime, one could find officials who disagreed with their government enough to lose their fear of the consequences for nonconformity.

"It's just like the old Albanian saying," Gezim said.

I smiled knowingly.

"Be careful when you try to dig a grave for others because you may actually be digging one for yourself."

When I heard those words again, I pondered their significance as if for the first time. That is exactly what happened to Sabri, the accountant who gave information against Xhemil. He was charged with treason and thrown in prison and never came out alive.

Gezim and I talked until we saw the morning sun shining through the window. Then it was time for my brother and me to return to our family. I stayed in Canada for almost a week. As much as I wanted to take them back with me, their asylum situations would not allow it. So I headed back to Connecticut alone. My brother's escape wasn't merely good news for my family. It was just one of the many early leaks that would lead to the dam break we had been waiting decades to see.

Chapter 24

O n every channel, the news was full of coverage from the Eastern Bloc. I found myself watching television almost around the clock. The Berlin Wall was coming down, and I knew that communism in many countries the world over would follow with falls of their own. It is a strange thing to watch such stirring images on the television and sit on the edge of your seat because you know that one day soon, they might lead to a reunion with your brothers and sisters. It was also surreal for me because I had read scripture that suggested regimes like these oppressive Communists could not stand forever, and yet I had also experienced more than thirty years of evidence to the contrary. During those decades, my faith would falter more than a few times. There were many nights when I thought that I would never see my siblings again.

Now as I watched those images flicker onscreen, I was reminded that my faith had been well placed. God had control of everything and everyone in the universe.

As the political unrest raged in the Eastern Bloc, I remained glued to the television, not wanting to miss a single broadcast of significance. It was almost as if I couldn't decide whether what I was watching was true or whether my life as a political prisoner and refugee had been one big dream from which I was about to wake up.

Not for the first time, as I pondered my allegiance to my birth country and my love for my new country, I felt like a child placed up for adoption by birth parents who couldn't care for him. I adored Albania, and all the fond memories I held of those lands before the Communists arrived, but it was my adoptive America that had provided the care, nurture, love, and protection during my most formative years. I loved both countries, but I felt betrayed by my countrymen who had joined the Communist regime.

One night, as I watched broadcasts of the unrest in Berlin, I thought about the many political meetings that Father and I had attended in the Albanian communities when I first moved to Waterbury. We loved talking politics and sharing views on what to expect from the superpowers of the world as they warred silently over the Soviet Union's oppressed territories. At one particular meeting, emotions were running extremely high. Everyone present was anxious to share their opinions about what was ahead for Albania. After a time, my father, who had been listening silently as we hotly debated our ideas, decided to speak.

"I must disagree with all of you," he said, his soft voice as profound as ever.

Everyone paused to give the elder the reverence he was due. Even the thick smoke from all the cigarettes in the room seemed to freeze as if to listen.

"Oh, I agree that communism is near an end," my father said. "And it will fall but not by the hands of anyone here tonight. We have neither the strategy nor the means to achieve that end by violence." He raised a finger to accentuate his point.

"On the day communism falls, not a shot will be fired."

A low rumble picked up as if there were some ready to object. But given his age and the wisdom in his eyes, no one would raise a voice to object until he had finished.

"We are given choices and are allowed to make decisions," Father continued. "But God alone will determine when we should be reunited with our families. It is he that controls this universe—not the soldiers you say we should raise. No, my friends, when communism falls, it will be by his hand, not ours."

When he was done, some of the men started chuckling. I could see that while they respected him enough to let him speak his mind, they also thought that he was a naïve old man and knew nothing about the situation.

Years later, news from the television delivered to my father his vindication. It all happened just as he had predicted.

The wall fell that night. I have known elation on many occasions in my life, but none of them have equaled that one.

With the yolk of communism pulling back from Europe, I knew there would be some huge obstacles ahead for my country. The first thing I needed to do was to help my father gain his official citizenship in the United States. My sisters and brothers would be allowed to come to America more quickly if their father were to sponsor them. I could try on my own, but visas were simpler matters if they came on the sponsorship of a parent. So I began the process of filling out the application and other necessary paperwork. Albania did not have an embassy in the United States, but Albanian representatives at the United Nations had an office in New York very near to the United Nations Building. This was the only office in America where Albanians felt their voices would be heard.

Around that same time, Albanian communities from all over the United States and Canada organized to hold a peaceful freedom demonstration on behalf of Albania and its people. They planned to stage the rally on the street in front of the Albanian representatives' office in New York. The demonstration would be in support of "the United States for a Free Albania." It was important to us to let our fellow Albanians know that even as the Communists in our homeland held tightly to their fleeting power, we had not forgotten about our native country or the families we had been separated from for many years.

The reports of the fall of communism in Albania began arriving daily not long after that. Then one day as I was watching CNN, I saw the report that approximately twenty-five thousand Albanians had charged the German embassy seeking asylum. This gave our group hope that it was only a matter of time now.

At our meetings, now instead of debating, we watched the news reports on CNN. More and more often, those reports would focus on Albania. Even though many of the reports downplayed the siege of the German Embassy as an act of vandalism by hoodlums and ex-prisoners, we knew better. Then came the reports of mass exodus.

Thousands upon thousands of Albanians were escaping to Italy by boat and some to Greece by land. They used any means available to break the barriers of the closed borders of Albania.

Those of us that had escaped the chains of communism years earlier knew how sweet was the taste of freedom. Very soon, all Albanians would live that same experience.

It seemed as if everyone had joined the uprising. Many were killed at the borders as the Communists tried desperately to maintain their grip, but it was too late. The power in numbers was simply too great. Finally, after all those years of torment and heartbreak and loss, Albanians joined together and made their stand against communism. This time, their call for freedom would not be stopped.

I spent much of this time feeling as if I were floating. My heart was so full of joy for my native country that I could hardly contain it. I was excited to be reunited with my family but was also overwhelmed with pride for all the Albanians that had chosen to stand up and take what was theirs. These people had been stripped of everything precious to them—their homes, their religion, their land, their families, even their self-esteem and dignity—but what communism would never take from them was their courage, their integrity, and their will to live in a free land.

The year was 1991. Only a few weeks had passed since the fall first began, but to me, with all the peaks and valleys of my emotions, it felt more like decades. The days that followed would drag by even slower as I anxiously awaited my first chance to speak with my sisters Lumka and Yllke and my brother Medi. When that day finally came, we found ourselves unable to utter a word. The tears we shed had simply been suppressed for too many years. We had spent our lives trying to contain our emotions, to remain strong for each other until the day our family could be together again. Now there was no holding back. It was the first time I had spoken with them in any form since my escape in 1957. The long, arduous battle was over, and soon, we would finally be together.

We had reclaimed our freedom, and yet it didn't much taste like victory. Our family had paid a dear price to reclaim something that should never have been taken from us in the first place. We paid with the lives of our brother, our mother, our uncles, our cousins, and our dear friends. And we paid with the loss of years together as a family.

When freedom came, Medi still found himself forced to live in the camp, as did many of the others who did not have homes to which they could return. For many, the camp was all they had known, and so leaving its walls was about as foreign and frightening a concept as boarding a spaceship to another planet. Medi's son Flamur had escaped a month earlier, but there had been no word on his whereabouts.

"I ask nothing for myself," Medi told me over the phone. "But if you would please see if you can get news of my son and whether his escape was successful, it would ease the pain I feel. I want him to be able to come to the United States and live as a free man. This is what I ask of you, my brother."

I promised him that I would make sure his son came to America. What Medi did not know was that my plans were to bring *all* them to America.

In 1992, I made the decision to return to the country of my birth. Father's health would not allow him to make the trip, and I didn't want to go alone, so I asked my cousin Syrja Topciu to make the trip with me. We flew to Italy, where I bought a car and arranged to have it shipped to Albania by boat. Then I made a call to my sister Yllke, who had been so young the last time I had seen her, and told her to let everyone know when we would arrive at the port.

The trip from Italy to Albania was one I will never forget. As I looked out over the glinting blue waters of the Mediterranean, I reflected on the past forty years—my father's escape, my brother's death, my escape. I thought that my dear brother Fejzi would have been proud to know that the stand he had taken so many years earlier was not in vain.

You won the battle for freedom, my brother, I thought. *I only wish you were here to celebrate the victory with us today. But we will remember you. You will never be forgotten.*

With the sea breeze caressing my face, I thought of Grandmother Aishe and the children and grandchildren she had lost in the battle for freedom. I thought of Mother and Father who for many years were never together but remained faithful to one another every day of their lives. Father often told me that the only thing keeping him alive for so many years was his undying love for his wife and the hope that one day they would be together again.

We all paid dearly for our freedom, not only with the lives that were lost but also with lost time. The years of separation had cost my family so many memories.

Mother went to her grave having never met her namesake, little Resmije. My children would never experience the joy of knowing their grandmother.

When the ship docked, I saw my sisters and my brother waiting for me. I was so excited that my hands were shaking as I went to the port office and signed off on the paperwork for the car.

The reunion was a tearful one. It was strange to be standing on Albanian soil once more, but as I hugged my family, there was no doubt that their embraces felt very much like home.

Then we piled into the car and headed to what my family had called their home for most of their lives, Saver. Even though the barriers were gone at the labor camp, there were still many families living there. Some of them couldn't imagine life beyond these walls, but most simply had no other place to go.

It had taken him some time, but with the help of a distant relative, Medi had secured a small house for his family in Lushnje. We all went to Medi's home after we had finished wandering that terrible place that had held us all for so long.

I had brought some gifts from the United States. They were things that for most of their lives, my family could have only dreamed of having—new clothes, makeup kits for the women, and watches for the men. My sisters were beautiful, and I knew that they had often dreamed to be made up as beautifully as they could be. Lumka and Yllke were very young when communism took over Albania, and they never had a chance to apply makeup.

As they opened the gifts, my cousin Myrset, who was now in her sixties, began telling the story of her engagement and marriage to her husband Shefqet. I had to fight back tears as she said, "Dear cousin, from the time I was a little girl, I have always dreamed of being a beautiful bride. But I would never get that chance. My wedding was in a small room within the camp. Our marriage was consummated in a honeymoon suite that doubled as a stall where the cows slept."

I hugged her as tears rolled down my cheeks. "That is a hardship," I said. "And a crime. But I know that you were a beautiful bride all the same." I pulled back to look at her. Her face was contorted into a look of tearful gratitude. "It is what's in a person's heart that determines their beauty. But we will make you a beautiful bride all over again right now. Would you like that?"

She nodded with the kind of excitement usually reserved for young girls.

I asked the other women to make up Myrset's face and do her hair as if she were preparing for her wedding day. As the women worked on my cousin, they all sang traditional love songs and wedding songs. It was a wonderful time for all of us and especially Myrset, who was beside herself when she saw how beautiful she looked!

That night, before prayers and bed, I reminded myself just how much God had blessed my life. I took time to thank him, not for the extravagant gifts I had received but for the very smallest of gifts, the simple things that so many of us take for granted.

The next day, I went to the cemetery to visit Mother's grave. I knelt at the graveside and prayed, asking God the merciful to bless her soul and give her peace in eternity. I told Mother that her husband had sent his forty-two years of undying love for her and told her to rest peacefully and not to worry any longer.

"Your family is united once more," I said. "We are all free now." Then I paused, thinking better of what I had said. "Albania is free from the bonds of communism, Mother, but the people are not yet free from the hatred that has engulfed our country. The ones stripped of their control and power hate the ones that took their power away from them. And the Albanian people hate the ones that kept them in bondage and treated them like slaves for over half a century."

Then I rose proudly, still speaking to her. "I promise you, my dear mother, that from this day on, no one will ever be able to hurt your children or grandchildren. I will take care of them and bring them to the safest place on Earth. I will bring them all to America.

And when the time comes that Father is united with you in eternity, I will find a way to bring you to America and bury you next to your loving husband so that your final resting place will be at his side once again."

Father had asked me to place a dozen white roses on his dear Resmije's grave. I gently laid the roses from Father on the ground. As I placed a single white rose on the grave in her honor for each of her children and grandchildren, I knew that there was one more promise she would want me to make.

"And, Mother, I give you my undying word, my BESA, that your children will search for our dear Fejzi's remains. If we find him, I will bring him to America to be buried by your side." I sighed. "But if we are unable to find Fejzi, we will build a monument in his honor so that everyone, for generations to come, will know of my brother's courage and bravery, the stand he took to protect his family and countrymen, and the sacrifice he made for freedom. Everyone who sees the monument will remember Fejzi Bylykbashi and will know of his bravery."

When I was finished, I stood in silence for a few moments to honor my dear mother Resmije for the bravery and courage she had shown throughout her life.

I stayed at my cousin Njiazi's house for a week. I visited the camp often and spent time with many families there. We were all much older now. It was nice to talk with them and rekindle the friendships. Each time I returned to the camp, the people living there would surround my car as if I were a celebrity. Before my arrival, they had never seen a private automobile, only the ones driven by the authorities.

I had memories of many of these people, good ones and bad ones, but those memories made it clear that something had changed for many of my Albanian countrymen. Their time in bondage had broken their spirit. Once when I visited a bar near the camp, a young man approached me, his eyes dark and fearful. From the look of him, it was clear he had been drinking for quite some time.

"Are you Pertef Bylykbashi?" he asked me softly.

"Yes," I replied.

He paused for a moment, his eyes welling with tears. "Are you here to kill me?"

I felt Medi's hand tug at my shoulder. "Just ignore him, Pertef," he insisted.

"He's just had too much to drink."

Normally, I would have heeded my brother, but I was curious to know how this man knew who I was and, more importantly, why he feared me so.

"Why would I want to kill you, son?" I could see that he was nervous, so I quickly added, "No, I'm not here to kill you, young man. I haven't any reason whatsoever to hurt you. Why do you think I would do such a terrible thing to a nice fellow like you?"

The young man's face became pale. He seemed unable to speak.

"Besides that, I don't even know you," I continued. "When I escaped Albania in 1957, I don't think you were even born yet."

"Well," he said finally, "when you find out who I am, you will change your mind."

"Then keep talking," I said, my curiosity reaching its peak. "We will find out."

"My grandfather was Commander Sterneci," the young man said. "He ran the labor camp where your family was confined."

At first, I furrowed my brow, but then I broke into a wide smile. "What a pleasant coincidence! Are you really his grandson?" I put my arm over his shoulders.

"I want to buy you a drink and tell you a story about your wonderful grandparents."

We sat at one of the rickety tables in the lounge, and I began to tell him the story of how his grandfather had saved my life by telling me to make my escape and how it was his grandmother who eased my mother's mind after the authorities claimed I had been killed by the border patrol. As I was telling the story, the people in the bar began to circle the table and listen passionately. When I finished, I hugged the young man and told him how wonderful his grandparents were. It touched my heart and made me feel proud that I could share this story with him. It appeared to lift a great weight from his shoulders.

Little did I know just how much healing of this sort my country would need over the years to come. In total, I spent six weeks with my family in Albania. It was truly one of the highlights in my life but also exhausting. The highs and lows of my emotions were just so draining. Then there was also the prospect of what still awaited us as we clawed our way back to normalcy.

When my trip came to an end, I vowed to continue the fight for my people and to make good on my promise to my mother. But I missed my family, and I missed America. For now, it was time to go home to the place where I could do the most good.

*****

On the way home, I tried to put everything that had happened into perspective. Albania had changed. The people I had left so many years ago were worn down. It had been a long struggle for them. You could look in their faces and see the hatred, jealousy, and suspicion they felt. Years of being degraded and humiliated had destroyed their self-esteem, and they had lost all trust in their fellow man. When you have no freedom to speak your mind, doing and saying anything to keep yourself alive becomes a way of life.

The news reports informed the world that Albania had won its freedom, but the truth was that they hadn't won anything. Even today, they practice at freedom, but it will take many years to fully undo what the Communists have done to them and to their country. Their traditions have been stripped. Their BESA gone.

I remembered Albania as a proud country with people like Uncle Nevrus, Gani Kulla, and Aidin Kulla, who did not hesitate to take a stand against a truckload of soldiers. I remembered my uncle and his friends who stood tall as they faced a firing squad. I remembered my dear brother Fejzi, who saved the last bullet for himself rather than give his enemies the satisfaction of a live capture and years of torture and imprisonment.

While thinking about all this, it occurred to me not for the first time how petty it was that so many Americans hated each other only for the color of their skin. They were all living in freedom, and they were all Americans regardless of their ancestral countries. Hatred is a terrible thing to hold onto. It's much like cancer, eating away until it has consumed your entire being. All Americans, including myself, have the same opportunities, but my visit to Albania helped me understand why the healing process has taken longer for certain cultures within the United States—particularly for African Americans. In Albania, the enemy was an ideology. When communism fell, the soldiers who had once served that oppressive regime traded their uniforms for civilian clothes and assimilated with their people. In the end, an Albanian was an Albanian. There was no way to recognize the Albanians that had succumbed to the horrible dictatorship of Enver Hoxha. Hatred didn't exist for a single person or group of people but rather for the ideology that had generated so much pain and suffering. When I see a soldier dressed in a Communist uniform, my blood begins to boil but not because of the person in the uniform. Rather, it is for the uniform itself. It causes me an intense hatred for the pain communism brought to my family.

The situation between black people and white people in America is much different. It isn't an ideology that imprisoned the black race. It was a way of life. Even though it was many years ago, the distrust bred by that way of life remains. Americans should never forget the past, for remembering the past will help them avoid the same mistakes in future generations. But they *must* leave the past behind and move forward so as not to be robbed of the opportunities this great country holds for their future.

A few days after I arrived home, we received a notice from the court in Hartford, Connecticut, that Father, at ninety-three years old, was to be sworn in for his citizenship. The oath would be administered to a group of about a hundred people applying for citizenship at the same time. I was as proud of my father as he was of himself. He stood tall as the judge entered the courtroom.

The judge saw my father and, realizing that he was very old, came over, took his hand, and led him to the front. He pulled up a chair beside his seat and asked my father to sit there with him. Before he began the oath, he pointed my father out to the others in the room, telling them that he was ninety-three years old and had never-theless endured the rigorous process to become an American citizen.

"We will be proud to have him as one of us," the judge said.

As proud as I was of my father, the comments made me prouder of America itself. Where else but the United States would an immigrant from another country receive the kindness shown by this judge?

I redoubled my efforts to bring the rest of my family to this great land in part because I knew it would be the best place for them to heal and in part because I could sense that my father didn't have much time left. I should not have underestimated his will to be reunited with his children. He lived for another eight years after gaining citizenship, and I suspect that what sustained him was a desire to know for certain that his family would always be free.

It saddens me to write that he made it only long enough to reunite with his two sons Medi and Gezim before he died. Father passed away at the age of 101. The last time they had seen their father, Lumka was sixteen, and Yllke was only a toddler, and they would never see him again. They came to America a few years after his death. Still all of us were glad to have accomplished what we had toward reassembling our family. Many of those that had escaped with my father were not fortunate enough to ever see any of their family again.

As it was with my uncle's funeral, the turnout of mourners when my father passed away proved staggering. He was highly respected by Albanians as well as Americans. People came from all over the United States and Canada to pay their final respects. Because he had lived for so many years, he had outlived most of his friends and relatives in his generation, but those in the generation behind him loved him just as well.

It was a sad time for me. He had lived a long, healthy life, but you never can ready yourself to lose a parent or loved one. I felt a sense of joy knowing that Medi, Gezim, Nazmi, Bedri, and Zyfer were standing there beside me. We each took our turn and individually paid our respects to Father. He was laid to rest in Waterbury, beside his brother Arif.

Chapter 25

When I visited Albania in 1992, I talked with each family member individually to determine who truly wanted to come to America. There was no question that I would sponsor any of them that wanted to come, but I needed them to understand that it would take time and patience. The amount of red tape allowing them passage to America would be enormous, making for a long, slow process. I wanted all them to understand also that the only way I would bring them to the United States was legally and that all the documents they provided would need to be authentic. It would be difficult enough just handling the correspondence involved, so I didn't want any of us to have to endure the additional task of having to verify the legality of documents.

As I had promised Medi, the first person I sponsored to bring to America was his son Flamur. We were all so proud to sponsor him. Nancy, the kids, and I worked hard to make him feel at home. I was anxious for him to love America as much as I did, given that he was now in a country with abundant opportunities and a democratic government, but the trust that had been stripped from the Albanian people was not easily regained. Flamur, like many Albanians who had spent their lives imprisoned, was suspicious of anyone who showed them kindness. I noticed this characteristic in my nephew almost immediately. We tried so hard to make him feel at home, but he never quite seemed comfortable or happy. Perhaps we tried too hard. Whatever the case, Flamur lasted three years with us before eventually going off on his own.

One evening, we received a call from the immigration and naturalization representative in New York. He said that they were holding a young man who was from Albania by the name of Bardhyl Agastra, who said he was my nephew. He told me that Bardhyl had acquired a fake picture identification and passport and had tried to enter the United States illegally. When he was caught and questioned, he insisted that his passport and ID were authentic, even though they were clearly forgeries. It had taken many hours of questioning before Bardhyl had finally come clean.

"That's when he told us he was your nephew," the representative explained. "He claims he is seeking political asylum. If you can identify him as your nephew, we'll release him into your custody, but you'll have to bring him back for his court hearing."

I agreed and packed a bag for New York. When I arrived at the immigrations office, I found Bardhyl waiting for me. He could see that I was very upset. This was exactly why I had told everyone that I wanted to bring them to the United States legally. I didn't want to have to deal with these kinds of problems, and more importantly, I didn't want one member of the family ruining the process for anyone else that might want to follow through the proper channels.

"Is this how you want to begin your new life in the United States?" I asked. "On a lie?"

He lowered his head, ashamed.

"When we go to your hearing," I said, "I want you to tell the court exactly what happened to you and to our family for the past forty-five years. The only way you'll win this case is by telling the truth, and that is the only way I'll agree to help you. Do you understand what I'm telling you?"

"I understand very well, Uncle," he said.

Bardhyl was the first one called for questioning on the day of his court hearing. He told the judge exactly what had happened to our family. It was clear that the prosecutor wanted to win this case and send him back to Albania, but as we had done for many years, my family worked together to stand up for what was right. Next, I was called for questioning. I mirrored Bardhyl's testimony and told exactly what had happened to my family over the years.

The prosecutor turned to the judge and said, "Your Honor, everyone in Albania was in the same situation, and we have received word from the State Department that Albania is a democratic government now."

I waited for him to finish talking before I spoke again. "Your Honor, the prosecutor has told this court that everyone suffered as my family suffered. But that is not so. The Communists killed my mother, the defendant's grandmother. They killed my brother, the defendant's uncle. My family has taken a stand against communism for as long as I can remember, and they've been doing so since I was not much older than a toddler. Members of my family were held in prison and in labor camps for many years. Your Honor, the Communists have tried to annihilate the entire Bylykbashi family, and we have had to fight our entire lives because of our stand for freedom. But they could not defeat us or break our spirit, no matter how hard they tried."

The judge gave me a frank stare.

"Now the prosecutor is saying that the State Department considers Albania a democratic government," I continued. "I have the utmost respect for our State Department, but I know for certain that the Albanian government right at this moment is not to be trusted. For fifty years, they have been lying to their people and to the entire world, so why should we believe them now? The truth is the Communists still reign in Albania."

"Your claim is conjecture," the prosecutor said.

The judge held up a hand to silence him.

I turned my attention to the prosecutor. "Wasn't it the State Department that went to Cuba and returned with the news that Fidel Castro was *not* a Communist?" The prosecutor appeared to lose his wind.

"Your Honor," I said, pointing to my nephew, "this boy's mother and father are already approved for visas and will soon be coming to the United States. I fully agree that what he did was wrong. He used poor judgment in trying to save himself, but doing whatever was necessary to save yourself has been a way of survival for him and for our family for years." I shrugged. "Now, Your Honor, the decision to allow him to remain in America will be up to you. Our family has been separated for over half a century. We are all getting older, and many of our family have died without being reunited. I plead with you, please take into consideration the suffering and the heartaches we have endured and give us a chance to be together for the last part of our lives."

The judge gave a pensive nod before excusing me. As I returned to my seat in the gallery, I glanced over to where Nancy and the rest of the family were sitting. I was filled with pride when I saw the expressions of approval on their faces. What I had told the judge had also touched their hearts.

"Your Honor," the prosecutor interjected, "there is no way to verify Mr. Bylykbashi's statement. We can't be sure that what he has told us is based on facts."

At the time, I had just started my autobiography, so I had decided to take the few completed pages with me to the hearing, along with a letter of encouragement that I had received years earlier from *Roots* author Alex Haley. Confidently, I held up the letter and the thirty or so pages I had written as I once again addressed the court.

"I can prove that everything I say is true. I have begun writing my autobiography. It tells the story of the Bylykbashi family."

"Let me see that," the judge said. "Can someone bring it to me?" My attorney took the pages and handed them to the judge.

After a few moments of waiting for the judge to finish reading, the prosecutor cleared his throat. "Your Honor, those pages could have been written last week as far as we all know."

The judge ignored him as she continued to read a moment longer. Then she looked up at me. "Do you have any proof that this story was written before the fall of communism, Mr. Bylykbashi?"

"Yes, Your Honor. You'll note the letter from Mr. Alex Haley, the author, encouraging me to finish the book. It's postmarked a good ten years before communism fell in my country. The book outlines exactly what I have told you today."

The judge quickly turned her attention to the letter. "I am going to approve the stay for Bardhyl Agastra," she said when she was finished reading. "Do you object, Mr. Prosecutor?"

"Yes, Your Honor, I object," he said, sounding downtrodden.

The judge sighed. "Mr. Bylykbashi, don't worry. Everything will be okay. I'll give my decision after I have researched all the information presented here today." With that, she dismissed us.

The judge ruled in our favor a few months later, and Bardhyl was granted political asylum. This was a big victory for my family—a victory for which we owe great thanks to our attorney Chris DeLucas, who did a wonderful job representing us.

After that first victory, it still took almost seven years to bring all of my siblings to the United States. The effort may have been grueling, but our reward was for the family to be together once again after more than half a century.

My sisters Lumka and Yllke, along with their husbands, were set to arrive at John F. Kennedy International Airport in New York. The night before, I went to bed early, but I was so filled with excitement that I couldn't sleep. Lumka and Yllke would be the last of my siblings to make the transition to America. They represented the end of an arduous journey and of a promise fulfilled. At last, we would all be together and in the United States no less. It seemed like a fairytale.

When Nancy noticed that I was having trouble sleeping, she suggested that we get up to mark the occasion instead. "Let's celebrate with a nice bottle of wine. We'll make a toast to welcome Lumka and Yllke to America."

That sounded good to me, so together, we went downstairs to find our best bottle. As I popped the cork, Nancy took a seat at the bar off the edge of our kitchen and smiled.

"I'm so happy for you, honey," she said with an awed little shake of her head. "You're a man of your word. You promised your mother that you would take good care of her children and bring all them to America. It seems to me that tomorrow, the promise you made to her will be fulfilled."

I knew that Mother would have been so happy to know that her children and grandchildren were making homes in America. My heart was full of happiness at the thought that I was able to keep my promise to her.

The next day, I called my nephews, Beni and Bardhyl, and told them their parents would be arriving at the airport at about six o'clock in the evening. Yllke's son Beni and his family had already settled in Plainville, Connecticut, and Lumka's son Bardhyl and his family had made their place in Waterbury. My sisters planned to live with their sons, so it was good to know that they would be close to where I lived with my family as well.

Before we left for the airport, I stopped by the florist to pick up a dozen roses for each of my sisters. We arrived at the airport about an hour before their touchdown. I spent that hour pacing the terminal again and again. I was so nervous I couldn't stand still.

Then just when I thought I could take no more of the waiting, I spotted Lumka and Yllke with their husbands coming out of the customs area. Their expressions as they examined their new surroundings made it seem as if they thought they had stepped onto another planet. I ran over to greet them.

"I would very much like to sit down for a moment," Lumka said, fanning herself. "Just to catch my breath. I still can't believe we're in America! Is this real, or am I dreaming?" Then she closed her eyes and kept them shut for a time before allowing them to flutter open and that old familiar smile to cross her lips. "This really is America," she said happily.

I handed each of them their roses. Then I threw my arms around them, and we held each other tight.

Life is unpredictable, and no one is promised tomorrow. To have that day and that moment gave me such an overwhelming sense of inner peace that I could only describe it as the touch of God. I had made my way in this country. I had enjoyed a wonderful life and raised a beautiful family. And now I had made good on my pledge to bring all my siblings into this country and the safety, opportunity, and happiness it afforded. Through it all, I had Nancy's support—a woman I could scarcely imagine how to live without. In all my life, I had never felt so blessed.

Chapter 26

On March 15, 2002, we received a call from Nancy's sister that their mother's health was rapidly declining and only had a few days to live at best. We were packing for a trip to Florida when Nancy complained of a tingling sensation in her left arm that was travelling down to her left leg.

This frightened me, for I had always heard that sort of thing to be the symptom of a heart attack. I wasted no time in taking her to UConn Hospital. The doctors and nurses immediately began what turned out to be dozens of tests on Nancy's heart and soon determined that all was well.

We had only a few short moments of relief. Even as we sighed happily about the clean bill of health for Nancy's heart, we had no idea how drastically our lives were about to change again.

"Mrs. Bylykbashi?" the doctor said. He was younger than I would have pictured a doctor of his caliber, I remember. He was fresh-faced and bright-eyed and clearly nervous about what he had to say.

"Yes?" Nancy said, her smile fading slowly.

"I'm afraid we found something else while we were running the tests."

I stopped breathing as the young doctor explained that they had found a brain tumor and that it appeared to be inoperable. He made every effort to explain the prognosis of her condition, but as he talked, I felt as if I had been suspended in time. The room—and my life along with it—was spinning. I couldn't believe there was any truth to what I was hearing. The notion that Nancy's situation was essentially hopeless just didn't register with me.

I was devastated. All the energy drained from my body. When the doctor asked us if we had any questions, it was as if my grief had stolen my ability to render language. I wanted to appear strong for Nancy. I wanted to find words to encourage her, just as she had given me words of encouragement throughout our lives. But there was nothing I could do and nothing I could say. Nancy didn't deserve this. She had so much life and love left to give.

Hand in hand, we left the doctor's office. I still hadn't managed to find words, and from the way I was hanging my head, she could clearly sense my fear and pain and sorrow. I don't know if it was the news finally catching up to me or just feeling my beloved's gaze on my cheek, but my eyes began to glaze with tears.

"Get a grip on yourself, Pertef," Nancy said flatly.

I looked at her wide-eyed, my tears retreating.

"You've been the pillar of our family," she insisted. "And I want you to continue to do so even after I'm gone. You must be strong for our sons and daughter and for Little Pertef. He is in a very awkward time in his life. Remember that you have to be there for our grand-children also." Then for a moment, she too became choked up. "I love them so."

"Come on," I said, feeling a strange new confidence pour out of me. "Stop talking that kind of nonsense. You're not going anywhere. I will take good care of you. I will keep you alive even if I have to give you my own last breath. I refuse to let you go. And besides that, if you leave, who the hell am I going to have to argue with?"

Even as my wife laughed, I tried to hide how I was still crying inside. We had endured so many trials and tribulations together and had always managed to come out on top, but this was one that neither of us could control. With no medical options to lean on, this would be in God's hands.

That night, after reading some scripture from the Bible and the Quran and saying my prayers, I had a dream that was more vivid and real than any dream I had ever experienced. I woke from it halfway through the night and found that I couldn't return to sleep because I was parsing every detail in the hopes of coming to the correct translation of what the vision had meant.

The next day, I waited until my wife and I had gotten back to the hospital for her biopsy appointment before I finally shared what was on my mind.

"Let me translate the dream I had last night," I said as we waited for the doctor.

"Oh, Pertef," she said with a roll of her eyes. I had thought that she was seeming more morose today than yesterday, and this was my confirmation. "You and your dreams! What can a dream have to do with everything that's going on right now? The tumor is here to stay. Didn't you hear what the doctor said? If you've forgotten, then let me remind you. The tumor is inoperable, and it will continue to grow until there isn't enough room in my skull, and it will ultimately take me out."

"Probably," I said with a shrug. "In the long run, it will take you out." She looked surprised that I was agreeing with her.

"But according to the translation of my dream," I continued, "you have a few more years left to spend with me, God willing. Then we will continue to pray that a cure can be found, and you and I will spend many years together and be able to grow older with our children and grandchildren."

She chuffed. "That's exactly what I am afraid of—having to spend a few more years with you. That scares me more than the tumor."

We feigned a glare at one another for a moment before my wife began to laugh, softly at first, but then she began laughing hysterically. Nancy's sense of humor was beyond measure. There was absolutely nothing that could keep her down.

She fixed those beautiful dark eyes straight on me. "Come over here and sit down. I promise I'll listen to your dream because I know you're dying to tell me."

"Yes, I am," I said. "You know my dreams have been right on the money all these years. And I know this one is too. Last night, after a shower and my nightly scripture, I knelt and prayed to God for your health. Later as I slept, I dreamed that you and I were in a fantastic high-rise building. We were on the fifth floor in a large, well-decorated room. There were a few people in the room with us, but I don't recall if it was anyone we knew. Suddenly, you called my name. 'Pertef,' you said, 'I'm going to jump out of the window.'" Nancy chuckled nervously.

"I was amazed to hear you say that," I continued. "And as I turned around to try and stop you, you were already walking toward the big picture window. You had on a beautiful blue dress and matching blue shoes. You were absolutely gorgeous."

She started to say something but then closed her mouth and waited for me to finish.

"The episode took only a couple of seconds," I explained. "You were standing on the windowsill, and then you jumped. I was devastated! I just knew that you were dead and thought that when I ran to the window to see what had happened to you, you would be in pieces. Instead, when I looked from the window, I saw that you had fallen into a large swimming pool. Soon, you came up from under the water. You were swimming around the pool but unable to come out. I was so relieved that you weren't hurt, but I couldn't understand why you wouldn't get out of the pool."

When the story was over, my wife and I shared a long stare. I could see that she was having trouble deciding how she should feel about my dream.

"And your translation is?" she said after a time.

I sighed. "This is what I think. The dream means that you will have at least five years left. And by then, who knows what might happen? So let's just take this five years at a time."

Before she could respond to that, the doctor entered the room.

"How are you doing, Nancy?" he asked in his soft, soothing voice. "Did you sleep well last night?"

"I did," Nancy said, ashen as she often was when speaking with the doctors. "But I'm less concerned about my sleep and more about my prognosis." She took a deep breath as if clearing her mind. "How long do I have? You can tell me. I'm a big girl, and I can take it."

The doctor looked down at his chart, an action he often took when trying to stall. Whenever he did this, I was reminded of just how young he seemed. There wasn't a laugh line or wrinkle anywhere on his youthful face. He held my wife's life in his hands, and he looked more boy than man.

"Well, Nancy, I'm afraid the prognosis is not good. With this type of tumor, the best we can project is about two months." My knees turned to rubber.

"I'm sorry, Nancy," the doctor was saying. "I wish I had some good news to tell you." Then he made his exit by explaining that another doctor would be coming in to talk to us about treatments and surgeries. As he departed, I felt utterly numb.

"There you go, Pertef," Nancy said once we were alone. "You heard it from the horse's mouth. Now what do you have to say about your dream translation?"

Finally, I managed to collect myself. "I don't believe that doctor," I said flatly.

"I'll stand by my dream translations any time. I've proven my dreams to you time and time again. Just like the others, you'll see that this is a true translation."

"Well, I guess your proof had better come soon because the judge just sentenced me to two months." She laughed.

I gave a soft scowl. "The doctor is very young and lacks the experience that comes with age. How could you really believe that diagnosis?" I pointed to my chest. "Because I don't believe him and I'll bet my life on my dream! You'll see that I'm right."

Before she could reply, the door opened once more. This time, a stocky, broad-shouldered, and decidedly older doctor entered the room. From the moment he began introducing himself, it was clear that his bedside manner left much to be desired.

"I'm here to take you for a biopsy," he said dispassionately as he finished off this breakfast bran muffin. "Are you ready?" Nancy looked to me with fear in her eyes.

"Doctor, would you please explain the procedure to us before my wife goes with you? How will the biopsy be done?"

"I figured the procedures had already been explained to you," the doctor said, remnants of muffin still on his face and hospital jacket. "But since you haven't been given the details, I'll tell you." He looked casually at my wife as he explained the horrifying procedure.

"We'll drill a hole about the size of a half-dollar through your skull and try to obtain some tissue from the tumor." Then he looked to me. "She'll be in recovery for a short time before we return her to her room."

I looked at Nancy, the question of whether she was ready written plainly in my gaze. I could see the fear of uncertainty on her face, and when she rolled her eyes, I knew that was her way of telling me to do whatever I thought was right.

"Doctor," I said, "I don't think I'll be letting anyone drill into my wife's head today. I'm taking her home."

As the doctor stared at me aghast, Nancy nodded with approval.

"You're right, honey," she said with a chuckle and smile. "Let's go home!"

Despite my desire to see her rest as much as possible, Nancy suggested that we continue as planned and drive to Orlando to see her mother. We went immediately, and it was a good thing because they were only able to spend two hours together before her mother passed away.

The next morning, as Nancy was helping prepare for the funeral, I received a call from my niece in Long Island, letting me know that my cousin Zyfer had passed away as well. I knew my place was with Nancy during this difficult time to help her deal with the pain of the loss of her mother—not to mention the news of her brain tumor that we were both still trying to absorb—but Nancy felt that one of us had to be with Zyfer's family, so she insisted I go to New York for his funeral while she stayed behind for her mother's funeral. I planned to fly back to Orlando the following week and drive us home, but by the time I had arrived in New York, she told me over the phone that she had already made arrangements with her sister Pam and her nephew Danny Jr. to drive her back to Connecticut.

So I spent the next week helping Zyfer's family through their loss and calling Nancy whenever I could.

Finally, the day came that they would leave Orlando. About halfway through their drive back, they decided to stop at a motel for the night in North Carolina. Their room was on the second floor, which meant that Nancy would have to navigate the concrete steps in her fragile condition. The next morning, as they were leaving, Nancy stepped on a broken pencil as she was coming down the stairs. She lost her footing, hit the top step with her head, and then rolled down the other nine steps like a soccer ball before landing at the bottom in the parking lot, unconscious.

My cell phone rang. "Pertef, I have some bad news," Pam said from the other end of the line. "Nancy fell down the stairs this morning. We called 911, and they took her to the hospital."

"Oh my," I said, losing the wind to speak.

"Her leg is broken for certain," Pam said. "And she took a hard hit on the head. The hospital didn't want to treat her because of the tumor, so they bandaged her up and helped us get her back into the car."

"Let me talk to her."

"She's heavily sedated." For the first time, I could hear that Pam was crying.

"But if you want to try talking to her—" I heard some shuffling.

I spoke first. "Nan, honey, are you hurt badly?" Then Nancy's voice came through. "I'm okay, Pertef," she said, her words slow and slurred from the sedative.

"I must say, though, I thought this morning was going to be my last day on this earth. It's a good thing Pam and Danny were behind me. If they'd been in front of me, I'd have crushed them like ants." She tried to laugh, but I could tell she was hurting too badly.

I felt utterly helpless and about a million miles away from where I should have been. "Nancy, I—"

"Don't worry about me," she interrupted. "I'll be all right. I love you and will see you tonight."

I reunited with my wife around ten o'clock that same evening. Her face was terribly swollen to the point where her eyes were completely shut. The bump on her head was as big as a melon.

As soon as they pulled in the driveway, I got into the car and we immediately drove her to UConn Hospital. The ER doctors put pins in Nancy's broken ankle and a cast on her leg. They treated and bandaged her head and set her up for a week's stay.

When it was all over, the doctors advised her to keep to bed rest for six weeks at least. It was grave counsel, considering the prognosis she had received just two weeks earlier that she didn't have much more than six weeks left to live.

Nancy's accident put the entire family into a different dimension. In a strange way, her physical wounds allowed us to forget about the tumor for a while. She went about her period of rest as if nothing was wrong, apart from the cast on her leg.

Eventually, I told myself that I had to stop buying into the charade. Time wasn't on our side. We needed to do anything and everything possible to prolong her life. I was still so certain that if she made it five years, there would be a cure for her awaiting us there.

So we went for a second opinion. I had spent much of my free time over the previous two weeks researching neurologists and cancer treatment centers. I spent hours on the computer, checking qualifications of doctors and facilities, doing anything I could to educate myself about her medical condition so that I could make sure Nancy got the best treatment available.

The more educated I became, the more discouraged I became. Everything I was reading provided little to no hope for Nancy's type of brain tumor. It would take a miracle from God for her to beat this, but we all knew it was in his hands anyway.

In the end, it was Resmije who found the right doctor for us. Through a friend of hers whose mother had been treated for a brain tumor, she learned the name of Dr. Fatel, a renowned neurologist based in New York City. She had already set up an appointment for Nancy for the following morning.

I was immediately impressed with Dr. Fatel's thoroughness as he carefully examined Nancy's x-rays and MRIs. Once he had made his evaluations, he recommended a neurosurgeon by the name of Dr. Isabelle Germano.

By then, I was weary of all this passing around of care. "How well do you know Dr. Germano?" I asked, my skepticism apparent in my tone.

Dr. Fatel nodded knowingly. "Mr. Bylykbashi, if anyone in my family needed a biopsy, I wouldn't hesitate for even a second to send them to Dr. Germano. She is one of the best."

A week later, when Nancy went for her biopsy, Resmije, Ron, and Rob came with us. Dr. Germano was waiting in her small, tidy office. She was a strong and assured woman, but I'm sure she could see the look of uncertainty on our faces, for she offered a reassuring gaze as I prepared myself to ask the question on all our minds.

"How many biopsies of this type have you performed?" I asked.

She gave me a warm smile. "I'm proud to say I have performed more than four thousand biopsies, and every one of them was successful." We all kept silent, impressed as we were.

"We will inject a small needle and remove some tissue from the tumor for the biopsy," Dr. Germano said. "There is very little to be concerned about. Did my answer satisfy you?" Again, she smiled.

I felt satisfied, but my primary concern was Nancy. I didn't want her to go under the knife with someone with whom she hadn't connected. Fortunately, I could tell by the way Nancy smiled at the doctor's response that she was comfortable in her care.

After the biopsy, Dr. Germano had some encouraging news. She explained that the tumor could have been present for quite some time and that it would not be unheard of for the tumor to remain dormant for another twenty years.

"But I have to warn you that Nancy isn't out of the woods yet," she advised.

"We'll need to monitor and treat the tumor consistently."

Delighted with this optimistic outlook, we thanked Dr. Germano with a big hug for a job well done.

*****

And so our lives went on with as much normalcy as possible. Nancy's future remained uncertain, but the knowledge that she was likely to live more than just a few months gave us all comfort. If Nancy herself ever feared death, she never let it show. I have never seen anyone with such courage and strength. It was almost as if death feared her. We spoke of death often, with Nancy usually the one to bring it up. She would tell me about the things she wanted done when her time came.

She would say, "Promise me, Pertef, that when it's my time to go, you will honor all my last requests."

"Of course, I will," I would reply.

She smiled for a moment. Then she gave me a grave look. "If I've ever been serious about anything in my life, I'm serious now. So please listen to me carefully. It's important that you understand these are my last requests in this world, and I want to know that you will fulfill them for me."

I looked into Nancy's eyes and saw that she was as serious as I had ever seen her. It was difficult for me to talk about this with her. My eyes began to tear up, despite my efforts to remain strong.

"Pertef, stop," she said. "I'm not dead yet! Cry when I'm gone. You'll have plenty of time then!" She chuckled. "Or maybe you're crying because I'm still around."

I laughed as I leaned in for a hug. "You know, Nancy, you really are a crazy woman."

We held our warm embrace for a long time after that, neither of us wanting to let go. Finally, it was Nancy who let her arms fall.

"Where were we?" she said as I wiped the tears from my eyes. "When my time comes, I want to be cremated. I want some of my ashes spread in Anniston, Alabama, and the children can place the rest of my ashes with you if you wish."

I wanted to interject, but she held up a hand to ask me to wait until she was finished.

"Next, you know I'm a donor. I want to donate every organ I have that can be useful. It will make me feel good while I'm alive to know that I might make a difference in some lives after I'm gone."

Again, I tried to speak, and again, she cut me off gently.

"I don't want to be kept alive with life support," she insisted. "Once it's certain there is no hope left, I want you to let me go. And last but most importantly, don't let my grandchildren forget about me." Now a tear rolled down her cheek. "That's about it. So do I have your word on this?"

I sighed and nodded. "My darling," I said, "not only do you have my word, but I give you my BESA that your last wishes will be fulfilled."

*****

New Year's Eve of 2006, five years after Nancy was diagnosed with a brain tumor, is a bittersweet memory for me. None of us knew that it would be the last time Nancy would ring in a new year with us. For as long as I can remember, Nancy and I had celebrated the occasion in our home with our children and our close friends.

A few days before New Year's Eve, Pam and Gani's son Pertef, who was called Little Peter, showed up. We had not seen him for over a year and had missed him terribly. His return sparked excitement in both Nancy and me. Neither of us could think of a better way to bring in the New Year than to celebrate with our whole family intact. I called Resmije and asked her not to make any plans for New Year's Eve because I wanted her and Seby to come to the house with the grandchildren. My next call was to Ron. I told him the same thing. Then I called Rob to tell him of the gathering, but he and Jennifer had already made plans for the evening.

I stayed busy the entire day, preparing a wonderful dinner for the family. Nancy was as excited as I was. It had been a while since we had cooked for the whole family.

We were just about to sit down for dinner when Rob surprised us and walked in. He had decided to cancel his previous plans and spend New Year's Eve with the family. Nancy was thrilled to have everyone together in our home. I think she knew her time was drawing near as if she had an intuition that this would be the last time we would all be together, but she did everything she could to hide that sentiment. That was my Nancy. Even if she had known it was her last day on this earth, she would have kept it to herself rather than risk spoiling the occasion for everyone.

That night was unforgettable. We passed the time laughing, joking, sharing, and generally acting silly. The love we shared was tangible. At midnight, I opened a couple bottles of Cristal champagne. With the arrival of 2007, my prayers, as well as my children's prayers, were that God would bless our family with another year together.

But that wasn't in God's plan.

On the night of January 9, around midnight, Nancy retired to the master bedroom to finish reading a book she had started a few days earlier. I went to the study to finish some work. Half an hour later, I was reading the news from an Albanian website when a strange feeling came over me. It was as if someone had touched my shoulder. I turned to see who it was, but no one was there. Still the sense that something was wrong lingered.

I decided to stop what I was doing and check on Nancy. To my relief, she was lying in bed reading.

"This book is phenomenal, Pertef," she said with wide eyes. "I really want you to read it sometime."

"I will," I replied. "When you're finished with it."

She started to climb out of bed. But then as she stood, she lost her balance and fell to the floor. The fall was a gentle one, but I rushed to her all the same.

"Are you hurt, honey?" I asked breathlessly.

"I'm okay," she replied with a half-hearted laugh.

"Well then, give me your hands so I can pull you up."

Now her half laugh swelled to a cackle. "With all the weight I've put on lately, I'm almost certain that instead of you pulling me up, I'm going to pull you down."

"That doesn't sound like such a bad idea," I joked.

Laughing, I sat down on the floor next to her. For the first time, I looked directly into her eyes, and immediately, I noticed that she didn't look well. "Nancy, are you sure you're okay?"

Again, she assured me that she was fine and hadn't hurt herself. "Just get me a glass of water, please."

Before I could even make the attempt to get up, she laid her head on my chest. I thought at first that she might be having a seizure, but then I saw a few drops of blood running out from her nose, and I knew that my beautiful Nancy was dying in my arms. It happened so quickly that neither of us realized what was taking place.

"Oh, God, it can't be this way," I said as I gently kissed her forehead. "It can't be this way!" I held her quietly in my arms for a few moments and reminisced over our time together, back to the first day we had met some forty years ago. As I pondered our past, I hoped that I would wake up and find that this moment had been just a bad dream, but Nancy was not responsive.

I picked up the phone and called Resmije. I told her what had happened and asked her to call the ambulance and also her brothers.

The paramedics took Nancy to UConn Hospital in Farmington, where the diagnosis was an aneurism, leaving no hope for revival. I called the children together and told them what the doctor had said. I shared Nancy's last wishes and explained that she had made me promise to fulfill them. She had given to her oldest son Ron the responsibility of making the decision to remove life support. This was a heavy burden to bear, but mothers know the capability of her children, their strengths and their weaknesses.

Ron talked with the doctor and expressed his mother's wishes. Before life support was removed, I asked all my children to step out of the room because I wanted to be alone with Nancy for a few minutes. When we were alone, I told her how much I loved her, and I reassured her that I would not let her grandchildren ever forget her. I held and kissed my wife one last time and told her I would be with her again someday. I began to smile to myself when I imagined what my dear Nancy would have said to that: "Be with me again? Over my dead body!"

In the midst of our grief, I had almost forgotten about Nancy's request to donate her organs. I notified the nurse's station that Nancy was an organ donor, and they immediately made the necessary contacts and preparations. Then with all of us standing beside Nancy and telling her how much we loved her, Ron called the nurse to the room, and life support was removed.

Fortunately, there is nothing that surpasses the love of a family. My children and grandchildren circled around me, and we immediately began drawing strength from one another.

Nancy's funeral service was held at Saint Patrick's Catholic Church in Farmington, Connecticut. Resmije gave her mother's eulogy. It was beautifully done and so fitting for our Nancy. Other family members came forward to say their last goodbyes, including Nancy's brother Danny. Our granddaughters Nicole and Katie read scripture as well.

Through the kindness and compassion she shared all her life, Nancy had found a place in many people's hearts. I know that she was proud of her family and the strength they displayed during their grief. She had taught them well. I, on the other hand, still had much to learn.

Chapter 27

Without Nancy, my life had lost all meaning. I had no passion or desire to continue. We had been together for over forty years. She was not only my wife but also my life.

For the first couple of months, the children and I operated in a strange sort of denial. We carried on with daily routines even as we tied up loose ends from Nancy's businesses, her medical bills, and all the other harsh finalities one faces when a loved one's life comes to an end.

For years, Nancy had often taken one or two of the grandchildren to the condo we had at Burr Mountain. The kids always loved going because there were indoor swimming facilities and other recreational activities. Even as I faced the reality of my wife's death, I would catch myself feeling as if she had just gone away for a few days to the condo and would be walking through the front door any moment.

My properties and businesses kept me busy, but the nights were difficult, given that I would have to spend them alone at home. Most of my life, I had lived with close family sharing the same roof. As a child—and even while locked away in the labor camp—there were always my siblings, parents, aunts, and uncles. As a grown man, there was Nancy, our children, Nancy's siblings, and their children. Our house was always full.

Now it was just me. I spent much of my time looking at the family pictures and surrounding myself in quiet memories. There is much to be said about the love of family. It was my children and grandchildren that got me through the first few months of pain. Resmije shouldered the responsibility of helping the rest of us heal rather than worry about her own sorrow and loss. She was just like her mother in that respect, always putting others before herself.

One day, I was having a cup of coffee at her house when suddenly she asked, "Babi, how would you like to move in with us?"

"Honey, Seby asked me the same thing, and I knew he meant it. He said, 'Babi, you know that your grandchildren are crazy about you. If you lived to be two hundred years old, they would still not be able to get enough of you. Resmije and I would be honored to have you live with us.'"

"We mean it, Babi," my daughter said, and in her eyes, I could see her mother smiling.

"You are a beautiful and fantastic daughter," I said, my voice dripping with gratitude. "Your mother and I knew that from the day you were born. You have no idea how proud it makes me to hear those kind words from you and Seby. I thank you from the bottom of my heart, but I will have to say no. I need to go home every day and face this new life head on. Time will heal the sorrow, and then only the good memories will linger."

In the end, it was just as Nancy had told me it would be: I would find my solace in our grandchildren. "After I am gone," she had said to me, "look at our grandchildren, and you will see me there because you know that every fiber of my being is in them."

And she was right. In my grandchildren, I found that spark of contagious laughter that had so marked my wife's personality. I saw that through our children and grandchildren, Nancy's legacy would live on.

It was Carrie who suggested that I find a project to focus on during my time alone. This way, I wouldn't have to suffer through my idle thoughts and loneliness every night.

"You need to begin work on your book again, she told me. You have an awesome story that needs to be told. It would be a tribute to you and your Albanian heritage, and it would also be a wonderful tribute to Nancy."

I had put together about two hundred pages at the time, but I was not skilled at typing. Not only did Carrie encourage me to continue the project but also offered her help in doing the research and helping with the editing and typing of the manuscript.

That was a turning point for me. In pouring myself into this story, I was able to begin healing my broken heart.

We immediately began working on my book, now titled *BESA*. Each night, we would spend hours on the phone. I would read what I had written, and she would type the story into the computer. As Carrie and I spent more time working together on the manuscript, I became more confident in knowing that my book would be finished. The story began to motivate me and bring me back to the suffering that my family had endured in Albania—suffering which for years had been the focal point of my thoughts. In the reminders of my youth, it began to occur to me that my book wouldn't be enough on its own. I still felt compelled to honor those who had gone before me in the cause of freedom.

I knew that it would take more than BESA for the memory of those that fought for freedom and democracy to be remembered. *I made a promise to my mother*, I thought. *I must do something to honor my brother Fejzi, my uncles, my mother, and all those who suffered and died for freedom. I have to build a monument that will be seen by many people—a monument to remind all Albanians, young and old, and for generations to come, that freedom is a precious thing.*

The thought forced me to stop writing and close my eyes so I could imagine the monument. The more I thought about it, the more excited I became. I called Gezim and Bedri to share my idea with them.

"I'm planning a trip to Albania to try and locate Fejzi's remains," I said. "I'll also be searching for Uncle Nevrus. I want to keep my promise to Mother. If I can't find them, I want to build a monument to honor them."

Gezim and Bedri loved the idea so much that both offered to join me on the trip.

From the day communism had fallen in our homeland, we had been enduring the process of trying to recover the properties the regime had confiscated from our family. But since they had been in government hands for so long, the only piece of our property that we were able to take back was our old store in the town of Bilisht. My original plan was to demolish the building and put the monument there, but I had no idea that the store had been reopened and was being operated by another member of my family. So the search began to find just the right piece of property that I could purchase outright.

Mondi Gjyli and Dani Lami worked for the local town hall. They found a vacant lot on the map and told me that I might be able to purchase it. I thanked them and then walked to the crossroads where they said it could be found. The moment I saw it in person, I knew that this was where the monument belonged.

So I went to the house that overlooked the lot and knocked on the door. A lady in her late fifties answered.

"My name is Pertef Bylykbashi," I told her. Then I pointed to my companions and introduced them. Gezim had come along and also our cousin Nijazi, who still lived in Albania. "I am from the United States. I'm here visiting my family. Are you the owner of the vacant lot down the street?"

The lady nodded. "Yes, the lot belongs to my husband."

Then a man came to the door and introduced himself. Even from the look of him, I could tell that we would be fast friends. "I am Gurali Skoti, and this is my wife, Mrs. Skoti. Please come in."

The couple kept a lovely home. It was modest, but everything seemed to have its right place. Mr. Skoti opened a bottle of raki as his wife made coffee. After a few minutes of small talk, I asked about the property.

"I understand that you are the owner of the vacant lot just down the street," I said.

"That's right," he replied.

My body began to feel all jittery with the conviction I held for the idea I was about to share. "I would like to purchase that lot. You see, Mr. Skoti, I escaped Albania in 1957 and was separated from my family for many years. My brother and uncle were killed by the Communists, and my mother died in the labor camp. I want to erect a monument to honor them, as well as other Albanians whose lives were sacrificed under the Communist regime. I want everyone to know what freedom means and how costly it is. I want to erect the monument here in Bilisht because this is the last place my brother's body was before the Communists dragged him away to an unknown location."

Mr. Skoti didn't answer at first. Instead, we talked about the past for some time.

"You know," I said, "it's possible you knew my brother. How old are you?"

"Sixty-seven," he told me. "What is your brother's name?"

"Fejzi." Just speaking his name in this place caused my heart to flutter.

"Fejzi Bylykbashi?" Mr. Skoti said, his eyes going wide.

I nodded eagerly.

"Pertef, come to the window. I want to show you something."

We walked over to the window just to the right of where we were sitting. Mr. Skoti pointed toward the vacant lot and about twenty-five feet beyond it to the other side of the road. "Yes, Pertef, I remember Fejzi. I was a shepherd boy of about thirteen years of age at that time. I came to that place over there and saw your brother's body lying on the ground. I had heard the stories of his bravery and of his stand for democracy. The townspeople spoke of him often but in secret." He shuddered through a sigh before continuing. "I watched his fellow Albanians stomping, kicking, and spitting on his lifeless body, some doing it because they were told to and some just out of fear and ignorance. They were cursing him and jeering with the soldiers urging them on. They stuffed rocks and sticks in his mouth and in his body. I remember thinking, even at the age of thirteen, *Go ahead, you cowardly bastards. You are the ones that know of his bravery. Do what you want to him, but if he were alive, you wouldn't be so brave. He would kill you all.*"

I wanted to speak but was unable to find the right words.

Mr. Skoti turned to face me. "Pertef, I will not sell you the lot for your monument. My conscience wouldn't let me do that." My heart sank.

"Instead," he continued, "I will give you the lot. I want to be a part of such a wonderful, noble cause. It will be my gift to you and your family. And it will honor all Albanians that died for the cause of democracy. My wife's uncle was also killed by the Communists. I would like to have his name placed on the monument if it would be possible."

I could hardly breathe, I was so grateful. Land was such a valuable commodity in Albania, and Mr. Skoti was giving us this piece of land at no cost. It was almost too much to believe.

"I don't know what to say, Mr. Skoti," I said with grateful tears in my eyes.

"Thank you just doesn't seem like enough."

"Create a beautiful monument to those we've lost," he said. "That will be thanks enough."

"Of course." I shook his hand vigorously. "Your wife's uncle will be listed on the monument, along with many others who fought and died for the freedom Albania enjoys today."

As we left the Skoti home, I was full of joy knowing that Fejzi's memory was still alive. Albania remembered. Now I could take the next steps to ensure that Albania would never forget.

*****

The next day, I met with the mayor. By now, we had quite a few supporters, all anxious to see the monument completed, and there were five or six men with me when I entered the mayor's office. Mayor Miza was about forty years old, short and stocky with a soft voice, intelligent and well-spoken. We began the conversation discussing both past and present political situations, with Mayor Miza explaining the difficulties Albania had encountered during the healing process. He proudly spoke of the "New Liberated Albania" and the progress they were making under the Democratic-Party-led government. I shared in his enthusiasm because I knew that my adopted country of America was responsible for the freedom that my birth country was enjoying.

Our conversation eventually led me to the reason for my visit. I asked Mayor Miza if there were any government funds available to erect a monument to honor the Albanians that had given their lives in the fight for freedom.

His response was honest and to the point. "A few years back, there was an allowance of such funds, but the government has since changed the policy. Right now, funding is not available for this type of project."

The reply didn't surprise me. Despite its relative freedoms, Albania was and is still an oppressed country. The documents of democracy may have been signed by government officials, but it will take years, even generations, for the remnants of communism to fade.

After a moment's pause, I knew what I must do. "Very well. I am willing to finance this entire project with my personal funds. I will oversee the construction from start to finish, and I will register the monument at the capital in Tirana as a landmark and historical monument. But I would like your guarantee that once the monument is completed, the town of Bilisht will be fully responsible for maintaining and keeping the site in good condition. I want to send a message to our younger generations that we should honor noble lives forever and that if you stand firm for what is right, your name will be remembered and spoken with honor and dignity."

Mayor Miza accepted the terms. It was documented that the monument would belong to the people of Albania and be maintained by the town of Bilisht.

On August 20, 2007, I returned to Connecticut. Throughout the next year, there were phone calls to make, contractors and engineers to find, and documents and legal papers to sign. My promise was becoming a reality.

Almost one year later, on June 12, 2008, I returned to Albania to fulfill what had been a lifelong dream. Gezim, cousin Bedri, and my nephew Bardhyl all agreed to make the trip to help me work on the project. Little did any of us know just how long the days would be and just how many weeks it would take to complete the job.

The two months we spent in Albania was a stressful time, due not only to the amount of work involved with the monument, but also because I began to notice that many Albanians had been damaged by their years under Communist dictatorship. I remembered an Albania that was a proud and generous country, rich in both resources and history. The Albanian people from my youth were caring and loving, family oriented, and held a strong love and belief in God. Now after communism and forced atheism, many of them seemed disoriented as if they had somehow lost their sense of pride, their spiritual and familial beliefs, and their self-esteem. Their spirit had been broken.

My prayer, both then and now, is that God will in some way help the Albanian people find a common ground that will allow them to live with each other in peace, harmony, and prosperity. And like the American people, they should never forget the past, for remembering will help them avoid the same mistakes as they rebuild their country. They too must leave the past behind and move forward so as not to be robbed of their future.

There are still pockets of corruption in the government that need to be dissolved. When Albania was liberated, the uniforms came off, making it impossible to see the enemy in the way we once did. But that only made it more difficult for some of the people to see who their true friends were. Many still need to be convinced that democracy is not the enemy. The corruption will need to be cleaned up; the evil that was done by individuals still in power needs to be addressed; and those responsible for that evil need to be held accountable for the suffering and degradation they caused. Then and only then will Albanians begin to put their trust in their government, their friends, and their neighbors, and then and only then will my birth country be on its way to building an honest and flourishing society. There was a time that BESA was the law of the land in my country and was a promise most dear to the Albanian people. My prayer is that BESA will once again be the law that our young people honor.

When the time to complete the monument finally came, I felt an overwhelming sense of personal gratification, and yet I also knew a sense of emptiness. It was as if I had come to the end of a long journey—a journey filled with so much happiness, love, and laughter yet mixed with years of sadness, tears, unnecessary death, and loss of friends and loved ones. There were memories I was never allowed to make with my parents and siblings, moments that I will never be able to recapture with my family, moments that so many families take for granted, moments that I have so many times longed to embrace.

The monument was spectacular—a truly beautiful sight. At its center was a list of the names of those who had fought bravely for our freedom. To its left, carved into the granite, was the Albanian flag. To the right was another flag, this one the symbol of the country that had made all this possible—the United States of America. I looked on in awe.

My mind drifted back to my days in the army. I recalled the times during basic training when we would go on training maneuvers, and I would imagine that I was marching somewhere in Albania, rifle in one hand and the American flag in the other, on my way to free my mother, brothers, and sisters from the bonds of communism. So many times in my life, my best friend would be my own imagination, for it was my imagination that never let me give up on the hope of someday being reunited with my family and being able to honor Fejzi and his courage. Now it was no longer a dream, no longer my imagination. The time had arrived. My family was free from the bonds of communism, and Fejzi's courage would always be remembered. I felt humbled by the knowledge that I did not accomplish this with a rifle in one hand and a flag in the other. Rather, I did it with a dozen roses set gently on my mother's grave—that and the flag of freedom, the American flag forever engraved in a marble monument, proudly displayed for all to see.

Fejzi's death was not in vain, I thought as a tear rolled down my cheek. *This is what he lived for and why he fought.* On that dreadful summer morning in 1952, as I looked on, Fejzi had bravely and courageously stood tall, one man against an army. He had made his last stand and courageously died for freedom for his homeland Albania. Now everyone who visited this monument would know, and all would remember.

With the building of the monument complete, now we could begin the preparations for the dedication ceremonies. We sent invitations to the families whose loved ones were remembered on the wall. We formally invited government officials and made special invitations for King Leka Zogu and the U.S. ambassador to Albania, John Withers.

The turnout for the dedication was more than expected. Many high-level officials were there, and even though the king had prior engagements, he sent a representative in his place and a special personal message in a letter to me.

We held the dedication ceremony for the monument on August 8, 2008, at 10:30 a.m. My nephew Shkelqim Bylykbashi served as officiant. The program began with both the Albanian and the American national anthems. There were quite a few guest speakers, and all them delivered stirring speeches.

When it was my turn to speak, the message I shared with the people that attended the dedication was one of hope, of courage, and of freedom:

> We must never forget the good deeds that these fallen patriots have done and the sacrifice they have made for Albania and their fellow countrymen as a whole. Freedom is very dear to everyone but especially dear to those of you that survived under dictatorship for over half a century. Those of you here today know firsthand the price of winning and protecting our freedom.
>
> We are here today to remember and honor these one hundred and twenty heroes that paid the ultimate price. As we honor these heroes today, we must not forget that we have lost hundreds of thousands of fellow countrymen that were killed or died in labor camps and prisons at the hands of communism.
>
> Albania and its people are very blessed to have as an ally and friend the United States of America, one of the most powerful countries in the world. They have shown to the Albanian people their love and compassion and did not hesitate to stand beside us, to stamp out the evils of communism, so that we could once again unite with our families and live our lives with dignity

and as free men. May God bless Albania and its people, and may God bless the United States of America.

What an honor it was to be a part of such a historical occasion! I have lived a life of so many "once in a lifetime" experiences, but this truly was one of my most memorable moments.

Now I have one last thing to do before I can close this chapter of my life, I thought as I strode down from the podium beside the monument I had envisioned for so long and now had made a reality. *The final chapter will close when I can bring Mother's remains to America—to freedom—and lay her to rest beside her beloved husband for all eternity.*

I knew that this was the final step to find closure for my family and for myself.

When the dedication of the monument was over and after the crowds had gone home, I took a few moments in the silence of the late afternoon to reflect on my life. I began to read each name on the monument one by one. I reached for a small ladder beside me, pulled it to the monument, and climbed up so that I could place my hand on Fejzi's name. As my hand rested on his name, I could not have been any happier or content. I felt Fejzi's spirit right there with me. I could feel the presence of my mother as if she too stood beside me. I was overwhelmed with an inner peace.

As I closed my eyes, suddenly, I saw myself as a little boy. From there, in a matter of a heartbeat, I watched as the events of my lifetime unfolded. I opened my eyes to realize that I had become an older man but an older man full of pride and contentment for having fulfilled the dream of finding freedom. My brother's memory would live on. Everyone who visited this monument would know of his bravery and his stand for freedom. My people lived a generation of torment and suffering, but the names forever etched on the monument would stand as a lesson to a brighter future.

About the Author

Pertef Bylykbashi was born July 1, 1938, in the village of Pilur in southern Albania. He was the fifth of seven children born to Zenel and Resmije Bylykbashi. As a very young child, Pertef dreamed of someday going to America. Through his dreams and imagination, he grew to love a country that as a child only existed in his mind.

During the communist takeover of Albania in the early forties, his father and uncle escaped to Greece with the intention of organizing other freedom fighters to go back to Albania and rescue their families. Their plan did not work out. As fate would have it, Pertef's life would take many turns, and it would be many years before he would reunite with his father.

(Continued on the next page)

In 1950, Pertef, along with his mother and other siblings, was arrested and sent to a communist labor camp. The authorities kept their mother but put the children out on their own. They somehow found their way back to their home in Pilur where they lived under virtual house arrest for the next four years with no adults to help them. They endured unspeakable hardship. Had it not been for their ingenuity, they would have starved or frozen to death.

In 1954, Pertef was again arrested and sent back to the labor camp, where he was tortured, beaten, and humiliated many times until he planned and executed his own escape into Greece in 1957. There he was recruited into the United States Army under the Lodge Act and sent to Fort Jackson, South Carolina, for training. He was nineteen years old and spoke no English. He learned English in the military language school and proudly served five years as a U.S. soldier.

On April 5, 1963, he received an honorable discharge from the Army and moved to Brooklyn, New York, where he lived a short while before relocating to Waterbury, Connecticut. It was there that he met and married his wife Nancy. In their forty-year marriage, they had three children and nine grandchildren.

Mr. Bylykbashi is a very successful businessman and entrepreneur. He currently resides in Farmington, Connecticut, where he enjoys spending time with his children and grandchildren. He is very proud of the fact that although he was denied an education beyond the fourth grade in Albania, he was able to earn a high school diploma and go on to earn a college degree in specialized business after he became an American citizen. His greatest pride, however, lies in the fact that he was allowed to serve five years in the United States Army.

"I will never be able to repay the debt I owe to this great country, but maybe in some small way my service in the military made a difference."